EMILIE BARNES'

15

MINUTE

Home and Family

ORGANIZER

EMILIE BARNES'

15

MINUTE

Home and Family

ORGANIZER

Two Bestselling Works Complete in One Volume

THE 15 MINUTE ORGANIZER

**15 MINUTE FAMILY
TRADITIONS AND MEMORIES**

Emilie Barnes

Inspirational Press

First Inspirational Press edition published in 1998.

Inspirational Press
A division of BBS Publishing Corporation
450 Raritan Center Parkway
Edison, NJ 08837

Inspirational Press is a registered trademark of BBS Publishing Corporation.

Published by arrangement with Harvest House Publishers, Eugene, Oregon 97402.

Distributed by World Publishing
Nashville, TN 37214
www.worldpublishing.com

Library of Congress Catalog Card Number: 97-77409

ISBN: 0-88486-362-X

Printed in the United States of America.

Contents

THE
15
MINUTE
Organizer

Dedication

This book is dedicated to the many readers of my series article, "The Sage Hen," that has appeared in *Virtue* magazine since 1983.

Over the years you have been a real encouragement to me with your many cards and letters. You have been a real inspiration to me by letting me know what information women want in order to make their lives more manageable.

Many of you are hustled, hassled, and hurried, and this book is written just for you. May your 15 minutes of reading give you many hours of peace.

I truly thank you for giving me the encouragement and motivation to address the topics of home and personal organization. You have truly helped me, and I thank you for that.

Emilie Barnes

Contents

FINANCES

HOLIDAY

FOODS AND KITCHEN

ORGANIZATION

AUTOMOBILE

TIME FOR YOU

MISCELLANEOUS

Introduction

We live in a very hurried-up society. There is not enough time for love, marriage, children, vacations, listening to music, and reading a good book. Our television programming has to fit into a 30-minute time allotment; a TV character must go from birth to death within this time period!

In a sense we are all in a hurry to get life over with. We demand instant cures, fast-food eating, and fast-forward buttons on our VCR's.

This book has been adapted from the last seven years of my articles of "The Sage Hen" in *Virtue* magazine for the person who needs to fit a lot of things into a short period of time. The purpose of this book is to provide brief but effective solutions to many of our basic organizational questions. Each chapter is short and to the point, especially designed for the person who has limited time to read a book.

This book can be read cover to cover, or else it can be used as a reference book to be placed on your bookshelf, to be read when you are looking for the answer to a particular question.

I have developed each chapter out of my own needs. Over the years I have met many people at our seminars who have had the same organizational needs that I have solved in my own life. I think you will find these ideas to be an encouragement to you as you become frustrated and cry out, "I can't seem to get organized, and my world is falling apart!"

Our motto is: "Fifteen minutes a day and you're on your way to having more hours in your day!" Make this a battle cry in your home, and you'll see how well it works!

Getting Started

Goal Setting Made Easy

> While they are still talking to me
> about their needs, I will go ahead
> and answer their prayers!
>
> —*Isaiah 65:24*

*D*O YOU WANT to set goals but shy away from it because of past failures in following through with your goals, or just because you don't know how to set a goal?

With a little information you can learn how to properly set goals for your life. Proverbs 29:18 states that if we have no vision we will perish. You are either moving ahead or falling back; there is no middle ground. I label the meaning of a goal as *a dream with a deadline*. Sometimes our goals aren't very achievable because they aren't very measurable. We have goals such as "I want to lose weight," "I want to eat better," "I want to be a better wife," or "I want to be more spiritual." These are all good desires, but we can't measure them and they don't have any deadlines.

There are two very important parts to goal-setting. Goals must include:

- A statement of quantity (how much)
- A date to complete (deadline)

A proper statement of a goal would be "I would like to lose 15 pounds by March 15." This way I can determine whether I have reached my goal. But remember that goals aren't cast in concrete; they just point you in the right direction. You can always rewrite, restate, or even cancel any goal.

As the beginning point of goal-setting, I recommend that you write down your goals that you want to accomplish within the next 90 days. As you get proficient in 90 days go out to six months, then nine months, then one year. Bite off little pieces at first; don't choke on a mouthful.

You might ask the same questions that a lot of people ask who come to my seminars: For what areas of my life should I write goals? In my own goal-setting I try to concentrate on eight areas:

1. Physical goals
2. Marriage/family goals
3. Financial goals
4. Professional goals
5. Mental goals
6. Social goals
7. Community support goals
8 Spiritual goals

These are not listed in any special priority, but are randomly listed for consideration when I want to get a grip on my life. An example of a 90-day goal for each of these areas would be:

1. I want to do 50 sit-ups by March 1.
2. I want to plan a 25th wedding anniversary party for my parents by April 15.
3. I want to save $250.00 by February 28.
4. I plan to enroll in an accounting class at the community college by April 2.
5. I plan to memorize the state capitals by May 5.
6. I plan on inviting the Merrihews, Planchons, and Hendricksens to a roller skating party on March 26.
7. I will take the Red Cross fliers to my neighbors on February 14.
8. I plan to read the Gospels of the New Testament by April 1.

Notice that each goal states a quantity and gives a date for completion. Each goal is measurable. As you complete each goal, take a pen and draw a line through that goal. This action will make you feel good about goal-setting.

As you complete each goal, you might want to write a new goal to take its place for the next 90 days.

Establishing Daily Priorities

Never be lazy in your work, but
serve the Lord enthusiastically.

—Romans 12:11

I'VE GOT so many things to do today
that I don't know where to begin!" Is
that how you feel on many days? This statement is shared by many
people because they have never learned to establish daily priorities.

This article will give you tools for solving the dilemma "what do I
do next?" Tools needed for this exercise are:

- Sheet of paper
- 3 x 5 cards
- Pen or pencil

Label your sheet of paper "TO DO" and list all the things you
have been requested to do for today. When you are requested to do
something, you need to ask yourself two basic questions:

1. Do I want to take advantage of this opportunity?
2. Shall I take part in this particular activity?

After asking the two questions you may answer in one of three
ways:

Yes   No   Maybe

You only want to deal with the items which you have written YES next to. The NO or MAYBE items can wait for another day. Deal only with the YES items today.

Using one 3 x 5 card for each activity, write out the activity you will do. Such activities might include:

- Get a haircut
- Go to the bank
- Pray for ten minutes
- Spend 30 minutes cleaning the kitchen
- Write a thank-you note to Sally
- See Mary's soccer game
- Prepare dinner for tonight

After all your activities have been written on separate 3 x 5 cards, sort them by the order of priority (what needs to be done first, second, third, etc.). Concentrate on only one activity at a time. After each has been completed, you can either toss out the 3 x 5 card or place it on the bottom of the stack of cards. When your children or mate come home and want to know what you've done all day, you can read off the various activities and they will be impressed!

Every request that comes your way doesn't have to be answered YES. It's okay to say NO. *You* need to control your schedule and not let others plan it for you.

12 Ways
to Put Off
Procrastinating

It is far better not to say you'll do
something than to say you will and
then not do it.

—Ecclesiastes 5:5

*T*HE NATIONAL Procrastination Club
was scheduled to meet in San Francisco
in early 1991, but the meeting was canceled because they weren't
able to plan it. Does that sound like you or a good friend or yours?
Most of us are caught up in the no-action mode of not getting started.

Many of us self-talk ourselves into procrastinating. We say things
like "I work best under pressure" or "The easy way is the best way"
or "I can still go shopping and get the assignment completed on
time." Does this sound familiar?

It's hard to measure procrastination because we measure performance by what we *do* and not by what we *don't do*. Procrastination
becomes a problem when we neglect or delay doing those things that
are important to us. Procrastination is the universal "effectiveness
killer." Putting things off takes an enormous toll. Some of these
include:

• *Continuous frustration.* We are always under the stress of
frustration. We say things like "I hope," "I wish," "Maybe things

17

will get better," and other such negative self-talk. We're always going to get it together *tomorrow*.

• *Boredom.* Boredom is a way of life, and a great escape for not using present moments constructively. Choosing boredom as a way of life is merely another way that the procrastinator structures her time.

• *Impotent goals.* We never get around to accomplishing our goals. Our speech is loaded with "I'm gonna's." But we never get around to actually putting into action our gonna's.

• *Always having unsolved problems.* We feel like a fireman trying to put out new fires. As we have one almost out, another one starts. We don't actually put any fires all the way out, and we're always tired because nothing is resolved. Unsolved problems tend to create more problems.

• *Waste of the present.* The past is history and tomorrow is only a vision, but the procrastinator wastes *today*. She is always living for tomorrow, and when tomorrow comes she starts waiting again for tomorrow.

• *Unfulfilled life.* Procrastination is an immobilizer that blocks fulfillment. There is always tomorrow, so today never has to count for anything. We fill our daily voids with less desirable things just to fill the void.

• *Poor health.* We put off next month to have a checkup for that lump in our breast. Then it is too late. Or we drive too long on bald tires, until we have a costly accident because we have a blowout on the freeway.

• *A life of indecision.* When we put off decisions we are forfeiting important opportunities. By not being able to make decisions we allow ourselves to become slaves to our future rather than masters of it.

• *Poor human relationships.* The people in our family, at our church, and at our work become restless around us if we aren't capable of doing anything. People don't want to be around us. We become the object of jokes and insults, which damage our relationships over time.

• *Fatigue.* With all the above energy drains working against us, no wonder we're tired at the end of the day!

How to Roll into Action

A human body at rest tends to remain at rest, and a body in motion tends to remain in motion. Procrastinators have a difficult time getting in motion, but once we get into motion we tend to stay in motion. If we gain momentum the task is well on its way to completion.

The following are a few ideas for creating momentum.

1. *Recognize the futility of procrastination as a way of living.* Do you really want a life of frustration, fatigue, and boredom?

2. *Break down overwhelming tasks into small tasks.* Try to limit them to five-to-ten-minute tasks. Write them on 3 x 5 cards for easy referral. Hardly anything is really hard if you divide it into small jobs.

3. *Face unpleasant tasks squarely.* Ignoring unpleasant tasks doesn't make them go away. Not doing it today only insures that you will feel equally burdened about it (plus other tasks) tomorrow.

4. *Do a start-up task.* Pick one or two of those instant tasks from number 2 above and begin to work on those. Just get started.

5. *Take advantage of your moods.* If there are tasks you don't feel like doing today, find those tasks you *do* feel like doing today. Take advantage of your moods. Get started.

6. *Think of something important that you have been putting off.* List the good things that could possibly happen by doing the task. Now list the disadvantages that could come about as a result of inaction. You will usually find that the advantages outweigh the disadvantages.

7. *Make a commitment to someone.* Enlist a friend to hold you accountable for getting started. Choose someone who is firm and won't let you off the hook.

8. *Give yourself a reward.* Find an important goal that you have been dodging and decide what would be a fitting reward for you when you achieve it. Make your reward commensurate with the size of the task.

9. *Give yourself deadlines.* Color-code the due date on your calendar so you can visually see that date each day. You might even color-code a few immediate dates along the way to make sure you are on track. Write down the due date.

10. *Resolve to make every day count.* Treat each day as a treasure. Self-talk yourself into accomplishing something new each day. Live for *today* without always anticipating tomorrow.

11. *Be decisive and have the courage to act.* Many times we're crippled by "what if," "I'm gonna," "I wish," "I want," "I hope," and so on. Make something happen!

12. *Refuse to be bored.* Get out of the rut you're living in. Buy some flowers, cook a new dish, replace the familiar with the unfamiliar. Take time to smell a new rose.

13. *Practice doing absolutely nothing.* When you're avoiding getting started, go sit in a chair and do absolutely nothing until you are motivated to begin. Most of us are poor at the art of doing nothing. You'll soon find yourself eager to get moving.

14. *Ask yourself, "What's the best use of my time and energy right now?"* If that's not what you are doing, then switch to a higher priority. What you are doing might be good, but is it the best?

15. *Ask yourself, "What is the greatest problem facing me, and what am I going to do about it today?"* Plan your action and get into motion.

As Christian women, we are directed in Proverbs 31:15, "She gets up before dawn to prepare breakfast for her household, and plans the day's work for her servant girls." This means we are to be women of action. Treat each day as being precious. When it's gone, it never comes back to you.

How to Stop Saying "I'll Do It Tomorrow"

Commit your work to the Lord, and
then it will succeed.

—*Proverbs 16:3*

*A*RE THERE things you really want and need to accomplish but keep putting off for another day? Do you often let little things slide until they pile up and become large problems? Guess what—there is hope. There are steps you can take to get going and get organized.

In reality most procrastinators suffer from nothing more than simple laziness. They just delay doing things that bore them.

The perfectionist puts off projects because if she cannot do it perfectly she won't do it at all. Susan is a typical example of a perfectionist. The things she does are exact, perfect, and "spit-shined." She analyzes her project, gathers her tools and materials, sets a time, and goes for it. However, Susan's house can be a total mess much of the time because she doesn't tackle part of a job. If she can't do it all and do it perfectly, she'd rather not do it at all. So because she doesn't have large blocks of time in her life, she gets very little accomplished.

We all at times put things off for later, but later may never come. Who loves to rake leaves every day? But if they don't get raked we may never see the front yard until spring. Reward yourself after those "hate-to-do" jobs. Take ten minutes to read a magazine or have a cup of tea or hot cocoa. Arrange some flowers or do something fun and something you love to do. Remember, life sometimes isn't easy; we have many responsibilities we may dislike doing.

Here are a few tips to help you get going.

1. *Set goals.* Set manageable goals. Start with small ones so that you feel a sense of accomplishment. If it's the hall closet that needs cleaning, plan to do it in three-to-fifteen-minute segments. If it's answering letters, don't do them all in one day; set a goal of 30 minutes a week until you're all caught up. Remember, break things up into small steps.

2. *Make a schedule.* Block out time for each day on your calendar to complete a task. Perhaps it's ironing; allot 30 minutes for the day, then STOP. Before long you will be all caught up. What you thought would take one whole day will only take 30 minutes a day for four days.

3. *Be realistic.* If you find that 30 minutes a day is too long, cut down the time by five or ten minutes. If you find that 30 minutes is not long enough, add ten or fifteen minutes. Remember that interruptions take place (children, phone, etc.), so be sure to allow for these.

4. *Take it easy.* If you feel overextended, trim down your commitments until you get caught up and have a workable, manageable load you can feel comfortable with.

5. *Get help.* Incorporate your family. Perhaps the garage or attic needs reorganizing. Ask, "What can you do to help mom and dad?" Plan a fun day working together, then reward the kids with their favorite chocolate cake and apple cider.

6. *Do it now.* Remember, it is more important to just *get it done now* than to do it perfectly later. *Now* gets results, and you'll feel great for accomplishing something.

7. *Be flexible with your goal.* Nothing is set in concrete. You may need to adjust your goals. Remember, setting a goal is a step in conquering procrastination.

8. *Remember to reward yourself along the way.* After that project is completed, all the letters answered, and the garage cleaned, get excited and take the family out to dinner or take a friend to lunch. How about an afternoon at the mall? Or feed the ducks with the children, ride bikes, fly kites, or cut pumpkins and make a pie. You know what you and your family love to do, so do it!

Give yourself time off. Even procrastinators deserve a little fun.

Thank the Lord each step of the way. God is interested in our successes and guides us through our failures.

Putting Everything in Its Place

There is an appointed time for
everything. And there is a time for
every event under heaven.

—*Ecclesiastes 3:1 NASB*

*W*ITH SPRING cleaning around the
corner, it's time to consider doing
something about the piles of stuff that have accumulated over the
winter days of holiday rush.

While we were busily celebrating Christmas and the New Year,
our closets, shelves, and drawers were mysteriously attracting all
sorts of odds and ends. These things have meaning to us and we don't
want to give or throw them away. But we do need places to put them
away. Here's a system that will get us organized.

The necessary basic equipment:

- 3 to 12 large cardboard boxes approximately 10 inches high, 12
  inches wide, and 16 inches long, lids preferred.
- One 3 x 5 plastic file card holder with 36 lined cards and seven
  divider tabs.
- One wide-tipped black felt marking pen.
- 8½ x 11 file folders

Take the large cardboard boxes and begin to fill them with the
items you want to save and store for future use.

Mark the front of each box with a number. Assign a 3 x 5 lined file card for each box. For each box write on the card what you have stored in that box. For example:

Box 1—Scrap sewing fabric
Box 2—Chad's baby toys and clothes
Box 3—Jenny's high school cheerleading uniform
Box 4—Ski clothes
Box 5—Gold-mining gear
Box 6—Snorkel gear with swim fins

Save Number 15 for your income tax records (April 15):

Box 15A—1987 records
Box 15B—1988 records
Box 15C—1989 records
Box 15D—1990 records
Box 15E—1991 records

Number 25 is a good one for your Christmas items:

Box 25A—Wreaths
Box 25B—Outdoor lights
Box 25C—Indoor lights
Box 25D—Tree decorations
Box 25E—Garlands & candles

By labeling your boxes A through Z you can add to your number sequence and keep all your items together. (It saves a lot of time when you need to retrieve those items.) Every two or three years go back through these boxes, cleaning them out and consolidating them.

On your 3 x 5 card write in the upper-right-hand corner where you have stored each box. Ideally, store these boxes in the garage, attic, or basement. If you don't have the luxury of lots of storage space, spray paint or wallpaper the boxes to fit in with the decor of your home (such as the laundry room, bedroom or bathroom).

When you get to the bottom of the "put away" pile, you will probably find many loose items of papers and records that need some type of storage for quick retrieval. This is where your 8½ x 11 file folders come in hand.

Label the folders with the following headings and then place each paper or receipt in the corresponding folder:

Insurance Papers
- Auto
- Health
- Homeowner's

Homeowner Papers
- Escrow papers
- Tax records (for current year)

Receipts
- Auto repairs
- Major purchases

Store these folders in a metal file cabinet or a storage box. If possible, keep these boxes near the office area in your home. Close accessibility to these files will save you extra footsteps when you need to get to them.

Give your young children storage boxes, file cards, and file folders to help them keep their rooms organized. This provides an excellent model for their future personal organization.

Just think of your satisfaction when a member of your family comes to you and asks where something is and you pull out your box, flip through your cards, and tell him or her to look in Box 5, which is located under the attic stairs. Won't he be impressed with the new organized you!

Four Tools
to an
Organized You

To fail to plan is to plan to fail.
—Unknown

*D*O YOU EVER look around your home, room, or office and just want to throw up your hands in disgust and say, "It's no use, I'll never get organized"? The old saying "Everything has a place and everything in its place" sounds great, but how do you make it work for you? Here are four simple tools to help you get your home organized for the new year.

- "To do" list
- Calendar
- Telephone/address list
- Simple filing system

A "To Do" List

Use the same size of paper for the first three tools (8½ x 11 or 5½ x 8½). This way you won't have to fight with different sizes of paper. After choosing your size of paper, write the words TO DO at the top of a piece of paper. Begin writing down all the things that you need to do.

When you finish each item during the day, relish the pleasure of crossing it off the list. At the end of the day, review your list and update any new things you need to add. If you have accomplished something that day that wasn't on your list, write it down. Everyone's life is full of interruptions, and you need to applaud yourself for what you *did* accomplish!

At the end of the week, consolidate your lists and start again on Monday with a fresh page. Eventually you will want to rank your TO DO items by importance. This added technique will help you maximize your time to it fullest potential.

A Calendar

I recommend two types of calendars. The first is a two-page "Month at a Glance" calendar. One glance will give you a good idea of the overview of the month. Details aren't written here, but do jot down broad engagements with times. For example, write down meetings, luncheons, basketball games, speaking engagements, and dental appointments.

The second type of calendar is a page for each day—"A Day at a Glance." On this calendar you write down more specific details, such as what you will be doing on the hour or half-hour. Be careful that you don't overload your calendar and jam your appointments too close together. Remember to schedule in time alone and time with God.

As a guideline, I suggest that if you've been someplace before and you know where you're going, allow 25 percent more time than you think it will take. If you estimate that a meeting will last one hour, block out one hour and fifteen minutes.

A Telephone/Address List

This list will become your personal telephone and address book. Using the same size paper as your TO DO list and calendar, design your own directory of information for home, work, and play. You might want to list certain numbers by broad headings, such as schools, attorneys, dentists, doctors, plumbers, carpenters, and restaurants. This helps you look up the specifics when you can't remember the person's last name. Use a pencil in writing down addresses and telephone numbers; since it is much easier to correct than ink if the information changes.

If you have a client or customer listed, you may want to mark down personal data about the person to review before your next meeting.

Some items to include are the client's spouse and children's names, sports of interest, and favorite foods and vacation spots. Your clients will be impressed that you remembered all that information about them.

The same system works well with guests in your home. Include some of the meals you served them, any particular food allergies they have, and whether they drank coffee or tea.

A Simple Filing System

The motto in our home is "Don't pile it, file it." This tool will make your home look like a new place! At your local stationery store, purchase about four dozen colored or manila 8½ x 14 file folders. I recommend colored file folders because they help you categorize your material and also add a little cheer to your day. I find that the legal-size folder (8½ x 14) are more functional, since they accommodate longer, nonstandardized pieces of paper.

Label each folder with a simple heading, such as Sales Slips, Auto, Insurance, School Papers, Maps, Warranties, Taxes, and Checks. Then take all the loose papers you find around your home and put them into their respective folders. If you have a filing cabinet to house these folders, that's great. If not, just get a cardboard storage box to get started.

After you have mastered these four tools to organization, you can branch out and acquire more skills. Remember, though, to give yourself time, since it takes 21 consecutive days to acquire a new habit.

How to Find More Time

All of us must quickly carry out the
tasks assigned to us by [God] . . .
for there is little time left before
the night falls.
—*John 9:4*

IF ONLY I could get organized!" "I
just don't have enough time in the day!"
Do you ever hear yourself making these statements?

Don't we all at some point in our lives find ourselves waiting until the last minute to fill out tax forms, wrap Christmas presents, or send a belated birthday card?

Here are a few ideas that will help you find more time for yourself and enable you to get all those little jobs done.

1. As you make a TO DO list, set small, manageable deadlines for yourself. For example, by October 2 I'll clean two drawers in the kitchen. By October 8 I'll sort through papers in my desk. On October 28 I'll select my Christmas cards.

Some other bite-sized chunks that will take 15 minutes a day are answering a letter, cleaning a bathroom, or changing the linen on one bed. If it helps, set a timer for 15 minutes. When the timer goes off, go back to your regular schedule.

2. Plan ahead for guests. Sometimes having guests come to your home can be overwhelming when you think about the preparation

involved. Doing things in 15-minute increments works wonders for your preparation. Write out a TO DO list about a week before your party, Sunday brunch, or arrival of weekend guests. Plan to do a little each day until your guests arrive.

For example, one day make up their bed with clean sheets. Wait until the next day to do the vacuuming and the following to do the baking. Remember, reward yourself or give yourself a break after each accomplishment. Pick some flowers, take a walk, polish your nails, or give yourself a facial.

3. Watch out for interruptions. They will be there, but try to avoid them. If you have an answering machine, turn it on. If you don't have a machine, tell the caller you will call back later, when you finish the project you're involved in. Wait until the baby is sleeping for certain projects. Put a note on the front door that reads "Available after 3 P.M."

4. Learn to say no at least until you've completed what you set out to do on your list. But remember to keep your list realistic and obtainable. Don't load yourself to the point that you feel overwhelmed and then give up and do nothing at all.

5. Get your family to help with odd jobs by giving them a chart. TO DO BY 5 P.M.: a) Sweep the driveway; b) Rake the leaves in the backyard; c) Set the table for the next meal; d) Take an apple break.

Let your family in on your 15-minute plan. They'll love working against time; it becomes a game. Reward, praise, and compliment them for a job well done. If each child works 15 minutes a day toward an organized home, look how many hours it will save you! This will give you time for yourself and at the same time teach your children to be responsible young people.

6. Reward yourself when projects are complete. Go out for lunch with a friend and share what you've accomplished. She'll be excited for you and probably go home and clean out her drawers too! Or sit down with a cup of tea or coffee and read a magazine or the Bible.

Cleaning

How to Get Housework Done in Record Time

Teach us to number our days and
recognize how few they are; help
us to spend them as we should.

—*Psalm 90:12*

*F*OR THE BUSY woman today, housework is a nuisance and not necessarily
her real concern. Today's woman does not have time to devote her
full time to cleaning, as did her grandmother. However, dirt doesn't
just blow away and seven dwarfs don't appear at night while we sleep
to clean up our messes. Wouldn't it be wonderful to have time to do
things with family and church instead of spending all day Saturday
cleaning, cleaning, cleaning? Here are some speedy tips to get the
job done and feel great about doing it.

Start with collecting the right supplies.

• Pail or bucket and mop.

• Broom and dustpan.

• Squeegee. Professionals use these exclusively. Never use newspaper or paper towels, since they contain fibers that leave the
windows messy. A good squeegee works fast and easy: Use a spray
bottle with rubbing alcohol; spray on window and squeegee off.

• Billy's old football knee pads. These are great protectors which
can be purchased at sporting goods stores (or similar work pads at

hardware stores) for cleaning floors and tubs. Soft pads keep knee work less painful.

• Clean dustcloths. Diapers are great, and so are 100 percent cotton dishcloths (well-washed and dried).

• Carry-all tray. A must for storing cleaning items such as wax, window spray, etc.

• Feather duster. A super item for moving small amounts of dust from a higher level to a lower level, where most of it can be vacuumed up. I have lots of cobwebs and knickknack items, and this is my quick lifesaver of dusting each item every time. Invest in a good ostrich duster. You can purchase one at a hardware or janitor supply store.

• Pumice stone. It gets that ugly ring out of the toilet bowl caused by rust and mineral deposits. It's amazing how fast a pumice stone will remove the scale; just rub it on the ring gently and it's gone. It also cleans ovens and removes the carbon buildup on grills and iron cookware, as well as removing paint from concrete and masonry walls and scale from swimming pools. Pumice stones can be purchased in hardware stores, janitor supply stores, and beauty supply stores.

• Toothbrush. Great for cleaning the hard corners of floors and showers and around faucets at the sink.

• Vacuum cleaner. An absolute must!

• Ammonia. An excellent cleaner (not the sudsy type) for floors.

• Powdered cleanser. For sinks and bathtubs.

• Oven cleaner.

• Rubber gloves. To protect your hands from the chemicals in household cleaners and detergents.

• Scraper. Use the razor-blade type to remove paint from tile or glass and decals or stickers from the shower door. Also, remove dried-on food after it gets hard, such as pancake batter or eggs. But be careful not to scratch the surface.

Fill your carry-all tray with many of the above items. It's ready to work when you are!

When you work, be sure to use the SPEEDY EASY METHOD:

1. Put on some music with a very fast beat. This will help your cleaning go faster plus take your mind off the drudgery.

2. Go in one direction. Work around your room from top to bottom and from right to left or left to right—whatever feels good to you. Also start at one end of your home and work toward the other end. Don't get sidetracked with this mess and that mess.

3. Before cleaning windowpanes, wipe or vacuum sills and wood cross-frames. Use your spray bottle with alcohol and squeegee and

cotton cloth. Use a horizontal stroke on the outside and a vertical stroke on the inside. That way you'll know if you missed a spot because you can tell which side the streak is on.

4. Use your hair dryer to blow off the dust from silk flowers. Your feather duster will work well to dust off soft fabric items, plants, picture frames, and lampshades. Remember, we're working from top to bottom in each room, so you'll be vacuuming up this dust soon.

5. After wiping clean your wastebaskets, give the inside bottom a quick coat of floor wax. This will prevent trash from sticking to the bottom of the wastebasket in the future.

6. Change your air conditioner and heater filters every six months for best performance. This will keep the dust and dirt from circulating through your rooms.

7. Wipe off the blades of your window and/or room fans quarterly to keep dirt and dust from flying around.

8. Try to avoid interruptions; take the phone message and call back when it is convenient.

9. Big question: Should you vacuum first or last? Last, of course.

Having the proper tools helps. Don't feel that everything has to be done in one work session. Set your timer and then work in 15-minute time slots. Work fast, but after each time and/or project, treat yourself to a cup of hot chocolate or iced tea, or put a mask on your face and enjoy a hot bath.

Then go to the garden and pick a fresh bouquet of flowers for your beautiful clean house.

Are You
a Pack Rat?

She watches carefully all that goes
on throughout her household, and is
never lazy.
—Proverbs 31:27

*A*NSWER YES OR NO to each question. You get a zero for every no and one point for every yes.

A zero is a perfect score and probably impossible. If your score is 10, you are a pack rat and you've come to the right place!

1. Do you find yourself complaining that you don't have enough room or space?

2. Do you have things piled up in cupboards and closets or stacked into corners because there is no place to put them?

3. Do you have magazines stacked around the house waiting to be read? Are you saving them for the day when you'll sit down and cut out articles, recipes, and patterns?

4. Do things often get "lost" in your house?

5. Do you think, "I'll just put this here for now and put it away later"?

6. Are things collecting on top of your refrigerator, dresser drawers in the bedroom, counters, end tables, coffee tables, and bookshelves?

7. Do you have things around your home that you haven't used for a long time or possibly don't even want?

8. Do you ever buy something you already have at home because you can't find it or don't want to look for it?

9. Do you often say, "It might come in handy someday"?

10. Do you have to move things around in your closet or cupboards to find a certain item?

Let's see how you did.

0-3	You're in pretty good shape.
4-7	You could use some improvement.
8-10	It's never too late, pack rat. However, I'd start with prayer. Philippians 4:13 says, "I can do all things through Christ who strengthens me" (NKJV).

Begin with a family meeting, saying that you have discovered a problem. Let them know that you are a collector of things and need help from all of them, along with their support, to help you get your house in order.

When we admit our problem, somehow it helps us to get started in organizing.

You didn't get to this problem point by yourself; surely the whole family is as guilty as you are. But *you* are the one admitting it, so let's start with you. You take the responsibility and work toward getting control. (Altogether too many homes today are controlling us instead of us being in control of our homes.)

Step 1 is to think of what area of your clutter is bothering you the most. Is it the top of the refrigerator?

Step 2 is to set a 10-to-15-minute time slot to take care of that clutter. Set your timer on the oven and go at it. You'll be surprised at what you can get done in 15-minute intervals!

Repeat steps 1 and 2 above with each area of your home clutter. It may take weeks to finish the project, but at least you'll be working toward organizing your pack rat clutter.

Begin to file away the piles of papers, letters, articles, etc. into a file cabinet or cardboard file box, keeping in mind **DON'T PUT IT DOWN, PUT IT AWAY!**

This will help you in the future to put things in their proper place.

If you have a difficult time deciding whether to *throw* something away or *store* it away, put those difficult-decision things into a box or baggie and put it in the garage, attic, or basement. Then if something is so important to you that you would go to the extreme of retrieving it from the box or baggie, that item should be stored nearby. But if those boxes or bags sit for several months untouched, it's a sure indication to give them away or throw them away.

"Out of sight, out of mind" is a good saying to remember. So *throw away* and *give away.*

After attending one of my seminars, one woman told me that in five weeks she had organized the things in her home into 62 cardboard boxes! She said, "I'm a pack rat, but at least I'm an organized one!"

Key to a
Clean House

In everything you do, put God first,
and he will direct you and crown
your efforts with success.
—*Proverbs 3:6*

*D*O YOU HAVE the type of home where every room you go into contains so many odd jobs to do (picking up yesterday's paper, washing off the refrigerator door, folding the last load of clothes) that you rush around all day never completing any one job?

If you struggle with getting household chores done, try this time-tested technique: *Break down big jobs into little jobs.* Here are a few ideas.

• Commit yourself to accomplishing a chore that shows. Start by picking up and putting away items in the living room that don't belong there (i.e., last week's TV listings or your son's Tonka truck). It will help you feel better if, as you walk into the house, at least the living room is in order. Take a minute to make a bed or pick up dirty dishes scattered throughout the house. The idea is to organize *at least one thing*, since this will take you only two minutes or less.

• *Buy a timer or use the one on your oven.* A woman once told me that she hated to mop her kitchen floor. It caused her anger and stress every time she thought of doing it, and even more stress every time she walked across a sticky floor.

I recommended that she time how long it took her to mop her floor. She reported that it only took her three minutes! Now when she thinks of mopping that floor she thinks of taking only three minutes to do the job, and she feels less stressed about it. We have many jobs around our homes that can be done in three to ten minutes.

• *List on a piece of paper the jobs that can be done in 15 minutes or less.* This will be easy to do once you get into the swing of timing your chores.

Because our normal tendency is to group work into big jobs, we make the excuse that we don't have time to do certain chores. For example, we may figure it takes 30 minutes to clean the refrigerator, and if we don't have 30 minutes to do it, we won't do it at all.

In reality it could take only seven minutes. Once you've timed this job, the next time the refrigerator needs cleaning it won't be that big a deal.

• *Profit from the precious minutes usually wasted while you wait for someone.* You are ready for Marci to pick you up for that meeting, but you have ten minutes before she comes. Instead of sitting on the stairs to wait for her, look around and find one simple task you can complete. One glance and you'll find jobs such as unloading the dishwasher, dusting a table, folding a load of laundry, putting a fresh load of clothes in the washer, or wiping around the bathroom sink.

• *Divide jobs into segments.* When cleaning the living room, divide it into three segments: dusting, picking up items, and vacuuming. The segment idea also goes for the bathroom: scrubbing the sink, shower, and toilet; mopping the floor; shaking out the throw rugs; polishing the mirrors.

• *Improve a room's appearance every time you go into it.* Simply putting the milk away or straightening a bath towel will make the room look better, and then you'll feel better about it. Remember, don't put it *down*, put it *away*.

• *Replace an item where it belongs after you use it.* (This is one idea that would be worth training the whole family to do.) Instead of leaving the toothpaste cap on the counter, put it back on the tube and place the toothpaste in a drawer or on the shelf.

Instead of tossing a towel on the floor or clothing on the bed, hang it back up on the towel rack, or on a hanger in the closet.

• *Do simple tasks right away.* For example, if you go to the grocery store and buy celery, don't put off cleaning it. Instead, as you're putting away your groceries, clean the celery, cut it up, put it in a container of water, and slip it into the refrigerator. Presto, the job is done!

This week commit yourself to nine things you can do in 15-minute time slots. When you do, you'll have accomplished 1½ hours of cleaning without even noticing it!

Do I Really Need This?

Teach a wise man, and he will be
wiser; teach a good man and he
will learn more.

—*Proverbs 9:9*

I HAVE A FRIEND who has 40 robes.
Now one woman cannot possibly wear
40 robes. "It's hard to throw things out," she says. Another woman
has saved her plastic baggies from the supermarket and at last count
had 320 of them!

We live in a world of mass production and marketing. We must
learn to sort and let go of certain things, or else we will need to build
a huge warehouse to contain everything, not to mention inventorying
the stock of collectibles so we know what we have and where it all is
located. Years ago, when we got something we kept it until it wore
out. But today it may never wear out before we tire of it. Yet it seems
just too good to dispose of.

We often have things not because of an active decision to keep
them but because we have not made the decision to get rid of them.

On an average, people keep things several years after their usefulness has passed. Perhaps we overbuy and have supplies, materials, and
tools left over. The things we liked years ago are not what we like or
enjoy today, but we hang onto them, thinking that someday we may use

them again. It's like we're obligated to keep them "just in case."

Toys and baby equipment are saved because someday they may be used for grandchildren. We store things for our adult children "someday."

Let's face the job of streamlining our possessions and ask ourselves some questions:

1. How long has it been since you used that item? My rule of thumb is if it hasn't been used in the past year I'm going to give it away, throw it away, or store it away.

I use trash bags for my throwaway items. A black one is best so *you* can't see in it, *your husband* can't see in it, and *your children* can't see in it. Those 320 baggies can go into the throwaway bags, along with broken toys, torn and stained clothing, and newspapers and jars you've been saving for the "someday" you might use them.

Keep tax records (including canceled checks) for seven years and then throw them out. (But keep *homebuying* and *homeselling* records permanently.) Throw out most receipts, check stubs, and utility bills after two or three years.

2. The irreplaceable items that I don't use go into storage boxes, such as my honeymoon suit, Bob's high school or college letterman's jackets, baby's first shoes, and other memorabilia. Those boxes I number 1, 2, 3, etc. I catalog these on a 3 x 5 card that is also numbered, and I put it into a small file box. Then these cards are ready to retrieve if I need them at a later date.

3. The only reasons to keep things for long periods should be for memories or perhaps to pass on to another member in the family someday, such as a lace tablecloth, a quilt, granddad's toolbox or pocket knife, or books that can benefit another member of the family or a friend.

Things you don't need to keep include old magazines (unless they could realistically become collector's items) or magazines that are recent. These could be placed in your doctor's office, convalescent hospitals, etc. Junk mail is a big source of clutter and needs to be thrown away. *"Don't put it away, throw it away"* is a good motto for that junk mail. If you have a pile now, stop and throw it away right now. It's a great feeling, isn't it? But a new pile will return in a few days, so do it again and again until you realize that throwing this junk mail away is not going to affect your life in any way other than making you feel great!

With other mail our motto is *"File it, don't pile it!"* Get some file folders and label them "Medical," "Insurance," "Bills," "House-hold," "Letters to Answer," etc. As the mail comes in, open it, read it, quickly highlight it with a yellow pen, and then file it into the proper folders. Those folders can then go into a file drawer or box.

Our children's school papers were kept for one week, with two papers chosen at the end of the week and put into a file folder. At the end of the month they were allowed to choose only two special "let's keep" papers. By the end of the year the file folder consisted of those special papers, photos, and report cards. Each year the folder was put into their own "keepsake" box, and by the time high school graduation came each person had a special box filled with special memories. (They still have these boxes.)

On my fiftieth birthday I received over 150 cards, each one from a special friend, with special notes in many cases. They would fill a box just by themselves. Not too many people are interested in those cards except me, and in 20 years certainly no one but me. With those that I could, I cut off the front side of the card and used them as postcards (if not written on). Special notes I kept and put into a memorable photo book with my birthday celebration pictures.

Cards that Bob and the children have sent me over the years I keep in a file folder, being careful only to keep those that are unusual or have notes. Now...hold your breath...I dumped all the others!

If you or your husband or your children are pack rats use my box and catalog system for storage. You may still be a pack rat, but at least you'll be an organized one!

Swish, Swash, How Do I Wash?

She is energetic, a hard worker.
—*Proverbs 31:17*

I WAS TALKING with a woman who had 15 children (all single births) who told me she pulled 60 socks out of her dryer one day and none of them matched! I was able to tell her about those plastic sock sorters you can buy that scoot onto the end of a pair of socks. Into the washer and dryer then go, and they stay together until you are ready to roll them and put them in a drawer. I have also had women tell me they keep a good supply of large safety pins by their laundry area so they can safety pin the socks together in pairs before putting them into the washer.

It has always amazed me how socks get totally lost from the washer to the dryer, and come out single and perhaps lost forever. I'm beginning to think that our appliances feed on socks, since they seem to get eaten in the laundry process!

The laundry needs organization as much as any other area of our homes.

In raising our children, I delegated much of the chores to the children themselves. By the time Jenny was ten years old she was doing all the laundry from sorting to ironing. It took time and training to get her to that point, however. I didn't just dump the laundry responsibility in her lap at ten years old and tell her to go to it. I began when they were two and three teaching both Jenny and Brad to sort the dirty clothes into three laundry bags. One was a colored bag made out of some bright calico print fabric that had lots of colors on it; all the *colored* clothes went into that bag. Another laundry bag was all white for the *white* clothes, and another one was navy or dark solid for the dirty *dark-colored* clothes.

Make a rule that what goes in the wash inside out (such as socks, underwear, and T-shirts) comes out inside out. Have everyone straighten his or her own clothes. King-size pillowcases make great laundry bags. You can string some shoe laces around the top and you have laundry bags—fast, simple, and not too expensive, if you buy the pillowcases on sale. Colored plastic trash cans make great laundry sorters also. With a fat felt pen you can write on the outside "COLORED," "WHITE," or "DARK." That way the family can simply sort their dirty clothes as they dump them in the proper bins.

Now that the clothes have been sorted and the socks paired up with your sock sorters, you can plan your washday.

Young mothers with several children may need to wash every day, others one to three times per week. But it is important to schedule your laundry days ahead and begin early in the day, or better yet, put in a load the night before. Many days I would have a load started the night before. On your way to bed, simply dump in one of the bags of sorted clothes. By morning they are ready to put into the dryer or basket for hanging out today, and you will be one load ahead of the game. When it was Jenny's responsibility for the laundry, I would put a load in on my way to bed as a little surprise to help her out with the chores.

If at all possible, use cold water, especially on colored clothes. The colors stay sharp longer and don't fade as quickly.

Wash full loads rather than small loads. That saves on energy for both you and the appliances. Remember, *do not* run the washing machine or dryer when no one is at home. If the machine leaks or shirt-circuits, you could have some big problems.

As soon as the dryer stops, take out the permanent press articles. Think toward no ironing, and that way you'll have less ironing than otherwise. Many articles can go without the iron if you remove them immediately from the dryer and put them on hangers. So . . . keep a good supply of hangers close to your laundry area!

Now let's talk about hangers. The plastic colored-type are really the best. They help prevent marks and creases on your clothing, plus you can color-code your whole family. If you have several children at home, plus mom and dad, you will use a lot of hangers.

An easy way it worked for us was to give each person in the family a color. Brad had blue, Jenny had yellow, mom had white, dad had red, etc. When the shirts or blouses were taken out of the dryer, they were hung on the appropriate-colored hangers. Then when the children came in from school, they picked up the hangers of their color, took them to their room, and hung them up.

You can also color-code underwear and socks as much as possible by giving each family member his or her color or pattern. Another great idea is to sew onto the garments (with a thread or embroidery thread) the person's color so he or she can identify the items. Color-coding also works well with folded clothes. One mom told me she had a shelf built in her laundry area, and on this shelf she placed colored plastic bins (the dishpan type). So if Brad's color is blue he gets a blue bin, Jenny gets yellow, etc. All the folded-type clothes go in at the time of folding and are taken to the person's room. If the bin is not returned to the laundry area, then no clean clothes until it is!

Another mom went a step further and gave each person his own colored towels. Again, Brad would now have blue towels. If a towel is left lying around and it's blue, we know who didn't hang up his towel or put it away!

Put a few hooks near the laundry area so they will be handy to hang the colored hangers on. If your laundry area is in the garage, a long nail works great. Or string a line from one rafter to the next. (It also makes a great clothesline for those drip-dry articles or rainy day hangups.)

Fold each load as you take it out of the dryer. Should you forget a load and it sets awhile, simply throw in a well-dampened towel and let it dry again for about ten minutes. The dampness from the towel will freshen up the load and take out any set wrinkles.

Set aside at least one day a week for ironing. Keeping ahead of ironing is the only way to keep your mind free of those "need to do" lists that grow longer and longer.

One husband shared with me that anytime he needed a fresh shirt to wear, it needed to be ironed. Surprise him, gals, and have a catch-up ironing day! How happy he will be when he goes to the closet and see *all* his shirts beautifully ironed on his colored hangers! Then keep it up. No more hurried ironing at 6:00 A.M. so hubby has a clean shirt to wear to work. It's another way of saying "I love you."

When folding linens and towels, fold them all in one direction. When they are placed on the linen closet shelf, they can be piled up neatly in an organized fashion.

Label your shelves in the linen closet so that whoever puts the linens away will know the right spot.

Buying different patterned sheets for each person's bed is great for instant recognition. One mother told me she buys solid sheets for twin beds, stripes for full or queen, and floral for the king-sized beds.

Let's Review

- Teach and delegate some laundry responsibilities to your family.
- Start washing loads early in the day or the night before.
- Color-code the family.
- Aim toward having no ironing.
- Fold each load as you take it out of the dryer.
- Iron weekly to prevent ironing build-up.
- Have family members put away their own laundry.
- Label linen-closet shelves for quick identification.
- Thank the Lord we have appliances to help us save time!

Household Remedies for Stubborn Stains

A home is built of loving deeds.

*H*OLIDAY TIME is busy enough without having to fight spots and stains. Do you wonder how you can get stubborn stains out? If the holiday tablecloth is stained and so are the cloth napkins—with lipstick—this can cause added stress for the holidays as well as any day.

Here are some hints on getting those stubborn stains out.

Candle wax. To remove from fabrics, simply place a paper towel under the spot and one on top of the spot. Press with a warm iron until the paper towel absorbs the melted wax. Move the paper towel frequently so it doesn't oversaturate.

Coffee or tea. Can be removed by rubbing the stain with a damp cloth dipped in baking soda.

Lipstick. Here are three ways to remove lipstick from fabric: 1) Rub it with a slice of white bread; 2) dab the smear with petroleum jelly, then apply a dry-cleaning solution; 3) pat with salad oil on the spot and launder the fabric after five minutes.

Makeup marks disappear from dark clothing if they are rubbed with bread.

Nail polish spots. If they get on fabric (which happens often to women with small children), lift the spot by applying remover to the fabric underside. (But first check on an inconspicuous place to make sure you won't damage the fabric.)

Grease. Remove grease from fabrics by applying cornstarch or dampening and then adding salt dissolved in ammonia.

Food stains. There are several ways to remove chocolate or cocoa stains from fabrics. You could soak the stains thoroughly with club soda before washing or else rub talcum powder into the stains to absorb them. Try applying milk to the stains, since milk keeps them from setting. A fourth way is to rub shortening into them, then launder. Remove fruit stains by pouring a mixture of detergent and boiling water through the fabric or sponge the stained area with lemon juice. You can also rub the cut sides of a lemon slice over the stain. To remove egg stains from fabric, soak the fabric for an hour in cold water before laundering.

Hardened stains. These can sometimes be loosened up by placing a pad dampened with stain remover on top of the stain and keeping the top pad damp by adding more stain remover as needed.

You can remove shoe polish from clothing by applying rubbing alcohol. If traces of polish remain, add a teaspoon of borax powder to the water when laundering.

To eliminate a tar spot on fabric, apply shortening and let the tar soften for ten mintues. Scrape it away and launder.

Hints on Treating Spots and Stains

Work fast! Treat the stains right away. The longer a stain stays on a fabric, the more likely it is to become permanent.

Handle stained items gently. Rubbing, folding, wringing, or squeezing can cause the stain to penetrate more deeply and may damage delicate fibers.

Keep a cool approach to stain removal, since heat can set a stain. Keep stained fabrics away from hot water, a dryer, or an iron. After washing a garment, be sure all stains are completely removed *before* ironing. Heat-set stains are often impossible to remove.

Remove as much of a stain-producing agent as possible before treating it with a stain-removal product. That way you'll avoid the the possibility of enlarging the stain.

Steps to Success

Pretest any stain-removing agent in an inconspicuous spot, such as the seam allowance or hem of a garment, the part of a rug that is hidden under a table or chair, or the upholstery under a seat cushion. Always run a sample test, since even water may damage some surfaces.

When you flush a stain, especially on a nonwashable fabric, carefully control the flow of flushing liquid with an adjustable plastic trigger spray bottle.

When stain-remover instructions call for sponging, place the fabric stained-side-down on an absorbent pad. Then dampen another pad with water or a stain remover and blot lightly from the center of the stain outward to the edge to minimize the formation of rings. Change the absorbent pads when there is any sign of the stain transferring to them so the stain won't be redeposited on the fabric. For ring-prone fabrics, barely touch the stain with the sponging pad so the stain absorbs the cleaner slowly. When the spot has been lifted, use a dry pad on either side to blot up as much excess moisture as possible.

Tamping is a good way to remove stains if the fabric is sturdy enough. Use a small dry brush or toothbrush. Use it as a small hammer with a light action until the stain is removed.

An effective way to loosen many stains is by scraping with a teaspoon. Place the stain directly on the work surface and grasp the spoon by the side of its bowl. After adding a stain remover to the stain, move the edge of the spoon's bowl back and forth in short strokes, without pressing hard on the spoon. This procedure shouldn't be used on delicate fabrics.

You'll get best results if you work from the center of the stain outward.

If, in the cleaning process, you have to use more than one stain-removal agent or method, thoroughly rinse after each one before applying the next.

Homemade Spot Removers

A soapless spot cleaner can be created by mixing two cups of isopropyl rubbing alcohol (70%) with ¾ cup of white vinegar. Pour the mixture into a clean bottle and cover tightly. *Label* the bottle. To use, blot the soiled area until it is dry, apply the cleaner with a cloth or sponge and let stand for several minutes, then blot the area dry again. Repeat if necessary. Blot with water after using.

To make a wet spotter for nongreasy stains, combine one cup of water with two tablespoons of glycerin and two tablespoons of liquid dishwashing detergent. Stir in a small bowl until the mixture is thoroughly blended. Pour into a clean bottle or squeeze bottle and cover the container tightly. *Label*. When using, blot the soiled area dry, apply the spotter, let the spotter stand for several minutes, and then blot the soiled area dry again. Repeat if necessary.

Tips
for Easier
Spring Cleaning

> In everything you do, put God first,
> and he will direct you and crown
> your efforts with success.
>
> —*Proverbs 3:6*

AS WINTER begins to melt away, we get excited and motivated to get our homes in order. But it takes a bit of organization and a few tips in order to get started toward completing the job. Just remember, it can take less time than you think. Jobs that you anticipate taking two hours can actually take only a few minutes.

So let's get started with these three thoughts in mind:

DO IT!
DO IT RIGHT!
DO IT RIGHT NOW!

Cleaning Products to Have on Hand

- All-purpose cleaner
- Floor products (waxes plus cleaners for vinyl or wood floors)
- Bathroom products (disinfectant, tile cleaner, mildew remover)
- Furniture polish
- Cleaning pads

- Scouring powders
- Metal polish
- Silver polish
- Window cleaner
- Dishwashing detergent or powder
- Rug and carpet cleaners
- Upholstery cleaners (Scotchguard after cleaning to protect against staining)
- Bleach, liquid or dry
- Fabric softener, liquid or sheets
- Prewash stain removers
- Oven cleaner (be sure to use rubber gloves with this type of cleaner)
- Drain cleaner
- Toilet bowl cleaner (a pumice stone is a must for removing the ring around the bowl)
- General cleaners (vinegar, ammonia, baking soda)

Cleaning Tools to Have on Hand

- Rubber gloves
- Vacuum cleaner, plus attachments for those hard-to-reach places (blinds, baseboards, radiators, shutters, corners in furniture, mattresses, ceilings, and walls)
- Dustcloth (100% cotton is best, such as towels, flannel, etc.)
- Feather duster
- Brushes for corners, tile, barbecue, etc.
- Paper towels
- Bucket
- Rags
- Broom and dustpan
- Stepladder or stepstool
- Mop
- Floor polisher or shampoo rug cleaner (optional)

Methods to Try

- Do one room at a time. Don't hurry; be thorough.
- Make a chart and delegate some of the jobs to the family: a) dad: windows; b) son: barbecue; c) daughter: pantry.
- Each week reward your family by making their favorite pie, cake, or dinner.
- Take short breaks and eat an apple or have a cup of tea or chocolate milk and cookies.

• Take cleaners with you from job to job and room to room by putting them in a bucket, a plastic type carry-all, or a basket.

• Turn on the radio for music to work by. Make it lively music so you can work faster.

• Time yourself by setting a timer. It's amazing what you can accomplish in 15 minutes.

• Upholstery furniture pieces can be brushed and vacuumed clean. This removes surface dirt and should be done four times a year.

• Drapes can be sent out for cleaning, or, depending on their fabric, they could be washed. Once-a-year cleaning is generally enough.

• Miniblinds can be removed and hosed down with sudsy water and ammonia. Then they can be maintained monthly with a feather duster.

• Wash windows quarterly (more often if needed).

• Baseboards should be checked monthly and cleaned if needed.

• Check air conditioner/heating unit. The filters need to be checked and replaced at least twice a year. These must be kept clean for maximum efficiency and lowest cost.

• Barbecue grill can be scrubbed with a hard brush. Oven cleaner works great, but make sure to use rubber gloves. Remember to remove ashes after each use.

• Keep your awnings clean by scrubbing with a long-handle brush. Use water and a mild soap. Rinse with a hose.

• Garage and cement driveways can be cleaned and scrubbed with detergent. Scrub with a stiff broom dipped in thick detergent suds. Repeat over the oil stains. Rinse by hosing with clean water.

Organizing Your Summer to Prevent Trouble

They that wait upon the Lord shall
renew their strength. They shall
mount up with wings like eagles.
—Isaiah 40:31

*T*HE NATIONAL Safety Council esti-
mates that more than half of all summer
accidents could be prevented if people took simple, common-sense
precautions.

Summer brings varied schedules and activities: day and summer
camp, skiing, swimming, biking, and many other activities which
may result in animal bites, heat exposure, sunburn, cuts, insect bites,
and much more. Unpredictable situations may be prevented by
following these helpful hints:

• Post emergency phone numbers in plain view by the telephone
for you and your children and the babysitter.

• Plan ahead by taking a first-aid class including CPR (cardio-
pulmonary resuscitation) from your local Red Cross chapter. Many
chapters offer the classes at no charge.

• Give your children swimming lessons at the earliest possible
age. Many YMCA's and YWCA's offer great programs for children.

• If you are in an area where no swimming classes are offered,
work with your children yourself. We started with our children at a

very young age by pouring water over their heads and having them hold their breath and blow bubbles underwater. Make it fun, and at the same time you will be helping them become comfortable in water.

• Common water-safety violations often result in injury. These include running, jumping, or sliding around a pool deck, diving without checking the water depth, and leaving a child unattended beside a pool, lake, or bathtub. (Purchase a cordless phone to keep with you at home so you won't leave the children unattended by pool or bathtub.) Go over safety rules with the family *often*: no running, never swim alone, etc.

• Purchase (or put together yourself) a first-aid kit for car travel. Keep it in a suitcase at the lake or pool area. This will keep it handy for you but out of the reach of children.

• Sunburn is very common, so use extra precautions. Sunscreen lotions are a must; keep them handy for small children and light-skinned people. Sunscreens are rated from 1 to 30; the higher the number, the more protection they give. A sun hat, visor, or bonnet is also recommended to prevent sunburned noses.

• Poison ivy, poison oak, and poison sumac are often found in uncultivated fields and wooded areas. Touching one of these plants (whose leaves often cluster three to a stalk) usually results within 24 hours in an oozy, itchy rash that may spread over much of the body. The trouble comes with infection caused by scratching the area. If your summer plans include hiking or picnicking in wooded or mountain areas, review with the family the facts about these poisonous plants. You may want to go to the library and find photos of the plants. Ask questions and inquire about these and other potential dangers in the area you plan to go to. Educate yourself and your family for a safer outing.

• Insect bites or stings can cause swelling, pain, redness, burning, or itching which can last from 48 to 72 hours. If you know you are allergic to bee stings, before leaving town be sure to consult your doctor about any medication you may need to take along. This is a good item to keep in your first-aid kit.

A honey bee leaves its stinger imbedded in the skin. It's best to remove the stinger with tweezers or by scraping with a fingernail. Wash the sting area with soap and water and apply ice or flush with cold water to reduce swelling and pain. Calamine lotion is available over-the-counter in drugstores. Baking soda works well by mixing with water to form a paste. (Baking soda is another good item for your first-aid kit.)

• Think ahead and plan ahead in order to be prepared for emergencies. When taking various foods on picnics, remember to keep the perishable items in coolers with lots of ice. Any food item containing mayonnaise is likely to go bad quickly. Don't let any food items sit in the hot sun. Eggs and uncooked meats need to be kept especially well-cooled.

• Take a car emergency kit. Some very good kits are available at auto parts stores. Or you can make up your own kit consisting of: flares, jumper cables, "HELP" sign, "CALL POLICE" sign, fire extinguisher, nylon rope, towel, flashlight, fuses, and an approved empty gasoline can. All of these can be put together in a plastic dishpan, which can also be used to carry water in an emergency.

• Buy and use a "Hide-A-Key" box. After the first time I locked my keys inside my car, the time I lost and the stress I endured sent me directly to a store to find a "Hide-A-Key" case and attach it to the car in a hidden place. (This makes an especially good gift for teen drivers.) For some reason keys locked inside a car cause lots of trouble to lots of people. So think ahead and prevent this kind of trouble!

Fall
Family
Organization

Don't act thoughtlessly, but try to
find out and do whatever the Lord
wants you to.
—*Ephesians 5:17*

*I*S GETTING the children organized a
problem for you after a summer of
irregular schedules? Here are a few steps to help you!

Step 1

Plan a back-to-school organizational day with each child. For the
working moms it may need to be a Saturday or an evening.

Step 2

With a child, go through his or her drawers and closets and throw
or give away summer clothing and outgrown shoes. A lot of the
summer clothing can be stored away for next summer. Put clothing
in boxes and label the boxes according to size, so when next summer
arrives, the clothing can be given to other members of the family or
to friends whom they will fit. That way you can recycle the children's
perfectly good clothes. The boxes can be stored in the basement,
garage, attic, or closets.

WARDROBE INVENTORY

Blouses	Pants	Skirts	Jackets	Sweaters

Dresses	Gowns	Lingerie	Shoes	Jewelry

Step 3

Take a wardrobe inventory! A checklist chart (Figure 1, page 60) like the one on the previous page will be helpful.

Step 4

Now comes the fun. Plan a time alone with each child to go over the inventory chart and to discuss needed new clothing to fill in the chart.

For moms that sew, take the child with you when picking out patterns and fabrics. If shopping from mail order catalogs, sit down and discuss the purchases with your child. Make it a togetherness time, and then he or she will feel part of the new wardrobe and the "I hate to wear that" syndrome will be eliminated. This method also teaches your children how to make decisions responsibly. Later on you'll find this guidance and time pay off as your children grow older and shop capably for themselves.

Step 5

Plan a family meeting to discuss home responsibilities. Make up a "Daily Work Planner Chart" (see Figure 2, page 62). Notice that mom's and dad's names are also listed on the chart. This shows that you work together as a family. Especially if mom is working outside the home, the family needs to support her all they can.

Step 6

Make a list of jobs the family can do to help around the house. (See Figure 3, page 63 with suggested jobs.) Put each item on a separate piece of paper and put each into a basket. You may need two baskets, one for children's jobs 3-7 years old and one for children 8-18. Then once a week the children will draw out two to five jobs. These jobs are put on the "Work Planner Chart."

As the children do their job, a happy face can be drawn by their name (or a sad face if they dropped the ball and neglected to do their job.) Stickers or stars can also be used. This makes for a colorful chart.

If they complete their jobs easily, they may draw another job from the basket and get extra credit or double stickers, stars, or happy faces. Children become excited about duties around the house and work toward a colorful chart for each week of the month.

DAILY WORK PLANNER CHART

Day of the Week	Mom	Dad	#1 Child	#2 Child	#3 Child	#4 Child	#5 Child
Saturday							
Sunday							
Monday							
Tuesday							
Wednesday							
Thursday							
Friday							

DAILY WORK PLANNER CHART

Day of the Week	Mom	Dad	#1 Child	#2 Child	#3 Child	#4 Child	#5 Child
Saturday	Clean House	Clean Garage	Bathe Dog	Mow Lawn	Clean Refrigerator		
Sunday	Plan Upcoming Week	Plan Upcoming Week	Set and Clear Table	Do Evening Dishes	Do Evening Dishes		
Monday	Menu Planning Grocery Shopping	Pick Up Dry Cleaning	Do Evening Dishes	Set and Clear Table	Empty Garbage Feed Dog		
Tuesday	Wash Clothes	Pick Up Rooms (clutter)	Fold and Distribute Clothes	Do Evening Dishes Feed Dog	Set and Clear Table		
Wednesday	Mop Floors	Clean Bathroom(s)	Set and Clear Table	Do Evening Dishes Feed Dog	Do Evening Dishes Feed Dog		
Thursday	Shopping Drop off Dry Cleaning	Vacuum	Do Evening Dishes Feed Dog	Set and Clear Table	Empty Garbage		
Friday	Change Bed Linens	Water Plants	Dust Furniture	Do Evening Dishes Feed Dog	Set and Clear Table		

Figure 3

At the end of the month you can plan a special family surprise as a reward for jobs well done. You might say, "This month we've worked together as a family. Now we're going to play together as a family." Plan a fun Saturday bike ride ending with a picnic lunch, or a Friday evening by the fire popping corn and playing a favorite family game.

Organizing for fall can be a creative and productive time in your homes. Let's begin.

• Wallpaper scraps. It's always a good idea to save wallpaper scraps in case sections of the paper need to be repaired later. To make a patch, tear (don't cut) a scrap into the approximate size and shape needed. The irregular torn edges will blend better with the paper already on the wall, making the patch less apparent than it would be if cut.

• Paint splatters. Here's an easy way to erase paint splatters from a brick fireplace. Get a broken brick the same color as the brick on the fireplace and scrub it back and forth over the spattered areas. Brick against brick will abrade away most of the paint. Any remaining paint will pick up the brick color and thus be camouflaged.

• Turning one pound of butter into two pounds with gelatin. Let the butter stand at room temperature until soft. Into $1\frac{1}{4}$ cup cold milk, soften one envelope of unflavored gelatin. Add $1\frac{3}{4}$ cups hot milk; stir until gelatin is dissolved. Cool until lukewarm. Whip into butter with electric mixer. Keep covered in refrigerator. Use within one week as a spread, not for baking.

• Clutter. Work better and faster by tossing out things that are no longer needed or have lost their usefulness, such as stacks of old magazines or receipts. If you don't want to throw them out, store them in a box.

• Unfinished work. Don't let work pile up. Decide which projects need to be completed.

• Lots of choices. Since your time is limited, choose to do things that you enjoy or find useful. Don't overload yourself with tasks or responsibilities. Always strive to simplify your life.

• Procrastination. Do the jobs you dislike *first*. Once you've got those unpleasant tasks out of your way, you'll find that the rest of the work will be somewhat easier.

• Racing through each day. Try to work smarter, not harder. Plan your day. Pace your energy and skills through the day like a disciplined athlete getting ready for the Olympics. At the end of the day you will have achieved more and won't feel so tired and stressed.

• Cleaning the grout. To clean the grout between the tiles in your kitchen or bathroom, mix up a paste of scouring powder and hydrogen peroxide (just enough to make a paste.) Apply with an old toothbrush, let sit 20 minutes, then wash off with hot water and a scrub brush. (Keep the windows open as you work!) Try a mildew stain remover you can buy in the hardware store or supermarket and apply according to the directions on the container.

• Whitening a porcelain sink. First fill the sink with two or three inches of warm water. Add detergent and half a cup of chlorine bleach. Let sit 15 minutes, then wash the entire sink with the solution. Rinse thoroughly with hot tapwater.

• Cleaning glass or plastic shower stall doors. Just put a little lemon oil furniture polish on a soft clean cloth and rub the doors clean. Be careful not to get any of the lemon oil polish on your tiles. (The whole problem of keeping the shower stall doors clean can be avoided if everyone wipes the doors dry after taking a shower!)

• Speeding up a sluggish drain. First run hot tapwater down the drain, then pour in three tablespoons of baking soda and half a cup of distilled white vinegar. Stop up the drain and wait 15 minutes. The baking soda and vinegar will foam up, reacting with each other and eating away at whatever is slowing the drain. Finally, flush the drain with hot tapwater.

• Removing candle wax from a tablecloth. Place the waxy section of the tablecloth between two thicknesses of paper toweling and press with a warm iron. If a greasy spot remains, treat it with a dry cleaning fluid.

• Removing candle wax from a candlestick. Try pouring boiling water into the candlestick socket to melt the wax. Once melted it will wipe out easily.

• Getting white rings off furniture. Dampen a cloth with a small amount of mineral oil and dab it in fireplace ashes. Wipe gently on the ring, then polish or wax the wood as usual.

• Eliminating cooking odors. Boil 1 tablespoon white vinegar in 1 cup water over stove. This will eliminate unpleasant cooking odors.

• Eliminating tobacco odors. During and after a party, place a small bowl of white vinegar in the room.

• Freshening laundry. Add $1/3$ cup baking soda to wash or rinse cycle. Clothes will be sweeter and cleaner smelling.

• Removing water spots from fabrics. Sponge entire stained area with white vinegar; let stand a few minutes. Rinse with clear, cool water and let dry.

• Removing lipstick, liquid makeup, or mascara from fabrics. Soak in dry-cleaning solution and let dry. Rinse and then wash.

• Freshening lunch boxes. Dampen a piece of fresh bread with white vinegar and put it in the lunch box overnight.

• Making your blankets fluffier. Add 2 cups white vinegar to a washer tub of rinse water.

• Removing dark or burned stains from an electric iron. Rub with equal amounts of white or cider vinegar and salt, heated first in a small aluminum pan. Polish in the same way you do silver.

• Removing decals. Paint them with several coats of white vinegar. Give the vinegar time to soak in. After several minutes the decals should wash off easily.

• Deodorizing refrigerator. Place one opened box of baking soda in the back of the refrigerator or in a shelf on the door. Change every other month.

• Freshening drains and garbage disposal. Use a discarded box of baking soda previously used in your refrigerator.

• Removing burned or baked on foods from your cookware. Scrub with baking soda sprinkled on a plastic scouring pad; rinse and dry. You might also try warm soda paste soaked on burned area; keep wet, then scrub as needed.

• Deodorizing your carpet. Sprinkle dry baking soda on the rug. Allow to set overnight, then vacuum. (Test for color fastness in an inconspicuous area.)

• Deodorizing cat litter. Cover the bottom of the litter pan with 1 part baking soda; then cover baking soda with 3 parts litter to absorb odors for up to a week. Litter won't need replacing as often.

• Disinfecting wood chopping surfaces. Scrub with a mild bleach solution, then rinse and rub it with a thin coat of mineral or salad oil.

Year 'Round
Clothing Care

She looks for wool and flax, and
works with her hands in delight.
—*Proverbs 31:13* NASB

*W*ITH THE COST of clothing and fabrics these days, we need to know what we can do to keep our clothing fresh and new, especially if we are spending money on fairly expensive clothing.

We live only one hour from the Los Angeles garment district, and 90 percent of all my clothing is bought from 40 to 70 percent off. I don't have time to shop very often, so I need to take especially good care of my clothing so it will look new and fresh for several years. Here are some fun ideas and tips to do just that.

First of all I start with three basic items in a solid color:
1. A blazer or jacket
2. A skirt
3. Pants

To these three basics I then add blouses in prints or solid colors that will coordinate. Next I add a few sweaters and several accessories, such as scarves, ribbon ties, boots, jewelry, and perhaps a silk flower. Finally I purchase two pairs of shoes, one for casual wear and one pair for dress (the church type).

Since I do a great deal of traveling, I take these six to nine items and a few accessories (plus one all-weather coat) and coordinate them into approximately 12 to 16 outfits that will last 7 to 14 days.

How to Make Clothing Last

1. Dry clean your garments every eight to ten wearings (or longer if possible). Dry cleaning is hard on fabrics.

2. Rotate your various items of clothing as much as possible so they can regain their shape. I have a friend who rotates her garments by hanging them after each wearing at the right end of the closet. The next day she picks the skirt or pants that are on the left end of the closet. That way she knows how often they are worn. This works especially well with men's suits.

3. As soon as you take off your garments, empty the pockets, shake the garment well, and hang up immediately.

4. Have you ever thought of Scotchguarding your new fabrics? It's very effective and will last until the garment is cleaned or washed. (Then just spray it again.) You can also use Scotchguard on your fabric shoes.

5. Mend your garments as soon as they are damaged. Sew on those buttons and repair those rips and loose hems. My Bob has a tendency to tear out the seat of his pants, so I triple-stitch and zigzag the seams when they are new, even before they are worn. That keeps embarrassing moments to a minimum.

6. Keep from snagging your hose by using hand lotion to soften your hands before putting your hose on.

7. Hang wrinkled clothes in the bathroom while showering. The steam will cause the wrinkles to come out.

8. Let perfumes and deodorants dry on your body before getting dressed in order to prevent garment damage.

9. I put a scarf over my head before pulling a garment over my head to prevent a messed hairdo and makeup smudges and stains.

10. Hang blazers and coats on padded hangers to avoid hanger marks.

11. Keep sweaters in a drawer or shelf rather than on a hanger (to prevent stretching).

12. Skirts and pants are best hung on hangers with clips; or you can use clothespins on wire hangers.

13. Even very good jewelry can discolor your clothing, so just dab the backs with clear nail polish. The polish can also be painted on jewelry with rough edges that could pull fibers of fabrics.

14. Some stickpins can make holes in delicate fabrics, so be careful and don't wear them if you are in doubt.

15. Be sure to have your good leather shoes polished to retain their shine. It also feeds and preserves the leather.

16. Brush suede shoes with a suede brush that brings up the nap. You can use a nail file to rub off any little spots.

17. Replace heels and soles on your shoes before they wear down completely.

18. If your shoes get wet, stuff them with paper towels or newspaper and allow to dry away from direct heat.

19. Shoe trees are great to keep the shape in your shoes.

20. When storing leather handbags or shoes, never put them into plastic bags, since this can cause the leather to dry out. Instead, use fabric shoe bags or wrap the shoes in tissue and put them into shoe boxes.

21 Washday Hints to Relieve Laundry Stress

She makes coverings for herself;
her clothing is fine linen and
purple.
—*Proverbs 31:22 NASB*

*D*OES WASHDAY come when there is nothing clean left to wear? Does your clothing need to be ironed before you can go out of the house, or do you go anyway looking wrinkled or crumpled? Do your children dash madly about in search of matching socks but are not able to find them because your washing machine ate them up or they fall out of a fitted sheet two weeks later, after you've thrown out the single one?

Sorting laundry can save time, stress, and energy. Children can be taught simple organizational techniques to save the family washday stress.

1. Divide your laundry into three cloth bags. These can be made from fabric or three large king-size pillowcases with a drawstring. Bag 1 is white for the soiled white clothes. Bag 2 is dark (brown, navy, black) for the dark soiled clothes (jeans, washcloths, etc.) Bag 3 is multicolored for the mixed-colored clothes. Colored plastic trash cans can also be used. Label the cans "colored," "white," and "dark." Show all members of the family how to sort their own dirty clothes by putting them in the proper bags or cans. Each child or

bedroom could have its own laundry bag. From there they take the clothes to the central sorting area, then sort their own into the three bags. (Or each day *all* dirty clothing goes to the sorting area.) On washdays or whenever the bags become full it's a simple matter of dumping bag 1 into the machine and swish, swash, the wash is done. To solve your missing-sock problem, invest in plastic sock sorters. These can be found in drug or variety stores. Safety pins are also great to keep socks paired during the wash and dry cycles. One mom purchased only white socks for the children, one size fits all. Remember, it's not what you *expect* but what you *inspect*. So be sure to teach the method and then inspect from time to time to see if they are doing it properly. Whatever goes *in* the bags inside out will come *out* inside out.

2. Each family member can also have his or her own bright-colored bin for clean folded clothes. Christine's is pink, Chad's is blue, Bevan's is white, mom's is red, and dad's is green. Or you can use all white bins (or dishpan-type bins) and color-code them with stick-on dots or colored felt markers with each family member's name on them.

3. Whoever folds the clothes places each person's items in his or her proper bin. It is then the responsibility of each family member to take his own bin to the drawers and empty the bin. Should the bin not return to the folding area, no clothes will be folded for that person.

4. Plan your washing days and start washing early in the day.

5. On washing day use cold water if possible, especially on colored clothes, as this will help them to stay bright longer.

6. Wash full loads rather than small ones. This saves energy and your appliances as well.

7. Never leave the washer or dryer running when you aren't home. A machine leak or short circuit can cause damage or, worse yet, start a fire.

8. If using a dryer, remove the clothes as soon as it stops, then hang and fold. This will save wrinkled items and many times save ironing items.

9. Forgot to take out the clothes in the dryer? Simply throw in a damp towel or washcloth and turn on the dryer again for five to ten minutes. The dampness from the towel will freshen the load and remove any wrinkles.

10. Hang as many clothes as possible on hangers, especially permanent-press garments. This will also help cut down on ironing. Put up a few hooks near the laundry area or string an indoor clothesline.

11. I recommend using plastic-colored hangers rather than metal ones. They prevent marks and creases on your garments. Using colored hangers can also color-code your family. Assign each person a different color. Then when you take the clothing out of the dryer, hang it on the appropriate-colored hanger: mom, white; dad, brown; Kevin, blue; Susie, yellow; etc.

12. Schedule at least one day a week for ironing, or three 15-minute slots per week. Keep ahead of your ironing; this will relieve your stress level and eliminate having to iron at the last minute before you leave the house.

13. To help ironing time go quickly, pray for the person whose clothing you are ironing. This way ironing can become a real joy and blessing.

14. Label your linen closet shelves so that whoever puts the sheets and towels away will know just the right spot for them. This prevents confusion, keeps your closet looking neat, and saves time in finding king-size or twin-size.

15. When your iron sticks, sprinkle a little salt onto a piece of waxed paper and run the hot iron over it. Rough, sticky spots will disappear as if by magic.

16. Always wash your throw rugs in cool or lukewarm water. (Hot water will cause the rubber backing to peel.) Let the rug dry on a line instead of in the dryer. You can fluff it up when it is dry in the no-heat cycle of your dryer.

17. Here's a little trick to make ironing easier: Using pieces of wax candles in an old cotton sock, swipe your iron every so often while ironing. The wax makes it glide smoothly, and your ironing goes faster.

18. Instead of using expensive fabric-softener sheets, pour one-fourth cup *white* vinegar in the last rinse of the washing cycle. This eliminates static cling, helps remove wrinkles, gives clothes a fresh smell by removing soap, and cleans the drains of the washer by removing soap scum and lint.

19. Another way to remove garment wrinkles: Hang wrinkled garments on the curtain rod in your bathroom and run very hot water from the shower. Close the bathroom door and let the water run for a couple of minutes. The steam will fade the wrinkles from your clothing. Great for those who travel!

20. If your steam iron clogs up, fill it with a mixture of one-fourth cup of vinegar and one cup of water and let it stand overnight. Heat the iron the next day. Remove the mixture and rinse with clear water.

Children

How to Get Your Children to Help Around the House

Train up a child in the way he
should go, and even when he is old
he will not depart from it.
—*Proverbs 22:6 NASB*

*A*S A MOTHER of five children under five years of age, at one time in my life it was easy to become overwhelmed and frustrated at trying to be Supermom. I needed help, and the help came from my family. I found a way to get my husband and children to help with the housework cheerfully. Even the toddlers helped.

Your children will benefit by one day becoming independent, responsible adults who are pleased with their accomplishments. So make the housework fun, give clearly defined directions, keep the jobs realistic, and avoid criticism. Above all, praise, praise, praise!

I wrote the jobs that they could do on individual pieces of paper and put them in a basket. Then they got to choose two or three jobs from that basket once a week. These jobs went onto a Work Planner Chart, which was posted. When jobs each day were completed they were marked with an "X" and a happy face or a sticker. By the end of the week the chart was full of marks; each child used a different-colored marking pen, and each loved to see his or her color appear often. Rewards came at the end of the week, with lots of praise!

Toddlers respond well to marks on a chart, and teens like to work on a point system. (So many points per job; add them up on Saturday and reward accordingly.) When our children got into junior high school, even their friends wanted their names on our Work Planner Chart. Why? Because we had a well-defined plan, we made it fun, and they were rewarded.

If you want your children to grow up believing that the mess belongs to the person who made it, don't teach them that they are helping mommy. Instead, applaud them for making *their* bed, dressing *themselves*, and putting *their* clothes away. Praise your children for keeping *their* room neat and putting *their* toys away. Thank them for doing a good job because they are such good workers. Help them to feel good about being a part of a family effort. Then they will learn that they are part of a family team in which each person contributes and each person appreciates the other.

Have the mindset that the child's room belongs to the child. Teach your children from an early age (one, two, three years old) to be responsible for their own clothes, bed, laundry, and toys. This way they will find out early that if they wish to live in a neat and clean room they will have to do the work themselves.

You ask, "What if they like to live in a mess?" You are still the winner because you are spared the time, energy, stress, and aggravation of doing it all.

At an early age, when they make their bed praise them for it! Praise will get you everywhere, and they'll want to do it again and again.

When they're ready to put away their toys, have boxes, bins, or low shelves available for them to use. Let them do it their own way, arranged by them and not you. Provide low hooks so they can hang their own sweaters, jammies, and jackets. Whenever possible, make a game of putting these things away.

One mom installed a wooden pole that went from the floor to the ceiling. Then she screwed cup hooks into the pole and sewed a plastic curtain ring onto each of the children's stuffed animals so the children could easily hang up their animals when they were finished with them. This arrangement also provided a creative decorator item, and the children loved hooking their teddy bears to the pole.

Make the chores fun and games. The children will want to work if you make it a happy time!

A toddler can set the table. Make a placemat out of paper and draw the shapes of the fork, plate, spoon, and glass. The child gets to put each item in its proper place. Soon Susie or Timmy will want to set the table for everyone.

Let them play policeman or trashman. Give them a pillowcase to pickup toys, trash, and papers around the house and even in the yard.

Toddlers can feel important this way and can learn to like the feeling of work. Congratulations are in order for a job well done!

Help your child dress independently. Keep solid bottoms in a low drawer with printed tops. If you buy coordinates, any top will go with any bottom. Even a young child can choose what to wear within reason and limitations.

Avoid uncomfortable or difficult clothing. If you want to have children who can dress themselves, they certainly can't cope with tight collars or fancy buttons. Snaps and loose tops help them not to feel frustrated. The Velcro used on shoes today is great for little fingers and makes the children feel proud of themselves as they put on their own shoes.

Yes, children can learn to love to do their fair share around the house!

20

How to Teach Your Children About Money

Steady plodding brings prosperity;
hasty speculation brings poverty.
— *Proverbs 21:5*

*W*E LIVE in a world where adults often find themselves in financial woes. Where do we learn about money? Usually by trial and error, since few families take the time to teach their children how to be smart with money. Yet at an early age, children should know about money and what it can do for them.

Children who learn about money at an early age will be ahead in this mystery game. Learning to deal with money properly will foster discipline, good work habits, and self-respect.

Here are eight ways in which you can help your children get a good handle on money.

1. **Start with an allowance.** Most experts advise that an allowance should not be tied directly to a child's daily chores. Children should help around the home not because they get paid for it but because they share responsibilities as members of a family. However, you might pay a child for doing *extra* jobs at home. This can develop his or her initiative. We know of parents who give stickers to their children when they do something that they haven't

specifically been asked to do. These stickers may then be redeemed for 25 cents each. This has been great for teaching not only initiative but also teamwork in the family.

An allowance is a vital tool for teaching children how to budget, save, and make their own decisions. Children learn from their mistakes when their own money has been lost or spent foolishly.

How large an allowance to give depends on your individual family status. It should be based on a fair budget that allows a reasonable amount for entertainment, snacks, lunch money, bus fare, and school supplies. Add some extra money to allow for church and savings. Be willing to hold your children responsible for living within their budget. Some weeks they may have to go without, particularly when they run out of money.

2. **Model the proper use of credit.** In today's society we see the results of individuals and couples using bad judgment regarding credit.

Explain to your children the conditions when it's necessary to use credit and the importance of paying their loan back on a timely basis. You can make this a great teaching tool. Give them practice in filling out credit forms. Their first loan might be from you to them for a special purchase. Go through all the mechanics that a bank would; have them fill out a credit application and sign a paper with all the information stated. Let them understand about interest, installment payments, balloon payments, late payment costs, etc. Teach them to be responsible to pay on time.

3. **Teach your children how to save.** In today's instant society it is hard to teach this lesson. At times we should deny our children certain material things so that they have a reason to save. As they get older they will want bicycles, stereos, a car, a big trip, etc. They need to learn the habit of saving so they can then buy these larger items.

One of the first ways to begin teaching the concept of saving is to give the children some form of piggy bank. Spare change or extra earnings can go into the piggy bank. When it gets full you might want to open an account at a local bank.

When your children are older you might want to establish a passbook account at a local bank so they can go to the bank and personally deposit money to their account. Most banks will not pay interest until the balance becomes larger, but at least this habit of depositing money will help your children begin thinking about saving.

In the end, children who learn how to save will better appreciate what they've worked to acquire.

4. Show them how to be wise in their spending. Take your children with you when you shop, and show them some cost comparisons. They will soon see that with a little effort they can save a lot of money. You might want to demonstrate this principle to them in a tangible way when they want to purchase a larger item for themselves. Go with them to several stores to look for that one item, writing down the highest price and the lowest price for that item. This way they can really see how much they can save by comparison shopping.

Clothing is an area where a lot of lessons on wise spending can be made. After awhile your children will realize that designer clothes cost a lot more just for that particular label or patch. Our daughter, Jenny, soon learned that outlet stores were great bargains for clothes dollars. To this day she can still find excellent bargains by comparison shopping.

5. Let them work part-time. There are many excellent part-time jobs waiting for your child. Fast-food outlets, markets, malls, babysitting, etc. can give valuable work experience to your children. Some entrepreneurial youngsters even begin a thriving business based on their skills and interest. These part-time jobs are real confidence boosters. Just remember to help your child keep a proper balance between work, home, church, and school. A limit of 10 to 15 hours per week might be a good guideline.

6. Let them help you with your budgeting. Encourage your children to help you budget for the family finances. This gives them experience in real-life money problems. They also get a better idea about your family's income and expenses. Children can have good suggestions about how to better utilize the family finances, and their experience can give them a better understanding of why your family can't afford certain luxuries.

7. Give them experience in handling adult expenses. As your children get older they need to experience real-life costs. Since children normally live at home, they don't always understand true-to-life expenses. Let them experience paying for their own telephone bill, car expenses, and clothing expenses. Depending upon the situation, having them pay a portion of the utility and household bills can be an invaluable experience for children who have left school and are still living at home.

8. Show them how to give to the Lord. At a very young stage in life, parents and children should talk about where things come from. The children should be aware that all things are given from God and that He is just letting us borrow them for a time. Children can understand that we are to return back to God what He has so abundantly given to us. This principle can be experienced through either Sunday school or their church offerings. When special projects at church come up, you might want to review these needs with your children so they can decide whether they want to give extra money above what they normally give to their church. Early training in this area provides a valuable basis for learning how to be a giver in life and not a taker.

Your children will learn about money from *you*, so be a good model. If you have good habits, they will reflect that; if you struggle with finances, so will they. One valuable lesson to teach them is that money doesn't reflect love. A hug, a smile, a kiss, or just time spent together is much more valuable than money.

Summertime Projects to Keep Your Children Busy

> Children are a gift from God; they are his reward.
> —*Psalm 127:3*

ONE JULY afternoon our Brad and Jenny echoed, "There's nothing to do, Mom. What can we do to have some fun?"

With a quick prayer and a lot of creativity we came up with our Summer Project Box. We scurried around the house to find just the right box. (The right box should be sturdy and made of cardboard. A shoebox, hatbox, or even a file-type box will do.) To keep our projects separate we made cardboard dividers (file folders will also do). On these dividers we listed summer projects which the children were interested in exploring. I found that they were very creative in their ideas.

Here are some of our projects that were successful. Your children may have other projects, depending upon their ages and interest.

Sports/Games

Set up a file on your favorite sports star. Include photos (you can send for them), articles from newspapers and magazines, and autographs.

Also include copies of letters which your children write to their favorite stars in football, baseball, hockey, skating, etc.

Organize a Summer Olympics in your neighborhood. Time the running events and relay races, and measure the long jumps. Design and create medals and/or rewards.

Set up a bowling alley in your backyard by using milk cartons for pins and a large rubber ball. Tell the children they can ask neighbors to save their milk cartons to contribute to this project.

Garden/Nature

Plant and care for a vegetable garden or flower garden. Children love to watch the plants come up and to eventually harvest the vegetables and pick the flowers. Keep records on plant growth, watering, and fertilizing.

Make a study of insects. Keep a record of what they eat and how they live. Make sketches of them. Take your children to the library and find books about insects and how to identify them.

Press wildflowers to use for art projects, Christmas cards, and/or thank-you notes.

Find rocks—smooth, round, and odd-shaped. Make creative items with them by painting them with flowers, people, and animals. One summer the children filled their wagons with the rocks they had painted and sold them door-to-door as paperweights.

Food

Set up a lemonade stand for the neighborhood. This is a great way for younger children to learn about running a small business. Have them make the posters, set the cost, and stock the stand with such items as lemonade, ice, and cups, and perhaps such additional items as muffins, cookies, licorice, and nuts. Garden vegetables could also be sold (corn, carrots, radishes, pumpkins, etc.).

Have your children choose a recipe and make something from scratch. Have them file a copy of the recipe in a box, with notes on how it came out.

Beach/Lake

Take pictures or make sketches of various kinds of boats. Collect shells and devise your own classification system. Take a field trip to the beach and discover the tidepools. List the different kinds of crabs, snails, starfish, etc.

Go lake or ocean fishing and bring home the catch for dinner.

Study nature, balances of life, tadpoles, and frogs.

Go sailing, canoeing, rowing. List the activity and what was learned. Put into the Project Box.

Vacations/Short Trips

Conduct research to find places in your area that would make good family trips. Write a short description of each place and include, if possible, a photo or drawing of the spot. Share your research with the family.

Make a file of activities for car, plane, train. List necessary items to take along. Include clothing, camera, etc. Collect maps, brochures, and postcards from your travels and file them in the Project Box.

The children may come up with more project categories to add to the Project Box. They will be excited by simply putting together their box. The summer will be fun, exciting, and a real learning time for your children as they choose a project on those days when they would otherwise say, "But, mom, there's nothing to do!"

Organizing Fun Ways for Your Children to Earn Money

Much is required from those to
whom much is given, for their
responsibility is greater.

—Luke 12:48

*T*O BE INDUSTRIOUS is what Proverbs 31 tells us women to strive to achieve. But do we teach that to our children? As our own children grew up, we thought of all kinds of ways to create money-earning ventures. One of the very first projects they did was at ages five and six. We lived in a beach area in Southern California and spent time collecting shells and rocks. We had so many that they overflowed the bedrooms. So one summer we had a rock-painting session in the garage with acrylic paints. The children made creative, colorful rocks and shells, and when they were finished they displayed their creations in their wagon, walking the neighborhood and selling their rocks and shells for five cents each. They were really excited to sell rocks and shells for cash!

It's hard for children to earn money by doing chores around the house. Even for money it just isn't the same as earning it independently. When children earn money for themselves it gives them a sense of responsibility. When the jobs are fun and helpful, everyone benefits.

How much should mom be involved? Plenty at first. Make sure you know the people who are hiring your child. Help match your child's age and ability to the job in question, and be sure the child is realistically paid for his or her time. After that pull back, relax, and watch your child blossom with the satisfaction of earning money for a job well done.

Over the years we came up with many moneymaking ideas. Here are some of the family-tested ones that WORK!

1. **Toy Sale.** This children's version of the garage sale works especially well when the prices are kept low, since most customers will be other children. Put pricetags on everything, post a sign at the bottom of the driveway, and place the most eye-catching items up front. Let the children take it from there. They will learn about making change, negotiating, and (after sitting for hours between customers) perseverance.

2. **Pet-sitting**. Many owners of birds, cats, and goldfish (and other pets that don't need walking) hire a sitter to come in every day to feed the animals, change what needs changing, and give the pets some love and affection. Depending on the child's age, you may have to help lock and unlock the pet owner's doors or gates. But once inside, it's the child's job, and it's a good one. Standard rates of pay for this service are between $1.50 and $4.00 per day.

3. **Yard Work.** Even before they're old enough to handle power equipment, children can help garden in other ways. Their young backs don't get nearly as tired from pulling weeds and planting flowers as adults' do, and children make great scouts for hidden rocks and branches that play havoc with the lawnmower. Rates should be a penny per rock for the tiny tots and more when the work is harder.

4. **Dog-Walking.** The size of the dog may dictate the size of the walker, but most kids can handle this job. People are surprisingly eager to pay someone else to walk their dog, especially when the weather is sloppy. Today's busy person is usually happy to pay $1.00 per walk.

5. **Assisting at Children's Birthday Parties.** The hired helper should be only a few years older than the party group. He can help pass out food, round up trash and wrapping paper, oversee the games, and provide a vital extra set of eyes and hands for those guests who wander off and search for something breakable. Rate of pay: $3.00 per party.

6. **Cleaning Out Crawl Spaces, Storage Sheds, Etc.** The more cramped the space, the better little bodies can help to clean it.

Children are surprisingly strong and endlessly curious about cluttered nooks and crannies. Though they can't sort through the things you've accumulated, it may be worth paying a few cents just for the company. Rate of pay: 50¢ per hour.

7. **Child-Walking.** An older child can walk a younger child to school every day, to a music lesson, or to the playground for a time of teeter-totter or swinging. Estimated rate of pay: 25¢ per day.

8. **Summer Stock.** This is always a fun time for children to express their talents. Plan a show where several children put on an act or talent show. Sing a song or lip sync to a record, tell a few jokes, play an instrument, juggle, write and then read a poem, do a dance, or teach the dog a trick and then have the dog do tricks. Sell tickets to the show. Suggested ticket price: 20¢ to 50¢ each, depending on the talents.

9. **Summer Camp.** This is great fun for several children to help in. Together they can supervise up to eight children—making crafts, running relay races, and conducting a story read-aloud hour.

Two hours is usually the maximum attention span for most children. Rates: from $2.00 to $4.00 per child, depending on the cost of necessary craft items, such as popsicle sticks, yarn, paints, cookies, juice, and other goodies.

10. **Car Wash.** Always a hit. Cloths, whisk broom, buckets, and window spray will be the equipment needed. Children can go door-to-door and make appointments. After the winter weather has thawed out and the spring rains are over is a good time to canvass the neighborhood. If they do a good job they could very well turn this into a weekly job. Rates range from $1.50 to $3.00 per car, depending on the size of the car and how well the job is completed.

11. **House-Sitting.** Many people like their home taken care of when out of town or on vacation. This is a good opportunity for the child to learn responsibility. The lawn and potted plants (indoor and outdoor) need watering, paper and mail taken inside, and lights turned on and off to make the situation seem normal. Pets can also be fed and watered. The rate of pay will depend on the amount of work done. Range: $1.00 to $5.00 per day.

Child Safety

In everything you do, stay away
from complaining and arguing.
—*Philippians 2:14*

*C*HARCOAL lighter fluid may not taste
good, but a thirsty child may easily grab a
can, put it to his mouth, and down a swallow in a matter of seconds.

I was reminded of this type of household accident (and others)
shortly after our three grandchildren were born. I realized once
again the importance of making my home safe for small children.

Accidents happen when we least expect them, and they are most
common within our own homes. The National Safety Council esti-
mates that there is a home accident every seven seconds.

Even if you don't have children, making your home safe for
visitors with small children is very important.

I've compiled a list to help you get started.

Kitchen Safety

- Keep knives in a knife holder on a wall or in a higher drawer.
- Put knives in dishwasher point down.
- Store cleaning items in a plastic bucket or a carry-all with a
handle. Place it on a shelf in the garage or the hall closet.

The bucket or carry-all can then be taken from room to room for cleaning and will free up the space under the kitchen sink for storing paper towels, napkins, paper plates, and cups.

• When cooking on your kitchen range, keep the handles of your pots turned *away* from the front of the stove. If you don't do this, children can easily dump a pot of boiling water or food on their heads by pulling on a handle or swinging a toy overhead.

• Always wrap broken glass in paper or place it in an old paper bag before throwing it into the trash. This goes for razor blades and jagged metal lids as well. A child may drop a toy into the trash and try to retrieve it, or may be taking out the trash and see an item he wants to look at or take out.

• When wiping up broken glass off the floor, use a dampened paper towel. This will ensure that you get all the pieces and will also protect your hands.

• Teach your children how to pour hot water slowly and to aim steam away from them so it doesn't gush out and burn them. Be sure to check the lid of a teapot or kettle to see that it fits tightly and won't fall into the cup and splash boiling hot water all over.

• Any poisons or extremely dangerous products should be kept in a locked cabinet on a very high shelf.

• Never store products in unlabeled jars or cans. It's just too easy to forget what's inside.

• For all electrical outlets, purchase cover caps for your child's safety. The caps are very inexpensive and can be purchased at drugstores, hardware stores and even children's shops.

• Never leave a cord plugged into a socket with the other end exposed for a child to put into his mouth. Use an empty toilet paper tube to wrap your cords around, and place the tube in a safe drawer.

Bathroom Safety

• Never leave children in the bathtub unattended; a lifeguard needs to be on duty at all times. Falling is just one of the hazards that younger children face in the tub. Don't answer the door or telephone without taking the child with you.

• Check the water temperature carefully before putting children in the tub or shower. It can start out warm but then get really hot if you accidentally brush the faucet handle with your hand. Never allow children to fiddle with the faucets. Scalds can happen very quickly.

• Never add hot water to the bathtub when the baby is in it. Be sure the hot water faucet is turned off tightly. Wrap a washcloth around the faucet for safety when the child is in the tub.

• Tell the whole family that shower valves should be turned to "OFF" after use. Otherwise a bather or bathtub cleaner may get scalding water on his or her head.

• Store all medications in a cool, dry place somewhere other than the bathroom. This way there is no danger of little hands reaching your medicine, and it will not be damaged by moisture.

Door Safety

• If you have small children in your home, keep your bathroom doors closed at all times. A latch placed up high where toddlers can't unlatch it should do the trick.

• Be careful of bathroom doors that lock from the inside. Be sure you have an emergency key that will open the door from the outside should junior become locked in and you locked out.

• Door gates can be used across bathroom or bedroom doors, stairs, and many other places that you want to keep away from children. These gates can be purchased in most stores that have baby departments. Look for them also at garage sales or in want ads in newspapers.

Miscellaneous Safety

• Post emergency phone numbers near your phone for both yourself and babysitters.

• Take a first-aid class that includes CPR (mouth-to-mouth resuscitation) at your local Red Cross chapter.

• Give your children swimming lessons at a very early age and/or teach them in the bathtub how to hold their breath underwater. Many community pools offer swimming lessons.

• If you don't already have a first-aid kit, get one or make up your own. Store it out of children's reach.

• Use side rails on small children's beds to keep infants from falling out. These can be purchased out of catalogs or in children's departments at most stores.

• Keep scissors, plastic bags, icepicks, and matches away from the reach of children.

• Warn children not to touch an electrical appliance plug with wet hands.

Remember, safety saves lives!

Preparing for Vacation Travel

> If you refuse to discipline your son,
> it proves you don't love him; for if
> you love him you will be prompt to
> punish him.
>
> —*Proverbs 13:24*

*B*ELIEVE IT or not, it can be a joy to travel with your children!

Granted, the preparation for a trip sometimes seems exhausting, and you may wonder if it is worth it all to leave the house, the pets, and a regular routine. But the excitement and wonder of children as they experience new sights will truly be ample reward for the effort involved.

Here are some hints for making your trip smoother for the whole family.

• **Prepare your child for the exciting adventure.** Talk with them about where you are going and what you will be doing. As a child grows out of the infant and toddler stages and as his world expands to include friends, some verbal preparation becomes very important.

Tell your youngsters about the fun that is in store for them. Show them books, maps, and photographs about your route and destination. Be sure to reassure them that you will soon return home and that the toys they didn't take with them will still be there when they get back.

• **Watch your tendency to overpack.** The rule of thumb for experienced travelers applies to children as well: *Take just what you need and no more.*

The length of the trip (adjusted for the dirt factor for your children) should give you a reasonable handle on the amount of clothing they will need each day. Bear in mind that a public laundromat will probably be available during your travels.

• **Pack only clothing that your children like.** Let them help you pack. Even a three-year old can learn to help. Lay out five items and let them choose two to take along. This is a great teaching tool.

In our family, our children eventually did all their own packing. I merely checked their items to be sure all the bases were covered. Sometimes we had to leave items behind because, as time and experience taught us, we learned we were wearing only half of what we took. However, always take a sweater or sweatshirt, since temperatures can sometimes change very quickly, even in tropical areas.

• **Take toys that your children enjoy.** Again, let your child help in this area. A toy that you consider mundane might provide considerable amusement to your child.

It's also a good idea to stash away a couple of new attention-getters—maybe a special surprise like a new toy that he or she has always wanted. But don't forget the tried and true, either. A special pillow, favorite blanket, cuddly stuffed teddy, or special doll are often comforting for a child sleeping in a strange bed for the first time.

• **Consider a backpack for the preschooler and older child.** This is a great way of limiting items or toys taken. Make a rule that your children can take along whatever fits into their backpack.

• **Bring along a surprise box**. Children love it when mom and dad have secrets for them. Your box can include such items as toys, food snacks, puzzles, books, and word games. Be creative but keep it a surprise, and when things get hectic or a child gets irritable, pull out the surprise box.

• **Remember car seats**. If you are renting a car for your trip, request a car seat for any child four years old and younger. Many rental agencies provide these seats, but the availability is sometimes limited, so it is important to reserve one.

• **Plan frequent stops.** This is very important if you are traveling by car with small children. Cramped legs and fidgety children will be the cause of many arguments if not taken care of sensibly.

Give your children plenty of opportunities to get out and run, skip, and jump for a few minutes, and also to use the restroom.

• **Always carry a small cooler with you.** Keep a cooler filled with milk, fruit juice, snacks, and fruit. This will be a pick-me-up, and the refreshment is always welcome. It will also prevent too many fast-food stops. Picnic whenever possible; it's cheaper and children love it.

• **Invest in a first-aid kit.** Fill an empty coffee can with Band-Aids, children's aspirin, antiseptic, thermometer, scissors, safety pins, tweezers, adhesive tape, gauze, and cotton balls. Try to cover all bases. Don't forget a good supply of handy wipes and a blanket.

• **Bring a flashlight.** Be sure to check the batteries before leaving home. When all else fails, children love to play with a flashlight. Take along an extra set of batteries.

• **Throw in your bathing suits**. Keep these in an easy-to-get-to place. Many motels and hotels have pools that are usable even in the winter months. They may also have hot tubs or Jacuzzis. Also, you may find yourself stopping by a lake or beach for a quick swim.

• **Give your children their own map.** Depending on the age of your children, give them a map so they can follow the route and tell you how far it is to the next stop or town. Older children can also keep a journal of the trip.

• **Send up a prayer for safety and patience.** Before we drive out of our driveway, we always offer a prayer for protection and patience. Prayer during the trips also helps to calm a tense situation.

Some of your most memorable times together as a family will come from traveling on vacation. With a little planning and preparation, those memories can be truly happy ones.

Off to School

Let the little children come to Me,
and do not forbid them, for of such
is the kingdom of God.

—*Mark 10:14 NKJV*

I CAN vividly remember when my niece, Keri, was living with us. We had done everything possible to make sure that she knew how to walk to school on that first day of kindergarten. We had even made dry runs, with her walking without us and us following behind in a car to make sure she got there. And in practice she did well.

On that first morning to school she left the house all dressed with new clothes, little knapsack, and a lunchbox. We were so excited on that first day of school. We kissed her goodbye, took a picture, and said goodbye. Off she walked in the direction of her new school. But in about 30 minutes the principal of the adjoining elementary school called and said, "Your niece Keri is here at the wrong school!"

No matter how hard we try, our efforts sometimes go unnoticed. However, there are certain steps we can take to make sure that the first school experience is at least somewhat successful.

Walk with your child to school or the bus stop at least once before the school year starts. Be sure the child understands any special arrangements you have made for his or her going to school and returning home. Practice the proper way to cross the street at every opportunity.

Be sure your child has seen and used a public toilet (including a urinal for boys) so that the school restrooms won't seem strange. Teach your children to use the correct words to ask to "go to the restroom or toilet." Emphasize the need to wash hands even when grownups are not around with reminders.

If your child will be eating lunch in the school cafeteria, take him or her to eat at a cafeteria-style restaurant, so that the procedures will be familiar. Let your child practice at home carrying a loaded food tray or using a lunchbox. Remind him or her to bring his lunchbox home each day.

It is very important for your child to know his or her full name, address, and home and work telephone numbers. (At least Keri did know how to get in touch with me.) An excellent way to teach these numbers is to set them to the tune of a nursery rhyme or a popular song. Be sure to give the school office your *work* number as well as your home number, plus the name and number of a parent substitute to call if you're not available in an emergency.

Make a safe place to keep any notes "to" and "from" the teacher. I inserted a manila envelope with holes punched on one side into my child's loose-leaf notebook. This way the notes to home didn't fall out and get lost.

Sick Days

Is your child too sick to go to school? This is a common cry heard by mom and dad. Talk to your child and carefully listen to what he or she is saying. The problem may not be stated in words but instead may be hidden beneath several unrelated answers. If you decide to allow your child to stay home from school, have a quiet talk showing a lot of love from mom.

If your child has too many pleas for sick days, consider causes other than illness, such as being teased, or frightened, fear of parental separation, etc. If you choose to keep your child home from school and in your judgment the child is not truly ill, staying home should not be a fun time. Put the child to bed for the day to "get well." If his pleas continue, make an appointment with your family doctor and your child's teachers. Both professionals might give you valuable feedback to why your child wants to stay home.

Reasons to Keep a Child Home From School

- A fever of 101 degrees or greater.
- Nausea and/or vomiting.
- Abdominal cramps.
- Diarrhea.
- A cold, when it is associated with a fever, frequent coughing, or heavy nasal congestion.
- A cough, when its symptoms aren't due to any allergy or the aftereffects of a recent illness.
- A sore throat, with fever.
- Any unidentified rash. This should be checked promptly by your doctor for the possibility of measles, chicken pox, or other infectious disease.
- Any infectious disease that your doctor has diagnosed.
- An earache.
- Conjunctivitis (pinkeye).
- Your own visual test or gut feeling that tells you your child really isn't well.
- Your child is overly tired or emotional.

Send your child off to school with a hug and a smile!

Finances

Keeping Your Utility Bills Down

My health fails; my spirits droop,
yet God remains. He is the strength
of my heart; he is mine forever!

—Psalm 73:26

$\mathscr{E}$NERGY BILLS are never fun to pay. Although some factors may be beyond your control (extreme weather conditions, home location, or illness in the family), there are ways to make your use of energy more efficient and to reduce your energy bills. Here are some tips and ideas to help stabilize those bills.

Heating

Your heating system is probably your home's biggest energy user in the winter. It can be an energy waster if you don't use it wisely.

1. Leave the thermostat alone. During the day set it at 65 degrees or below. You raise operating costs 5 percent every time you raise the thermostat two degrees. Turn it down to 55 degrees or off at bedtime for more energy savings.

2. Proper insulation keeps your home warm in winter and cool in summer. In fact, up to 20 percent of your heating energy can be lost through an uninsulated ceiling.

3. Cut more heat loss by weatherstripping doors and windows. Close the damper when not using the fireplace or else heat will escape. Close off rooms not in use, along with heating vents, though not in more than 30 percent of the house. (Make sure you leave the vent open nearest the thermostat to insure proper temperature sensing.) Turn off individual thermostats.

4. Close draperies at night to keep out the cold. Open them during the day to let the sun shine through.

Lighting

Although individual lights don't use much energy, because houses are full of them and they get so much use (especially in winter), lighting costs can add up. Here are some ideas on keeping lighting costs down.

1. Fluorescent lights provide three times the light for the same amount of electricity as incandescent lights. They are very economical for bathrooms and kitchens, last ten times as long as incandescent bulbs, and produce less wasted heat.

2. Dimmer switches can multiply bulb life up to 12 times while they reduce electricity use.

3. Turn lights off when you're leaving a room and advise your family to do the same.

4. Let the light shine through. Lampshades lined in white give the best light. Tall, narrow shades or short, dark-colored ones waste watts. (Dirt and dust absorb light too, so add bulb-dusting to your cleaning list.)

5. One properly situated light in a room will do the work of three or four carelessly placed fixtures. Rearrange your room so the light is used more efficiently. If you're redecorating, use light colors. Dark colors absorb light.

6. Don't use infrared heating lights for night lights or general lighting.

7. Use lower-watt bulbs.

8. Turn off all outdoor lights except those necessary for safety and security.

Hot Water

Although hot water is the third-largest energy user in the average household, its use can be cut down painlessly.

1. Consider flow-restricting devices. These devices can cut water consumption in half.

2. Buy a water heater insulation blanket. This saves up to 9 percent of your water heater costs.

3. Fix the drips on all faucets. One drip a second can waste up to 700 gallons of hot water a year!

4. Take showers instead of baths. The shower's the winner for less hot water use if you keep your shower time under five minutes. (If you need to wash your hair, do it in the sink. A shower just to shampoo is a hot water waster.)

5. Monitor the use of the dishwasher. Run it once a day or less. It uses about 13 gallons each time instead of the 10 gallons each time you wash dishes by hand.

6. Use cold water for the garbage disposal. It solidifies the grease and flushes it away easily.

7. Turn down the temperature on your hot water heater to 140 degrees. (That's a "medium" setting if your dial isn't numbered.) If you don't have a dishwasher, 120 degrees may be adequate.

When you go away on vacation, set the pilot setting on "low" or turn it off altogether. If you have an electric water heater, it may be the type on which the upper thermostat can be set 10 degrees lower than the bottom one.

Energy-Saving Tips
Around the Home

Always be joyful. Always keep on
praying. No matter what happens,
always be thankful, for this is
God's will for you.
—1 Thessalonians 5:16-18

*I*T SOMETIMES seems surprising how
those energy bills can jump around
from month to month. What can you do to stabilize those bills and
hold down the energy costs?

Some factors may be beyond your control: extreme weather,
location of home, illness in family, old or less efficient appliances,
etc. Additional houseguests, entertaining, building around the
house, special projects, and vacations can often contribute to fluctu-
ation in your energy usage.

Most energy users in the home are easily recognized, and many
times you can make these more efficient. Here are some tips and
ideas to help you stabilize those energy bills.

Refrigerator/Freezer

Your refrigerator/freezer is probably one of the biggest energy
users in your home. Here are some ways to beat the cost of keeping
things cool.

1. *Keep it clean.* In a manual-defrost model more than half an inch of frost can build up and make the appliance work harder, so *defrost regularly.* Vacuum clean the condenser coils below or at the back of the refrigerator/freezer three or four times a year. Clean coils keep it running efficiently and help save energy.

2. *Keep it closed.* The time for decisions is not when you have the door open. Get everything you need for a sandwich or recipe in one trip.

3. *Keep it full.* Frozen food helps keep the air cool in your freezer. But don't overpack food in either refrigerator or freezer, or the cold air won't have space to circulate properly.

4. *Heat has no business in the refrigerator.* Cool dishes before you store them so your appliance won't have to work so hard.

5. *Investigate before you buy.* A frost-free refrigerator/freezer may use 30 percent more electricity than a manual-defrost unit. Also, be sure to choose the correct cubic footage for your family, since a too-full or too-empty refrigerator/freezer wastes energy.

6. *Unplug your second refrigerator.* Refrigerators are big energy users, so if your second refrigerator is not being used to full capacity, unplug it. It could save you $15 a month or more, depending on its size.

Range/Oven

Your food budget shouldn't stop at the checkout counter. These days the cost of preparing the food can add up. Here are some tips on holding down cooking costs.

1. *Pots and pans are important.* Pans with flared sides or that are smaller than your burner let heat escape. If they're too big or have warped bottoms, food won't cook evenly. (For most foods, a medium-weight aluminum pan cooks fast and efficiently. Save your heavy pans for foods that require slow, steady cooking.)

2. *Cover up.* Use pan covers, since trapped steam cooks food quickly. Also, thaw foods completely before cooking.

3. *Preheating is out.* Unless you're baking things like breads and cakes, preheating isn't necessary and is very costly. Casseroles and broiled foods don't need it.

4. *Plan all-oven meals.* A meal like meat loaf, baked tomatoes, scalloped potatoes, and baked apples can all cook at the same time and temperature.

5. *Limit your boiling.* Water doesn't get any hotter with prolonged boiling. Therefore when you need to bring water to a boil

(e.g. for making drip coffee), turn off your range once the water has started to boil.

6. *Keep that oven door closed.* Every time you open the door, you lose 25 degrees of heat. Get yourself a timer and just be patient.

7. *Use your free heat.* A gas oven retains heat for up to 15 minutes, an electric oven for up to half an hour, and an electric range-top element for three to five minutes. Use that free heat to warm up desserts or rolls or to freshen crackers and cookies.

8. *Keep it clean.* A range free of grease and baked-on residue works better and costs you less.

9. *Use a microwave oven.* A microwave oven uses about the same amount of energy per hour as a conventional electric oven but cooks most foods in less than half the time. This can mean big savings on the cooking portion of your bill.

10. *Use your electric skillet.* Use your broiler oven or toaster oven instead of your electric range's oven for cooking and baking in small quantities. These can use as little as half the energy and won't heat up the kitchen nearly as much.

Washer/Dryer

Here's how to get the most out of that costly hot water.

1. *Wash full loads.* Washing two or three large items (like sheets) with a number of small ones (but don't pack them in) will give you a clean wash without taxing your washer's motor. If it is necessary to wash less than a full load, adjust the water-level settings accordingly.

2. *Sort by fabric, color, and degree of soil.* Use hot water only for whites, hard-to-clean items, and sterilizing. Use cold and warm water on all the rest. Your clothes will be just as clean, will fade less, and will have fewer wrinkles (which might save you some ironing).

3. *Check hose and faucet connections.* If the hose is cracked or the faucet connection is loose, you're probably losing hot water.

4. *Don't overkill.* Don't overdo it on soap, washing cycle, or drying. An oversudsed machine uses more energy. Regular clothes need only a 10- to 15-minute washing cycle. And overdrying will age your clothes and make them stiff and wrinkled.

5. *Get the lint out.* Clean the filters on the dryer after every use. Besides making your clothes more attractive, a lint-free machine works more efficiently.

6. *Use your clothesline.* It will save you 100 percent of the energy otherwise consumed by your gas or electric dryer. This could

amount to between $2 and $9 of the average $70 bill paid monthly in some areas of the country.

Small Appliances

Some small appliances can do the same jobs with half the energy use as their full-sized counterparts. Use them whenever practical.

1. *Use small appliances.* Small appliances use less energy if you remember to turn them off when you're through. Pull the plug on your coffeepot, iron, electric skillet, and curling iron. (A memory lapse will waste energy and might ruin the appliance.)

2. *Little appliances are okay.* You needn't be guilt-stricken about enjoying the luxury of an electric toothbrush or carving knife. (A continuous-charge toothbrush usually uses less than five cents a month and a carving knife less than ten cents a year.) Cut down instead on the *big* appliances. They're the ones that add up on your electric bill.

Air Conditioning

In many areas keeping cool in summer can cost a lot more than keeping warm in winter. Here are some things you can do to hold down the cost.

1. *Watch your degree of comfort.* Set your thermostat at 78 degrees or above. A setting of 78 instead of 73 saves 20 to 25 percent of your AC operating costs.

2. *Keep the cool air inside.* Close doors and windows. Check the weather-stripping. Seal up cracks. Insulate. These measures will help cut heating costs in the winter as well.

3. *Don't block vents.* Move furniture away from vents and window units. Trim shrubbery outside, too.

4. *Close drapes or blinds.* This helps keep the sun's heat out. Solar screens and shades can also effectively block a large amount of the sun's heat before it enters your home.

5. *Check your filters.* Do this once a month during cooling season. Vacuum or replace them as necessary.

6. *Grow deciduous trees.* Plant them where they will shade your house from the sun's hottest rays in the summer and let warming sun through in the winter.

7. *Check the EER before you buy.* Some systems use less energy than others—sometimes only half as much. Find the Energy Efficiency Rating (EER) on the yellow energy-guide label. The higher

the EER, the more efficient the unit. An EER of 10 will consume half the energy of a similar unit rated 5.

Swimming Pool

If you have a pool, a major portion of your energy outlay is the cost of operating it. Here are some ways to get control of swimming pool energy costs.

1. *Lower your pool's temperature.* Lowering your pool heater setting just two degrees can reduce your pool heating substantially. (A reduction from 80 degrees to 78 degrees could save up to 20 percent of heating costs.) The lower temperature saves on chemicals, too.

2. *Use a swimming pool cover.* You can save as much as 80 percent on your summer pool-heating bill by using a pool cover.

3. *Heat early in the morning.* The sun and the pool heater work together most efficiently during the morning hours.

4. *Protect your pool from wind.* Wind has the same effect on your pool as blowing on hot soup: It cools it. Hedges, fences, and cabanas help keep wind down.

5. *Don't overfilter.* Most pools require only four to five hours of filtering a day in summer and two to three hours in the winter. Reducing your filtration by 50 percent may save you more than $20 per month. Be sure to filter before 11 A.M. and/or after 5 P.M.

6. *Keep filter, skimmer, and strainer basket clean.* When your pump motor doesn't work as hard, it costs less to operate.

7. *Don't overclean.* Automatic pool-sweeping devices can usually get the job done in three to four hours a day in the summer and two to three hours a day during the off-season. But remember to set the cleaner to start 15 minutes before your filter. Again, try to operate the sweep outside the hours of 11 A.M. to 5 P.M.

Waterbed

Improperly controlled, waterbed energy costs could make you lose sleep. These tips will save you a lot of money.

1. *Don't unplug the bed during the day.* Getting the bed up to temperature every night uses more energy than operating the bed continuously with thermostat control.

2. *Make the bed every morning.* Controlled tests have shown that

beds with mattress pad sheets, cotton quilt, one blanket, and one-inch foam rubber mat between mattress and pad save about $15 a month over one covered by just sheets.

As you begin to put these various tips into practice, you will begin to see real savings on your monthly energy bills!

Saving Time and Money

A man who refuses to admit his
mistakes can never be successful.
But if he confesses and forsakes
them, he gets another chance.

—Proverbs 28:13

IME AND MONEY: We never seem to
have enough of either of them, do we?
Actually, we can control both time and money so that they work
efficiently for us.

Here are some practical household tips that can help you save both
time and money on a daily basis.

Saving Time

1. Plan a weekly menu and base your shopping list just on those
menus. Then add to your list those staples which are getting low.
Make sure your list is complete before you go shopping; it will save
you time and gasoline.

2. Avoid trips to the market for single items.

3. Never shop for food when you're hungry; you may be tempted
to deviate from your shopping list!

4. Plan your timetable for meal preparation so that your broccoli
is not done ten minutes before the chicken and thereby loses color,
texture, flavor, and nutritive value.

5. If you have such conveniences as a microwave oven or food processor, take advantage of them by incorporating them into your time schedule and menu for the week.

6. Organize your kitchen and save steps. Keep your most-used cookbooks and utensils in an area close at hand.

7. Save salad preparation time by washing and tearing salad greens once a week. Store them in an airtight container such as Tupperware.

8. Learn to do two things at the same time. When talking on the telephone you can: load the dishwasher, clean the refrigerator, cook a meal, bake a cake, mop the floor, or clean under the kitchen sink. I do recommend getting a long extension cord on your telephone!

9. Shell and chop your fresh pecans and walnuts while watching television. Then store them in the freezer or refrigerate them in airtight bags. When baking day arrives you'll be all set.

10. Convenience foods are worth their extra cost when time is short. A stock of frozen pastry shells, for example, will enable you to make a quiche or cream pie in very little time.

Saving Money

Here are some tips to keep in mind when planning your weekly menu.

1. Seasonal produce is usually your best buy. Green beans, in season, cost less per serving than canned beans and offer much more nutrition. Fresh produce also has better flavor and fewer additives.

2. High-ticket items are placed at eye level at most grocery stores. Check the top and bottom shelves for similar items with lower price tags.

3. Avoid impulse buying, if it's not on your list, don't buy it.

4. Check your local newspaper ads for sales, especially in the meat section.

5. When things are on sale, consider buying them in larger quantities. For example, a dozen cans of tuna can be stored indefinitely.

6. Stay within your budget. Take a small notepad or calculator to the store so that you can keep a running total.

7. Take advantage of coupons, but only buy the product if it is already on your shopping list. Although this seems tedious, I know women who save $5.00 and more on their weekly grocery bill by using coupons.

8. Buy cheese in bricks. Slice or grate it at home to save the cost of handling and packaging.

9. Compare prices. For example, whole chicken breasts with ribs are about half the price of boned chicken breasts. If you want boned chicken, buy whole chicken breasts and parboil them for 10 to 12 minutes, and the meat will peel right off the bone.

10. Turn your unused bread crusts or not-quite-fresh bread and crackers into crumbs by using your blender. Use your crumbs in stuffing, casseroles, and meatloaf.

11. Save the oil from deep-frying. Strain it through cheesecloth and then refrigerate it.

12. Citrus fruit yields more juice when stored at room temperature.

13. Look into using special services and conveniences that don't cost extra money. For example, shopping from catalogs is one way to streamline your schedule and save time.

By putting even half of these ideas into action, you'll be surprised at how much time and money you'll save!

Great
Fund-Raising
Ideas

Happiness comes to those who are
fair to others and are always just
and good.

—Psalm 106:3

ANY OF US are members of churches,
clubs, fraternities, or sororities that are
looking for ways to raise funds. About the time we realize there is a
need to raise funds, we scratch our heads to think of creative ways to
supplement our budget. Our minds go blank! Some of these ideas
from our readers can help you.

• **Service, Time, and Talent Auction.** In this auction you don't
sell material possessions but pledges for service, time, and talent.
Items you might include: baby-sitting, a resort area condominium,
home-baked cookies once a month for a year, car service to and from
the airport for a future plane trip. Each donation is the generous
giving of self.

• **Cleanup Crew.** A great high school or teenage project is to take
the place of professional street cleaners when you need to clean the
streets of the fall leaves. Charge the neighbors or business tenants a
fair wage scale. It doesn't take many students to earn a substantial
amount of money for their special project.

• **Hill of Beans.** Here's a fund-raiser that's literally a hill of beans—kidneys, pintos, lentils, split peas, garbanzos, limas, and more. Members of your club can donate these beans. Combine them into a colorful, flavorful mix, which are then bagged in plastic baggies of two cups each and sold for $2.00 along with instructions for rinsing, soaking, and making soup. Tie a colorful ribbon at the top of your bag to provide colorful eye appeal.

• **Lip Sync.** Hold a lip-sync show. While a recording of a real singer plays, each child performs one or two songs, imitating the artist's style and mouthing the lyrics. Have rehearsals so the students can pool the songs, tapes, records, and lyrics. You can even make costumes with materials on hand and such finishing touches as feathers or jewelry. Sell tickets or take a freewill offering. This is a good source for added funds.

• **Krazy Kalendar.** For your special fund-raiser, make up a unique calendar where you can preprint for specific days of the month specified money to put away for this fund-raising idea. For example, during a typical week in July ask for 50 cents on Sunday "if you didn't go to church tonight," followed by "one cent for each year of your age above 21" on Monday, "ten cents if you have a patio or deck" on Tuesday, "25 cents if you turned on the air conditioner" on Wednesday, "five cents for each glass of water you drank" on Thursday, "one cent for each page of a book you read" on Friday, and "ten cents if you drank lemonade" on Saturday. Deposit the money in a jar and contribute jointly for your special fund-raiser.

• **House Numbers.** Raise extra money by painting street numbers on the curbs of your neighborhood streets. Be sure to clear the idea with your local police department. Call on the neighbors to presell the orders. Depending on the economic level of your neighborhood, a fair price would be in the $3.00 to $5.00 range. Stencil black numbers in white 6 x 10 inch rectangles on curbs, steps, and sidewalks. You might even have local merchants donate the paint. You will find that the police and fire departments are usually delighted with the easy-to-read addresses.

• **Tasting Bee.** If you are passing up the usual barbecues, fish fries, pancake breakfasts, etc. you might want to try something different to make money— a "May Tasting Bee." At theme tables decorated with flowers, flags, and costumed dolls representing various parts of the world, you can serve portions of a variety of American, European, Mexican, and Oriental foods. For a fixed price you can sample food from as many tables as you wish. The dessert table could be an extra cost if you wish. The only eating utensils needed should be teaspoons and toothpicks. You could also preprint the food recipes and sell them for a nominal cost.

• **20 Talents.** Give your group of 20 youngsters $1.00 each to purchase supplies for a craft or baking project. You can also pool your money for larger projects. You can even contribute a little extra money on your own if you like. You can also use materials found around the house. In three or four weeks you can bring the crafts or baked goods to a central area in which they can be sold. You can turn the original $20.00 into much more than this by selling or auctioning off cookies, cakes, holiday decorations, aprons, stuffed toys, baby quilts, or covered photograph albums.

• **Seesaw Marathon.** Schedule a seesaw contest within your group and seesaw from a Friday afternoon until Sunday afternoon. You can presell pledges from you neighbors, friends, and family based on the number of hours the students can keep going. The students can teeter-totter in three-hour shifts.

Use your own creative imagination in creating your fund-raising projects. These efforts bring out the organizational ability of the various members and tend to bring the members closer together. Those who participate in these projects also become more familiar in the sponsoring group's purposes.

Fund-raising can be fun!

Organizing and Retrieving Records for Your Income Tax Report

> Better is a little with righteousness
> than vast revenues without justice.
> —*Proverbs 16:18 NKJV*

*J*ENNY, where are the canceled checks for Dr. Merrihew?" Does this sound familiar around your home as you prepare for the annual April 15 deadline? Much unnecessary stress is caused in our households when we don't properly plan organizational details to help us as we prepare for our yearly IRS reports.

For many of us, we can complete the short form and claim the standard deductions and mail the forms off. However, for those who itemize our deductions, we have the responsibility to keep thorough records.

Beginning with 1987 and going through 1989 we found ourselves adapting to new tax laws (and it looks like the changes will continue). For those of you who have figured your own tax forms in the past, now might be the time to look into a professional tax-preparer.

Several years ago my husband, Bob, and I searched for a qualified tax professional who was a CPA, and we have been pleased with the additional refunds we have received because that person thoroughly understands the tax laws. With the coming changes, a professional preparer can more than save you the service charge to properly figure your new tax forms. Since his or her time usually costs by the number of schedules to prepare and the length of time it takes, you will save many dollars by having your records complete when you meet for your appointment. A little planning will save you a lot in the end.

Many of us have different styles of organization. Sally Sanguine can't be bothered each month to keep accurate records, so she tosses all her receipts, pay stubs, bank statements, canceled checks, and receipts (cash and charge) into a drawer or shoe box until tax time. At the end of the year she dumps all her materials on a tabletop or the floor and begins to sort. This type of record-keeping takes four to six hours to process. If you have several schedules with a small business, rental property, stock transactions, etc. you might spend up to three or four days to complete the forms.

If this is your style (and it can work) you can simplify the task by filing the receipts in an accordion file folder or large 9 x 12 envelopes. Total and staple each category and write the total at the top sheet of the category. Then record your totals on a worksheet. At this point you are ready to complete your own tax forms, or you can meet with your tax-preparer. Treat yourself to a bowl of ice cream or popcorn. In order to function under this method you have to have the right mindset. You are making a trade-off of small increments of time each month for a larger block of time once a year.

Many of us function better by staying on top of our record-keeping in smaller blocks of time. Some people prefer daily, some weekly, and some monthly. Whatever your desire, you need some basic tools to start your record-keeping.

- Regular or legal-size manila file folders (multicolored make the task cheerier and brightens up the task).
- A metal file cabinet (two-drawer minimum).
- Your local stationery store carries standard-size boxes to house such yearly records.
- Accordion-type file folder.
- Regular or legal-size envelopes.
- Wide felt pen for labeling your headings.
- Highlighter pen for marking receipt totals (for ease in identification when summarizing).

There are several ways to categorize your records. Select one that best fits your style of organization. Make a list of all items that will be income items and all expenses that are tax-deductible.

Income

- Salary—head of household
- Salary—spouse
  These records must include total wages, federal tax withheld, FICA, and state and local taxes. This information should appear on your W-2 form.
- Income listed on a 1099 form should be included.
- Alimony received (excluding child support)
- Interest and dividend income
- Income from sale of property, stocks, mutual funds, etc. Consult your tax-preparer for short-term or capital-gains implication.
- Royalties, commissions, fees
- Bonuses and prizes
- Tips and gratuities
- Annuities and pension income
- Lump-sum distribution from retirement plans
- Unemployment compensation. Note this even though it may not be taxable.
- Social Security benefits
- Veteran's benefits
- Workman's Compensation
- Other income

Expenses and Deductions

- Adoption expenses
- Alimony paid
- Casualty losses. Include auto accidents, fire, theft, storms, property damage, etc. List the loss, the value, and insurance payment, if any.
- Charitable work. Document expenses such as transportation, special clothing, and food and lodging if out of town.
- Childcare and dependent-care expenses
- Contributions, including tithes and offerings. List the name of the organization and the amount. Keep a receipt or canceled check.
- Doctors and dentists. This includes the amount of the bill as well as transportation or mileage on all trips.
- Finance charges on contracts
- Interest paid on all loans or mortgages
- Investment expenses. Include supplies, publications, transportation, cost of safe deposit box.

- Job-related expenses. This could include auto, special shoes, tools, uniforms, union dues, education expenses, professional dues and journals, safety equipment, transportation to a second job, job-seeking expenses, and employment agency fees.
- Medical insurance (premiums)
- Medication and drugs. Include prescriptions, vitamins/diet supplements if prescribed, and some over-the-counter drugs.
- Other medical expenses. Include eye exams, eyeglasses, ambulance, artificial limbs, hearing aids, lab tests, X-rays, acupuncture, chiropractors, nursing care, etc.
- Service charges and carrying charges on credit cards, cash reserves, etc.
- Tax (income, sales, state, and estimated taxes paid during the year)
- Tax-preparation costs

Some of these expense deductions will change in future years under new tax laws. It is always a good idea to check with the IRS literature for the next year. Call 1 (800) 829-1040 for IRS questions.

Once you have determined which of the income and expense items relate to your family's organizational needs, you can:

- Label a file folder for each income or deductible topic. When you have an item to file away, you can use the front of the envelope as a journal for writing down the date, to whom, and the amount of the entry. At the end of the year you just total the items listed on the front of the envelope and you have the totals for that entry. Inside your envelope you have all the receipts and stubs to back up your final total.
- Store these envelopes in your metal file folder, your cardboard box that you purchased from the local stationery store, or your accordion file. The method you use will be determined by how complicated your tax returns will be.

I have found that household receipts can be organized in a very simple way by using a regular legal-size folder. Just open it flat and glue onto each side of the folder three legal-size white envelopes. Label each envelope for the receipts:

A. utilities   D. medical
B. donations   E. insurance
C. credit cards   F. food

Set up one of these file folders for each month of the year, using your wide felt pen to label one folder for each month of the year. Each month as you pay bills, just slip the receipts into the proper envelope and file away. One added step speeds up the year-end process: Total the receipts in each envelope each month and write the total of the contents on the front of each of the individual envelopes. When tax time comes you will have all you need and can retrieve it quickly.

The IRS requires that you keep your records for a minimum of six years for most records. However, you will need to keep real estate and investment records longer if you will need to verify purchase prices in the future. Take particular care when relocating your residence. You do not want to lose these records in transit; in case of an audit you will find the reconstruction of your records to be very time-consuming and in some cases quite costly.

With a little thought and preparation you can have a system that is easy and that reduces stress and tension when your husband asks you to find where Dr. Merrihew's canceled checks are. He too will be able to retrieve this information quickly. Review together if you are married, because none of us knows when an emergency might occur for the other partner. Let's not keep our records a mystery!

Seven Steps
to Financial Cleanup
at Tax Time

A prudent man foresees the
difficulties ahead and
prepares for them.

—Proverbs 22:3

*Y*OU CAN DO a great financial cleanup yourself by breaking the job down into logical steps. Throwing everything out and making a clean start isn't the answer. Discarding salary stubs, last year's tax return, or current receipts for medical or business expenses will only bring you problems further down the road.

One of the biggest mistakes people make is not retaining records. Throwing away records that later turn out to be important cause people a lot of unnecessary work and worry. Well-kept financial records will pay off during emergencies. Should an accident occur, a friend or family member can quickly locate your insurance policy and the papers needed for vital information.

Here are seven steps to help have "More Hours in Your Day" during tax-return time.

1. *Know what to keep.* Keep permanent, lifetime records. These would include personal documents required for credit, job-qualification papers, Social Security and government program papers, birth and marriage certificates, Social Security number

cards, property records, college credits, diplomas, and licenses. Also keep *transitory records*. These pertain to your current circumstances: employee benefits, receipts for major purchases (auto, stock, jewelry, art), tax returns, insurance policies, credit union information, and canceled checks relating directly to home improvements.

The IRS has the right to audit within six years. Let this be a measure of how long you keep receipts, etc.

2. Set up your personal system according to your natural organization. If you are disorganized, your system should be simple. Keep it uncomplicated.

The less time you have, the simpler your system should be. If you like working with numbers and are good in math, your system can be more complex.

The simplest way to begin is to obtain two folders for receipts. Use the first folder for probable deductions and the second folder for questionable deductions. At tax time match deductible items or set up a system with folders for various deductions: medical, business, taxes, home, etc. When you pay a bill or get a receipt, simply drop it in the proper folder.

3. Set aside a spot for your records. Obtain a safe deposit box for permanent documents plus a fireproof and waterproof file cabinet for home use.

4. Let someone know where your records are kept. Make a list of the location of your insurance policies and give it to a family member, a friend, or even your pastor.

5. Get professional advice when you need it. Expert advice can go a long way and in the long run save you time and money. Accountants are a great source of information and many times save much more than their cost. Financial planners are helpful if your past history has been a financial disaster, and they can benefit you by helping you avoid future mistakes.

6. Change your system depending upon your season of life, such as marriage, self-employment, or vocational change. What works now may not work five years from now. What worked last year may need some revisions this year.

7. Record-keeping requires time set aside. You must discipline yourself to set aside a time each month on a consistent basis to go over your financial records so you won't be overwhelmed in April when you have to file your tax return. Some people update weekly when paying bills or when reconciling checking accounts.

Great record-keeping gives mental benefits as well as "More Hours" to do things you enjoy doing.

God will honor and bless you as you keep order in your financial life.

Holidays

Holiday Safety Survival Checklist

Suddenly there appeared with the angel a multitude of the heavenly host, praising God and saying, "Glory to God in the highest, and on earth peace among men with whom He is pleased."

—*Luke 2:13,14*

*T*HE HOLIDAYS are supposed to be fun, relaxing, spiritual, and festive.

This Christmas safety checklist will help you and your family have a safe and merry Christmas! Taking these simple safety precautions throughout the season will prevent mishaps and help you enjoy the holidays even more.

Tips:

- Don't overload electrical circuits.
- Use only the replacement bulbs and fuses recommended by the manufacturer.
- Replace broken or burned-out bulbs in old strings of lights, unplugging them before you do.
- Keep strings of lights unplugged when hanging them on the tree.
- Use clips specially made for hanging lights on the house. Misdirected nails and staples can damage or expose wires.
- Don't use indoor lights outside.

- Do not use lights with worn or frayed cords, exposed wires, broken or cracked sockets, or loose connections.
- Check all electrical lights, cords, and connections before you decorate.
- Use a heavy-duty extension cord with a ground, and never string more than three standard-size sets of lights per single extension cord.
- Follow the directions and heed the cautions on the packaging of any lighting products you purchase.
- Safety experts recommend using electrical fixtures that carry the approval label of Underwriters Laboratory (UL).
- The Red Cross warns that many holiday plants are poisonous and can cause serious illness. Holly, mistletoe, yew, and Jerusalem cherry plants should never be chewed or swallowed.
- All parts of the poinsettia also are dangerous, they contain toxins that can irritate the mouth, throat, stomach and eyes. If swallowed, seek prompt medical attention. Keep all holiday plants out of the reach of children.
- To avoid electrical shock, do not use electrical decorations on trees with metallic needles, leaves, or branches. Use color spotlights above or beside a metallic tree.
- Burning evergreens in a fireplace is dangerous; flames can flare out and send sparks flying about the room. Give your tree to the garbage collector.
- Equip your home with a UL-listed, ABC-rated fire extinguisher and smoke or heat detectors. They make good stocking stuffers.
- Be careful with fire salts, which produce colored flames on wood fires. They cause severe stomach disorders if swallowed. Keep them away from children.
- Make sure your tree is fresh when you buy it. As the needles turn brown and begin to break off easily, the tree becomes a greater fire risk. Keep the tree-base holder filled with water at all times. Place the tree in a location away from the fireplace, radiator, and other heat sources. Be sure it is out of your home traffic pattern and doesn't block a doorway.
- Never use lighted candles on a tree or near evergreens or draperies.
- Never use aluminum foil or differently-rated fuses to replace burned-out electric fuses.
- If you buy an artificial tree, make sure it has been UL-tested for flammability.
- Buy toys for infants and toddlers that are too large to fit into their mouths. Be sure the eyes on dolls and the buttons on stuffed animals are secure.

- Buy toys appropriate for a child's age and development.
- Be sure electrical toys are tested for safety. Look for the UL mark.
- Throw away gift wrappings immediately. Don't burn them in the fireplace. They can ignite suddenly and cause a flash fire.
- Always turn off tree lights before leaving home or going to bed.
- When removing your tree lights, wind them around the tube from a roll of paper towels. Start collecting tubes now. It will make for fast, easy storage and easy tree trimming next year.
- Store ornaments in apple-type boxes; layer newspaper or tissue paper between ornaments to prevent breakage.
- Store extension cords in toilet paper tubes and keep them with your tree lights so you'll have them when needed next year.
- Don't forget wrapping paper, cards, and Christmas ribbons go on sale the week after Christmas at 50 to 70 percent off, so stock up for next year and save money.

Blessings for a happy holiday and a safe New Year!

Fall Harvest Pumpkin Times

If we are living in the light of
God's presence, just as Christ does,
then we have wonderful fellowship
and joy with each other.

—1 John 1:7

*S*UMMER IS about over and as the nip hits
the air and the leaves begin to turn burnt
red and orange, it's time to hang the corn on your door and put Mr.
Pumpkin in place for the fall season.

Even though we live in the city our home is country. By mid-
September our corn season is about over and the stalks from our
summer garden are tied and placed around the front door of the
house. One package of pumpkin seeds planted last May gave us an
overabundant supply of fresh, bright orange pumpkins. We not only
had enough for our home but enough to supply the neighborhood. We
then made Mr. Scarecrow out of an old pair of Bob's blue jeans and a
plaid shirt stuffed with newspapers . . . so easy. A pair of garden
gloves for his hands and a pumpkin for his head—we painted the face
and placed a straw hat to top it off! All the children loved our harvest
scene and it was enjoyed until late November.

Harvest ideas are a treat to create. Take your pick of these ideas
and establish your own family traditions.

1. If you are proud of your carved harvest pumpkins and want to

keep them in firm shape indefinitely, simply spray their insides and outsides with an antiseptic, repeating periodically as necessary. The antiseptic destroys the bacteria that normally grow and soften the pumpkins.

2. Don't throw out the pumpkin seeds when you are through carving. Salt the seeds and dry them in the oven on a cookie sheet for a tasty, nutritious snack the whole family will love.

3. A hollowed pumpkin makes a creative punch bowl for apple cider. It can also be used for a harvest soup tureen. There are recipes for pumpkin soup and spiced tea in my book *The Complete Holiday Organizer* (Harvest House).

4. Many local churches, parks, recreation departments, and community centers provide fun harvest activities, a phone call can give you the schedule of events.

5. Take your family to a local pumpkin patch. There are many commercial pumpkin fields in various areas across the country. Often you can harvest your own pumpkin right from the grower's field. If not, consider planting your own patch next year like we did.

No thumping is necessary to determine pumpkin ripeness: Once it is orange a pumpkin is ready to use. It will last for months if not cut or broken or cracked. It's best not to lift pumpkins by the stem as they often break off.

Take home several for Halloween carving and Thanksgiving pumpkin pies.

This is a fun outing particularly for city families. Many of these patches will have cornstalks, gourds, and Indian corn, which make excellent materials for harvest decoration both at the front door and dining room table. Ask the farmer if you could bring a picnic lunch and share a family time in the midst of the vines.

6. Carving faces on the pumpkins is a fun experience for the family. Children love to be involved in making funny faces, but care needs to be taken when carving. A sharp knife used by either a child who is too young or by a child who hasn't been shown the proper use of a knife can ruin a good time. Colored paint-pens are a great option and can be purchased at craft and art supply stores.

7. Plan a neighborhood pumpkin carving or pumpkin painting party:

• Spread several layers of newspapers on the driveway, kitchen countertop, garage floor, or basement (depending on the weather).

• Carve or draw faces on the pumpkins, each person creating his or her own masterpiece. Children can use the paint pens or felt marking pens.

• Cut into the pumpkin and separate seeds from pulp. (See number 2 above on how to roast seeds.)

• After each pumpkin is carved, put a candle inside. In the bottom of the pumpkin carve a shallow hole so the candle will fit in an upright position. A little melted wax in the hole will also help secure the candle. A votive candle in a glass container works best if available.

• Display your pumpkin in the window, on the table, or on your front porch. Make sure there is no fire danger near the candle.

• After the carving session you might want to finish off the evening with hot apple cider, popcorn, and your roasted pumpkin seeds. Truly an evening to remember.

• For baby pumpkins use oranges. A fun project is to decorate with faces using, again, the marking pens. The decorated oranges can also be used as a nutritious snack and put into lunch sacks during the harvest season.

• Make pumpkin faces on a cheese sandwich. Cut the jack-o'-lantern face on one side of bread. Add cheese and second slice of bread. Serve plain or toasted under the broiler. A cleaner combination is dark rye bread with yellow cheese.

• Create these and other fun memories during this special harvest pumpkin time. Plan several harvest walks as a family and collect leaves, acorns, pods, and berries. These can all be placed around your pumpkins on the table for your harvest centerpiece.

The Busy Person's Thanksgiving Dinner

Let us not get tired of doing what is
right, for after a while we will reap
a harvest of blessing.

—Galatians 6:9

*T*ODAY'S BUSY WOMEN just don't have
the time to do what great grandma did.
She cooked for days until Thanksgiving arrived. Last Thanksgiving
I found myself in the middle of a busy holiday seminar schedule. The
thought of roasting a turkey, cleaning the house, and getting the
trimmings together for Thanksgiving dinner caused my stress level
to elevate to dangerous heights!

I stopped to take a deep breath and think long enough to come up
with a solution to my busyness. I decided to make our harvest dinner
a potluck. I made a few phone calls and quickly organized a simple
meal.

Here are some of the steps I took. Try them out this year for your
best-ever Thanksgiving.

Step 1

Develop your Thanksgiving dinner menu. Here is a sample menu:

Turkey, dressing, cranberry sauce: You will do this.
Vegetable: Auntie Syd
Potato or rice: Grandma Gertie
Rolls: Uncle Blair
Relish dish: Brad and Marie
Pumpkin pie: Craig and Jenny

Step 2

Phone your guests to invite them for a Busy Person's Thanksgiving Dinner. For your own reference, make a simple chart or list with their name and what item they will be bringing. (For example: Vegetable—Aunt Amy; Relish dish—Sister Sue.)

Ask them to please call an RSVP to you at least 10 days before Thanksgiving dinner. This way you'll still have time to adjust things if someone can't make it after all.

Step 3

Get your family involved. Assign the name cards to one child or to your husband to write a Scripture verse on the back or inside of each individual card. These verses should fit the Thanksgiving holiday; for example, Ephesians 5:20, "Always giving thanks for all things in the name of our Lord Jesus Christ" (NASB).

Use a 3 x 5 card folded in half, placing the name on the front and the Scripture inside. These will be read aloud by each person before your meal.

Step 4

Have another child make cards titled "I'm thankful for. . . ." These should be given to your guests when they first arrive at your home, so they have time to think about their response.

After dinner each guest will read their thankful card. This is a great way to focus on the positive things God provides for us. Or you could have a person interview each guest, asking the question, "What is the best thing that has happened to you this year (month, week, today)?" This exercise has given our family many great times of communication and often brought tears from each of us.

Step 5

Make out your grocery list for what you will need for the big day. As hostess you will be providing the turkey, dressing, and cranberry sauce.

Step 6

A few days before turkey day, make sure you have everything you will need for setting the table—including a centerpiece. Keep it simple by using a pumpkin surrounded by fresh fruit or three candles in autumn colors with designed holders. (Votive candles floating in a glass or bowl of water also work well as a centerpiece.) To save time, try to use something you already have on hand.

Step 7

Prepare your thawed turkey for roasting in the late afternoon on the day before Thanksgiving.

I recommend my "Perfect Every Time Turkey Recipe." I have found it to be a lifesaver for the busy woman. I've adapted the recipe from Adelle Davis' book *Let's Cook It Right* (New American Library, 1947). I've used this recipe for 32 years and never had it fail me yet!

Recipe

Preheat oven to 350 degrees.

Wash turkey well and remove the neck and giblets. Dry turkey with paper towels, salt the cavity, and stuff with dressing of your choice. Rub the outside of the turkey with pure olive oil. Stick a meat thermometer into the turkey.

Place the turkey breast-down in the roasting pan on a rack (this way the breast bastes itself, keeping the meat moist). Roast the turkey one hour at 350 degrees to destroy bacteria on the surface. Then adjust the heat to 180 or 200 degrees for any size turkey. The turkey can roast in the oven on this low temperature 15 to 30 hours before you eat it. A good rule for timing is to allow about one hour per pound of meat.

For example, a 20-pound turkey that takes 15 minutes per pound to roast would take five hours by the conventional, fast-cooking method. The slow method is one hour per pound, so it would take 20 hours to roast.

I usually begin roasting a 22-pound turkey at 5 P.M. Thanksgiving Eve. I put the turkey in the oven and leave it uncovered until it's done the next day between 1 P.M. and 3 P.M.

Although the amount of cooking time seems startling at first, the meat turns out amazingly delicious, juicy, and tender. It slices beautifully, barely shrinks in size, and vitamins and proteins are not harmed because of the low cooking temperature.

Once the turkey is done, it will not overcook. You can leave it in an additional three to six hours, and it will still not dry out. It browns perfectly and you'll get wonderful drippings for gravy.

Thanksgiving
Countdown

> Happy is the generous man, the one
> who feeds the poor.
> —*Proverbs 22:9*

*T*HE FIRST national Thanksgiving proclamation was issued by George Washington in 1789. In 1863 President Abraham Lincoln made a Thanksgiving Day proclamation to establish this as a national holiday of thanksgiving to be observed on the last Thursday in November. In 1941 Congress changed the day to the fourth Thursday in November, which is where it has stayed.

For the last 100 years in America, we have been developing meaningful traditions to make this one of the most memorable of all holidays.

Thanksgiving is warm hearts, good food, family, and *lots* of conversation.

It is said that 60 percent of our stress is caused by disorganization. If Thanksgiving brings stress to your mind, it could very well be because of disorganization. So let's relieve that stress. Step by step let's count down the things we can do to make this holiday season stress-less. This will give us time and energy to build memories with our families and friends.

First Week in November

Activity   *Done (X)*
- Polish silver ....
- Plan guest list ....
- Send invitations ....
  (or a cheery phone invitation is always welcome)

Second Week in November

Activity   *Done (X)*
- Plan menu ....
- Begin marketing list ....
- Plan table setting............................
- Plan centerpiece ....
- List what you may need to borrow and
  reserve those items ....

Third Week in November

Activity   *Done (X)*
- Make name place cards. As a family you can each find verses with a thankful theme. Take a 3 x 5 card, fold it in half and stand it up on the table. On the front write the name of the person who will sit at that place and inside write the thankful verse of Scripture. When everyone is seated on Thanksgiving Day, each person reads his verse. This can serve as the blessing ....
- Have prepared 3 x 5 cards and a pen at each person's seat and have the person write something for which they are thankful. These can be read during or before or after the meal ....
- Begin to buy some of the staples at the market you will need for that Thanksgiving feast. It will help the budget that last week. Canned cranberry sauce, dressing mix, canned green beans, etc. ....
- Plan your baking day ....

Fourth Week in November

By now I'm really excited about all the things that I've done and so thankful I've already accomplished so much toward our special day.

Activity	Done (X)
• Plan and organize serving dishes	
• Make out a 3 x 5 card for each dish and list on the card what will go into the empty dish. This way you don't have to remember at the last minute what goes where. It also makes it easy for guests to help with the final preparations	
• Check marketing list to be sure you've got on it just what you'll need for each recipe	
• The day before Thanksgiving set the table and set centerpiece on the table	
• Place Scripture name cards at each place	
• Put serving silverware on the table to be put into each serving dish	
• Bake pies	
• Check menu and recipes one more time	

Perhaps you are not preparing a Thanksgiving dinner yourself, but may be taking a dish to someone's home. Your organization will be simpler but should also be planned ahead of time. Ingredients purchased and time set aside for preparation and cooking can be planned ahead as well. Even if you aren't taking food, a hostess gift is always nice: a bouquet of flowers, small plant, stationery, jar of jam, crackers and cheese, etc. Remember, even if you gave a verbal thank-you it is always good manners to follow up with a written note.

As you gather around the Thanksgiving table, holding hands can make this a special family and friendship time. "We give thanks to God, the Father of our Lord Jesus Christ" (Colossians 1:3). Have a beautiful turkey day filled with love and thanksgiving to God—and don't forget to serve the cranberry sauce and garnish the platter with parsley.

Week After Thanksgiving

Activity	Done (X)
• Put away fall decorations	
• Start thinking toward Christmas	

Activity	Done (X)
• Week 1	
• Week 2	
• Week 3	
• Week of	
• Week after	

Christmas Countdown

Unto us a Child is born; unto us a
Son is given.... His royal titles:
"Wonderful," "Counselor," "The
Mighty God."

—*Isaiah 9:6*

*B*EING BUSY homemakers, with many women also working outside the home, puts added pressure on us as the holiday season arrives. However, if we can plan ahead and organize our holidays, we will find it a joy instead of feeling, "Oh no, not Christmas again!" Proverbs 16:3 says that we are to commit our works to the Lord, and our *plans* will be established.

As we begin this Holiday Countdown let's first give these next weeks to our Lord, remembering to give thanks for *all* things and trusting Him to help us establish our holiday plans and priorities.

Take time to share the true meaning of the holidays with your friends and family.

December Countdown

Christmas is a loving and giving time. Take time to love: Send a card to a shut-in; sing a song at a convalescent home; smile a greeting as you shop.

• Address Christmas cards and mail early in the month.

- Make Christmas gift list.
- Plan baking days for the month. Include at least one baking day for the children to help with cookies and candies.
- Plan a craft day for the family to make tree ornaments. Felt, noodles, ice cream sticks, pine cones, and thread spools can all be used to create ornaments. String popcorn and cranberries for the tree. Keep in mind the family unit working together.
- Shop early.
- Wrap gifts early.
- Keep in mind giving handmade and homemade items such as jams, breads, pot holders, and tree ornaments as gifts.
- Attend a Christmas boutique. There you will be able to purchase beautiful handmade items at reasonable prices.
- Decorate your home early in the month so you can enjoy the holiday as long as possible.
- Decorate your front door with a wreath made of pine branches, pine cones, and ribbon, and incorporate a small nativity scene keeping Christ in Christmas. Your front door will give a warm welcome to all who enter your loving home, apartment, mobile home, condominium, or whatever place you call home.

Suggested Stocking Stuffers

- Small stuffed teddy bears
- Paint sets and brushes
- Colored pens or pencils
- Art paper for projects
- Puzzles, books, small Bible
- Marbles, jacks
- Subscription to magazine
- Clothing items such as socks, tights, hosiery, belts, barrettes, headbands, or other hair items
- Music tapes
- Photos (framed)
- Posters
- Theater tickets for a special play, amusement park tickets (Disneyland, etc.)
- Balloons with a dollar bill tucked inside
- Nuts and fruits
- Toothbrush, shampoo, curling iron, hand lotion, perfume or cologne
- Kitchen items for mom
- Small garden tools and packaged seeds for dad

- Any hobby items
- Barbecue tools, picnic accessories
- Tupperware
- Flashlight
- Measuring tape
- Apron, kitchen towels
- Golf balls
- Tennis balls
- Etc. etc. etc.... This should get you started with suggested ideas!
- Plan a family "Happy Birthday Jesus" party:
    Bake a cake with candles.
    Read the Christmas story.
    Share memorable Christmases.
    Have a family communion.
    Sing "Happy Birthday" to Jesus.
- Make a Christmas Love Basket filled with food items, toys, clothing, and needed items for a needy family in your church or community. Sharing our Lord's love with others is what Christmas is all about.

Stressless
Christmas

Not by might, nor by power, but by
my Spirit, says the Lord
Almighty—you will succeed
because of my Spirit.

—*Zechariah 4:6*

*H*OW FUN and relaxed you will be
when you have stacked up creative
gifts made by you and ready to give throughout this holiday season.

From the time I was a little girl, my mother taught me how to
make fun, inexpensive gifts. Here are a few of those ideas to help you
get gift-organized for Christmas.

- Give your favorite recipe written on a cute card and include two
  or three of the ingredients. Example: Chocolate chip oatmeal
  cookie recipe—include one package chocolate chips, one package nuts and several cups oatmeal in a zip-lock bag.
- Package in a zip-lock bag five to seven different kinds of dry
  beans and include your favorite bean soup recipe.
- Take baby food jars and apply cute stickers to the front. Three of
  these make a great gift for storing cotton balls, bath salts,
  Q-Tips, etc.
- Paint "Honey Pot" on the front of a jar and fill with honey. Tie a
  cute ribbon around the lid with a bow.

- Make Christmas ornaments out of different kinds of noodles, using Elmer's white glue.
- Cover shoeboxes with wrapping paper, wallpaper, contact paper, etc., and use as a gift box. Fill with stationery items—glue stick, small scissors, paper clips, marking pens, memo pad, and thank-you notes. Any mom, dad, grandparent, or teacher would love such a gift.
- How about covering a box with road maps and filling the box with more road maps, a first-aid kit, a teaching tape or your favorite music tape, jumper cables, flares, or any kind of item associated with travel and/or the car?
- Baskets make great gifts filled with items:

> Bath—soaps, shower cap, bubble bath, bath oil, washcloth
>
> Reading—book for each family member, bookmarks
>
> Kitchen—wooden spoons, measuring cups, can opener, etc.
>
> Toys—games, books, teddy bear, dolls, truck, puzzles, etc.
>
> Grandma—bib to use for grandbabies, toy, rattle, book of short stories, baby items, etc.
>
> Gardening—seeds, garden tools, gloves, pruners/clippers, hand shovel, fertilizer, potted plants
>
> Sewing—measuring tape, scissors, pins, jar of buttons, elastic lace, ribbon, tape, etc.
>
> Laundry—bleach, laundry powder or liquid, fabric softener, spray spot remover, small spot brush
>
> For men—car wax, chamois, Armor-all, trash bags, litter bag for car

Food items always make great gifts. Use resources that are in your area and available to you. Every year we receive a bag of raw peanuts. Oh, how we love and enjoy them for several months! Here are more food ideas:

- Popcorn
- Breads—banana, zucchini
- Nuts—almonds, walnuts
- Carmel corn
- Pure natural maple syrup
- Fruits—We have several orange trees on our property, so I fill a box or basket with oranges and send them to my uncle. He especially loves this gift and looks forward to it.

Avocados
Dried fruits
- Basket of natural foods such as granola mix, raisins, three-to-seven-grain cereal mix
- Bread starters

Many of these gift ideas can be prepared far ahead of time so that you will be able to relax and enjoy the holidays. Organization of gifts is one of the keys to a stressless Christmas. So plan and prepare ahead for a pleasant, organized holiday.

38

Holiday Hints
for You
and the Children

This is the day which the Lord hath
made; we will rejoice and be glad
in it.

—Psalm 118:24 NKJV

*H*OLIDAY TIMES can be a fun time for children. It can also be a very hectic time for parents. What with presents, entertaining, cooking, and shopping . . . the children get so-o-o excited and seem to have more energy than at any other time of the year. This can be a season of learning for those energetic little ones as we channel that energy into helping us relieve the stress of the holiday "frenzies." Here are some Holiday Helps to bless you and the children.

Plan one or two baking days when the children help with holiday breads, cookies, or pies. Christ-centered cookie cutters such as stars, angels, crosses, and even Christmas trees are available. As you cut the cookies discuss with the little ones the Christmas story from the star to the wise men to the gifts the wise men brought. You can relate that one of the reasons we give gifts to others is to give our love to others as did the wise men gone to the Christ child. The Christmas and lights signify the shining stars and a place to put the gifts. As they decorate the cookies you can sing Christmas carols or play a holiday musical tape.

The cookies can be frozen for later use. A plate of cookies given to friends or neighbors can teach the children to give of their talents and the fruits of their labor. Plus what an outreach to those who receive Christ-centered cookies.

Depending upon the ages of the children they can help wrap presents. Comic strip sections from newspapers make good wrapping paper, or use white paper or tissue paper the children can rubber-stamp. Again, find a Christ-centered stamp with a manger scene or perhaps stars. Glue on candy kisses, candy canes, M & M's. Get creative—anything goes. If the gift is a cookbook or kitchen item, wrap it in a tea towel. If it's an educational book, use roadmaps as the paper. If it's handsewn, a measuring tape makes a cute bow. Get out lace pieces and rickrack to glue on and decorate the top. The children can design a lace collar for mom's gift, and for dad, a tie or bow tie. The children will be excited and invent all sorts of unusual gift wraps.

Make your own gift tags out of wrapping paper pieces or construction paper in red, green, or white; rubber-stamped to match the papers. You can also use wooden spoon ornaments, paper dolls, cookie cutters, key chains, shells, bookmarks, etc. Paint pens (which can be bought at craft or art supply stores) will write on almost anything and the color and print won't come off.

Capitalize if possible, on the hobby or vocation of the person whose gift you are wrapping. For the golfer, use golf tees tied onto the bow. For an artist, a new paint brush. For the mechanic, a new tool; the gardener, a new pair of gloves or seeds. For the craft lady or knitter, knitting needles or embroidery thread tied onto the bow.

Children will love this gift idea: Roll up a dollar bill and insert it into a balloon. Mail it along with a card and instructions to blow up the balloon and then pop it. Out comes the bill!

When planning your holiday party, buffet, open house, or family dinner, let the older children extend themselves by helping out with the little ones to give you extra time to shop and prepare. They can then have the privilege of taking part in greeting the guests, taking their coats, being polite, and using manners with a smile. They should also remember to say thank you and please. They can pass out hors d'oeuvres, pour water, coffee, tea, clear off tables, serve dessert, and blow out the candles. Cleanup help can also be part of learning. Throw some coins into the bottom of the kitchen sink beneath the sudsy water as a reward. One hundred pennies, four to eight quarters, 20 nickels, etc. On their pillow pin a big thank-you note saying, "Good job, well done!"

If you don't have children, borrow some just to help teach them manners and proper ways of entertaining.

A great gift that children can make is a personalized pillow or pillowcase. They can use paint pens in assorted colors or nontoxic acrylic paints to list a friend's important personal dates and memory places or perhaps his or her favorite Bible verse on the pillow. Grandparents' names can be put along with the children's handprints. Aprons also make great personalized gifts with the grandchildren's names printed on and/or their handprints. This is also a nice idea for teachers at school or Sunday school.

Homemade Christmas cards that children have cut out or colored are always appreciated. Last year's cards can be cut up and glued onto construction paper. Children can use stencils, rubber stamps, or their own creative designs. These can also be made into placemats. I've found that heavy-duty plastic, oval-shaped placemats (on sale) in a variety of colors work well. Or make the placemats out of heavy poster board and cover with clear plastic contact paper.

Let your and the children's creative juices flow as you guide them into helping you relieve some of the stress the holiday brings.

They will receive the blessings and you will be blessed as you watch their talents develop.

Organizing
Holiday Meals

*The more lowly your service to
others, the greater you are. To be
the greatest, be a servant.*

—*Matthew 23:11*

*T*HE CRISP DAYS of late autumn bring on
memories of holiday happenings, roast
turkey, cranberry sauce, hot apple cider, family gatherings—and lest
you forget, a lot of hard work. But with a bit of organization, holiday
planning can be more stress-free and a lot of fun.

I've prepared a Hospitality Sheet for you on page 147 (Figure 4)
that can be clipped out or easily reproduced for your convenience.

To show you how the chart works, here are a few ideas about how
to fill it in.

One Week Before
- Prepare your menu.
- Make your shopping list.

Three Days Before
- Polish silver.
- Clean house as needed.

One Day Before
- Shop for groceries.
- Clean and prepare vegetables, grate cheese, and chop nuts.

- Set table and also place centerpiece, candles, and other decorations.

Day Of

- Cook your meal.
- Give yourself time to relax and dress before the guests arrive.

Last Minute

- Check your menu to see that you haven't forgotten anything such as the cranberry sauce or pickles.
- Enjoy your time with family and friends.

HOSPITALITY SHEET

Date _____   Place _____
Time _____   Number of Guests _____
Event _____   Theme _____

Menu	Recipe Preparation Time	Things To Do	✓
Hors D'Oeuvres/Appetizer		One Week Before	
Entree		Three Days Before	
Side Dishes		One Day Before	
Salad		Day of	
Dessert			
Drinks		Last Minute	

Guest List	RSVP Yes	RSVP No	★ Notes ★	Supplies
				Tables/Chairs
				Dishes
				Silver
				Glasses

Figure 4

Holiday
Kitchen Hints

The Lord himself will choose the
sign—a child shall be born to a
virgin! And she shall call him
Immanuel (meaning, "God is
with us").

—*Isaiah 7:14*

*T*HE HOLIDAY SEASON is a great time to renew old acquaintances, reconcile broken relationships, and reinforce existing friendships. It's a time for growing—growing through giving, through sharing, through serving. But most of all, it's a time to give thanks to a loving Father for all the little things we take for granted.

Hints

- If bread or cake browns too quickly before it is thoroughly baked, place a pan of warm water on the rack above it in the oven.
- To prevent icing from running off cake, dust a little cornstarch over the cake before icing.
- To add a new taste to oatmeal cookies, add a small amount of grated orange peel to the next batch.
- If you cover dried fruit or nuts with flour before adding them to the cake batter, they will not sink to the bottom during baking.
- The yolk of an egg will keep for several days if it is covered with cold water and placed in the refrigerator in a covered dish.

- Either parboil sausages or roll them in flour before frying to prevent them from bursting.
- If you have used too much salt while cooking, add a raw potato. This will absorb much of the salt.
- Tie herbs and spices in a piece of wet muslin or cheesecloth before adding them to soup or stew so that they may be easily removed when finished.
- Save the rinds of the oranges you squeezed for breakfast. Pile mounds of mashed sweet potatoes on them, then brown them in the oven.
- To keep old potatoes from darkening when they are boiling, add a small amount of milk to the cooking water.
- Pancakes will remain hot longer if the bottle of syrup which is to be served with them is first heated in hot water.
- Adding a pinch of salt in the basket will relieve some of the acid taste in perked coffee. For clear coffee, put egg shells in after perking. And remember, always start with cold water.
- Adding about 1½ teaspoonfuls of lemon juice to a cup of rice while cooking will keep the kernels separated.
- Baking apples or stuffed peppers in a well-greased muffin tin will help them keep their shape and look more attractive when served.
- Combining the juices from canned vegetables with soups will increase the quantity and flavor.
- Lumpy gravy? Pour it in your blender and in seconds it will be smooth.
- You'll shed fewer tears if you cut the root end of the onion off last.
- To eliminate spattering and sticking when pan-frying or sautéing, heat your pan before adding butter or oil. Not even eggs stick with this method.
- Muffins sticking to the tin pan? Place the hot pan on a wet towel. The muffins will slide right out.
- To tenderize tough meat or game: Make a marinade of equal parts cooking vinegar and heated bouillon. Marinate for two hours.
- To stew an old hen, soak it in vinegar for several hours before cooking. It will taste like a spring chicken!
- Instant white sauce: Blend together one cup soft butter and one cup flour. Spread in a 16-cube ice cube tray and chill. Store cubes in a plastic bag in the freezer. For medium thick sauce, drop one cube into one cup of milk and heat slowly, stirring as it thickens.

- Unmolding gelatin: Rinse the mold in cold water and coat with salad oil. Your molded salad will drop out easily and will have an appealing luster.
- Ridding the ham of the rind: Slit the rind lengthwise on the underside before placing ham in the roasting pan. As the ham bakes, the rind will pull away and can be removed easily without lifting ham.
- To keep olives or pimentos from spoiling, cover them with a brine solution of one teaspoonful of salt to one cup of water. Then float just enough salad oil over the top to form a layer about 1/8-inch thick. Store them in the refrigerator.

Blessed holidays to all!

Surviving
the Stress
of Shopping

I will call upon the Lord, who is
worthy to be praised; he will save
me from all my enemies.
—*2 Samuel 22:4*

*M*ANY OF US who keep a busy schedule right through the holidays usually
don't find time to shop for Christmas until after Thanksgiving.

With limited time to spend shopping, every minute must count—
and organization is a key. Before you begin, plan your shopping
strategy so that you can accomplish the majority of your shopping in
one trip.

1. Review all the stores in the mall or downtown area you plan to
shop in—such as jewelry, clothing, book, china, and hardware stores.
(If you are really ambitious, write them all down.)

2. Decide before you go out what types of gifts you plan to
purchase this year. For example, are you going to buy one big gift for
each person or lots of little things? Each year I do things a bit
differently.

3. Make your gift list based on the order of the shops within the
particular shopping area you choose. Work your way around mentally, jotting down specific people and gift ideas.

4. Take advantage of wrapping services and/or gift boxes with ribbon and tissue. As much as possible, take home gifts that are ready to place under the tree.

5. Do two things at the same time. If, for example, you purchase clothing for more than one person at a store which offers gift wrapping, allow the clerk to finish the packages while you visit other shops. Circle back at the end of the day and collect your packages.

6. Think in categories. How many golfers, skiers, or tennis players are on your list? When buying for one, buy for the others. What about duplicate gifts? Can you give all your neighbors gourmet cheese in a can or spiced mustard in a jar? Why not?

7. Make use of your phone. Call your florist to make up a silk flower arrangement or a basket of soaps and hand creams. Or order a pretty holiday arrangement with a candle for the Christmas table centerpiece. Many times a florist will wrap and deliver your gift for you.

8. Give gift certificates to the hard-to-please people who have everything. Certificates for restaurants, ice-cream shops, and fast-food drive-ins (children love those) are always a hit.

9. Present a magazine subscription. Often magazines offer a gift subscription at a reduced price for the holidays. Include a current issue with your gift card.

10. Take a few breaks during your shopping to review your list and thoughts. Plan a coffee, tea, or lunch break. If you find yourself weighed down by too many packages, make a trip to lock them in the car.

11. Avoid retracing your steps or making second trips by not leaving a shopping area until you are sure you have accomplished all you wanted to do in that spot.

12. Assign shopping to a teenager or a friend who loves to shop.

13. Remember to keep your shopping simple. It is the love you put into each gift that will last rather than the gift alone. And more importantly, remember to make Christ the center of all your activities this Christmas.

Gift Wrap
Organization
for Gift-Giving

Today in the city of David there has
been born for you a Savior, who is
Christ the Lord.

—Luke 2:11 NASB

*G*IFT GIVING really goes on all year. It
is one of the major parts of our lives.
The love of giving gifts goes on and on
and on and on throughout the year.

Being creative with gift wrap is easy and can be inexpensive—
like using newsprint to wrap dad's gift. The stock market, sports,
travel, comic, or business section with Christmas ribbon is easy and
original.

Perhaps you've saved those little pieces of wrapping paper thinking someday you would use them. Use them now! Simply tape
together the pieces and make a patchwork gift wrap. Creative,
original, and inexpensive.

Your plain paper or butcher paper can be used as a background for
rubber-stamping, stickers, or vegetable prints. To make a potato
print, cut a potato in half and carve a design into the potato; a heart,
an angel, a Christmas tree, a star, a teddy bear, etc. Dip the potato
into acrylic paint thinned with water, then stamp onto the brown
paper. Thumbprint designs are unique and handprints are always

fun. Collages can be made from old Christmas cards, pictures cut out of magazines, and newspapers. These can be taped or glued to plain paper and used as gift wrap.

Instead of bows on kitchen gifts, use a colored plastic or copper scouring pad, or colorful plastic measuring spoons. The name tag can be a wooden spoon with the "to" and "from" written on the handle with a felt pen.

Baby's gift can be wrapped in a clean disposable diaper or a cloth diaper. An ornament for baby's first Christmas can be tied to the package.

Gifts for sewing buffs can be wrapped in a remnant of fabric, tied with a tape measure, and pinned together (rather than using tape).

At the after-Christmas supplies sales you will find most gift wrap supplies marked down at least 50 percent. This is the time to buy— try to hit the sales this year and relieve the stress for next year. Talking about stress, let's take the pressure out of gift wrapping by organizing all the supplies we need to do the job creatively and quickly.

The perfect tool to help the busy woman out of the gift wrapping dilemma is a "Perfect Gift Wrap Organizer." (This can be purchased mail order. See information on page 296.)

This organizer is the center of your wrapping experience and should include the tools needed to wrap those instant gifts. So begin to collect the following products:

- Shelf paper
- Wallpaper
- Newspaper—funnies, sports page, stock market section, travel section
- Fabric
- Tissue paper—white (great for rubber-stamping), colors, plain, pin-dot, graph, or patterned
- Gift boxes—enameled, fold-up, acrylic, or Lucite
- Gift bags and totes—lunch bags, enamel bags, cellophane bags, window bags, small bottle and jar bags
- Tags or enclosure cards
- Ribbon—satin, plaid, taffeta, curling ribbon, curly satin, fabric, rickrack, shoelaces, measuring tape, lace, jute
- Stickers
- Mailing labels
- Glue gun, glue sticks

- Chenille stems—use on your make-ahead bows and store in a Perfect box
- Rubber stamps, stamp pad, or brush markers

Hints for Use of Old Wrapping Paper and Bows

- Make used wrapping paper new again by lightly spraying the wrong side with spray starch and pressing with a warm iron.
- Run wrinkled ribbon through a hot curling iron to take out old creases. I keep an old one in my "Perfect Gift Wrap Organizer."
- Ribbons—Make your own with pieces of leftover fabric. Almost any type of fabric can be cut to the desired width and length. Striped materials are great to cut into even widths. Press fabric strips between sheets of wax paper with a hot iron. This will keep the strips from unraveling and provide enough stiffness for the ribbon to hold its shape when making it into a bow.

More Wrapping Ideas

Cellophane
- For those "How am I going to wrap that?" gifts. It will always get you out of a jam.
- For a basket, bucket, pail, or small wagon toy filled with goodies—tied with a fluffy bow and a sprig of holly or pine, or decorative stickers.
- For your gifts of food—cookies on a Christmas plate, breads wrapped with cellophane and Christmas ribbon, a homemade quiche, a basket of muffins in a checked napkin or muffins in a muffin tin.
- For a plant.
- For fresh bouquet of flowers—tied with a beautiful bow and a special note inside.

Gift Bags
A wonderful idea for a quick, easy, and decorative way to wrap! They are reusable too!

Line bag with contrasting tissue or wrap your gift item or items in tissue. Add a bow to the handle with a gift tag. Add Tissue Toss on top for a festive look. (Tissue Toss: Use any color combination of tissue depending on the time of the year. Cut tissue into ¼-inch strips, then toss like a green salad and you've made Tissue Toss.)

Decorate bag with stickers, banners, or cutouts from old Christmas cards.

Large silver or black or green plastic garbage bags may be just the thing to hide a large gift. Add a banner, large bow, and stickers. It will look just like Santa's pack. Reuse your bags for lunches or to hold your needlework.

Gift Boxes and Containers

- The decorated ones need only a ribbon! Always get a courtesy box, tissue, and ribbon whenever you buy anything at a department store or where the gift wrap is free. Save them in your gift wrap center for the times you need them. Usually they fold flat and are easy to store.
- Wrap a lid separate from the bottom to use again and again.
- Use tins, ceramic containers, Lucite or acrylic boxes, flowerpots, buckets, pails, and baskets.

Gift Certificates

- Purchase from stores
- Make your own with calligraphy, sticker art, or rubber-stamp art and then laminate them. Have certificates redeemable for:

Babysitting	Day of shopping and lunch
Dinners in your home	Trip to the zoo
Frozen yogurt	Plays

These ideas should help to stimulate your creative juices in making the gift wrapping in your life a happy, pleasant experience.

Foods and Kitchen

43

How to Save Money at the Supermarket

Plans fail for lack of counsel, but
with many advisers they succeed.
—*Proverbs 15:22 NIV*

*T*ODAY in our busy society we find that
much of our stress is caused by how we
provide nutrition for our family. At one time in our society there was
much emphasis upon the family spending quality time around the
dining room table. Many times in years gone by we could expect to
have at least two of the three meals (breakfast and dinner) together.
The dinner table was a great place to have a "summit conference" or
just to catch up on the day's happenings.

Today with our hustled, hassled, and hurried society, we have
stopped or seriously neglected this tradition. I encourage each family to seriously evaluate their family time and see if at least one meal
can be shared together. If you do make this commitment, try to make
the meal a pleasant time for the family. You want it to be a rewarding
experience. This is not the time to be negative. Make it an uplifting
time, one where everyone will go away wanting to get back together
again.

Many busy families have surrendered to the fast-food phenome-
non and very rarely cook at home. This is fine occasionally but

should be viewed cautiously for regular meals. Those who find themselves on tight budgets will soon find the fast-food compromise most expensive. In many cases, it also deprives your family of balanced nutrition.

Don't view food preparation as drudgery, but delight in providing meals for your family. There are excellent cookbooks available that simplify food preparation. To ease your planning you might make up 3 x 5 cards giving you about seven different recipes for breakfast, lunch, and dinner. By rotating the cards, you can have variety and not get bored with your meals. Try to introduce a new recipe occasionally. If you have teenagers, they can be of great assistance. They can set the table, shop, clean vegetables, start the meal, serve the food, clean the table, and even load the dishwasher (if you have one). This is an excellent opportunity to teach your children many lessons for the adult life: meal planning, shopping for bargains, budget preparation, nutritional balance, table etiquette, time management in cooking meals, and meal cleanup.

I have a friend who took one summer to teach her teenage sons how to survive—she called it "Survival Summer." At the end of the summer she felt comfortable and self-assured that her boys could take care of themselves in an emergency. An added benefit is that she now has help to relieve her of her expanding responsibilities.

One word of caution is that busy teenagers carrying a heavy college-prep academic load must have time for the studies; however, this doesn't mean that they don't carry some responsibilities for family functions.

To help you save money at the supermarket I have listed several helpful hints for you. These should not only make shopping more efficient, but also save you some money.

1. *Shop with a purpose and with a list.* Plan your menus for the entire week (or two) and then organize your shopping list so that you have to pass through each section of the supermarket only once. You might even make a list of standard products, arranged to correspond to the flow of your normal supermarket. (See page 174 for a sample of a marketing list.) If you have to return to the first aisle to pick up just one thing, you may find yourself attracted by other items. This will push you over your food budget and cause you added stress.

2. *Try to control your impulse buying.* Studies have estimated that almost 50 percent of purchases are entirely unplanned (not on your list). Be especially careful at the start of your shopping trip when your cart is nearly empty. You're more susceptible to high-priced, unplanned purchases then.

3. *Get your shopping done within a half hour.* This means you don't shop during rush hour. Shopping at busy times will hurry you up, and you will have a greater tendency to just pull items from the shelves without really shopping comparatively for the best product. Supermarkets are often very comfortable places to linger, but one study suggests that customers spend at least 75 cents a minute after a half-hour in the store.

4. *Shop alone if you can.* Children and even dads can cause you to compromise from your lists as they try to help you with unplanned purchases. Television advertising can cause great stress when your children go with you. They want to make sure they have the latest cereal, even though it is loaded with sugar and has very little nutritional value.

5. *Never shop when hungry.* Enough said. The psychology is obvious.

6. *Use coupons wisely.* Food companies often use coupon offers to promote either new products or old products that haven't been selling well. Ask yourself if you would have bought the item had there been no coupon, and compare prices with competing brands to see if you're really saving money.

7. *Be a smart shopper.* Be aware that grocery stores stock the highest-priced items at eye level. The lower-priced staples like flour, sugar, and salt are often below eye level, as are bulk quantities of many items. More and more specialty stores are carrying bulk food, which can give you excellent cost savings if you are buying for a large family or joint-purchasing for several families or even for a picnic. One word of caution is that even though you might save money on bulk buying, you might really spend more because your family doesn't consume the item fast enough; you find that it spoils and you end up throwing away excess. This can be expensive and not a savings. Also, be aware that foods displayed at the end of an aisle may appear to be on sale, but often are not.

8. *Use unit pricing.* Purchase a small, inexpensive pocket calculator to take with you to the market. This way you can divide the price or the item by the number of units in the package to find the cost per unit. This way you can compare apples with apples. The lowest-priced container does not always have the cheapest price per unit.

9. *Avoid foods that are packaged as individual servings.* Extra packaging usually boosts the price of the product. This becomes too expensive for families. In some cases a one- or two-member family might be able to buy in this portion; however, for the general buying

of American families you would not find this an economical way to purchase food.

10. *When buying meat consider the amount of lean meat in the cut as well as the price per pound.* A relatively high-priced cut with little or no waste may provide more meat for your money than a low-priced cut with a great deal of bone, gristle, or fat. Chicken, turkey, and fish are often good bargains for the budget buyer.

11. *Buy vegetables and fruits in season* since they'll be at their peak of quality and their lowest price. Never buy the first crop; prices are sure to go down. You might even want to consider planning an "old-time canning weekend." Canning produce yourself gives you the greatest economy and lets you enjoy these delicacies all during the year.

As an informed consumer you need to become more and more aware of what the labels on your products mean. Remember that manufacturers have to add additives and preservatives to give color and longer shelf-life to their products. As a buyer you may not be willing to make that trade-off. There are a lot of natural foods on the market and these can certainly help protect your family from the side effects of additives. Labels can tip you off to what's in the jar or the carton, so it's wise to know how to read them.

What Food Labels Tell You

• *Ingredients.* Ingredients must be listed in descending order of prominence by weight. The first ingredients listed are the main ingredients in that product.

• *Colors and flavors.* Added colors and flavors do not have to be listed by name, but the use of artificial colors or flavors must be indicated.

• *Serving content.* For each serving: the serving size; the number of calories per serving; the amount of protein, carbohydrates, and fat in a serving; the percentage of the U.S. Recommended Daily Allowance (USRDA) for protein and seven important vitamins and minerals.

• *Optional information.* Some labels also contain the following: the percentage of the USRDA for any of 12 additional vitamins and minerals: the amount of saturated and unsaturated fat and cholesterol in a serving; and the amount of sodium furnished by a serving.

What Food Labels Don't Tell You

• *What standardized foods contain.* Over 350 foods, including common ones like enriched white bread and catsup, are classified as "standardized." The Food and Drug Administration (FDA) has established guidelines for these products and manufacturers are therefore not required to list ingredients.

• *How much sugar is in some products.* Sugar and sweeteners come in a variety of forms (white sugar, brown sugar, corn syrup, dextrose, sucrose, maltose, corn sweeteners), and if they're all listed separately, it's nearly impossible to know the true amount of sugar contained in a labeled product.

• *How "natural" a product is.* The FDA's policy on using the word "natural" on a food label is loose. The product may, in fact, be highly processed and full of additives.

• *Specific ingredients that may be harmful.* Because coloring or spices that don't have to be listed by name can cause nausea, dizziness, or hives in certain people, people with food or additive allergies may have trouble knowing which products they need to avoid.

As an informed shopper you have more control over your purchase style and habits. Much of your budget goes to food. Become a good steward of God's money and get the most in return for it. Be knowledgeable in all phases of living.

Turning Coupons into Cash

Trust in your money and down
you go! Trust in God and flourish
as a tree!
—*Proverbs 11:28*

*M*ANY SMART WOMEN are saving
money by couponing.

Today's household is certainly concerned with finances.

I've talked with several women who are a part of a coupon club in their church. They meet monthly to exchange coupons and rebate forms. These women have a well-organized file system for their coupons. They bring in magazines and newspapers given to them by other people so the time can be spent in cutting out coupons and filing away or exchanging them with each other.

I've found that an accordion 9 x 5½ file is a great tool for organizing your coupons. Your topics could include:

Personal/health	Mixes
Laundry	Frozen
Poultry/meats	Cleaners
Cereals	Baking products
Baby	Soda pop
Dairy	Dry goods

164

Breads	Snacks
Garden	Cookies
Charcoal	Salad seasoning
Soups	Package mixes
Sauces	Jams
Rice	Coffee/tea
Lunch meats	Miscellaneous
Paper products	

When cutting out a coupon, run a yellow highlighter pen over the expiration date. That way your eye will catch the date quickly.

I met a beautiful young mother who told me she saved $850.00 last year by couponing. Another working woman saved $1,100 couponing in one year.

These women struck my interest and I asked them to share with me some of their ideas that helped save them that kind of money. Here are some of those ideas:

• A store will run a special ad in the local newspaper; for example, coffee at $1.99. You have a coffee coupon for 50 cents off. This week you also cut out a coupon that entitles you to a double discount on any coupon. You then can purchase that $1.99 can of coffee for only 99 cents.

• Whenever possible use double coupons. If your market is not honoring double coupons, it could be worth driving to another local market that is.

• You can cut out coupons for "luxury" items (freezer baggies, an expensive brand of disposable diapers, pie crust mix, etc.) and many times end up finding these things on a clearance table, either discontinued by the market or the manufacturer, or damaged. Then, with your coupon doubled you can get it free or at a minimal price. (Homemade-type mix for rye bread, clearance priced at 90 cents, with a 40-cent doubled coupon cost me 10 cents.) On items used a lot that are costly (disposable diapers, soda pop, or coffee for some people) *drive* to another neighborhood market for a great deal. The savings are far worth it. Stock up as much as your budget and number of double coupons will allow. When a meat item is priced well, stock up on it at a different store. If you eat a lot of poultry and prefer breast meat only, go elsewhere when you can save 60 to 70 cents per pound. Because you stock up, you won't have to do this very often. Also, there are many poultry coupons available; double them for more savings.

• What is hard to understand is that in double-couponing the *smaller* quantity is usually the better buy because you can get it for a few cents, if not free. Just buy two or three dish detergents, and you'll have enough until another brand goes on special.

• Switch brands of most items regularly. Couponing lets you try lots of products. Obviously there are some things you won't care for, so don't buy them again. But on the average you can switch peanut butter, jelly, rice, margarine, coffee, soda pop, paper towels, toilet paper, etc. You might find a better product in the sampling. Because of couponing, generic is *not* always the best buy. If you can get a superior product for the same price or less, then use a coupon. Stock up on staples and paper products. (If you don't have very much storage, you can put things in the garage or even under the beds.) Most important is getting hold of coupons and filing them. Throw *nothing* away, even if you get two major papers on Thursday (or whatever day is food section day for you!) Tucked into our throwaway neighborhood advertising paper is Safeway's advertising circular. My market is currently doubling *all* other market's coupons, so I cut out Safeway's coupons and keep them for that week. Friends and neighbors can even give you leftover coupons that are mailed to them. You can use many of these as well. However, go through your file once or twice a month to discard those which have gone beyond their expiration date.

• Refunding is complicated, or can be, so you may set up rules for yourself. Get all refunding forms from newspapers or magazines because most markets don't stock them. Don't buy the required number of products *unless* you have the refund form. (It's easy to have the advertiser say the refund form is available at your grocer's, but it rarely is, unfortunately.) Try to combine your refunds with purchasing the item on sale, with a doubled coupon, or, better, both! It must be something you use often, not a new, untried product. (Who wants three boxes of terrible-tasting cereal in your cupboards with another free one on the way!) Many people save all box tops and wrappings. I've tried it and it simply was not worth it. Most refunds are for combinations of foods I don't buy or use. Therefore, wait until you see the requirements and then decide if it is worth the effort and postage.

Where can you get coupons? Many places—a lot come through the mail. I used to throw out junk mail and not even look at it. Now I quickly finger through the pages and cut the coupons—before tossing the rest.

Major and local newspapers run coupons every week.

Friends can cut coupons and save them for you. My auntie cuts coupons; it gives her a purpose to help plus any coupons she doesn't use she passes on to me, and any I don't use I then pass on to our married daughter, Jenny.

Grandmas and grandpas use couponing as a great project.

Neighbors', friends', and relatives' cast-off magazines are also a great source of coupons.

Cutting out, filing, and organizing will take you no more than a half-hour per week, and this could very well save you $13.00 to $20.00 per week on your grocery bill. This pays you four to six times minimum wage. It's fun, too, and very rewarding.

Try it—you'll love it. It's another way of being a good steward of your money.

One woman shared with me that she would write her check at the checkout stand for the total amount and then pocket her savings from coupons, thus giving her money which she spent on Christmas presents. Her husband was so excited about what she did that he told everyone how proud he was of a wife who looks well into her household, being a Proverbs 31 woman.

Remember, coupons give savings!

Planning Meals
Saves Stress

Let each of you look out not only
for his own interests, but also for
the interests of others.

—*Philippians 2:4 NKJV*

*T*HE AVERAGE WOMAN cooks, plans, markets, chops, pares, cleans up or eats out over 750 meals a year. If this is anywhere close to true, doesn't it stand to reason this is an area we need to organize? Feeding our families certainly is a big part of our lives—not to mention feeding them with good nutrition. We will gravitate to foods that have been planned and prepared. Here are easy steps and hints to successful meals.

1. Make a simple meal-planner chart. On an 8½ x 11 sheet of paper list the days of the week. Start on the left side from top to bottom. Then across the top list "Breakfast," "Lunch," "Dinner." These will form an easy chart as you draw lines dividing each day and meal time. A sample chart (Figure 5) is included on the following page.

2. From your meal planner, make out a marketing list. Start by listing items needed as they appear on the aisles in your supermarket. This will prevent backtracking in the market. You want to get in and get out. A study showed after the first half-hour

WEEKLY MENUS

Date **Jan 7–13**

Day of week	Breakfast	Lunch	Dinner
Monday			
Tuesday	Hot cereal	Salami sandwich	Chicken
Wednesday			
Thursday	Granola + bananas	Turkey– cheese sandwich	Lasagna casserole
Friday			
Saturday	Pancakes	Turkey hot dogs	Tacos
Sunday			

Figure 5

in the market a woman will spend at least 75 cents per minute. Stick to your list and use coupons.

3. Post your meal-planner chart so all family members can see it. Should you be late arriving home, older family members can check the planner and start dinner for you.

4. Don't forget Tupper Suppers—premade meals that have been prepared ahead of time and are stored in Tupperware or containers in the freezer or refrigerator.

5. Plan family favorites into each week.

6. Remember to include things still in the freezer from previous month plan-overs or leftovers.

7. Also listed on your menu planner you can schedule which person in the family sets the table that day or week; also who clears off. Our rule was whoever set the table also cleared it off.

8. Teach creativity in setting the table by allowing each person, when it's their turn, to use paper or cloth napkins, paper or glass dishes, a candle, a few fresh flowers, Teddy Bear, a pumpkin, or whatever they think of for a centerpiece.

9. To quickly remove water from the lettuce greens that you have just washed, simply put into a clean pillowcase or lingerie bag and spin in your washing machine for two minutes. Remove from the bag and tear lettuce, making a big salad. Store in refrigerator for up to two weeks.

10. Make up your own TV dinners. Use containers purchased in your market for microwave or regular ovens. Then put your leftovers in sections of the trays and freeze. Great for dad and children when mom's away.

11. Keep parsley fresh and crisp. Wash the parsley and put a bunch of sprigs into a jar, stem ends down. Pour in an inch or two of cold water, enough for the stems to stand in without the leaves touching the water. Tighten the lid, set the jar in the refrigerator, and enjoy crisp parsley for up to two weeks.

12. To speed up baking potatoes, simply put a clean nail through the potato. It will cook in half the time.

13. A piece of lettuce dropped into a pot of soup will soak up the excess grease. Remove the lettuce as soon as it has absorbed the grease.

14. Our family loves BLT (bacon, lettuce, and tomato) sandwiches. Whenever I fry or microwave bacon, I cook a few extra

pieces and put them into a plastic freezer bag and freeze. They are ready for the next BLT sandwich.

15. Leftover pancakes or waffles? Don't discard them—pop them into the toaster or oven for a quick and easy breakfast or afterschool snack.

16. For the two of us I bake six large potatoes. We eat them baked the first night. The second serving is sliced and fried in a bit of butter. The last two potatoes are cubed and served in a cream sauce with some cheese.

17. To get more juice out of a lemon, place it in a microwave oven for 30 seconds. Squeeze the lemon and you will get twice as much juice. Vitamins won't be destroyed.

18. Frozen foods have a definite freezer life; it is important to use the food within the specified period of time. The easiest way to mark meat and other frozen foods is to put a "use by" date on a label or on the package. Your market does this and it makes good sense.

19. Freeze lunchbox sandwiches. They can be made up by the week. Put on all the ingredients except lettuce. It will save time and trouble.

20. You can make your own convenience foods. Chop large batches of onion, green pepper, or nuts, and freeze them in small units. Grate a week's or month's worth of cheese, then freeze it in recipe-size portions. Shape ground meat or ground turkey into patties so you can thaw a few at a time. Freeze homemade casseroles, soups, stews, and chilies in serving-size portions for faster thawing and reheating.

21. No need to boil those lasagna noodles anymore! Just spread sauce in the bottom of the pan, place hard, uncooked noodles on top and spread sauce on top of noodles. Continue with the other layers, finishing with noodles and sauce. Cover with foil and bake at 350 degrees for 1 hour and 15 minutes. This will probably be the best hint you'll ever get.

22. Before freezing fresh bagels, cut them in half. When you're ready to use them, they will defrost faster and can even be toasted while they are still frozen.

23. Fruit prepared ahead of time will keep well if you squeeze lemon juice over it and refrigerate. The juice of half a lemon is enough for up to two quarts of cut fruit.

By spending a little time preparing your food and planning your meals, you'll save even more time for the other things you need to do.

Pantry Organization

You must love and help your
neighbors just as much as you love
and take care of yourself.

—James 2:8

 HE LAST TIME I visited my aunt's
house, I was looking for the dry cereal
one morning. "Oh, you'll find it in the pantry next to the cat food,"
my aunt said as she nodded her head in the direction of a colorful blue
door.

I opened the door, ducking just in time to narrowly miss an
avalanche of half-folded grocery sacks that came tumbling down. I
wasn't as lucky with the mop handle which bopped me a good one!
Buried deep in the recesses, I did manage to locate a box of Cheerios.

Although my aunt's pantry seemed more like a war zone than a
pantry, your pantry can be a storehouse of confidence at your fingertips.

All it takes is some simple planning and organizing and the pantry
will become your best friend.

I suggest stocking your pantry primarily with staple foods including starches, sweets, condiments, and canned or bottled items.
These will last for six months or longer.

Perishable goods can also be stored in a pantry. The only difference is, of course, that they will have to be replenished more often. The chart (Figure 6) on page 174 will help you keep track of the basics.

Arranging Your Pantry

1. When stocking your pantry, organize your staples and canned goods by category. For example, put canned fruit in one row and dry cereal in another, or organize everything alphabetically.

2. To help keep your food items in the right place, label your pantry shelves accordingly. This is also on excellent way to keep your spices in order.

3. Sort your packaged items such as dry taco mix, salad dressing, and gravy mix in a large jar or small shoebox covered with contact paper.

4. Store as much as possible in jars—everything from tea bags to flour and noodles to coffee filters. Products are protected from moisture and tend to stay fresh longer when placed in jars.

5. For convenience, save one shelf for appliances and group them according to function. For example, keep your mixing bowls, mixers, and measuring cups together.

6. As you plan your weekly menus, check your staple and perishable foods and replenish if necessary.

Other Helpful Hints

• Use freezer and storage space well. If you take advantage of sales and coupons to stock up and save money, you can avoid many of those "emergency" trips to the supermarket when unexpected company arrives.

• Plan a "cooking marathon" with a friend or your family. Bake or cook a few entrees such as breads, cakes, casseroles and soups. Freeze the items, some in family portions and some in individual servings. Remember to date and label each item. Now, on a day when mom's sick or there's no time to cook a meal, you can open your freezer and take your pick!

• Make your own TV dinners by using a sectional paper plate or pie tin and adding leftovers to each section throughout the week. Then freeze the whole plate. Your kids will be able to fend for themselves on the nights you can't be home.

You'll be surprised at how a little organization in your pantry will not only save you precious time, but will relieve a potential area of stress as well.

PANTRY STOCKING LIST

Date _____

Qty.	Cost	Starches
____	____	Flour
____	____	Cornmeal
____	____	Oatmeal
____	____	Pasta
____	____	White rice
____	____	Brown rice
____	____	Potatoes
____	____	
____	____	
____	____	
____	____	
____	____	

Qty.	Cost	Sweet-based staples
____	____	Brown sugar
____	____	White sugar
____	____	Powdered sugar
____	____	Honey
____	____	Maple syrup
____	____	Jams/jellies
____	____	
____	____	
____	____	
____	____	

Qty.	Cost	Canned & bottled goods
____	____	Tuna
____	____	Juices
____	____	Peanut butter
____	____	Tomato sauce
____	____	Tomato paste
____	____	Dried fruit
____	____	Dried mixes (i.e. salad dressing, taco mix)
____	____	Canned vegetables
____	____	Canned fruit
____	____	Pancake mix

Qty.	Cost	
____	____	Jello
____	____	Pudding mix
____	____	Soup
____	____	
____	____	

Qty.	Cost	Condiments
____	____	Ketchup
____	____	Vinegar
____	____	Capers
____	____	Brown mustard
____	____	Yellow mustard
____	____	Oil
____	____	Tabasco sauce
____	____	Worchestershire sauce
____	____	
____	____	
____	____	

Qty.	Cost	Perishable foods
____	____	Fresh garlic
____	____	Ginger
____	____	Green peppers
____	____	Celery
____	____	Eggs
____	____	Nuts
____	____	Green onions
____	____	Yellow onions
____	____	White onions
____	____	Tomatoes
____	____	Carrots
____	____	White cheese
____	____	Yellow cheese
____	____	Lemons
____	____	
____	____	
____	____	

Figure 6

Kitchen Organization

Happy are those who are strong in
the Lord, who want above all else
to follow your steps.

—Psalm 84:5

*A*MERICAN KITCHENS are busy places. Today's women spend an average of 1,092 hours a year there, along with everyone from husbands to friends to teenagers to dinner guests to babysitters. That little room puts up with a lot of traffic, and organization is essential. But how, how, *how* do we do it?

It takes time, but it is well worth it. Organization frees you from your kitchen mess and gives you total rest in this big area of your life. Here's a plan to get you started.

What You Need

Jars (assorted sizes), covered plastic containers, lazy Susans, large cardboard box marked "kitchen overflow," contact paper, trash bag, markers, and labels. Most important, you need a two-to-three-hour slot of time and some help from your family. When family members help get the kitchen in order, they're more likely to help keep it that way.

Cupboards

Begin with the cupboard closest to the sink and methodically go around the kitchen. Take everything out of each cupboard. Wipe shelves and re-paper if necessary. Throw away or set aside anything that is not used daily or every other day. Pile the seldom-used items in the "kitchen overflow" box.

Put "prime time" equipment such as frequently used spices, glasses, dishes, and pots and pans back into the cupboards, placing seldom-used items toward the back or on the highest levels. Set broken appliances aside to be repaired or thrown away.

Overflow, such as odd vases, dishes, platters, pans, canned goods, seldom-used appliances, and camping equipment (which could be boxed separately) should be stored in the garage or basement to reduce kitchen clutter.

Gadgets and utensils such as wooden spoons, ladles, long-handled spoons, forks, and potato mashers can be stashed into a crock or ceramic pot to save space. Either sharpen dull knives or throw them out. Try a plastic divider (usually used for flatware) in the junk drawer for storing a small hammer, tacks, screwdriver, nails, batteries, glue, etc.

Pots and Pans

To keep pots and pans in neat order, try lining the shelves with plain or light-colored paper and drawing an exaggerated outline of each item. Then store each pot or pan in its designated space. You'll be surprised at how easy it will be to find things.

Refrigerator

Don't let your refrigerator intimidate you; just think of it as another closet. Store fruits and vegetables in covered plastic containers, baggies, or refrigerator drawers to insure freshness. Keep meats and cheeses on the coldest shelf, and rotate eggs so that you use the oldest first. Lazy Susans are great refrigerator space-savers and can be used to hold sour cream, cottage cheese, jellies, peanut butter, mustard, and whatever else is cluttering up your refrigerator. You can also buy dispensers and bottle racks which attach to refrigerator shelves.

Freezer

The cardinal rule for freezer organization is to date and label *everything*. Be sure to avoid mystery packages! Shape hamburger into patties, freeze on a cookie sheet, and then transfer to plastic bags. They won't stick together and will thaw quickly for meatloaf, burgers, tacos, casseroles, or spaghetti. Keep ahead of ice cubes by periodically bagging up a bunch. Frozen packaged vegetables go together in the freezer as do ice cream and frozen desserts. Potato chips, corn chips, nuts, breads, muffins, wheat flour, and tortillas (corn and flour), even candies, all freeze well. Your freezer can be a real time-saver if you make dinners ahead. Lasagna, noodle and cheese casseroles, soups, beans, spaghetti sauce, and enchiladas are yummy freeze-ahead meals. If you're freezing in jars, be sure to leave 1½ inches at the top for expansion.

Planning Your Kitchen

I will reject all selfishness and stay away from every evil. I will not tolerate anyone who secretly slanders his neighbors.

—Psalm 101:4,5

A WELL-PLANNED KITCHEN is the envy of all those whose kitchens are an obstacle course to efficient cooking. No matter how large or small, any kitchen can be tailored to suit your lifestyle if thought is given to your cooking habits and needs.

Here are some helps for a well-planned kitchen.

1. Invest in a good selection of pans and utensils to accomplish your culinary pursuits. These should include:

- One 10-inch skillet w/lid
- One 8-to 10-inch omelet pan
- A set of covered casserole dishes
- A roasting pan with rack
- Bread pans
- Two cookie sheets
- Double boiler
- One muffin pan with 6 to 12 cups
- Dutch oven or similar type of pan

Basic Utensils

Begin with a good set of knives. Bob and I have been married almost 35 years and just this year we invested in knives. This should have been done years ago. These items are all great ideas for shower and wedding gifts for the bride and groom. Be sure to include a steel knife sharpener for proper maintenance of your knife set investment.

Other Necessary Items for the Kitchen

- A set of measuring cups
- Wooden spoons—a variety of sizes.
- A mallet for tenderizing less expensive cuts of meat.
- Spatula—I like the rubber type.
- Shears—great for cutting parsley, green onions and meat.
- Rolling pin
- Storage bowls (such as Tupperware)
- Cleaner
- Cheese slicer
- Tongs
- Garlic press—I use this often.

Gadgets

- Grater
- Colander
- Sifter
- Vegetable steamer
- Food grinder
- Eggbeater
- Whisk
- Egg slicer—makes pretty slices for salads.

Optional Larger Gadgets

- Mixer
- Blender
- Food processor
- Toaster oven
- Microwave oven
- Freezer

2. Plan a logical work space for yourself and be sure that all utensils have a definite place. For example, if you bake a lot, set up a

baking center. It could be on the counter top near a convenient cupboard, or even on a mobile kitchen worktable.

Your mixer, baking pans, utensils, and canisters should be readily accessible to that area.

Things That Work Together Should Be Stored Together. This is a good rule to remember when organizing your kitchen. Think through your daily work pattern and plan your space accordingly.

Items seldom used, such as a turkey platter, deviled egg dish, roasting pan, seasonal tableware, serving dishes, and picnic gear should be kept on higher shelves.

If you get a new set of flatware, keep the old to use for parties or to loan out when friends have buffets or church socials.

Spices can be retrieved quickly if stored in alphabetical order: Store on a "lazy Susan" or have your helpful handyman make a wooden spice rack to hang on your wall.

Here's a cute idea for that bridal shower. Have each guest bring (or tie on the top of their package) a spice. Specify a name brand so the spices will be uniform. You could even specify the type of spice on the invitation to prevent repetition.

Use a crock to store your utensils; place on the stove for quick retrieval. It's also a space saver that can take the place of a drawer. It can include your wooden spoons, whisks, meat mallet, ladles, and spatula.

Appliances

The many compact appliances available today are perfect for newlyweds looking to use time and space in the kitchen efficiently.

Mini food-processors and compact mincer-choppers, for instance, are suited for cooking meals for two or three people and are easier to clean than their full counterparts. They also take less space and less time.

Toaster ovens are handy for small meals. To save space they can be mounted under a cabinet. Rechargeable, hand-held beaters can be mounted on the wall. And some new coffee makers on the market brew a single mug at a time.

Several factors should be considered with purchasing appliances:

• Space: If you are short on counter space, look at undercabinet models.

• Convenience: Look for cordless products. They rest in a recharger base and are always ready to use.

• Weight comfort: Make sure hand-held appliances such as mixers and cordless knives are lightweight and easy to grip.

• Ease of operation: Push-button controls simplify use. Certain controls, such as a pulse control, regulate the amount of processing.

• Automatic shutoff: For peace of mind and for added safety, look for appliances that shut off automatically, including irons and coffee makers.

• Dishwasher safety: For maximum convenience, look for products with parts that can be easily disassembled and put into the dishwasher.

Other Handy Tips

• Glue a 12-inch square of cork to the inside of the cabinet door over your kitchen work area. On the cork tack the recipe card you are using and newspaper clippings of recipes you plan to try within a few days. It keeps them at eye level and they stay spatter-free.

• When using your electric can opener, help save your fingers from cuts by placing a refrigerator magnet on top of the can before opening it. This magnet will give you a good grip when you lift off the lid.

• Increase your efficiency with an extra-long phone cord that will reach to all corners of your kitchen. Instead of wasting time while on the phone, you can cook, set the table, or clean out a drawer. A speaker phone provides similar freedom.

• Meat slices easier if it's partially frozen.

• Want to mix frozen juice in a hurry without using the blender? Use your potato masher on the concentrate.

• You can peel garlic cloves faster if you mash them lightly with the side of the blade of a chef's knife.

• To keep bugs out of your flour canister, put a stick of spearmint gum in the flour and it will stay bug-free.

• Mark your bowls and their covers with the same number, using a marking pencil. Then you won't always be looking for a matching cover for the bowl when you're putting away leftovers. All you have to do is match the numbers.

• Arrange your kitchen for maximum efficiency. Position often-used utensils in convenient drawers and cupboards. Make your dishes do double duty. Use a saucepan as mixing bowl; then use the same pan for the cooking.

• Cut the lid off an egg carton and place the cups in a kitchen drawer. You can organize your cup hooks, small nails, paper clips, thumbtacks, and other small items. No more junky drawers.

• When you are in need of extra ice cubes for party or summer use, simply fill your egg cartons with water and freeze.

• If wax has built up on the felt pads of your floor polisher, place the pads between several thicknesses of paper toweling and press with a warm iron. The towels will quickly absorb the old wax.

• Place the plastic lids from coffee cans under bottles of cooking oil to keep cabinets clean. When the lids get dirty, just throw them away.

• A rubber jar-opener (or rubber gloves) gives you easy access to anything in a tightly closed jar.

• To cover kitchen cabinet shelves, apply easy-to-install vinyl floor squares by just peeling off the backing. They are particularly good for lower shelves where pots and pans are usually stored. They cut easily and do not tear or wrinkle.

• One of the best appliances you can have for your busy schedule is a slow cooker (crockpot). Prepare the meal early in the morning and when you come home from shopping or work, you will find your main dish for dinner ready.

• At least once a year pull the plug on your refrigerator and give it a thorough cleaning. Rinse with clean water after cleaning with baking soda (one tablespoon baking soda to one quart water). Let it air-dry.

• A trash can under the kitchen sink takes up some very valuable storage space. Take a large decorative basket and line it with a plastic bag. The bag is easy to lift out when full. Train several family members to take the trash out.

Remember, your kitchen is for *cooking*, not clutter!

Eggs, Eggs, and More Eggs

I will also meditate on all Your
work, and talk of Your deeds.

—*Psalm 77:12 NKJV*

$\mathcal{S}$UE GREGG and I in our book *Eating Right* (Harvest House) wrote a chapter dealing with the misunderstanding about eggs in our diet. The controversy and confusion over eggs focuses on the high cholesterol content of egg yolks. Media advertising, news articles, magazines, nutrition books, cookbooks, doctors, and nutritionists would have us believe that food cholesterol raises blood cholesterol. Yet there is no adequate research to substantiate this claim. Researchers are not agreed at all on this issue. The classic study that relates egg yolk cholesterol to blood cholesterol was conducted in 1913 by Nikolai Anichkov, a Russian pathologist, on rabbits. He fed rabbits the equivalent in human consumption of 60 eggs per day. The rabbits developed cholesterol deposits on their arteries. But rabbits are total vegetarians and do not eat eggs. There is nothing in their metabolism to handle eggs.

No human study shows a clear relationship between food cholesterol content and blood cholesterol, whereas research does indicate a clearer relationship to total fat consumption, especially to saturated fat. Yet eggs are lower in saturated fat than both meat and poultry, about the same as lowfat yogurt, and contain one-third of the amount that is in ¼ cup of cheddar cheese.

Advertising and popular news articles repeatedly reinforce the notion that food cholesterol raises blood cholesterol levels. "No cholesterol" labels are printed on vegetable oils and advertised everywhere. The message is effectively communicated, "Cholesterol in foods must be bad!"

Time magazine, March 26, 1984, reported the most extensive research project ever conducted on cholesterol in medical history. This project was declared ". . . a turning point in cholesterol-heart disease research," because it clearly demonstrated that high blood cholesterol contributes to heart disease and cardiac deaths. Ten years and $150 million were spent on 3,806 men, ages 35 to 39 with cholesterol levels of 265 milligrams. A cholesterol-lowering drug was used in the study. Those receiving the drug experienced an 8.5 percent drop in cholesterol, 19 percent fewer heart attacks, and 24 percent fewer cardiac deaths. Yet nothing was changed in their diets. The study had nothing to do with the cholesterol content of any foods.

The editors of *Time* magazine placed a "sad-face" picture on the front cover of this same issue, using two fried eggs for eyes and a slice of bacon for the mouth, with the overcaption: "Cholesterol . . . And Now the Bad News." The article was titled, "Hold the Eggs and Butter" (page 56). The message conveyed to the reader was "Eggs and butter contribute to heart disease." Yet the research project reviewed by *Time* had nothing to do with the effects of food on cholesterol! This kind of media influence confuses important nutritional issues of the American public. Of this research project Edward Ahrens, researcher at Rockefeller University, said, "Since this was basically a drug study we can conclude nothing about diet; such extrapolation is unwarranted, unscientific and wishful thinking" (*Time* magazine, March 26, 1984, page 58).

Only 20 to 30 percent of our cholesterol comes from food. Our bodies manufacture the rest. There are many other influences on blood cholesterol levels besides total fat intake, such as exercise, stress, inherited genes, prepackaged foods high in fats and refined carbohydrates, lack of dietary fiber, and inadequate vitamins and minerals. Rather than focus on egg yolks as a dietary disaster, we should develop a balance of real whole foods.

Eggs are a real food. They can readily be used in baking and a couple of times a week for meals. Two breakfasts or an egg main dish will not raise the total fat intake to over 30 percent of daily calories. Eggs are our best protein source because their amino acid pattern most nearly matches that needed for human growth and health. They are excellent sources of trace minerals; unsaturated fatty acids; iron; phosphorus; vitamin B-complex; and vitamins A, E, K, and even some D. Most of these reside in the egg yolk! Yolks also are the highest food source of choline, a component of lecithin that assists in keeping cholesterol liquid in the bloodstream. There is some question as to whether the lecithin is effective in this way, however.

If you do not want to eat egg yolks or are allergic to eggs, be encouraged. There are easy alternatives! You can use two egg whites in place of a whole egg in almost any baking recipe. Unfortunately that wastes the egg yolks, so we prefer using 1/4 cup tofu in place of an egg. Mixing it in the blender with other liquid ingredients works best. If you cannot find a real food to give taste pleasure, we recommend doing without.

Consider the value of fertile eggs. Fertile eggs come from hens, living with roosters, that are allowed to grow and peck on the ground. They receive no drugs as chickens raised in close quarters do. We don't really know what the nutritional difference between fertile eggs and sterile eggs is even though some people make claims for the nutritional superiority of fertile eggs. The clearest advantage is that fertile eggs are free of chemical residues. In general, fertile eggs also taste fresher but are also slightly more expensive. Many health food stores carry them. People who raise their own chickens also often sell them.

Mankind has eaten eggs for centuries. Even Job ate eggs: ". . . is there flavor in the white of an egg! I refuse to touch it; such food makes me ill" (Job 6:6,7 NIV). Yet heart disease was not reported in scientific literature until 1986. You decide. We still believe eggs are an economical blessing from God given to us to enjoy in moderation.

Organization

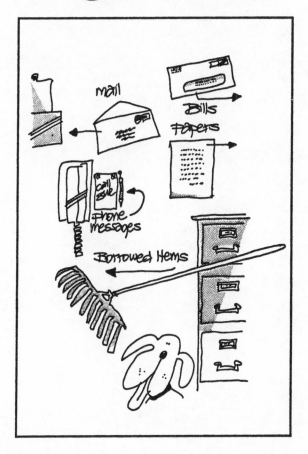

Telephone Tips to Give You More Time for Yourself

> Set your affection on the things
> above, not on things on the earth.
>
> —*Colossians 3:2 KJV*

*H*OW MANY times have you been stuck on the telephone trying to get off but unable to end the conversation? How often have you been put on hold for what seemed like an eternity and sometimes by people who have called *you*? How many times have you finally gotten a good start on a project at home or work only to be interrupted by a telephone call you really didn't want to take?

Our telephone can be a terrific time-saver. However, it also can rule our lives if we allow calls to interrupt meals or delay departures, causing late schedules, missed appointments, etc.

Here are some tips to help you control the telephone so it doesn't control you.

1. Organize a telephone center so you can make and receive calls efficiently. Next to every phone in your home or business should be a pad and pen. Keep extra pads in a drawer or on a shelf and pencils and/or pens too. It's amazing how they wander off, so a supply is important. Your calendar, phone book, area-code map and personal address book also needs to be close by for easy reference.

2. Organize your calls so that you can make several calls at one sitting when possible. You'll be apt to make your calls shorter and get more done. List your calls, questions to ask, and points to be discussed. Date your calls and take notes for future reference. I have a personal code by each call. If the party I'm calling is not home or there's no answer I put an "O"; if the line is busy I put a wavy line. If I leave a message to call back I put a jagged line. Make up your own code that will work for you.

3. Learn how to end conversations. Getting off the phone can truly be an art. Some people ignore all the signals you give and just keep talking. To free yourself more quickly, warn people in advance that your time is limited. For example, "Your trip sounds exciting but I've got to leave in five minutes, can you tell me briefly?" Or you might insert this, "Before we hang up. . . ." It is a reminder that your call will end soon. You might say, "I really can't spend a lot of time on the phone. Let's speak briefly and meet for lunch (coffee, tea) instead."

4. The investment of an answering machine will be money well spent. You can receive calls when you're away and return calls at your convenience. Some messages will be left as reminders of appointments with no return call needed. You can also screen calls, and if it is urgent you can answer it. If not, return the call later. You can also turn on the machine while showering, bathing the baby, eating meals, doing homework, or 15 minutes before you must leave for an appointment. That way you won't be delayed by any last-minute calls that can wait.

5. If you don't have an answering machine, enlist your husband or an older child to answer the phone for an afternoon or evening when you need a block of uninterrupted time.

6. Turn off the phone or unplug it when you don't want to be disturbed during dinnertime, special projects, sewing, ironing, or family meetings.

7. Avoid phone tag. When you leave a message for someone to call you, give a time when you'll be available. If you have to get back to people, ask them when they are able to receive calls.

8. When leaving messages give as much information as possible so you can eliminate another call.

9. Return phone calls. You'll build credibility as you do.

10. If you have children take messages for you, ask them to repeat names and numbers back to callers to be sure the information is taken correctly.

11. Put a long extension cord on your telephone or consider buying a cordless phone. You will then be free to move about, clean a

bathroom, check on children, etc. This can help you do two things at once.

Using these ideas will help you to do your work more efficiently and enable you to have more hours in your day to do some things you really enjoy doing.

15 Minutes a Day and You're on Your Way

> Seek first the kingdom of God and His righteousness, and all these things shall be added to you.
>
> —*Matthew 6:33 NKJV*

ONE OF THE number one frustrations facing all women—single, married, career, homemakers, college students—is how we can get organized enough to eliminate all the mess within our four walls, regardless how little or large those four walls are.

Who wants to spend all their waking hours cleaning their home? Is there a way to live after a messy house? Yes. You don't have to be a slave to your home. Give me at least 15 minutes a day for five weeks and I can have you on top of the pile.

As with any task, you need some basic equipment:

- 3 large 30-gallon trash bags
- 3 to 12 large cardboard boxes (approximately 10 x 12 x 16) preferably with lids
- 1 wide-tip black felt marking pen

You might ask, where do I find these materials? Check with your local stationery store. In some cases your market has leftover boxes of some sort to get you started. Try to have all the boxes uniform in size.

Before you start this project, commit it unto the Lord. Matthew 6:33 is a good verse for this phase of the program. Ask the Lord to provide you with the desire and energy to complete the project. In this program you will clean one room a week for five weeks. If you have fewer rooms it will take you less time and if you have a larger house it will take more than five weeks.

Step 1

Start by marking the three large trash bags as follows:
• Put Away
• Throw Away
• Give Away

Step 2

Start at the front door and go through your whole house. Start with the hall closet and proceed through the living room, dining room, bedrooms, and bathrooms. End in your kitchen because you need all the experience you can get to clean that room.

Step 3

For each room's closets, drawers, and shelves you are to wash, scrub, paint, and repaper everything. Take everything out of and off of these areas and clean thoroughly.

A close friend is a great help at this point in assisting you in deciding what to throw away. Try not to become emotionally attached to any items.

A good rule to help you decide whether to keep an item is if you haven't used it for a year, it must be thrown away, given away, or stored away. Exceptions to this would be treasured keepsakes, photos, or very special things you'll want to pass down to your children someday.

Magazines, papers, scrap material, clothing, and extra dishes and pans must go.

As you pull these items off your shelves and out of your closets, they can be put into the appropriately labeled trash bags. What's left will be put back into the proper closet or drawer, or onto the proper shelf.

After the last room is finished, you will have at least three very fat trash bags.

- The *Throw Away* bag goes out to the trash area for pickup.
- The *Give Away* bag can be sorted out, divided up among needy friends, or given to a thrift store, relatives, or the Salvation Army.
- The *Put Away* bag will be the most fun of all. Take the large cardboard boxes and begin to use them for storage of the items you'll want to save for future use. (See Chapter 5 for a refresher on how to label and store these boxes.)

Just *15 minutes a day* for five weeks has cleaned out all the clutter in your home!

Maintaining Your Five-Week Program

The Holy Spirit helps us with our
daily problems and in our praying.
For we don't even know what we
should pray for.
—*Romans 8:26*

*Y*OU NOW HAVE your home clean—
washed, dusted, sorted out, and
painted through this Five-Week Pro-
ram—and it feels good. Everything has a place in a cupboard,
dresser, closet, or on a shelf; all your boxes are marked and properly
filed away. Within a short time you can locate anything. Oh, that
feels good. The pressure is off!

It's a big accomplishment, but you're not quite through. It's a
matter of maintaining what you've worked so hard on the past five
weeks. This is the easiest part when applied.

For this phase of your program you will need:
- One 3 x 5 file box
- 36 lined 3 x 5 file cards
- Seven divider tabs

Step 1

Set-up your 3 x 5 file box with dividers.

Step 2

Label the dividers in the file box as follows:
1. Daily
2. Weekly
3. Monthly
4. Quarterly
5. Biannually
6. Annually
7. Storage (You will already have done this from a previous chapter.)

Step 3

Under each tab heading you now make a list of the jobs needing to be done on each file card. Some suggestions are:

A. *Daily*
    1. Wash dishes
    2. Make beds
    3. Sweep kitchen floor
    4. Pick up rooms
    5. Tidy bathrooms
    6. Make meal preparations, etc.
    Note: After a very short time these will become automatic and you won't need to write them down.

B. *Weekly*
    1. Monday—wash
    2. Tuesday—iron, water house plants
    3. Wednesday—mop floor, dust
    4. Thursday—vacuum, marketing
    5. Friday—change bed linens
    6. Saturday—yard work
    7. Sunday—church, free
    Note: If you skip a job on the allotted day, *DO NOT DO IT*. Skip it until the next scheduled time and put that card behind the proper tab in the file. You may have an item listed under two or more days.

C. *Monthly*
    Week 1—Clean refrigerator; clean bathrooms
    Week 2—Clean oven; wash living room windows
    Week 3—Mend clothing; wash bedroom windows
    Week 4—Clean and dust baseboards; wax kitchen floor

D. *Quarterly*
   1. Clean dresser drawers
   2. Clean out closets
   3. Move living room furniture and vacuum underneath
   4. Clean china cabinet glass
   5. Clean, rearrange, and organize cupboards in kitchen
E. *Biannually*
   1. Hose off screens
   2. Change filter in furnace
   3. Rearrange furniture
   4. Clean garage, basement, or attic (schedule the whole family on this project)
F. *Annually*
   1. Wash shear curtains
   2. Clean drapes if needed
   3. Shampoo carpet
   4. Wash walls and woodwork
   5. Paint chips or blisters on house

The above schedule is only a sample. Your particular projects can be inserted where needed. Living in different sections of our country will put different demands on your maintenance schedule. Get in the habit of staying on top of your schedule so you don't get buried again with your clutter and stress.

A Place for Everything

I will trust and not be afraid, for the Lord is my strength and song; he is my salvation.

—Isaiah 12:2

CRAFT AND sewing projects are fun hobbies, but if you've dabbled in them at all you've probably struggled with where and how to store patterns, leftover fabric, straw flowers, glue, and other odds and ends.

Before you let this clutter overwhelm you, try these simple organizational hints:

• Begin collecting storage boxes such as shoe boxes, cardboard boxes, or Perfect boxes. (Perfect storage boxes are available from More Hours In My Day—see order information at back of book.) Other containers that will work well for storing your craft items are plastic bins or stacking trays, laundry baskets, and small jars (baby food jars are great).

• Store patterns in boxes organized according to sizes and types: play clothes, dressy outfits, costumes, sportswear, blouses, and pants. Many fabric stores carry cardboard boxes made specifically for storing patterns, and you can buy these boxes at a very low price.

• Put fabrics in piles according to colors (prints, solids, and stripes) or types (wools, linens, and polyesters). Then place each pile in a separate cardboard Perfect box and number your boxes 1, 2, 3, 4, etc.

Make out a 3 x 5 file card and list on the card what type of fabric you stored in your Perfect box. On top of the card write the same number that is on the box. For example:

Box 1—Calico fabrics—reds and pinks

Box 2—Solid fabrics—blues, browns, blacks

Box 3—Stripes, polka dots

Box 4—Remnants and a yard or less of scraps

This can also be done with art and craft items. By keeping your 3 x 5 cards in a recipe box, you can quickly retrieve any item simply by looking up its card and finding the corresponding box.

• Organize buttons by color or size by stringing them onto safety pins, pipe cleaners, or plastic twist ties, or stick loose buttons and snaps on strips of transparent tape.

• Store bias tape, piping, and hem tape in a labeled shoebox.

• Keep hooks-and-eyes and snaps in baby food jars and line them up on a shelf or store them in shoe boxes, again labeled accordingly.

• String your sewing machine bobbins on pipe cleaners or keep them in a plastic ice cube tray (specialty bobbin boxes are also available at most fabric stores or drugstores).

• Organize spools of thread by grouping the spools according to color and laying them on their sides in the lids of shoe boxes. Stack the box tops so that frequently used colors are on top and stick them into a drawer or onto a shelf.

• Store fabric fill, stuffing, quilting materials, and straw or silk flowers in cardboard or Perfect boxes by using the numbering system.

• Use egg cartons for other odds and ends such as pins, small craft items, paper clips, and stamps.

• Clamp pattern pieces together with a clothespin until you finish the project or garment and then return them to the envelope.

• Large envelopes are also a great way to organize small items. The contents can be listed on the outside and stored in Perfect boxes or in a drawer. Suggested items to store are small scraps of fabric, ribbons, pipe cleaners, lace, bias tape, elastic, zippers, and stencils.

• Baskets are a fun way to store art and craft materials such as pin cushions and pins, scissors, measuring tape, ribbons, lace, and elastic.

The above items could be put into one basket and given as a gift to a creative craft friend for Christmas.

Another cute idea is to spray-glue one of the Perfect storage boxes and apply a patchwork of fabric pieces. It looks country and creative. It could be used as a gift or a storage box for fabrics.

How to Organize Your Closet

Anyone who wants to follow me
must put aside his own desires and
conveniences . . . every day and keep
close to me!

—*Luke 9:23*

*I*S YOUR closet a disaster that gives you the feeling of stress and confusion? Take heart, here's a sensible, easy way to clean it out and put every inch of space to good use. A well-put-together closet makes you more organized and your life just a little bit easier.

Cleaning the Closet

Step 1: Sort clothes into three piles. Hold each item up and ask yourself three questions. Be honest and take time to evaluate. 1) "Do I love it and wear it?" 2) "Do I feel good in it?" You seldom wear clothes you don't feel good in. You hang on to them because you think you are throwing money away if you get rid of them, or because they remind you of the past or because you *may* wear them in the future. Everyone does this. 3) "Am I willing to recycle this?" These are clothes you never wear.

Step 2: Remove the recycle pile. Here are three ways to do this: 1) take the clothes to a used clothing store and earn some extra money, 2) give the clothes to a charity, thrift store, Salvation Army, etc.

(getting a receipt will give you a tax deduction), 3) give the clothes to friends or needy families.

Step 3: Create an ambivalence center. Put the clothes you can't decide about out of the way in storage boxes in an attic, basement, garage, or storage closet. You may decide later to recycle these clothes after all, but for now it may be too emotional.

Step 4: You have now only the "I love to wear" pile to deal with. But why put your clothes back in the same old closet? It may be part of the reason your wardrobe seems to get so disorganized. Let's think about it.

The average closet consists of one long pole beneath one long shelf. The old-fashioned single-pole system wastes usable space. Far more efficient is a system with at least three poles and several shelves. By placing poles at different heights, you increase the number of items you can hang in a given area. In a his-and-her's closet, this technique can quadruple space (see illustrations on the following pages). By discarding the one pole you free space for more shelves. Use these shelves for foldable clothes (enough shelves can eliminate your need for a dresser). By keeping shoes off the floor, you'll eliminate jumbled dusty shoes. Hats and purses go on shelves to make your closet workable and pleasant.

You may want to add a light if there is none. If you have the option, avoid sliding doors. It's best to be able to see all your clothes at once. The floor may need a new look. Try inexpensive self-stick vinyl tiles or carpet remnants. Pretty up your closet with wallpaper, wallpaper borders, paint, posters, or eyelet lace glued on the edge of your shelves. Your new closet will save you both time and money. You'll know exactly where to find things and better yet where to put them back. It will be easier to mix and match outfits when you know what you have and can see everything clearly. You'll be able to expand your wardrobe using what you already own. Now you will enjoy your organized closet. Here are some additional tips:

• One of the reasons most closets are a mess is because people forget about closet organizers. Buy them in notions departments, hardware or dime stores, or use your imagination. These ideas will get you started.

• Mugracks. Good for jewelry, scarves, small purses. Hang vertically or horizontally on closet wall or door.

• Shoebags. Not just for shoes! Use for storing scarves, gloves, stockings . . . anything.

• Hanging baskets. A decorative way to store socks and small, light items.

Figure 7

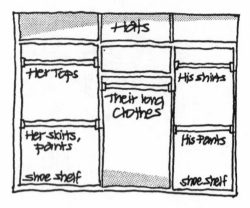

Figure 8

• Kitchen towel racks. Two to four hung on the back of your closet door are great for scarves. Use the thick rounded racks for pants.

• Colorful ceramic hooks. They fit anywhere—for hats, belts, bags, jewelry.

• Pegboards. Hang belts, hats, jewelry—you name it. They are great all-purpose organizers.

• Men's tie and belt racks. Ideal for leotards or lingerie.

• Overhead shoe chests. Ones with dividers and clear plastic zip fronts are an easy way to organize your handbags.

• Shoe boxes. For shoes! Write a description of each pair on the outside. To make them pretty, cover your shoe boxes with wallpaper.

• Plastic bags. *Beware*—do not use for leather bags, furs, boots, shoes, silks, or down vests. These accessories need to breathe.

How to Manage Your Mail

There is a time for everything,
and a season for every activity
under heaven.
—*Ecclesiastes 3:1* NIV

*M*ANY OF US can't wait for the mail to come each day. The thought of receiving news from afar is exciting and fresh. At the same time, however, the thought of processing it all can be depressing. Making decisions about what to throw away, what to save, where to put the mail for hubby to read if and when he gets around to it . . . and then, again, what to throw away!

I've discovered three easy steps that have helped me manage my mountains of mail. I hope they work for you too!

1. Designate one area where you open and process all your mail. It could be a desk, a table by a chair, or the kitchen counter. If you use the kitchen counter, however, be careful not to use it as a catchall. One woman told me she put her mail on top of her refrigerator, but it piled up so high it took her three weeks to go through it.

2. Don't let it pile up! Set a time each day when you process your mail. If you can't get to it when you receive your mail, then plan a time when you can. Do it daily.

3. Make decisions. Don't put it down; put it away, and don't be a

mail scooter. It's easy to scoot mail and papers from one area to another, one room to the next, or from one pile to another. Sort out your mail into categories:

- *Throwaway mail*—junk mail, advertisements, etc.
- *Mail you need to read*, but don't have time for now.
- *Mail you need to file away*, such as bills, insurance papers, and receipts.
- *Mail you need to ask someone about*—husband, children, etc.
- *Mail that needs a phone call*. Perhaps you have a question or need a clearer explanation than the letter gave. Many times people ask me questions by letter. If the person is relatively close, I will call rather than write. It is quicker and I can get that letter taken care of faster.
- *Mail to be answered*. Personal letters, forms to be filled out and returned, RSVP's for invitations.

All these categories can be labeled on file folders and put into a file box or metal file cabinet. As soon as the mail comes in, simply slip it into its proper place. Then when your husband comes home you can hand him his folder of mail to read and process.

One woman told me she covered shoeboxes with wallpaper and labeled them, set them in a row on a shelf and processed her mail very quickly. Remember, however, that with file folders or boxes, you still have to beware of pile-ups.

Junk mail is a time waster, so toss it! Don't let yourself say, "I'll probably use this someday," because you very likely will *not*.

On mail that requires other people's input, mark notes or question marks so both of you can discuss it.

There are times when you don't have time to read publications, missionary letters, and magazines. I slip them into a file folder and take the folder along with me in the car. When I have to wait in the doctor's office, for children, or even in a long line, I use that time to catch up on my mail reading. I make notes on it, and then process it according to its category.

Address changes should be made immediately upon receipt, making sure that you dispose of the old address. Also, an RSVP should be answered as soon as you know your plans. This is a common courtesy to your host or hostess; he or she will appreciate your promptness. If you can't give a yes/no answer, then let that be known also.

Mark dates on your calendar as soon as the invitations arrive. Also write down appointments, birthdays, and other significant days. With our busy, busy lives, we can't always depend upon our memories.

56

What to Do
with Those Piles
of Papers

A wise man thinks ahead; a fool
doesn't, and even brags about it!

—*Proverbs 13:16*

$\mathcal{E}$VERY DAY we make decisions about
paper—from personal mail to children's
papers, newspapers to magazines to Sunday School papers. We must
sort through mountains of paper each week, accumulated from day
to day, week to week, and month to month. Some of us find ourselves
buried in years of collected, often-forgotten papers.

One woman who attended my seminar shared that she finally had
to hire a person to help her organize her papers. A former school
teacher, she had acquired volumes of miscellaneous papers.

She and her helper worked three hours a day, five days a week, for
three months during summer vacation just organizing paper; a total
of 180 hours each!

A lot of time and expense can be avoided if paper is dealt with
when it arrives. Rather than stacking it on counters, appliance tops,
tables, dressers, or even on the floor until it takes up nearly every
empty space in our homes, we need to file and/or dispose of paper as
soon as it is received.

Another lady confessed that she couldn't use her dining room table without a major paper transfer before entertaining company. Still another woman shared that her husband threatened, "It's either me or the papers that go." Needless to say, she began a major paper-filing program and quickly got the paper epidemic under control.

Paper disorganization often begins in subtle ways. With only insurance policies, checking account statements, and canceled checks, car registrations, apartment rental agreements, birth certificates, a marriage license, diplomas, and a few other miscellaneous papers, a person often reasons that a full-fledged filing system is not necessary. Thus the file often consists of merely a cardboard shoebox or metal, fireproof box which can easily be stored away on a closet shelf.

As the years go by, however, there are "his" papers, "her" papers, appliance warranties, and instruction booklets on the television, the toaster, and the lawn mower (along with other gadgets too numerous to mention). The result is paper chaos.

Don't despair. Help is on the way. Here are six simple steps to effective paper-management.

1. *Schedule set times* for sorting through papers.
2. *Collect materials* you will need to help you get organized.
   - Metal file cabinet or file boxes.
   - Plastic trash bags.
   - File folders. (I prefer bright colored folders, but plain manila will do.)
   - Black felt marking pen.
3. *Begin.*
   - Start with whatever room annoys you the most. Work your way through every pile of paper; go through drawers and closets. Then move on to rooms where other papers have accumulated. Continue at set times until your project is completed.
4. *Throw away.*
   - Be determined. Make decisions. Throw away the clutter.
   - Perhaps you have lots of articles, recipes, or children's school papers and artwork which you have been saving for that special "someday." In each category, choose five pieces to keep and get rid of the rest! Try not to be too sentimental.
   - Keep the saving of papers to a minimum. Put the throwaway papers into bags and carry them out to the trash. Don't wait. It's a good feeling!
   - Don't get bogged down rereading old letters, recipes, articles, etc. It's easy to spend too much time reminiscing and get sidetracked from your purpose of streamlining your paper-filing system.

• Keep legal papers a minimum of seven years.

• If you have trouble determining what to throw away, ask a friend to help you make some of those decisions. Friends tend to be more objective and you can return the favor when they discover how "organized" you are.

5. *File.*

• Keep your filing system as simple as possible. If it is too detailed and complex, you may be easily discouraged.

• Categorize the papers you want to save (i.e., magazine articles, Bible study notes/outlines, family information, IRS papers, bank statements/ canceled checks, charge accounts, utilities, taxes, house, and investments).

• Label the file folders with a felt pen.

• Within each category, mark a folder or envelope for each separate account. For example, in the utilities, water, gasoline, and telephone. In the insurance folder, it is helpful to designate separate envelopes for life, health, car and house insurance.

• Label a folder for each member of the family. These can be used for keeping health records, report cards, notes, drawings, awards, and other special remembrances.

• Other suggestions for categories: vacation possibilities, Christmas card lists, home improvement ideas, warranties, instruction booklets, photos/negatives, and car/home repair receipts.

• File papers in appropriate folders. *Do it at the time they are received and/or paid.* (Especially take care to file away your check stubs, paid receipts, and other budget records on the day you receive your paycheck.)

• Place files in cabinet or boxes and store.

6. *Store.*

• Store files (cabinets or boxes) in a closet, garage, attic, or some other area that is out of sight, yet easily accessible.

• Be sure to label the file boxes. (I use a 3 x 5 card stapled on the end of the box with the contents written on the card. Then if I empty the box at a later date, I can easily tear off the card and replace it with another card, or use the box for other items.)

Remember, you don't need to buy a home computer to help you get organized. You do, however, need to start right where you are . . . tackling your own mountains of paper by filing and storing the information you want, and disposing of the clutter that depresses and discourages you.

57

Babysitting Survival Guide

Don't copy the behavior and
customs of this world, but be a new
and different person with a fresh
newness in all you do and think.

—Romans 12:2

*S*IXTEEN-YEAR OLD Lynn arrives at
the Merrihew home, eager to take care of
Craig and Jenny's three adorable children. Craig, Jenny, and Lynn
chat briefly, and then Craig and Jenny go out the door, delighted to
have their first date alone in six weeks.

About 45 minutes later, two-year old Christine is still crying and
screaming, "Mommy!" Lynn remembers that Craig and Jenny were
going to be at three different places during the evening, but she can't
remember what time they were to be where. She's not even sure if
she should call them.

Meanwhile Craig and Jenny keep remembering things they
wished they had told Lynn. Their intimate conversation is interrupted by an ongoing debate as to whether to call home.

Whether your babysitter is 16 or 66, there are certain steps you
can take to insure a smoother and more enjoyable evening for sitter
and parents alike. I call these "survival hints."

For Mom and Dad

• Agree on an hourly fee with your sitter when you make the babysitting arrangement.

• Ask a first-time sitter to arrive early so you and your children can get acquainted with the sitter. This gives your sitter the chance to become familiar with your home before you leave.

• Explain your home rules about snacking, visitors, television, and the stereo.

• Tell the sitter what time each child is to go to bed and whether your child has any special needs, such as a favorite toy, blanket, or story.

• Show the sitter, if necessary, procedures for feeding, warming a bottle, and changing a diaper.

• Write down the instructions as to time and dosage for any medications your child may be taking. Leave these next to the bottle with a measuring spoon or dropper nearby.

• Let your sitter know at the time of hiring whether he or she will be expected to prepare and serve a meal.

• Make special arrangements at the time you hire your sitter if you want him or her to do any housework. Most parents pay extra for that service.

• Place a flashlight in a handy place in case of power failure.

• Leave a pad and pen by the phone for phone messages and notes of the evening's events.

• Call home periodically if the sitter will not be able to reach you easily.

• Phone your sitter if you will be arriving home later than you had planned. Let him or her know when you expect to arrive.

• Pay your sitter the previously agreed-upon fee when you return home, unless you have worked out another payment arrangement ahead of time. Be aware that checks are sometimes hard for teen-agers to cash. Some parents pay extra for hours after midnight. (If you must cancel a sitter at the last minute, it is courteous to pay the sitter for part of the time he or she was planning on working for you.)

For the Babysitter

• Be sure you understand what is expected of you. Don't count on your memory; write instructions down if the list gets too long.

• Be sure you know where parents or other adults such as grand-parents or aunts and uncles can be reached at all times.

• Request that the children be present when parents give you instructions so you all understand the rules.

- Don't open the doors for strangers. (Any deliveries can be left outside or delivered later when the parents are home.)
- Keep all outside doors locked at all times.
- Don't tell telephone callers that parents are not at home. Take a message if possible, and tell the caller that they will return the call when they are able to come to the phone.
- Keep your own phone calls brief.
- Clean up your own mess. Any extra effort you make will encourage the parents to call you again.
- Don't snoop in closets or drawers. Even though you are working in the home, you are still a guest.
- Try to stay alert and awake unless it is a long, late evening.
- Inform the parents of any illness or accident, however minor, or any item broken while they were gone. Accidents do happen, and most parents allow for this.
- Tell parents as soon as possible if you have to cancel.
- Take a first-aid course at your local YWCA, Red Cross, or Community Service Department. Some cities have regular classes designed for babysitters. If not, buy a first-aid handbook.

58

Garage Sale Organization

> Fear not, for I am with you. Do not
> be dismayed. I am your God. I will
> strengthen you; I will help you; I
> will uphold you.
>
> —*Isaiah 41:10*

*A*S SUMMER comes to an end and you need something to keep your restless children busy, why not plan a garage sale? Tell them that they can keep the money from the sale of their items, and you'll be surprised at how quickly they get motivated to clean their rooms and get rid of clutter.

Not only will a garage sale tidy up your home, it can also be quite profitable. Our children often use their money to buy back-to-school supplies and new clothes. Another good idea is to give the money to a church project or a missionary family. After you help your children decide how they want to use the money they make, put on your grubbies, roll up your sleeves, and start planning.

Set your date. The first step is to set your garage sale date. It is best to plan a one-day sale, either on a Friday or Saturday. Once that is set, call the newspaper or community shopper handout and place an advertisement.

Your ad should be short, to the point, and should *not* include your phone number. You don't need to answer a lot of phone calls and silly questions. Here is a sample ad:

> Garage Sale—Saturday, Sept. 6, 9 A.M. to 5 P.M.
> Bookcase—toys—antiques—appliances—clothing—
> bike—tools and lots of goodies. 6256 Windemere Way,
> Chicago at Ransom Road.

Make your signs. Use heavy cardboard or brightly colored poster board and bold felt pens in contrasting colors. Keep it simple. Merely write: "GARAGE SALE," your house address, and street name. Most people don't need too much prompting to drive by a garage sale. My car goes on automatic when it sees a garage sale sign, and stops dead-center in front of the house!

When placing your signs, make sure they are in a prominent location. Use your own stakes. Do not put them on top of a street sign or speed-limit sign. Always go back and remove your signs the day after your sale.

Make your decisions. Now comes the cleaning out and decision-making process. Spend time with each child going over the items they begin to pull out of their rooms. They sometimes get so excited that they want to sell their bed, favorite teddy bear, and even the dog or cat.

You'll have to watch yourself too. I got so excited at one of our garage sales that I sold our refrigerator! People were coming and buying so fast that I got all caught up in it. I didn't like our refrigerator anyway and thought a new one would be great. Besides, it looked like we were selling plenty and bringing in a lot of money. A couple asked me what else I had for sale and I said, "How about the refrigerator?" They bought it.

I was thrilled—until my husband, Bob, came home. I learned a good lesson: Keep your cool and don't lose your head!

Organize. Display items in categories. For example, put all the toys in one place, and glassware and kitchen utensils in another. Place breakable items on tables if possible.

Have an extension cord available from your garden or house outlet so people can check electrical appliances such as a popcorn popper, iron, razor, or clock. If the item does not work, tell the truth. Your interested customer may still buy it. Many garage shoppers are handymen who can fix anything or can use the parts from a nonworking item.

Hospitality gives a garage sale an added touch. Try serving fresh coffee, tea, or iced tea.

Set your price. Pricing takes a lot of time and thought. As a general rule, keep your prices down. Never mark your price directly on the article. If your husband's shirt doesn't sell, he may go to the office one day with $1.50 inked on his cuff or pocket. It is best to use stick-on labels, round stickers, or masking tape.

If individual family members are going to keep the money from the sale of particular items, be sure to mark them with appropriate initials or a color code (Linda has the blue label, Tom has the green).

I always price everything in increments of 50 cents—$1.50, $2.50, etc. That way you have some bargaining power. People love bargains.

It's a good idea to have separate boxes containing items priced at five cents, ten cents, and 25 cents. This will save you from having to mark each item separately. Children love these boxes because then they can shop while mom and dad look around. You can even have a box marked "FREE."

Have one person, preferably an adult, be the cashier. All purchases must go through that person. Take a large sheet of poster board and list each person who is selling at your sale. As each item is sold, take off the price sticker and place it under his or her name or write the price in the appropriate column. At the end of the day, simply add up each column. It's best to accept only cash from your customer.

Make time count. On the day of the sale, get up early and commit the day to the sale. Eat a good breakfast; you'll need a clear mind for bargain decisions. Since people interested in antiques and valuable items will come by early, it is best to have everything set up the day before. Then all you have to do on the morning of the sale is to move your tables of items outside on the walkway, patio, or driveway.

Pack lunches the night before for you and your children. You won't have time to make lunch with people in your yard all day. Aim toward having a calm, loving spirit, and keep the family involved and available to help. Remember, this is a family project.

By the end of the day, you'll be ready for a hot bath and a chance to relax. Pop some popcorn, sit down with your family, and enjoy discussing the day's activities and the way you'll use your profits.

59

You're
Moving...
Again?

What is faith? It is the confident
assurance that something we want
is going to happen.
—*Hebrews 11:1*

I HAVE A friend whose husband serves
in the U.S. Army. Every time she
finally finishes unpacking the last box and begins to feel somewhat
acclimated to her new surroundings, her husband comes home from
work and says, "Well, it's time to pack up, we're moving next
month." In the past 11 years they've moved 11 times.

To most people, the thought of moving does not exactly bring
cheers or happy memories. It can, however, be an easy and smooth
process if preplanned and organized.

Before you even begin to organize your move, however, two
questions need to be answered clearly: 1) How long do you have to
plan your move—one week, one month, or six months? 2) How are
you going to move—a "do it yourself" move, a moving company, or
a combination of both?

Once you know when and how you are moving, you are ready to
begin.

Step 1: Household Check off List

There are so many details to remember before moving time, and often important things are forgotten until it's too late. Here is a checklist of the essential details that must be taken care of:

Transfer of Records
- School records
- Auto registration and driver's license
- Bank—savings and checking accounts
- Medical records from doctors and dentists
- Eyeglass prescription
- Pet immunization records
- Legal documents
- Church and other organizations
- Insurance

Services to Be Discontinued
- Telephone company
- Electric, gas, and water company
- Layaway purchases
- Cleaners—don't move without picking up all your clothes
- Fuel company
- Milk delivery
- Newspaper delivery
- Cable television
- Pest control
- Water softener or bottled water
- Garbage service
- Diaper service

Change of Address
- Local post office
- Magazines
- Friends and relatives
- Insurance company
- Creditors and charge accounts
- Lawyer
- Church

Step 2: Getting Ready

- Reserve a moving company if needed.
- Prepare to pack by enlisting some volunteers. Neighbors or friends from church are likely candidates and usually very willing to help.

• Collect boxes from local supermarkets and drugstores. Be sure to go to stores early in the day before the boxes are flattened and thrown out. Some moving companies will loan you boxes such as wardrobe boxes.

• Buy felt marking pens to color-code your boxes. (More details on how to do this later.)

• Prepare a work area such as a card table that can be used for wrapping and packing your goods.

• Clean and air the refrigerator and kitchen range.

• Be sure that gas appliances are properly disconnected.

• Make a list of items that need special care when being packed, such as your antique lamp or china cup-and-saucer collection.

• Discard flammable materials—empty gas tanks on mowers and chain saw.

• Be sure to leave space open in your driveway or on the street for your truck, trailer, or moving van.

• Keep handy a small box of tools to dismantle furniture with a bucket, rags, and cleaning products to clean your home after it is empty.

Step 3: Packing

Packing your goods properly is the most important part of your move. A little care on your part can assure that none of your things will be damaged.

Use good, sturdy boxes that you can depend on for protection, and be generous in padding your belongings with paper. Packing paper can be purchased at low cost at your local newspaper plant. This unprinted paper is super for wrapping dishes and glassware.

• Begin packing boxes, if possible, two weeks ahead of moving day.

• Either use colored pens or a number system and mark each box to identify its contents and the room where it is to go. For example: yellow—kitchen; green—garden and garage; blue—Brad's bedroom.

Or number your boxes 1, 2, 3, etc. Then make out 3 x 5 cards and number them Box 1, Box 2, etc. List on each card what is in each box and to which room it belongs. Put your 3 x 5 cards in a small box. On moving day, as each numbered box is carried into the house, direct it to the appropriate room.

Because you know by your numbered cards what is in each box without opening it, you can unpack the priority boxes first. This is also a great method for organizing the goods you plan to store in your basement or attic.

• Moving is a good time to weed out things you need to get rid of. Although some items should just be thrown out, other things such as old clothing can be given to churches, orphanages, or the Salvation Army.

Other ways to get rid of excess items are to run an ad in your local paper, or hold a garage sale.

Remember, when you give away items to nonprofit groups, you can use the net value as a deduction from your income tax. Be sure to get a signed receipt.

• Don't pack fragile and heavy items in the same box.

• Use smaller boxes for heavier items and larger boxes for lightweight, bulky items.

• Fill each box completely and compactly. Don't overfill or underfill.

• When packing glass dishes, put a paper plate between each plate as a protector. Stack plates on end (not flat). They seem to take the pressure better when packed that way.

• Popcorn is another good packing agent for china cups and crystal glasses. Fill the cups and glasses with popcorn and wrap them in your unprinted paper. Foam padding also works well to protect your breakables.

• To protect your mirrors and paintings, cut cardboard to fit around them, bind them with tape and label them "FRAGILE."

• When packing your tables, if possible remove their legs and pack them on edge. If this is not possible, load tables with their surface down and legs up. Take care to protect the finish with blankets or other padding.

Furniture pads can be wrapped around items and tied together or sewn together temporarily with heavy thread.

• Seal boxes with packing tape, or put the boxes into trash bags and then tape.

• Move your dresser drawers with the clothes inside.

• Be sure bathroom items, medicines, and cleaning agents are packed and sealed immediately so small children cannot get to them.

Loading Your Van, Truck, or Trailer

• Park next to the widest door of your home and leave enough room to extend a ramp if necessary.

• Load your vehicle one quarter at a time, using all the space from floor to ceiling. Try to load weight evenly from side to side to prevent it from shifting.

• Put heaviest items in front.

• Tie off each quarter with rope. This will keep your goods from banging up against each other and getting damaged.

• Use a dolly for the heavy items. (These can be rented from rental equipment or moving companies.) CAUTION: When lifting heavy objects, bend your knees and use your leg muscles. Keep your back as straight as possible.

• Fit bicycles and other odd-shaped items along the walls of the truck or on top of stacked items.

Finish cleaning up your house, lock your door, and you're on your way!

60

Corralling
the Chaos

> She watches carefully all that goes
> on throughout her household, and is
> never lazy.
> —*Proverbs 31:27*

*O*NE SUNDAY after church service my
husband, Bob, and I were visiting with
some friends. When one woman asked me about my "More Hours In
My Day" ministry, I told her about some of the recent seminars I had
conducted around the country.

All of a sudden, a man who was listening to our conversation
grabbed my arm. "Emilie, our family lives in a cesspool," he
complained. Thankfully, his wife was not within earshot.

"My wife doesn't work. We have three children; two of them are
in school. Yet she says she doesn't have time to clean the house."

Do you think this is an isolated case? It isn't. In today's hectic
society, men and women are so busy that often there is no time left to
plan and execute the daily routines of life.

For many people, life is lived in a constant panic, trying to stay on
top of the house, family, and career. With more women in the work
force, there has never been a greater need for basic organizational
skills in our homes.

Establishing the Target

If you don't have a goal for organizing your home and life, you can never know if you have hit or missed the target. Much time is wasted because we don't know where we're going.

Early in our marriage Bob and I felt it was important to set goals. We dreamed of the type of home and family we wanted. We realized that in order to achieve those dreams we needed a plan. That plan became the "Barnes' Family Life Goals."

We talked often of those goals, and periodically we adjusted them as our lives changed. The biggest change came as we began to mature in our Christian faith. That's when our goals became more Christ-centered.

Goal-setting doesn't just happen. You must take time to think long-range in order to effectively plan for the next few years. And your goals must be important enough to work at making them happen.

Bob and I have set ten-year goals and then we've broken those down into smaller goals. Where do we want to be in five years if we're to fulfill our ten-year goals? What about three years? One year? Six months? Three months? One month? Today?

See the progression? How can we plan today if we don't know where we're headed? Sure, we can fill our time with activities; that's easy. But by goal-setting, everything we do is directed toward a purpose that we've set.

Priorities—What Comes First?

Jean had set her goals and organized her days according to those goals. But she never was able to complete her daily TO DO list.

I asked Jean to show me a typical list of her day's priorities. With 16 activities written on her list, Jean realized she could not possibly do every one of them. She needed to divide these options into three categories:

Yes: I will do this.

Maybe: I will do this if there is time.

No: I will not attempt this today.

Notice the last option? You must learn to say "NO!" Too many women assume that their only options are "yes" and "maybe." If we can't say no to some things, we become overcommitted and wind up carrying heavy loads of guilt because of unfulfilled commitments.

Making Decisions Using Priorities

Just how does a Christian proceed with decisions when the answers are not obvious?

Priority 1: GOD

According to Matthew 6:33, our first priority is to seek and know God. This is a lifelong pursuit. When God has first place in our lives, deciding among the other alternatives is easier.

When I feel hassled or hurried, it's often because this priority is out of order. Usually I need to adjust my schedule in order to spend time with God. When I allow Him to fill my heart, I can relax and have a clearer perspective on the rest of my activities.

Priority 2: FAMILY

In Proverbs 31 we read about the woman who "watches carefully all that goes on throughout her household, and is never lazy. Her children stand and bless her; so does her husband" (verses 27,28).

How does a woman receive such praise from her family? The answer is by providing a home setting full of warmth, love, and respect.

Priority 3: CHURCH-RELATED ACTIVITIES

Hebrews 10:25 tells us to be involved in our church, but that is not at the expense of the first two priorities.

Priority 4: ALL OTHER AREAS

This includes job, exercise, classes, clubs, and other activities. Some people are amazed that there is time for any of these items. But there is.

God wants you to live a balanced life, and that means you need time for work and time for recreation—time to cut some flowers, drink a cup of tea, or go shopping with a friend. These activities can revitalize you for the responsibilities of home and church.

With these priorities in mind, Jean attacked her list of activities, beginning with the junk mail. "I think I'll just toss the whole pile," she said. By eliminating three more activities and putting four in the "maybe" category, Jean was immediately more relaxed.

I encouraged her to cross off the "yes" activities as she completed each one to give herself the satisfaction of seeing the list shrink during the day. If time permitted, she could do the "maybe" activities, but if she didn't, some of them might become "yes" activities on another day.

Of course, not all decisions can be made swiftly—some require more time and consideration. I've made Paul Little's five-point outline from his booklet *Affirming the Will of God* my criteria when I have trouble establishing my priorities:

1. Pray with an attitude of obedience to the Lord. God's promise to us is, "I will instruct you and teach you in the way you should go; I will counsel you and watch over you" (Psalm 32:8 NIV).

2. What does the Bible say that might guide me in making the decision? "Be diligent to present yourself approved to God as a workman . . . handling accurately the word of truth" (2 Timothy 2:15 NASB).

3. Obtain information from competent sources in order to gain all the pertinent facts. "A wise man's heart directs him toward the right" (Ecclesiastes 10:2 NASB).

4. Obtain advice from people knowledgeable about the issue. It's best if our counselors are fellow Christians who can pray with and for us. "Iron sharpens iron, so one man sharpens another" (Proverbs 27:17 NASB).

5. Make the decision without second-guessing God. "He who trusts in the Lord will prosper" (Proverbs 28:25 NASB).

The purpose of establishing priorities is to avoid becoming over-extended. If you know you are always doing the most important activities first, you can relax even when you cannot complete everything on your TO DO list.

Family Conference Time

Probably the number-one question women ask me when I give a seminar is "How do I get my husband and children involved?" That's a tough question to answer because each family is different.

One mistake many women make is that they assume every family member understands his or her role. They never discuss their expectations with their husband or children. With many mothers working, it is often necessary for other family members to assume some of the responsibilities that are traditionally the woman's. The family needs to understand the concept of *teamwork*.

Mom is not the only player in the family—everyone plays a valuable part. So I first recommend that moms stop carrying the whole team. That only leads to tired, burned-out, frustrated women.

It did not take the Barnes family long to realize that we need a regular time to discuss important topics. One of our long-range goals was to raise independent and responsible children, and Bob and I felt that one way to achieve this goal was to allow our children to be part of the decision-making process.

Yet how could we set aside more time when everyone was already busy with many activities? Our solution also resolved another chronic problem in our home.

Probably the most hectic time for our family was Sunday morning before church. Mom and dad often had a few cross words because we were late. By the time we drove into the church parking lot, we were rarely in a mood for worship.

In order to solve our two problems—stressful Sundays and the need for family meetings—we decided to start going out for breakfast on Sunday mornings before church. Overnight we saw improvement.

Eating breakfast out eliminated the problem of food preparation and cleanup, and it gave us time to discuss various aspects of our family life. We established Sunday breakfasts as part of our regular monthly budget, and all of us looked forward to this time together.

Our family activities and conference times played a valuable part in establishing harmony, respect, and pride within our family. Not every meeting and activity was a success, but we usually gained greater respect for one another.

Family Work Planner

One idea that helped our family better distribute the housework was to establish a "Daily Work Planner." We would write the weekly chores on separate slips of paper, place them in a basket, and every Saturday each of us drew one or more slips to learn our duties for the upcoming week.

As each assignment was drawn, it was recorded on the Daily Work Planner, which was posted in a conspicuous place. Each family member was responsible to complete his assignment. Mom and dad also drew their chores from the basket—this was a team effort.

If your children range widely in their ages, you may want to use two baskets—one for smaller children and one for the rest of the family. In this way, the younger children do not draw jobs that are too difficult for them.

It is also important that mom and dad inspect the work to make sure chores are being done properly. Occasionally, give a special reward for a job well done.

Please note that I am not suggesting that children assume the load in maintaining a house. As parents you must allow your children to participate in their own activities. They need time to get involved in sports, music, homework, and other school and church activities.

You also need to recognize your priorities in relating to your mate. When my children were still at home, I often remembered the saying, "You were a wife to your husband before you were a mother to your children." Our children will grow up and leave home (hopefully). However, we will still have our mate after the nest is empty.

A couple needs to spend quality time with each other without the children. You must not use the excuse that you can't afford to do it. You can't afford *not* to. Bob and I plan times together and reserve those days on our calendar just as we would any other appointment. We protect those times and don't cancel them unless there is an emergency.

For single parents who are raising children alone, the pressures are even more intense, especially when the children are young. I believe the family conference time and division of responsibilities can help relieve some of the pressure. However, sometimes as a parent—whether married, single, or widowed—you may have to leave some things unfinished rather than continue to tax your spirit.

There are no rules on how a home should be run; each family needs to set its own standards. My family enjoys working together as we set joint goals, but it is a process that takes time.

In his first letter, the apostle Peter wrote that wives could influence their husbands: "Even if any of them are disobedient to the word, they may be won without a word by the behavior of their wives" (1 Peter 3:1 NASB).

Even though the context of this verse deals with salvation, Peter provides an excellent principle. In our society, the mother sets the tone for the family and home. Many times, dad and junior are not as excited about the home as mom is. If you are aware of this truth, you will be disappointed less often because you will not have as many expectations.

We need to remind ourselves that it is not our role to change our husband and children. God will do that in His time. We must be faithful to the Scriptures and love our family even when they may not return that love.

It is important to realize that there are many areas of stress that you can relieve. I have attempted to give some practical helps in many of those areas. Implementing these organizational techniques can help you enjoy more hours in your day and experience more joy in your home.

Keeping Track
of Loaned
and Borrowed Items

To err is human, to forgive, divine.

$\mathcal{F}$OR MANY YEARS I loaned items to my friends thinking I would surely remember who had my turkey platter, Tupperware bowls, picnic basket, and the children's sleeping bags. You know what? I forgot after a short period of time. There was no way I could remember, no matter how hard I tried.

It's even more embarrassing to find you have items that don't belong to you and you can't remember who you borrowed them from.

We once had some brick masonry work done on our home and in talking with our contractor he said he had loaned over $500.00 worth of tools to friends but couldn't remember who the friends were. I showed him the form I use and he thought it would be of real value to him (see page 229, Figure 9).

This form will fit very nicely into your 8½ x 5½ organizer notebook for ease in keeping track of all your records.

Remember to form new habits you must be consistent in using your new organization tools.

228

ITEMS LOANED/BORROWED

Month/Year January – February 1991

Date	Item	Who	Returned
1/3	Cake plate	Church	✓
1/4	Screwdriver	Charlie	✓
1/7	Circular saw	Jimmy	✓
1/15	Plastic cups (10)	Brownies	✓
1/22	Lawn mower	George	✓
1/27	Card table	Christine	✓
1/29	Diving mask	Youth group	✓
2/4	Tent	Scout troop	✓
2/5	Posthole digger	Mr. Brown	✓
2/9	Snow White video	daughter	✓
2/12	Pewter pitcher	Georgia	✓

Figure 9

One other reminder is to personally identify items you loan with your name and telephone number. This technique will also help get back those missing items.

Make them loaned, not lost!

Keeping Track of Those On-Order Products

*H*AVE YOU forgotten which manufacturer's rebate coupons you have sent
in for a refund, or that blouse you have on order from your favorite
catalogue? Well, now you can spend a few minutes recording those
"on-order" items that need to be tracked until they have been
received (see page 233, Figure 10). I even use this form to track
refunds from my Visa card and the utility companies.

Add this form to your organizer notebook along with an index tab
for easy location and you can keep an easy record.

There are two rules to remember when using an organizer to help
you stay on track:
• You must write it down.
• You must read it.

It takes 21 days to form a new habit, so continue to write down
what's on order. There are many good commercially manufactured
organizer notebooks, for which you can pay anywhere from $40.00
to $250.00. Or you can be industrious and make your own organizer.
All you need is:

- one 8½ x 5½ three-ring binder
- ten 8½ x 5½ index tabs for labeling and dividing your paper by sections
- fifty 8½ x 5½ lined paper
- one 8½ x 5½ month-at-a-glance calendar on two pages
- thirty 8½ x 5½ daily calendar pages to help you through each day

ON ORDER

Date Ordered	Item	Company	Date Due	Received
1/6	white blouse	Lands End	1/20	✓
1/6	red socks	"	1/20	✓
1/6	plaid slacks	"	1/20	BO
2/3	crib sheets	J.C. Penny	2/17	✓
2/3	crib mattress	"	2/17	✓
2/15	Patio lights $1.00 rebate	Malibu Lights		
2/18	Gas rebate $12.00	Southern CA Gas Co.	3/1	✓
2/22	Credit $17.00	Bank Visa	3/10	✓
2/27	Coupon rebate $1.50	Campbell Soup		
3/2	T-shirts	Sears	3/14	
3/2	white socks	"	3/14	
3/2	Levis	"	3/14	

Figure 10

Setting Up a Desk and Work Area

The effective prayer of a righteous
man can accomplish much.

—*James 5:16* NASB

*A*S I BEGAN to get my home in order
and to eliminate all the clutter I soon
realized that I didn't have an area to handle all the mail and paper that
came into our home. We have had several mottos to help us focus in
on our home organization.

One was **"Don't put it down, put it away."** Much of our clutter
was little piles of materials that needed to be put away, but we just
temporarily put it down until we could put it where it belonged. At
the end of the day we had piles sitting all around the home. Now we
take the material back to where we found it. Amazing how the piles
have disappeared.

Another motto was **"Don't pile it, file it."** Somewhere in the
corner of the home we had piles of paper that were in no organized
fashion. In our new program we have taken manila folders and given
them one-word headings such as: insurance, car, home, foods, patio,
children, utilities, taxes. Now we file, not pile our papers.

During all this change in our home, we still had no central desk or
work area. Yet we had recognized that we needed one in order to

function properly and with maximum efficiency.

Paper-handling depends upon a good physical setting with a practical location furnished with a comfortable working surface and a good inventory of supplies. Ideally, this office will become a permanent fixture where the business life of your home is done. It should be accessible, with supplies and files, and located where other household operations do not interfere. However, if your desk/work area can't be this ideal, don't let this stop you from getting started. Your work area might have to be portable, but that's okay. The important thing is to *just get started*.

Since a desk or work area is so basic to a well-functioning lifestyle, we will give you some practical steps in setting up this area in your home.

Choosing the Location

Where your office will be should depend upon how long you plan to spend in your office daily. If you operate a business out of your home you will need to use different criteria in selecting that special site, giving preference to the needs of the business over those of the person who needs a place to open mail, answer mail, pay bills, and file papers. In either case, you want to choose a location that agrees with your spirit. If after a short while you find you aren't using your new space, but rather find yourself working in the room with a big window, you may have initially selected the wrong location. Make sure the location meets your needs. In order to help you choose that ideal setting, you might ask yourself these questions:

• Do you need to be in a place where it's quiet, or is it better for you to be near people?

• Do big windows distract you, or do you like being near windows?

• Do you prefer a sunny room or a shaded one?

• Do you prefer to work in the morning or in the afternoon?

These last two questions are related because different rooms receive varying amounts of light at different times of the day.

The answer to these questions helps narrow your alternatives. Walk around your home to see which areas meet the answers to your four questions. After selecting at least two locations, you might ask yourself another set of questions:

• Are there enough electrical outlets and telephone jacks?

• Is there enough space for a desk?

• Is this location out of the way of other household functions? If not, can the activities be shifted so they won't interfere with your office hours?

• Is the area structurally sound?

Again, add the answers to these questions to your previously selected alternatives and narrow your choices to a final selection. Do you feel good about this selection? Live with it a few days before making a final decision. Walk to and through it several times to make sure it feels good. Sit down in the area and read a magazine or book. If it still feels good, then you will probably like your choice.

Don't begin tearing out walls, adding electrical outlets, moving phone jacks, or building bookcases until you are sure it's the right location.

Selection of Desk, Equipment, and Supplies

After you have selected the location for your office, you need to take a sheet of paper and make a diagram of the floor plan with the dimensions listed. You will use this information when you want to make or select furniture for your new work area.

The Desk

In actuality, all one really needs is a writing surface of some type. In some cases a piece of plywood is all you may have or need. Look around. You may already have around your home a suitable desk or table which would fit into the dimensions of the work area.

If you find a table, it should be sturdy, high enough to write comfortably, and large enough to hold various implements on its surface.

If you can't find a desk or table in your home, buy a desk. It is an investment you won't regret. Check your local classified ads to find a good bargain. Another good place to look is in the yellow pages of your phone book under "Office Furniture—Used." You need not pay full price, and many times these stores will deliver to your home free or with a minimum charge.

You should have no trouble finding a desk which has the practical characteristics of office models, but is still attractive in your home. Here are a few specifications to keep in mind.

1. *Writing surface:* Your desk should be sturdy and comfortable to use, with a surface that doesn't wobble.

2. *Place for supplies:* Your desk should have at least one large drawer in which paper and envelopes can be kept in folders. If you find a desk with large drawers on each side, so much the better. There needs to be a shallow drawer with compartments for paper clips, rubber bands, and other supplies. Or you can purchase small trays with dividers that can store these small items at your local stationery store.

3. *Files and records:* A home office seldom has need for more than one file drawer, or sometimes two. If your desk has at least one drawer big enough to contain letter-size file folders (legal-size accommodation is preferable), all your files will probably fit. If you can't purchase a file cabinet at this time, use Perfect boxes until you are able to purchase a file cabinet. Watch your newspaper for stationery "sale" offerings.

4. *Typing platform:* If you have a typewriter or a personal computer and plan to use it in your work area, try to get a desk with a built-in platform for these to rest on. If you have enough room in your office you might want to designate separate areas for these two functions.

If you don't have enough space for a regular stationery desk in your home, look into portable storage to house your stationery and supplies. Go again to your local office supply store and have them recommend products that will service this need. You will still need a file cabinet or its short-term substitute (the Perfect Box) and a sturdy swivel chair just for the office area. The swivel chair permits you to turn from one position to another without getting up.

Other Storage Ideas

• Wall organizers are helpful for pads, pens, calendars, and other supplies.

• Paper, pencils, and supplies can be kept in stackable plastic or vinyl storage cubes kept under the desk.

• Use an extra bookcase shelf for a portable typewriter, a basket of supplies, or some files.

• Decorative objects such as a ceramic mug look attractive holding pencils and pens.

• Use stackable plastic bins that can be added to as your needs expand. Use the small style for stationery and papers, and a larger size (a vegetable bin) for magazines and newspapers.

Supplies

For your shopping convenience I have given you a checklist of supplies that you will need to stock your office. Again, try to purchase these items on sale or at an office supply discount store. Watch your local paper for these sales. Or again, let the yellow pages do the walking for you. Look under "Office Supplies." Many times bulk buying is where you will get your best prices.

____ *Address book or Rolodex.* I personally like both; the address book I take with me when I'm traveling or on business, and a Rolodex is permanently housed on my desk. The Rolodex also has more room for adding other information you might want to use when addressing a particular person/business.

_____ *Appointment calendar.* Ideally the calendar should be small enough to carry around with your notebook, as well as for use at your desk. If you search around you can find a combination notebook and calendar that isn't too bulky to carry around in your briefcase or handbag. The date squares should be large enough to list appointments comfortably. In our *Working Woman's Seminars* we offer an excellent organizer called the *Harper House/Day Runner.* This product does an excellent job meeting this need.

_____ *Bulletin board.* This is a good place to collect notes and reminders to yourself. Attach notes with push pins.

_____ *Business cards.* A must time-saver.

_____ *Carbon paper.* Make a carbon copy of every business letter you write. Your office supply store can help you with this selection. Every year new formats come on the market.

_____ *Desk lamp.* A three-way bulb will give you a choice of light.

_____ *Dictionary and/or electronic spell-checker.*

_____ *File folders.* I use colored "third-cut" folders in which the stick-up tabs are staggered so they don't block my view of other folders. The colors give a more attractive appearance to my file drawer.

_____ *Letter opener.*

_____ *Marking pens.* It is useful to have on hand a few marking pens in different colors. I do a lot of color-coding on my calendar. I also use a yellow highlighter when I want some information to pop out at me for rereading.

_____ *Paper clips.* Regular and large.

_____ *Postcards.* Saves money on your mailing.

_____ *Pencil sharpener.* If you use a lot of pencils, I recommend a desktop electric model.

_____ *Pencils and pens.*

_____ *Postage scale.* A small inexpensive type.

_____ *Rubber bands.* Mixed sizes.

_____ *Rubber stamp and inkpad.* There are all kinds of rubber stamps that you can use in your office. These are much cheaper than printed stationery or labels. If you use a certain one over and over, you might consider having a self-inking stamp made for you. A great time-saver.

____ *Ruler.*

____ *Scissors.*

____ *Scratch paper.* Use lined pads for this. Post-it-Notes are also great.

____ *Scotch tape and dispenser.*

____ *Stamps.* In addition to regular stamps, keep appropriate postage on hand for additional weight and special handling if you have special needs regularly. Postcards will save you money on certain types of correspondence.

____ *Stapler, staples, staple remover.* If you do a lot of stapling you might consider an electric model. Saves time and the palm of your hand.

____ *Stationery and envelopes.* Usually 8½ x 11 plain white paper with matching business-size envelopes is all you need. If you use printed letterhead stationery you will need to get some plain white or matching colored second sheets. I find 9 x 6 and 9 x 12 manila envelopes good for mailing bulk documents, books, or magazines. Sometimes padded envelopes are needed to ship items that need some protection from rough handling in transit.

____ *Telephone.* An extension right at your desk is great. I use my cordless telephone and it works just fine. Not as good as a permanent phone, but a good alternative.

____ *Typewriter.* If you have the skills.

____ *Typewriter correction fluid or paper.*

____ *Wastebasket.*

You now have an office space that can function to your maximum. This addition to your lifestyle should certainly make you more efficient in other areas of your life. It will give you a feeling of accomplishment.

Automobile

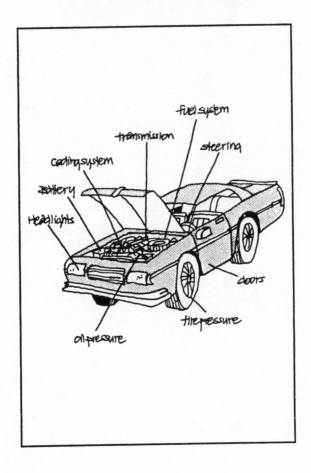

A Checklist for Your Car Before Taking a Trip

Stay away from any Christian who
spends his days in laziness and does
not follow the ideal of hard work.
—*2 Thessalonians 3:6*

*A*S IN ALL phases of life the three most important parts of any project are to PLAN, PLAN, PLAN. Usually things go wrong when we don't spend enough time in our planning phase. Don't be in such a hurry that you forget to plan. Plan to have your car regularly checked by a reliable mechanic and before starting off on that all-important trip. Many times we think of vacations only in the summer months, but depending upon your schedule flexibility you might well take your trip any time of the year.

Having your car checked regularly is the best way to prevent major car problems down the road when you are really counting on your car to perform properly. A combination of getting your car in shape and then paying close attention to the warning signals your car gives to you are key in assuring a car's smooth performance and longevity.

How do you know when your car needs attention? The Car Care Council gives some very practical suggestions.

1. Watch to see if your engine is hard to start, uses too much gas, seems sluggish, smokes, or is excessively noisy.

2. Be sure that your cooling and heating systems are in good condition. Be sure to check your hoses, belts, and anti-freeze/coolant.

3. How about those tires of yours? Heavy loads at high speeds are hard on tires. Make sure tires have plenty of tread and are properly inflated.

4. How's your oil? Oil is not only a lubricant, it is also a coolant. Clean, well-filtered oil will help your engine survive the heat as well as the cold.

5. Be sure to check your transmission. Does it slip when you shift gears? Is it noisy? Does it shift erratically? If you are towing a trailer, it is especially vital for your transmission to be in the best working order possible.

6. Be sure that the brakes stop evenly and are not making any strange noises.

7. Watch to see that all lights are working and that they are focused correctly. Also check turn signals and windshield wiper blades (for smearing or streaking).

After checking these areas of your car, you can feel more assured of a problem-free trip, barring unforeseen mechanical failure. If you do find yourself in car trouble in an unknown town and don't know of a good, reputable mechanic, you can look in the yellow pages under "Automotive Repairs" for ASE-certified technicians. These technicians have taken the proper courses to be certified by the National Institute for Automotive Service Excellence. This is an organization that is highly respected in the automotive industry, and is an independent, non-profit group which gives voluntary certification exams to technicians.

65

Pay Me Now
or Pay Me Later

*A*S CARS become more expensive it is to your advantage to keep a regular maintenance log on each of your cars. If you purchase a new car you will receive an owner's manual that will specify at what intervals you need to service your car and what maintenance is covered by your warranty. However, many people purchase older cars which are no longer covered by the new-car warranty.

As the old saying goes, "Pay me now or pay me later." You can either invest in preventative maintenance or pay more to repair breakdowns due to improper service on your automobile. A well-maintained car will bring greater driving pleasure; it will also be worth more when it is time to sell the older car to buy a newer model.

Place the following form (page 246, Figure 11) in a plastic divider in your glove compartment. Use one column each time the car is serviced. Your mechanic will tell you how often or how many miles you should service your car.

Automotive Information and Servicing Schedule

Model _____   Make _____   License Number _____

Serial # _____   Insurance Company _____   Telephone # (____) _____

Use one column each time car is serviced	Date Mileage	Date Mileage	Date Mileage	Date Mileage	Date Mileage	Date Mileage	Date Mileage
Oil Change							
Lubrication							
Change oil Filter							
Clean Air Filter							
Service Cooling System							
Rotate Tires							
Replace Tires							
Service Brakes							
Plugs, Points, Condenser							
Engine Tune-up							
Change Trans. Fluid							
Total Cost	$	$	$	$	$	$	$

66

What to Do When Your Car Won't Start

*Jehovah himself is caring for you!
He is your defender. He protects
you day and night.*
—Psalm 121:5,6

*Y*OU'RE DRESSED in your finest Sunday clothes waiting for the family to join you in the car for church. You jump in your car, turn the key—and the car plays dead. If you've ever had that happen to you, you know the empty feeling you have.

The children arrive on the scene and of course ask 100 questions, which makes matters worse. What are you to do? Call a friend? A neighbor? A taxi? Or cancel the church service?

The American Automobile Association says failure of cars to start was the most common emergency last year.

Two ways a car can fail to start are 1) the starter motor may turn, but the engine refuses to catch, or 2) the starter motor may be sluggish, perhaps not turning at all.

Let's deal with the second case first.

If you twist the key and you hear only a click, at least you know the ignition switch works. If there was a click and your car has an automatic transmission, move the shift lever into neutral and then back to park and try starting the car again. Sometimes a little switch that prevents you from starting your car while it's in gear, sticks.

Still no start? See if the headlights light and the horn honks. If they seem weak, the battery is either dead or has a bad connection.

1. Find where the battery is—usually under the hood.

2. Look closely at the two terminals and the ends of the two cables, positive (+) and negative (–), that attach to them.

3. Are they clean and firmly secured?

4. If not, remove the negative (–) cable (it's usually black) *first,* followed by the positive (+) cable (usually red).

5. Scrape them with a knife or screwdriver and firmly reattach them.

If your car still won't start, you can either push-start it (but only if it has a stick shift) or jump-start it using cables attached to another car's battery. To push-start, you'll need:

1. A couple of strong children or neighbors, *or*

2. An experienced driver who is willing to give you a push from the rear of the car.

3. Get in the car; turn on the ignition.

4. Put your foot on the clutch and put the shift lever in second gear.

5. When the car reaches about 5 mph, let out the clutch and the car should start.

If you are attempting to jump-start your car, be sure to refer to the owner's manual. Great care should be taken when jump-starting your car.

After the car starts, drive to your mechanic's to check out why the battery was low and wouldn't start the engine. You may need a new battery or it may just need to be charged.

The second area to check if your starter turns, but the engine won't start, is the fuel or the ignition system. Be sure to check that you have gas in your tank!

If your car has fuel injection, you will probably want to have the car towed to your mechanic, because these are very hard to service by the average layman. But if it has a carbureted engine:

1. Pump the throttle pedal three times and try to start the car.

2. Still no response? Open the hood.

3. If you smell gas, you have flooded the carburetor.

4. Wait a few minutes.

5. Press the gas pedal all the way to the floor. Hold it there— *don't pump!*

6. The engine should sputter a bit and then start up.

Cold and damp weather present special challenges to a slumbering engine. On a cold day if the starter turns and if you have a carbureted engine:

1. Open the hood and find the air cleaner (usually big and round on top of engine, although sometimes rectangular).

2. Take off the wing nut or retaining clips and lift off the cover of the air cleaner.

3. Spray a little ether starter fluid (available at auto parts stores) down the carburetor throat.

Another useful elixir to carry in your trunk is WD-40; it absorbs moisture. On a damp day, spray some on the coil, some on the spark-plug wires and on the distributor, and some inside the distributor—if you can get the lid off. Then give the starter another turn.

If on a hot day your car refuses to start after it's been running, it may have a "vapor lock." If your car has a mechanical fuel pump (most carbureted engines do), pour cold water on the pump and nearby gas lines, and that should get you on your way.

If you don't have a very difficult problem, you should get to church in time to participate in the services. Try to relax and not get too uptight.

Car-Care Checklist

> O Lord, you are worthy to receive
> the glory and the honor and
> the power, for you have
> created all things.
>
> —*Revelation 4:11*

*W*ITHOUT GIVING it a second thought, we jump into our car, turn the key in the ignition and expect our faithful buggy to start up and take us wherever we want to go.

But a car is an expensive piece of machinery, and, like our bodies, it needs care to run well. Being stuck with car trouble is no fun and can often be avoided.

Here is a checklist to help you keep your car in tiptop shape. It's especially important to give your car a checkup before going on a vacation or an extended trip.

Basic Checklist Before Taking a Trip

Don't be afraid to look over the service attendant's shoulder as he or she checks your car. You'll learn a great deal and can ask questions. Be sure the mechanic checks the following: engine oil level; coolant level (add only if below "add" mark); battery electrolyte level; windshield washer fluid level; and drive belt tension and condition.

Warning!

Do not remove the radiator cap quickly when the engine is hot, especially if the air conditioner has been used. Turn the cap slowly to let the steam escape. Otherwise you will be severely burned by hot water and steam.

Routine Maintenance Checklist

The following items need to be checked, especially before taking a long trip or vacation. Other than taking a trip, check these things twice a year. (The frequency of checkups depends somewhat on the type of climate you live in.)

If you take your car to a service station, don't assume that they automatically check these items. You'll need to ask for some of these services:

- Engine oil changed and filter replaced
- Air filter cleaned or replaced
- Emission control devices checked
- Headlights and brake lights inspected and adjusted
- Differential fluid level checked and changed (if applicable for your car)
- Transmission fluid level checked
- Wheel bearings inspected and repacked (once a year)
- Brakes inspected (once a year)
- Air-conditioning system checked and serviced once a year
- Cooling system hoses checked and coolant/antifreeze replaced once a year
- Power steering fluid level checked
- Shock absorbers tested
- Battery inspected
- Drive belts checked
- Windshield wipers. Even in summer you will need to replace if needed, in case of summer rainstorms.
- Tire tread depth and inflation pressure checked
- Exhaust system inspected for leaks
- Tune-up. Refer to owner's manual for manufacturer's suggestion for how often a tune-up is needed.

Emergency Organization List

These items should be carried in your car at all times in case of emergency:

- Fire extinguisher
- Jumper cables
- First-aid kit (bee-sting kit)
- Towel(s)
- Flashlight with extra batteries
- Ice scraper
- Spare fuses for electrical system
- Can of tire inflater/sealer
- Flares and/or highway triangular warning signs
- Spare drive belts, fan belts, air-conditioner belts, and air pump belts
- An empty approved gasoline container. *Do not carry extra gasoline in the trunk.*
- Container of water
- Warm blanket
- Metal or wire coat hanger
- Distress flag
- Plastic dropcloth for working under car
- Toolbox with the following: Pliers; screwdriver; adjustable wrench; small socket wrenches; hammer; cleanup wipes for hands; clean rag

Winter Tools

Chains, small shovel, can of sand, extra blankets or heavy coat for emergencies, heavy boots, and gloves.

It may seem overwhelming at first to furnish your car with these items, but it's well worth it. Being prepared could save a life or get you out of a dangerous or difficult situation. Besides, being ready for emergencies and keeping your car tuned up will relieve another whole area of stress in your life.

Automobile Organization— Travel Smart!

> Love forgets mistakes; nagging
> about them parts the best of
> friends.
>
> —*Proverbs 17:9*

*M*ANY WOMEN today are primarily responsible for their automobiles and need to know the basics of travel safety.

Be Prepared

Here is a helpful checklist of items to take with you in your car so you'll be prepared and ready to prevent minor roadside difficulties from becoming major ones.

Plan Ahead

Glove Compartment
- Maps
- Notepad and pen
- Tire-pressure gauge
- Cleanup wipes
- Sunglasses
- Mirror (best placed above sun visor)

- Extra pair of nylon hosiery for that unexpected run.
- Reading material, Bible—you can enjoy prayer and Bible reading during waiting times in the car.
- Can opener
- Plastic fork and spoon, for those yummy stops
- Change for phone calls
  Business cards
- Bandaids
- Matches
- Stationery—again, waiting can be used constructively to catch up on correspondence.
- Scissors, nail clippers
- Children's books and/or games

Trunk

(See "Emergency Organization List" on page 247–249 for car-care items that should be carried in case of emergencies.)

Protect Your Ownership

- Hide a key for the times you lock your keys inside the car. Caution: Don't put it under the hood if you have an inside hood-release.
- A good idea to prove ownership of your car is to print your name, address, and phone number on a 3 x 5 file card or use your business card and slide it down your car window-frame on the driver's side. If the car is lost or stolen, it is easier to prove the auto is yours.
- If you live in a potentially snowy area, keep a bag of kitty litter in your trunk. This will help give you traction if you are stuck in the snow.
- Your rubber carmats can be used to keep windshields from freezing. Put them on the outside of windows under your wipers to hold them in place, and presto . . . clean windows and no scraping either.
- Your car may not start if your battery terminals become corroded. Simply scrub them with a mixture of one cup of baking soda and two cups water. Presto! It cleans them right up.
- To remove decals and price lists from windows, simply sponge with plenty of white vinegar. Allow vinegar to soak in and stickers should come off easily.
- A rechargeable, battery-run, hand vacuum cleaner is very handy to have. It can be used to clean inside the car, carpet, and seats.

Time for You

Time for You–
Personal Grooming

Rejoice in the Lord, ye righteous;
and give thanks at the
remembrance of his holiness.

—*Psalm 97:12 KJV*

*T*HE OLD ADAGE "You only get one time to make a first impression" is certainly true. We live in a time in history that stresses personal grooming. As Christians we need to keep moderation in mind and not be out of balance, but we must also be aware that we often conduct ourselves based on how we feel about our personal grooming. As I go shopping, I realize as I look at people that it takes so little to be above average. God wants us to be groomed properly as we go out into the secular world to be ambassadors for Him. Because how we look can affect our personal witness of who we are, I trust that some of these ideas will be helpful for your improved grooming.

Shampooing Your Hair

Lather hair twice only if very oily or very dirty. Otherwise you'll strip your hair of natural oils.

Don't be surprised if your favorite shampoo seems to leave your hair less bouncy after months of satisfactory performance. No one is exactly sure why but "shampoo fatigue" may be due to a buildup of proteins or other conditioning ingredients. Many people switch brands, only to perceive a drop in performance with the new shampoo within several months. At that point try switching back to the old one.

When you need a dry shampoo, try bran, dry oatmeal, baby powder, or cornstarch. Use a large-holed shaker or an empty baby-powder container to apply. Wash through hair with your fingers and brush out thoroughly.

Conditioning Your Hair

If you have an oily scalp, but dry or damaged hair, condition hair before you shampoo. Wet your hair, towel it dry, and then apply conditioner, starting an inch from your scalp. Work conditioner through your hair, wait five minutes, and rinse. Then shampoo as usual.

To revitalize and give luster to all types of hair: Beat three eggs; add two tablespoons olive or safflower oil and one teaspoon vinegar. Apply mixture to hair and cover with plastic cap. Wait half an hour and then shampoo well.

Here's a hair conditioner that is bound to draw raves! Combine ³/₄ cup olive oil, ¹/₂ cup honey, and the juice of one lemon and set aside. Rinse hair with water and towel dry. Work in a small amount of conditioner (store leftovers in the refrigerator), comb to distribute evenly, and cover with a plastic cap for 30 minutes. Shampoo and rinse thoroughly.

When swimming daily in chlorinated or salt water, alternate hair care, using shampoo one day and conditioner the next.

Skin Products

A patch test for skin-care products: If you suspect you may be allergic to any substance, put a dab of it inside your wrist or elbow, cover it with an adhesive bandage, and leave it on for 24 hours. If no redness or irritation is evident, the product is probably safe. Because you can become allergic to something you have used regularly repeat this test whenever you haven't used a substance in several weeks and are concerned about a reaction from that product.

Change brands if you are experiencing a rash or lesions, or think you have an allergic reaction.

Cleansing Your Skin

To cleanse your face thoroughly, try the following method: Fill a clean sink with warm water, dip facial soap into the water, and rub ιne bar over your face. Dip the soap back into the water and make a lather in your hands. Massage this lather over your face. Rinse 15 to 20 times with the soapy water. Finish off with several cold-water rinses. Blot your face dry with a towel.

Excessive stinging or drying are signs that your toner, astringent, or aftershave lotion is too strong. Change brands or add one teaspoon of mineral water to each ounce of the product.

Hot weather tip: Refrigerator your facial toner, freshener, or astringent for a cool skin treat.

Bathing

In winter, your bath or shower water should be tepid—not hot, since hot water inflames the skin and increases moisture loss afterwards. Apply a moisturizing lotion right after bathing while your skin is still damp.

A simple but effective way to relieve dry skin and winter itch is to completely dissolve one cup of salt in a tub of water and bathe as usual. (For a more luxurious bath, try sea salt.) Bathing in salt often works better than using expensive bath oils, but if you really want to use oil, a plain mineral oil will generally fulfill your needs.

Moisturizing Your Skin

Always apply a moisturizer right after cleansing to prevent the surface moisture from evaporating. Moisturizers should last about ten hours. If your face feels tight before that time, freshen it with a toner and reapply your moisturizer. You may need a richer moisturizer.

Don't forget to moisturize your throat area. If this area is especially dry, heat peanut oil until warm and massage upward into your skin.

To avoid that cracked, flaky look on your elbows, make it a habit to pay special attention to them at the same time you lubricate the rest of your body.

If you have begun to get lines around your eyes and want to make them less obvious, rub eye cream between your fingertips to warm it before patting it around the eye area. This makes it easier for the skin to absorb the cream. Do not pull or stretch the skin around the eyes.

Sun Protection

Give your skin time to absorb a sunblock's ingredients before you need them. Apply sunscreen a half-hour before you go outdoors;

reapply after you swim or if you perspire heavily.

Take a long lunch hour away from outdoor exposure. The sun is highest in the sky and is most intense between the hours of 10:00 in the morning and 2:00 in the afternoon.

If you're planning on spending some time outdoors, use a moisturizing sunblock or sunscreen along with your regular moisturizer. Choose an SPF (sun protection factor) keyed to your skin's response to the sun. A fair person needs an SPF of 12 to 15.

Makeup Foundation

If you never seem to buy the right shade of foundation, try applying it just under the jawline rather than on the wrist. It should be just slightly lighter than your skin tone.

To transform a heavy, oil-based foundation into one that glides on more smoothly, add a bit of moisturizer or salt-free mineral water to the foundation. Use your palm or a small dish—not the makeup container—to do the mixing.

Blushers and Powders

For those "gray" days, mix a drop of liquid blusher with your foundation. Spread this instant glow all over your skin.

When you're feeling tired and dragged out, use blusher very lightly around the entire outer contour of your face, from the hairline to the chin, blending with a cosmetic sponge.

Under fluorescent lights, which destroy the rosy tones in the skin and give a yellowish look, apply your blusher a little darker and use a little deeper-colored lipstick.

Store loose powder in an old salt or pepper shaker so that you can shake it into your palm. Then dip a makeup brush or puff into the powder and dust it on.

Eye Makeup

Eye makeup is perishable. Bacteria from your eyes can be introduced to the product. Wash applicators frequently or use cotton swabs. Also, label shadows, pencils, and mascaras with their purchase dates. Replace your shadows and pencils every six months, your mascara every three months.

If you use liquid eyeliner, try dotting it on along the lash line. It will look less harsh than a solid line.

To get the sharpest point on your eyebrow, eyeliner, and lip pencils, put them in the freezer for an hour before sharpening.

Tame unruly eyebrows with a little bit of styling gel or mousse applied with an eyebrow brush.

Lip Care

Your lipstick will stay on much longer if you use the following method. Layer on in this order: face powder, lipstick, powder, lipstick. Wipe off excess powder with a damp washcloth or a tissue.

Remove Makeup

Never go to sleep without removing every trace of your makeup—except on your wedding night! Habitually sleeping with a layer of dirt, debris, and dead skin cells stuck to your face will leave your complexion looking muddy and dull.

When you're removing mascara, if it seems to get all over your face, wrap a tissue around your index finger and hold it just under the lower lashes. Remove eye makeup as usual with the other hand.

You are now well on your way of making that first good impression—may it wear well on you!

Organizing Your Prayer Time

Be anxious for nothing, but in
everything by prayer and
supplication, with thanksgiving,
let your requests be made known
to God.

—*Philippians 4:6 NKJV*

*D*URING MY early years of motherhood, I became frustrated about my
personal prayer time. I wanted to spend quality time with my Lord
but due to a busy schedule it just never worked out in a practical way.

One day through some trial and error I came up with a prayer
organization that worked for me. Here's what I did.

1. *Prayer Noteboook.* I purchased an inexpensive binder (5½ x
8½), one package of tabs, and one package of lined paper. The tabs
were labeled "Monday," "Tuesday," "Wednesday," etc. Next I
made a list of all things I wanted to pray for—family, finances,
church, missionaries, etc. I then delegated these requests into my
prayer notebook behind each tab. On Monday I now pray for each
member of the family. On Tuesday I pray for our church, the pastor,
the staff, etc. On Wednesday, I pray for people who are ill, and so on.
The Sunday tab is for sermon notes and outlines. I filter any prayer
requests into the weekly tabs so my prayer time does not overwhelm
me. I spend time reading my Bible, then I open my prayer notebook
to the tab for that day. I pray for the items behind that tab. The next

day I do the same, moving on through the next week.

    2. *Prayer Basket.* Try the following steps:

      a. Purchase a medium-size basket with a handle.

      b. Place in your basket your Bible, prayer notebook, a few postcards, a box of tissue, and a small bunch of silk flowers.

      c. Place your basket in an area you pass daily, perhaps on a table, the kitchen counter, your desk, or in the bathroom, etc.

      d. Schedule a daily time to spend time with your prayer basket in the morning, afternoon, or evening. Plan this time (five to 50 minutes) to pick up your basket and take it to a quiet place where you will use the ingredients during your prayer time.

- The Bible—read God's Word daily.
- Pray for the daily requests.
- Write a short note to someone who needs encouragement on your postcards. Or you might simply say, "I prayed for you today." Some days I cry through my whole prayer time. My tissue is right there in my basket. The flowers give encouragement and lighten my heart as I look at God's creation.

My prayer basket is so personal and special to me. Some days I walk by my basket and it may be three o'clock in the afternoon. It says to me, "Emilie, you haven't picked me up today." What a reminder and what a challenge to my heart and spirit to pick up my prayer basket, putting it to use every day in spending special time with my Lord.

Proverbs 16:3 says, "Commit your works to the Lord, and your plans will be established" (NASB).

The days I pick up my prayer basket, my day, my life, and my organization as a busy woman go so much smoother. I have strength to meet the schedules and stresses that usually come.

New Year Organization

Oh, give thanks to the Lord, for he
is good; his love and his kindness
go on forever.
—*1 Chronicles 16:34*

*R*ECENTLY AFTER finishing a seminar on how to organize your household, I talked to a young mother who said, "I loved all the organizational ideas and tips you gave for the family and the home, but what about me—my personal organization?" I gave her a copy of *My Daily Planner*, a tool I have used for years to get me through each day, week, month, and year of my life. Organization really does begin with our own personal lives. Once we have ourselves organized, we can move into the other areas of our lives such as our home or job.

Here are the tools you need to make your own daily planner. (If you would rather purchase a premade planner, *My Daily Planner* is published annually by Harvest House.)

- A small purse-size binder with paper
- Blank tabs you can label yourself
- A calendar

Label your tabs in the following way.

Tab 1: Goals

List long-range and short-range goals including daily, weekly, monthly, and yearly priorities. This will help you get your priorities in order. Include the following: Scriptures to read, prayer requests, priorities to accomplish, and family goals, as well as spiritual, household, work-related, financial, and budget goals.

Tab 2: Calendar

Purchase a small month-at-a-glance calendar at a stationery store and insert it into your binder. As you learn to write activities and commitments down, you will be surprised at how much less complicated your life becomes.

Tab 3: Daily Planner

In this section, list your daily appointments from morning to evening. This is not only useful for the mother who works outside her home but also for the homemaker who wants to get her daily household duties done in a more orderly manner.

Tab 4: To Do, To Buy

Make a note here of all the things you need to do when you have an errand day, such as:
- Pick up winter coat at the cleaners.
- Go to the grocery store for birthday candles.
- Take package to the post office.
- Buy vitamins at health food store.

Tab 5: Notes

Here is a place to write down notes from:
- Speakers and sermons
- Meetings and Bible studies
  Projects

Tab 6: Miscellaneous

Keep topical lists in this section such as:
- Emergency phone numbers
- Dentist/physician
- Babysitters' phone numbers

- Favorite restaurant phone numbers
- Books and music recommended

Tab 7: Expense Account

This section is especially for work-related expense outside the home.
- Who it was for and the amount and how it was paid for (cash, credit card, or check)
- What it was for: transportation, parking, food, promotion, or gas

Tab 8: Prayer Requests

Make colored insert tabs for each day of the week, Sunday through Saturday. Then write a comprehensive list of your prayer requests along with those of your friends and family, and divide them into five special lists. Assign each list to one day for one week, Monday through Friday. Leave Saturday as a swing day for immediate prayer requests.

Sunday's section should be left open for the pastor's sermon. That way you have a history of Scripture and content for later reference or study. If someone mentions a prayer request at church, you can assign it to a special day of the week when you get home.

In this way you can cover your prayer needs over a week's time. Date the request when you enter it into your book and then record the date when it is answered. Over a period of time you will have a history of how God has worked in your life. Remember, too, that not all prayers are immediately answered by "yes" or "no." Some are put "on hold" for awhile.

I'll guarantee that by implementing these few helpful ideas into your new year, you'll be on your way to the "organized you."

How to Organize Your Handbag

Keep alert and pray. Otherwise
temptation will overpower you. For
the spirit indeed is willing, but how
weak the body is!

—*Matthew 26:41*

*R*EMEMBER THE last time you rummaged through your handbag digging through old receipts, papers, tissue, half-used lipsticks, unwrapped Lifesavers, and that unmailed letter you thought was lost months ago? Handbags have a way of becoming catchalls, places where you have everything and can find nothing. You can get your handbag into top shape with just a little effort and organization. If you keep a well-organized handbag, it will be so simple to change bags and do it quickly.

Materials Needed

A nice-size handbag for everyday and three to seven small purses in various colors and sizes. (The small purses can be of quilted fabric, denim, or corduroy prints with zipper or velcro fasteners.)

How to Organize

1. *Wallet*
   Money/check book

267

Change compartment
Pen/credit cards
Pictures (most-used)
Driver's license
Calendar (current)

2. *Makeup Bag 1*
Lipstick
Comb/small brush
Blush
Mirror
Dime or quarter (phone change)

3. *Makeup Bag 2*
Nail file
Small perfume
Hand cream
Nail clippers
Scissors (small)
Tissues
Breath mints/gum/cough drops
Matches

4. *Eyeglass Case*
For sunglasses

5. *Eyeglass Case*
For reading/spare glasses

6. *Small Bag 1*
Business cards—yours & your husband's, hair dresser, insurance agent, auto club, doctor, health plan
Library card
Seldom-used credit cards
Small calculator
Tea bag/artificial sweetener/aspirin

7 *Small Bag 2*
Reading material—small Bible, paperback book
Toothbrush
Cleanup wipes
Needle/thread/pins/thimble
Band-Aid
Toothpicks
Tape measure
Feminine protection

By taking some time to set it up you can organize your purse and avoid last minute frustration and stress.

Planning a Picnic for Happy Memories

Create in me a new, clean heart, O
God, filled with clean thoughts and
right desires.
—*Psalm 51:10*

*F*UN-FILLED memories of special family
times can happen by taking a picnic meal
to the park, lake, mountains, beach, desert, or favorite picnic area.

I was four years old when we took a picnic lunch to the desert
under a yucca tree. The setting doesn't sound real exciting but I can
still remember the green-and-white checkered tablecloth my mother
pulled out and spread on the ground, along with plates, glasses,
silver utensils, and delicious food. She took me by the hand and we
picked a few wild desert flowers for the table. Later we took a nature
walk and collected fun memories.

Picnics are for everyone and loved by everyone, and they can be
planned for any time of the year (though as the weather begins to
warm up, the creative picnics seem to warm up too). Early American
picnics were called "frolics" and consisted of games, music, flirta-
tions, and good food. Keep this in mind as you keep your American
picnics filled with the same ingredients.

You can plan themes around your region or other regions of our
country or even the world. Some ideas might be:

- A Vermont Snow Snack
- A New England Clam Bake
- A Hawaiian Luau
- An Abalone Steak Picnic
- A San Francisco Crab Lunch
- An Indian Summer Brunch
- Mexican Memories
- A Mardi Gras Feast
- A Pumpkin Patch Picnic

These themes are starting points to plan our food selections. Draw the family into this planning and research for what food you are going to take along for this special event. Don't make this just a mom's project—involve the whole family. The Mardi Gras feast might include chicken gumbo, steamed rice, marinated green beans, and New Orleans King Cake.

The pantry is a good source for the basic food selections. If you need to make a market run to purchase special items, do so at a time when the store is less crowded. Try early in the morning or late in the evening. Stay away from peak shopping hours.

Keeping Foods Cold

Once you have purchased and/or prepared your food, you need to plan how to keep your food cold. The length of time in which food can spoil is relative to the temperature outdoors, but it also depends upon the way the food was cooked, chilled, wrapped, and carried. Foods containing mayonnaise, eggs, cream, sour cream, yogurt, or fish are safe unrefrigerated up to two hours if the weather is fairly cool. If it will be more than two hours before you eat, plan to carry along a refrigerated cooler. Cool dishes as quickly as possible after preparing them and leave them in the refrigerator until just before time to leave. *Remember: Never take anything on a picnic that could possibly spoil unless you can provide effective portable refrigeration.*

There are a lot of excellent commercial coolers on the market. Select a size that will be adequate for your family's need. You can chill food in the cooler by using ice cubes, crushed or chipped ice, blocks from ice machines, or blocks frozen in clean milk cartons or other containers. Or you can fill plastic bottles (two-thirds full) with water to allow for expansion and freeze them overnight. These frozen containers eliminate the mess of melted ice.

Packing, Transporting, and Safe-Storing Tips

Prepare all food as close to departure time as comfortably possible for you. Don't cook in advance earlier than the time recommended in the recipe unless the item can be frozen successfully.

Try to pack your hamper or other carryall in reverse order from the way in which you'll use each item at the site. Place your food containers right-side-up to prevent spills and breakage.

Breakable glassware can be wrapped in the tablecloth, napkins, kitchen towels, or newspaper.

Foods such as pies, tarts, cakes, muffins, mousses, molded salads, or home-baked breads that crumble easily can be carried in the pans in which they were prepared. If the supplies do not fill the hamper, fill in with rolled newspaper or paper towels to prevent foods from overturning or bumping together.

Bags

Shopping bags are excellent for holding many items for a simple picnic. Use those fancy, attractive bags for transporting excess items that won't fit into the main picnic hamper. You might also want to carry along a large bag for your unwanted trash. Leave the site clean.

Ground Covers and Tablecloths

Choose a blanket, patchwork quilt, bedspread, sheet, comforter, afghan, or any large piece of fabric for a ground cover and tablecloth. Top it, if you like, with a decorative second cloth that fits the mood of the picnic you've planned.

No-iron cotton or synthetic fabric is easy to keep clean and ready for traveling. Other choices to consider are beach towels, bamboo or reed matting, nylon parachute fabric, flannel shirt material, or lengths of easy-care fabric stitched at each end.

Purchase one or two plastic painters' drop cloths or carry a canvas tarpaulin to put down before you spread the tablecloth if the ground is damp, dusty, or snow-covered.

Baskets/Hampers

Wicker baskets or hampers are the traditional picnic carryalls. However, anything goes these days. Import shops sell baskets made in many different shapes, sizes, and price ranges.

The important thing is the time spent with your family and friends sharing your love together.

Beating
Jet Lag
in Travel

Praise ye the Lord. O give thanks
unto the Lord, for he is good, for
his mercy endureth forever.

—*Psalm 106:1*

*W*E LIVE in a fast-paced world of travel, and many times our body suffers as a result. We find ourselves unable to function as we should even though we have important business and social functions to perform.

As I travel throughout our continent I do certain things that help me minimize the effects of jet lag on my speaking schedule.

Jet lag is caused by rapid air travel over multiple time zones. The sudden change in time upsets synchronized body rhythms, resulting in physical and mental confusion. Research shows that the human body clock, set by stimuli like light and diet, can be "tricked" into adjusting to a new schedule. Here are some facts about jet lag and tips to avoid it.

Effects on the Body Clock

Many of our body cycles are affected by jet lag. We find rapid increases in our heartbeat, breathing, cell division, eye blinking, and swallowing. Our daily cycles of blood pressure, eyesight, mental ability, physical ability, sleep/wake rhythm, digestion, reproduction, temperature, metabolism, and sense of time are also disturbed.

Symptoms of Jet Lag

Some of the early signs of jet lag are fatigue, disorientation, reduced physical ability, reduced mental ability, upset appetite, and off-schedule bowel and urinary movements. Later symptoms of constipation or diarrhea, insomnia, acute fatigue, loss of appetite, headaches, lack of sexual interest, and slowed response-time to visual stimulation are also negative side effects.

Fighting Off Jet Lag

• *Diet.* Eating certain foods helps adjust the body clock. Foods high in carbohydrates induce sleep; those high in protein produce wakefulness. On a typical seven-hour flight over several time zones, you might try the following schedule to help reduce jet lag.

• *Three days before flight.* Eat a high-protein breakfast and lunch, a high-carbohydrate dinner, and caffeinated drinks (if you use) between 3:00 P.M. and 4:30 P.M. only.

• *Day of flight.* Get up earlier than usual, eat a high protein breakfast and lunch, a high-carbohydrate dinner, and shortly after 6:00 P.M., drink two to three cups of black coffee. Reset watch to destination time.

• *During flight, day of arrival.* Don't oversleep. A half-hour before breakfast (destination time) activate your body and brain, eat a high-protein breakfast and lunch, a high-carbohydrate dinner, drink, no caffeine, avoid napping, and go to sleep at 10:00 P.M. (destination time).

• *Consult an aircraft seating chart.* Request bulkhead or emergency exit seats, which have more leg room.

• *Don't drink alcohol.* It causes dehydration. Drink water.

• *Sleep and eat on your destination time schedule.* Ask the flight attendant to serve your meals at your specified time.

• *Avoid big meals.* Air pressure causes gas in the intestines to expand.

• *Request a special meal.* Do this 24 hours in advance from the airline if needed.

• *Don't wear contact lenses.* On long flights, they dry out.

• *Bring a game or book.* This will provide mental stimulation.

• *Don't cross your legs.* This interferes with blood circulation.

75

Tips to Start and Organize a Home Business

> She considers a field and
> buys it; out of her earnings
> she plants a vineyard.
> —*Proverbs 31:16 NKJV*

*T*ODAY'S WOMAN approaches the 1990's with much excitement. We've come a long way, women. The 80's found us making a lot of changes from home to work, with accompanying stress, frustration, disorganization, and fatigue. For some of us, our priorities went out the window along with our organized homes and meals. We gave up our children to babysitters and daycare and our meals to fast-food stores. Our spiritual life moved into low gear— not for everyone, but for many. However, new changes are coming into focus. We are tired of the tired 80's. More women are feeling the desire to be at-home mothers and career women. That's exciting. We are beginning to see the working woman find balance between work and home, with a new interest in home business (85 percent of new businesses are started by women in their homes). Many women will make a personal choice to be at home in the 90's, while many will continue jobs outside due to need or desire.

My mother became a single working parent when my father died. I was 11 years old. She opened a small dress shop and we lived in the back in a small, three-room apartment. Home and career were mixed. Mom not only sold clothing but worked late into the night doing alterations. Bookkeeping was also done after hours. We survived because we all helped in a time of need. When our children were small I developed a small business out of our home; the extra money was for extra things. I was able to do that because I felt somewhat organized and in control of our home.

This may very well be the year God will bring into your life the desire to be an at-home woman and develop a from-home business. Yes, to be successful it does take time, creativity, balance and desire. Our ministry, "More Hours In My Day," began in our home and has stayed there for over nine years. Books have been written, seminars given, and mail orders sent from our door to many of yours.

Our typist, Sheri, runs a typing service from her home and is enjoying better profits than ever before. A dear and longtime friend, Rose, has a small business called "Tiffany Touch" where she goes into other people's homes in her area and does everything from organizing drawers to hanging pictures. A mother with a new baby designed a slip-over-the-head bib that is sold all over the country out of her home. Still another mom created designer baby bottles—she changed baby diapers into cash of over $1 million.

Connie Lund, out of Olympia, Washington created a small devotional flip chart of inspiration called "Reaching Up to God" and through their sales is sending her daughter through college. When her daughter comes home for vacations she helps collate and tie the charts. Most at-home businesses develop family oneness, with everyone working together to help one another.

Direct sales are popular and profitable. Tupperware, Avon, Shaklee, Amway, Mary Kay, Home Interiors, Christmas Around the World, Successful Living Books, Choice Books—from home parties to door-to-door, these are just a few.

One woman I read about shops for working women, buying groceries and gifts, and running errands from picking up dry cleaning to buying stamps at the post office. She even delivered a lunch to a schoolchild who forgot it at home.

Another creative mom started gift wrapping for people (men in offices), which led to food baskets and then homemade wreaths and flower arrangements.

Another mom advertised her famous chili recipe for $1—and sold enough to buy Christmas presents for the whole family. She was very pleased and surprised. Aimee made colorful earrings. Women saw them on her and wanted a pair for themselves. From friends to boutique shops, sales multiplied.

All kinds of arts and crafts have created many added funds for the family income.

I was visiting some friends who received an adorable loaf of bread shaped like a teddy bear, a novelty gift that is now being shipped all over the state.

Nancy is a single parent who quit her computer job and started her own service in her home. She is able to be home with her three children and still run a very successful business.

Nancy and Elizabeth teamed up and are designing and selling Christian greeting cards, business cards, and Christmas cards, and are doing very well.

Some women are working at home as employees—sales reps, technical service reps, claim adjusters, and many others who are unsalaried employees but who spend most of their time in the field. Their employers typically don't provide an office so their files, desk phone, etc. are in their homes. Many other women could do part-time employment in the same way. Naturally you have to ask yourself if you have the space in your home for such types of employment.

I have a friend who represents designer clothing out of her home four times a year. She sends out invitations with days and hours, then books appointments and helps the women coordinate their wardrobes.

The 90's woman, I believe, will get back to home shopping and parties from jewelry to clothing to household products.

As we move further this year, set your desires high and chart out your goals for your future this year. Where would you like to be next year at this time? What will you need to accomplish to get there?

When can you start? Possibly now. 1) Your desire is to be working from home—by next year. 2) Make calls and talk with friends, family, and business associates. 3) Perhaps you need to take a class on business, sales, design, etc.

Many of you may be happy just working where you are. Others may want to cut hours to be at home a little more. Whatever you want to accomplish this year you can do with a positive attitude, desire, and creativity wrapped with prayer.

My desire is to see the busy woman get back to traditional values and to use her God-given creativity wherever she may be—in or out of the home. Changes will come in the future as they have in the past, but yours can come with a positive outlook and priorities of God, family, and career.

The following are some ideas and tips on how to implement or begin a business at home.

Research

1. Find others who are in your same field of home business and talk with them. They can provide a wealth of information.
2. Will it benefit you to advertise in your local telephone book?
3. What kind of advertising should you use other than word of mouth?

Goals

1. Determine a time schedule to be at home with your business. Example: Within one year.
2. Sign up for a class at your local community college on simple business bookeeping.

Finances

1. Draw up a projected budget for yourself. What will be your credits, your debits? How much money do you need to launch your business?
2. Consider the costs involved in advertising.
3. Set aside some money for start-up expenses and supplies such as a typewriter, copy machine, furniture, and for small desktop items, such as stapler, scissors, etc.
4. Start writing down hidden costs. There will always be expenses that you did not count on so the more research you do the less likely you will be to have a lot of surprises.

Home Preparation

1. What area will you use and how much space do you need?
2. Can you use your same phone system?
3. Do you need a desk, work tables, file cabinets, etc.?
4. Will any carpentry work be required?

Legalities

1. Get information on what legal matters need to be considered. Some home businesses will require a business license. Check with your local county records department.
2. Obtain a resale number if needed.
3. What kind of deductions are you eligible for? It is advisable to contact a CPA who is knowledgeable in the field of home business deductions.

Hours

1. Think through how many hours you will reasonably be able to work per day, per week, per month.
2. Will you need to work around children's schedules?
3. Will you have regular business hours?
4. When will you clean your home, cook meals, etc.?
5. Don't forget you—schedule time to do a few things for yourself, such as hair appointments, shopping, church, friends, Bible studies, etc.

Like many situations, there will be a lot of trial and error. You'll learn much as you grow along, and the benefits will be great!

Miscellaneous

76

27 Things to Help You Survive an Earthquake

We are hard-pressed on every side,
yet not crushed.

—*2 Corinthians 4:8 NKJV*

*I*N CALIFORNIA we are always concerned about the earth moving. Animals often hear the rumble of the earth before their owners sense that something is about to happen. It is truly an experience that a person will never forget—his or her first earthquake and every one thereafter.

If you live in California or some other earthquake-prone area, or are planning to visit such an area for business or pleasure, you may want to become familiar with the following recommendations as suggested by the American Red Cross.

Basics to Do During an Earthquake

1. Stay CALM.
2. *Inside:* Stand in a doorway, or crouch under a desk or table, away from windows or glass dividers.
3. *Outside:* Stand away from buildings, trees, and telephone and electric lines.

4. *On the Road:* Drive away from underpasses, overpasses; stop in safe area; stay in vehicle.

Basics to Do After an Earthquake

1. Check for injuries—provide first aid.
2. Check for safety—check for gas, water, and sewage breaks; check for downed electric lines and shorts; turn off appropriate utilities; check for building damage and potential safety problems during aftershocks, such as cracks around chimney and foundation.
3. Clean up dangerous spills.
4. Wear shoes.
5. Turn on radio and listen for instructions from public safety agencies.
6. Use the telephone only in emergency situations.

Basic Survival Items to Keep on Hand

1. Portable radio with extra batteries.
2. Flashlight with extra batteries.
3. First-aid kit, including specified medicines needed for members of your household.
4. First-aid book.
5. Fire extinguisher.
6. Adjustable wrench for turning off gas and water.
7. Smoke detectors properly installed.
8. Portable fire escape ladder for homes and apartments with multiple floors.
9. Bottled water sufficient for the number of members in your household for a week.
10. Canned and dried foods sufficient for a week for each member of your household. *Note:* Both water and food should be rotated into normal meals of household so as to keep freshness. Canned goods have a normal shelf-life of one year for maximum freshness.
11. Nonelectrical can openei.
12. Portable stove such as butane or charcoal. *Note:* Use of such stoves should not take place until it is determined that there is no gas leak in the area. Charcoal should be burned only out of doors. Use of charcoal indoors will lead to carbon monoxide poisoning.
13. Several dozen candles. The same caution should be taken as in the above note on portable stoves.

14. Matches.
15. Telephone numbers of police, fire, and doctor.

Basics You Need to Know

1. How to turn off gas, water, and electricity.
2. Basic first aid.
3. Plan for reuniting your family.

As with any emergency program that you have for your family, you must review it every three months to make sure the members of your family know what to do in case of an earthquake. The plan for evacuating the home and the plan for reuniting the family if the various members of the family are away from home should be walked through so the instructions are thoroughly understood by all members of the family.

Remember,

THE BEST SURVIVAL
IS A PREPARED SURVIVAL!

Record-Keeping Made Simple

No one can become my disciple
unless he first sits down and counts
his blessings—and then renounces
them all for me.

—Luke 14:33

*T*HIS IS THE YEAR to get our records,
bills, and receipts out of shoeboxes,
closets, drawers, and old envelopes. I found that I could clean out my
wardrobe closet fairly easily. I could toss an old skirt, stained blouse,
or a misfit jacket with little difficulty; however, where and when I
should toss old financial records was very difficult. I didn't want to
do the wrong thing, so I kept saving—usually too long.

At income-tax time my neck always got stiff because I knew Bob
was going to ask for a canceled check or a paid invoice and I wasn't
sure if I had it or not. At that point, I made a decision to get my
record-keeping in order so that it was a very easy process to keep my
records up-to-date.

I sat down and looked at the whole process of record-keeping and
began to break it down into logical steps. My first step was to decide
to keep my records. Since I like things to be in order with the
minimum amount of paperwork, I had a tendency to throw away
records that should have been saved. I found that throwing away
Bob's salary stubs, last year's tax return, or current receipts for

medical or business expenses would only bring problems further down the road.

Our CPA says that throwing away financial records is the biggest mistake that people make. Throwing away records that later turn out to be important causes people a lot of unnecessary work and worry, he cautioned. When you have an IRS audit and you can't prove your deductions by a canceled check, or a paid invoice, you will lose that deduction for that year, and be subject to a fine and interest due as well. Records are very important.

Good financial records help you make decisions very quickly. In just a few moments you can retrieve valuable information so that a decision can be made for budget planning, future purchases, or just anticipated future income.

As I began to develop a plan to establish good record-keeping, I came up with a seven-step program.

STEP 1: Know what to keep

I discovered that records generally fall into two categories: PERMANENT records (important to keep throughout your life) and TRANSITORY records (dealing with your current circumstances).

Permanent records would include personal documents required in applying for credit, qualifying for a job, or proving entitlement to Social Security and other government programs. Birth and marriage certificates, Social Security cards, property records, college transcripts, diplomas, and licenses all fall into this category.

Deciding how long to retain transitory records can be more difficult because often you don't know how long you'll need them. As a rule of thumb I suggest you keep all employment records until you leave the job. Other transitory records you want to keep include receipts for any major purchases you have made—jewelry, autos, art—stock certificates, tax returns and receipts (for at least six years), health insurance policies, credit union membership and company stock ownership plans. Canceled checks not relating directly to specifics like nome improvements should be kept for a minimum of three years in case of a tax audit; however, I will usually keep them five to six years just to make sure I'm not throwing any records away that I might need on a tax audit.

If you own your home, apartment, or mobile home, be sure to retain the receipts for any improvements you make until you sell the property. They become proof that you added to the property's value and will reduce any capital gains you might owe. Don't discard these receipts or tax returns from the year in which you paid for the improvements. I usually make a copy of this kind of receipt and keep a permanent copy in my "Home" folder. I have found that this saves a lot of valuable time when I need to justify each record. In my "Home" folder I also keep a running log with date, improvement made, cost, and receipt for each expenditure. At any given time we know how much money we have invested in our home. This information really helps when you get ready to sell your home and you want to establish a sales price.

Your tax return, wage statements, and other papers supporting your income and deductions should be kept at least six years (that's the IRS statute of limitations for examining your return). However, you will need to keep real estate and investment records longer if you will need to verify purchase prices in the future. I retain our records for six years, because the IRS has the right to audit within six years if they believe you omitted an item accounting for more than 25 percent of your reported income, or indefinitely if they believe you committed fraud.

STEP 2: Know yourself when you set up your system

Try to keep your system as simple as you can. I have found that the more disorganized you are, the simpler the system should be. It doesn't make sense to set up an elaborate filing system if it is too complicated for you to follow.

I suggest that you consider these points when setting up your system:

- How much time can you devote to record-keeping? The less time you have, the simpler your system should be.
- Do you like working with numbers? Are you good at math? If so, your system can be more complex.
- How familiar are you with tax deductions and financial planning? If you are a beginner, set up a simple system.
- Will anyone else be contributing records to the system?

This last point is a very important consideration if you are married. Mates may have a different opinion on what type of system you should have. I have found among married couples that it usually works best when you determine who is most gifted in this area and let that person take care of the records. Bob and I get along very well in this area. I write the checks for our home expenses and balance this account's checking statement. Then I forward the material to Bob for record-keeping. In our family he is the most gifted in this area of our life.

We have found that the simplest way to organize receipts for tax purposes is to keep two file folders, one for deduction items and another for questionable items. At tax time all you have to do is total up each category and fill in the blank. Be sure to double-check the other entries for overlooked possibilities.

If your return is more complex, set up a system with individual folders for the various deductions you claim: medical and dental expenses, business, travel, entertainment, property taxes, interest on loans, childcare services. When you pay a bill, drop the receipt into the right folder. At the end of the year, you'll be able to tally the receipts and be set to enter the totals on your tax forms.

Be sure to take your questionable-deduction folder with you when you go to see your CPA. Go over each item to see if it is eligible for a deduction. As you can tell by reading this chapter, I strongly endorse using a professional tax-preparer. Tax returns have become so difficult and the tax laws so complex that good stewardship of your money may require that you go to a professional. Tax-preparers will save you much more than you will spend for their services.

Your checkbook can be your best record-keeper if you check off entries that might count as tax deductions. If you have a personal computer at home, you have a wide selection of software programs to help you keep track of these records.

STEP 3: Set aside a spot for your records

Generally, home rather than office is the best place for personal documents. A fireproof, waterproof file cabinet or desk drawer is excellent for transitory records. However, I use and have thousands of other ladies all across the United States using our Perfect Boxes to store records.

Permanent documents generally should be kept in a safe-deposit box However, your will and important final instructions should be kept in a different place because in many states, safe-deposit boxes are sealed following the owner's death, even if someone else has a key.

STEP 4: Tell someone where your records are

As I travel around the country conducting seminars, many of the ladies tell me they don't know where their husbands have anything written down in case of death. None of us like to think about death because it is so far away, but we must share this important information with those people who will need to know.

Each year Bob reviews with me his "data sheet" listing all the information regarding insurance policies, stocks and investments, mortgage locations, banking account information, contents in safe-deposit boxes, etc. That information is very helpful and reassuring to me in case of any changes in our status.

Even if you're a whiz at keeping financial records, the records are not very useful if no one else knows where any of them are located. As a family, make up a list noting where your records are located and give it to a family member or trusted friend.

STEP 5: Get professional advice on handling records

As I've shared previously in this chapter, Bob and I recommend that you seek professional advice on how better records can translate into tax savings in the future. The expense is well worth the investment of time and money. You can also go to your local bookstore and purchase any number of good paperback books on this topic. Be a reader and a learner. It will serve you well.

STEP 6: Change your record-keeping system when you make a life change

Major life shifts—a job move, marriage, death, divorce, separation—signal a time to revamp your records. Starting a home-based business also means it's time to talk to the professional regarding new tax allowances. A life change usually necessitates a change in record-keeping.

The costs of looking for a new job in the same field and a job-related move can mean you're eligible for a new tax deduction, so be sure to file all receipts.

STEP 7: Set aside time for your record-keeping

Try to set a regular time each month to go over your financial records so that you won't be a wreck come April when you have to file your tax return. The best system in the world won't work if you don't use it or keep it current.

Many people prefer to update records when they pay bills. Others file receipts, update a ledger of expenses, and look over permanent records once a month when reconciling a checking account. Whatever works best for you is what's important. You should update at least once a month. If not, you will create a lot of stress playing catch-up. The goal of simple record-keeping is to reduce stress in our lives, not to increase the stress.

I have found that time is worth money. When I can reduce time, I can increase money because my energy is better spent on constructive efforts rather than always dealing with emergencies and putting out fires.

Home Fire Safety Survey

*I will bless the Lord and not forget
the glorious things he does for me.*

—*Psalm 103:2*

*A*FTER SPEAKING at a seminar one
evening, a lovely woman shared with
me her story of how a simple grease fire in the kitchen burned down
her whole house. I had given a hint about using baking soda to put out
kitchen fires, and about keeping a coffee can filled with baking soda
close at hand by the stove. She said until that night she had never
heard of that. I was totally surprised because I grew up knowing to
use baking soda in case of household fires. Because of her story, I
thought we needed to alert all homemakers to home fire safety. Many
city and town fire departments will provide free inspections to help
you identify any fire hazards in your home or business. Just give
them a call and ask their help. Here is a fire safety survey for you who
would like to do it yourself. It very well could save a life or the life of
your home.

DO-IT-YOURSELF
HOME FIRE SAFETY SURVEY

Kitchen

YES / NO

- Are stove and vent clean of grease buildup? ⎯⎯ ⎯⎯
- Are curtains or towel racks close to the stove? ⎯⎯ ⎯⎯
- Are flammable liquids (cleaning fluids, etc.) ⎯⎯ ⎯⎯
  stored near a heat source? Remember, even
  a pilot light can set vapors on fire.
- Is baking soda close at hand? ⎯⎯ ⎯⎯

Bedrooms

- Are smoke detectors installed and tested monthly? ⎯⎯ ⎯⎯
- Are there two ways out of the room? ⎯⎯ ⎯⎯
- If the bedroom is on the second floor, is there ⎯⎯ ⎯⎯
  an escape ladder by the window?

Halls and Stairways

- Are smoke detectors installed and tested monthly? ⎯⎯ ⎯⎯

Living and Dining Rooms

- Is there insufficient air space around TV and ⎯⎯ ⎯⎯
  stereo that could cause them to overheat?
- Are curtains, furniture, or papers near a space ⎯⎯ ⎯⎯
  heater? (Kerosene heaters are not allowed in
  living quarters.)
- Is there a spark screen on the fireplace? ⎯⎯ ⎯⎯

Garage

- Are gasoline, paint thinners, and/or other flam- ⎯⎯ ⎯⎯
  mable liquids stored in a ventilated area away
  from open flames? (hot water heater, furnace)
- Are flammable liquids stored in an approved ⎯⎯ ⎯⎯
  safety container?
- Is the hot water heater clear of any storage ⎯⎯ ⎯⎯
  within 18 inches?
- Is the furnace clear of any storage within 18 ⎯⎯ ⎯⎯
  inches and are filters changed on a regular basis?

- Is there a fire extinguisher nearby? ___ ___
- Are oil-soaked rags stored in a covered metal ___ ___
    container?

Outside

- Are house numbers visible from the street? ___ ___
- Are numbers painted on curb? ___ ___
- Are front and rear yards clear of debris? ___ ___
    Are trees well-trimmed? ___ ___
- Is the chimney spark arrester in place? ___ ___

General

- Are multiplug adapters used with appliances? ___ ___
- Are electrical cords in good condition? ___ ___
- Are there overloaded outlets or extension cords? ___ ___
- Are any extension cords run under rugs or ___ ___
    carpets or looped over nails or other sharp
    objects that could cause them to fray? (The
    fire department discourages the use of
    extension cords. However, if using portable
    or temporary extension cords, check listing
    label on both cord and appliance to
    determine appropriate size and configuration
    of extension cord needed.)
- Are matches and lighters out of reach of young ___ ___
    children?
- Has an emergency exit been planned, ___ ___
    developed, and practiced?
- Is clothes dryer free of lint? ___ ___
- Is firewood or lumber stored no less than ten ___ ___
    feet from house?
- Is the 9-1-1 emergency number on or by phone? ___ ___

These safeguards cannot guarantee you will not have a fire,
but they will reduce the chances of a fire starting or spreading.

79

House-Hunting Checklist

Lovest thou me more than these?
—John 21:15 KJV

*B*UYING OR RENTING a house, apartment, condo (or tent!) can sometimes
be a source of stress. By midsummer, the anxiety of being settled
before school starts can cause you to make the wrong decisions when
house hunting in a hurry.

The checklist (page 293, Figure 12) will be helpful in keeping
track of the special features of the homes that you've seen. Use it to
compare them and single out that special house you want to make
your home.

This organized shopping list can be kept and copies made. It will
enable you to look back and compare!

If you have a Polaroid camera, take a picture of each home and
attach it to the back of each checklist form.

This type of organization will certainly give you more credibility
with the realtor and home-seller. They both will give you the benefit
of being a wise buyer.

HOUSE HUNT RECORD

Date _____
Address of home _____ Age _____
Best route to take _____

Owner of Home _____ Phone # _____
Salesperson _____
House design _____
House color _____
No. of square feet _____ Size of lot _____
Asking price _____ Down payment $ _____
Monthly payment $ _____
Type of utilities _____ Cost per month $ _____
Other costs _____
Garage? ☐ 1 Car ☐ 2Car ☐ Larger ☐ Carport
Condition/type of roof _____
Living room: Size _____ Flooring _____
Kitchen: Size _____ Flooring _____
Dining room: Size _____ Flooring _____
Storage space: Adequate? ☐ Yes ☐ No
Husband's first impression _____

Bedrooms: Number _____ Sizes _____
Bathrooms: Number _____ Sizes _____ Colors _____
Fixtures and tile condition _____
Water pressure check _____
Family room: Size _____ Flooring _____
Foyer: Size _____ Closet space _____
Game room: Size _____ Flooring _____
Basement: Size _____ ☐ Finished ☐ Unfinished
Laundry room: Size _____ Flooring _____
Other _____
☐ Central Air ☐ Fireplace Location(s) _____
Overall interior condition _____
☐ Patio ☐ Pool ☐ Pantry _____
Distance from work: Miles _____ Time _____
Distance from shopping: Miles _____ Time _____
Neighborhood rating _____
Overall rating of home and property _____
Schools: Quality _____ Distance from home _____
Comments _____
Wife's first impression _____

Figure 12

80

Pool Owner's Checklist— Safety First

Happy are thy men, and happy are
these thy servants, which stand
continually before thee, and hear
thy wisdom.

—*2 Chronicles 9:7 KJV*

*A*S MORE AND more homes, apartments, condominiums, and mobile home parks offer swimming facilities of all types—above-ground pools, spas, vinyl lining, and conventional gunite pools— we must become more conscious of safety around water. Since there are so many opportunities to go swimming, we can't let down our alertness when we supervise our youngsters.

Nothing is more tragic than to lose a child to drowning or to a life of brain damage because we became complacent with water and its many dangers.

One scenario of a drowning might go like this: A three-year-old child is at home with one parent. A door to the swimming pool is unlocked. There is a fence around the yard per city code, but there is no interior fence around the pool. An outsider can't get to the pool easily, but the child at home is in trouble because he can get to the pool with no problem.

Mom answers the phone or goes to the bathroom. Supervision is interrupted for a minute or two. The child spots a plastic ball at the pool edge and quickly goes out the unlocked door and falls into the water trying to get the ball.

You may think it can't happen to you and your child, but many fire department personnel can give witness that it only takes one or two unattended moments.

Here is a pool safety checklist:

- Never leave a child alone near or in a pool or bathtub. Your quick phone call or trip to another part of the house leaves plenty of time for your unattended child to fall into the pool or tub.
- Give your child swimming lessons. (However, lessons don't replace constant supervision.)
- Call the local Red Cross chapter and enroll in a CPR class.
- Build a fence around all sides of the pool. Use nonclimbable material so the children can't climb over. Be sure to have a self-closing, self-latching gate. Fence should be at least four to five feet high.
- Doors leading to the pool should always be locked. Locks should be out of a child's reach. Kids can crawl through pet doors too.
- If a child can't swim he or she should not be allowed to dive head first into water, play on floats, play on inner tubes unattached to their bodies, or hold onto other children while in the water.
- Don't rely on flotation devices for protection.
- Consider door or floating pool alarms.
- Consider keeping a vinyl cover on your pool when it's not in use.
- Tell your babysitters or other guardians about drowning precautions. Encourage your babysitters to know CPR.
- Keep toys away from the pool. They are too tempting.
- Have a poolside phone with emergency telephone numbers.
- Have a long pole with a hook on it next to the pool so you could extend it to a child who might need some assistance.
- Do you know how to swim? If not, take lessons so you will personally feel confident around water.
- Spas, bathtubs, ponds, lakes, beaches, and toilets are potential drowning pools too.
- Purchase a long extension or cordless phone to take with you into the bathroom. Don't be tempted to leave your child unattended while in the tub.

SAFETY AROUND CHILDREN EXTENDS LIFE!

See *Survival For Busy Women*, also published by Harvest House, for many samples of useful charts.

"MORE HOURS IN MY DAY" can provide many of the organizational materials that are recommended in this book and others written by Emilie Barnes. You may obtain a price list and seminar information by sending your request and a stamped, self-addressed business envelope to:

MORE HOURS IN MY DAY
2838 Rumsey Drive
Riverside, California 92506

15
MINUTE

Family
TRADITIONS
& MEMORIES

Dedication

To my Bob, who has encouraged me to be the woman God wants me to be. He has helped me to use my creativity in making our home a warm and happy place to live. We have made some beautiful memories and started warm traditions together which we have passed down to our children and grandchildren.

Being raised in a Jewish home, I had many traditions, but it wasn't until my Bob led me to the Messiah that our real holiday traditions were created, thus making this book possible. I am grateful for my Jewish heritage which is now complete in Christ, who brings joy to our hearts and homes.

Contents

Measure Your Moments . . .
Treasure Your Memories

As we live in this hectic world that says, "Faster, faster, you must go faster," our souls cry out, "Slower, slower, I must go slower." What a conflict between what we hear and what we want to do!

In Romans 12:2 (NIV) Paul writes, "Do not conform any longer to the pattern of this world, but be transformed by the renewing of your mind. Then you will be able to test and approve what God's will is—his good, pleasing and perfect will."

When we take time in our hurried lives to create memories through the things we do, we are in essence saying, "Lord, what is important for me and my family's life? Show me what is important for everyday living. How can I beat the system?"

There was no Christmas, no tree, no parties, no gifts, no cookie exchange, no ornaments hung or given, no excitement, no wish list—just one little girl looking out a window, longing to be involved in the most beautiful season of the year.

I was raised in a Jewish home. Yes, there was love, there was food, and there was Hanukkah. I was different, but I wanted to be like everyone else—enjoying Christmas carols, Christmas shopping, Santa, sleigh bells, reindeer and, most of all, Christmas traditions.

I was 11 when my father died. My mother became even stronger in the Jewish faith, and I went weekly to Hebrew school and temple. It wasn't kosher to celebrate Christmas. God, however, had other plans for me. God brought a young man into my life who did celebrate Christmas, did believe in Jesus as Messiah, and did participate in all the beautiful traditions of the Christmas holiday. My heart was touched by Christ's love as Bob shared the true Christmas story with me one evening: that God did have a Son, His name is Jesus, and He is the Messiah our people are waiting for. Bob shared how Jesus said, "I am the way, and the truth, and the life; no one comes to the Father but through Me" (John 14:6), and "I came that they might have life, and might have it abundantly" (John 10:10).

Bob's Christian heritage and upbringing surfaced strongly during those early dating months and, through his loving influence, I received Christ into my heart and became a believing Christian. We were married a year later, and I'll never forget our first Christmas together—for me the very first Christmas of my life. Money was short, but we had a tree and gave each other ornaments, which became a tradition for our family.

Holidays are wonderful opportunities to develop lasting memories built around family traditions. Traditions are similar to habits. They may be either detrimental or beneficial. We need to understand why certain traditions are observed, the messages that they convey, and how they affect our lives.

In Proverbs 24:3,4 (NIV) we read, "By wisdom a house is built, and through understanding it is established; through knowledge its rooms are filled with rare and beautiful treasures." The writer encourages us to use wisdom, understanding, and knowledge to create homes filled with rare and beautiful treasures. These words of encouragement certainly put us into action.

This book, *15 Minute Family Traditions and Memories,* is written to help you, the reader, to measure your moments and treasure your memories. Creating family traditions isn't done in a vacuum, but through activities year-round. Be an observer of life. Seek ways to teach on a variety of occasions. In Deuteronomy 6:7, Moses instructs the people when he says, "You shall teach them diligently to your sons and shall talk of them when you sit in your house and when you walk by the way and when you lie down and when you rise up."

We are to live life with a godly purpose. For many years I thought I was raising children for the moment, not realizing that I was teaching for generations to come. The things I taught my children are now being taught by them to my grandchildren. Time flees from us so quickly. We pause for a moment, take several deep breaths, and find ourselves to be grandparents and great-grandparents.

Use this book to give you wisdom, understanding, and knowledge in raising those children so they can truly say, "I treasure my memories. The traditions that I learned and lived with while growing up have made me the person who I am today."

Learn to Create Treasured Memories

*I*N OUR HECTIC efforts to make a living and meet all the demands upon our 24 hours per day, we are often too exhausted to spend quality time together as a family to create treasured memories. When a slower day comes, we just want to lay back and do nothing. It becomes a catch-up day so we can be ready to start again. We continually ask, "How do I get off this treadmill?" We have to do it on purpose. Learn to create treasured memories! They don't happen by chance. For the family to endure today, we have to plan for success. Let's take time to live life with a purpose.

I want to give special encouragement to Mom and Dad to work as a team to make life meaningful. Children love to see their parents working with a plan. If Dad is reluctant to get involved, then Mom will have to carry the extra load to live life with a purpose. Planning ahead for memories will also give single parents an extra spurt of energy for living life with a quality of memories.

You don't need money to create memories; you just need a desire. As adults, many of our memories are from our childhood or from when we were first married. Looking back to our early married life, Bob and I had very little money, but we have many fond memories. Now we have much more financial independence, but our early memories are still very vivid. Someone shared with me once, "Successful people do what unsuccessful people aren't willing to do." That statement had a real impact on my life. From that day on, I began to identify what those things were. One that was brought to mind was that successful people planned their lives. I wasn't planning my life very well at the time. Since then, I have learned to create treasured memories.

A memory-builder doesn't have to be limited to one season of the year or a certain holiday. It can be any event that later becomes a happy memory—a family ritual, a season, a tradition, or even the creation of a memorable event out of an ordinary day. A memory-builder might be:

- Having a "Bowl Game Party" each New Year's Day.
- Thanksgiving Day at Grandma's house with her favorite turkey recipe.
- Trout fishing the last two weeks of August in Idaho.
- A tea party with Grammy in the garden.
- Ice fishing on the lake each December with Uncle Bill.
- Boiling and coloring eggs for Easter baskets.
- Going to the beach for the Fourth of July and roasting hot dogs and watching a fireworks display.
- Telephoning a family member each year on his or her birthday at the exact time the person was born.
- Flying a special birthday flag by the front door when someone in the family has a birthday.
- Eating off a special plate for that special occasion.
- Having Dad read the Christmas story in the Gospel of Luke before the main meal on Christmas Day.
- Having Mom place lit candles on the table at dinnertime.
- Spending a week at a lake in a cabin each summer.
- Swimming in the ocean each January along with the rest of the members of the local Polar Bear Club.
- Going to Mexico each summer on the church's work trip to help missionaries.
- Helping feed the homeless in the city on Thanksgiving Day.

Develop Family Traditions

I often question ladies who attend my seminars about traditions they had in their families while growing up—traditions that set them apart as belonging to that unique family (a sign, a thumbs-up, a kiss on the nose, a pinch of the cheek). I found that most people had no such traditions. Some even asked, "What's a tradition?" or said "We had no traditions at all, even at Christmastime, birthdays, or anniversaries."

From reading my books, you know very well that I am a strong believer in family traditions. I have found that it takes only a small gesture to bring families closer. Traditions help you connect with your family and maintain those ties.

Many of these traditions have been used by our own family or are ones that have been shared by many of the ladies who attend my seminars or read my books. There are more ideas than you can use. Select a few that interest you and try them on your family members. My Bob tells me that you are never too old to start a new tradition. So let's start now. . . .

A Butterfly Kiss

My Bob gives the grandchildren a "butterfly kiss" by fluttering his eyelashes on the children's cheeks. They just love it. Another one (which I won't describe) is a "car-wash kiss." You can guess what that's like.

A Special Handshake

My Bob greets a certain male friend and his two grown sons with a special greeting. They shake hands, slip down to a clasp of the fingertips, quickly move into a thumb grip, shift to a knock on the elbow, and finish with a big smile. Only men will probably want to do that—it's not very dainty for women.

Silent Communication

Invent a silent symbol of your family's camaraderie. For example, a thumbs-up, a wink, or a tug on the earlobe.

Kid Fix

Request a "kid fix"—a hefty hug and a big kiss—whenever you feel the need. Let your youngsters know it makes you feel much better.

Once a Day

Tell your children you love them at least once every 24 hours—when you send them off to school, when they come home, when you pray with them at night, or anytime.

Go Ahead, Try It

Encourage your child to try new things: taste unusual foods, enter contests, write for information on subjects that interest him or her.

Double Desserts

Once a month, surprise your family by announcing double-dessert night.

Yogurt Run

During the summer or when the children don't have school the next day, go into their rooms just before they fall asleep and announce a "yogurt run." They will think you have flipped out, but they will always remember the special times when you got them out of bed and went to get some delightful yogurt.

You Are Special Today

We have a large red plate which has inscribed on it: "You Are Special Today." We are always honoring a member of the family or guest who comes to dinner. We've even taken this plate to restaurants, on a picnic, and to a beach party. We let the special person use that special plate. We also take a photograph of that person and place the picture in a special photo album that houses pictures of our recipients.

Sharing a Secret

You can have a lot of fun by sharing a secret and keeping up the suspense until Christmas or a birthday comes. It's also good training to teach the children how to keep a secret.

What's the Best Thing That Happened to You Today?

Quite often we ask this question toward the end of our meal, and the discussion that follows keeps the family for a longer time at the table and keeps us talking. No TV is allowed during dinner.

Mom's Canned Questions

We have a jar of 150 questions that are great for the family to answer in a constructive way during any mealtime. Many times we even use this jar of questions when our adult friends come to visit.

Cooking Class

At least once a month set aside a special afternoon where the children are invited to the kitchen to prepare a meal or a portion of a meal. Desserts are always a winner. Bring out the aprons and chef's hat. If they dress like cooks, they will really get involved in the process.

Bravo!

Three cheers for success! Honor a child who does well in an activity, on a test, a term report, or by completing a chore. Make it a big deal—you might even cook the person's favorite meal.

Young Decorator

When sprucing up your children's rooms, allow them to pick the color theme, paint, sheets, curtains, or towels. If that's too risky, give them specific choices (several wallpaper designs, three or four paints, or choices of several bedspreads).

Study Hall

Select that special area at home (a table, a couch, a chair) to review materials to be covered in a test tomorrow. Have your children cozy up and get comfortable in their special "study hall."

What a Fine Family We Have

I'm one for framing family pictures all over tne house: individuals and group pictures from last summer's vacation, a winter ski trip, or a Christmas group picture. Be sure to share these pictures in the children's rooms, too. This gives them a great sense of family identity.

Cowbell

I have an old cowbell that is positioned by our kitchen door. Two minutes before a meal is to be served, I go out and ring that bell very firmly. This is a signal to the members of the family that the food is ready. They have two minutes to get to the table.

How Pretty

Let your children wear your old jewelry and dress up when they have playtime.

Sorry

Admit when you're wrong. Your family members know when you've blown it as well as you do.

Pet Names

As the children get older, don't drop those pet names, but use them privately to avoid embarrassing the kids.

Those School Projects

Use those special clay vases that are brought home as flower vases or to hold paper clips.

I'm Like Dad

Lend your son a tie to wear on special occasions.

I Choose You

Tell your children how much you enjoy being their parents. Kids like to hear they are loved.

A Warm Bear Hug

There's nothing like going to bed on a cold night with a warm teddy bear at your side. Sew flannel, fake fur, or other cuddly material into a teddy bear that will fit around a hot-water-bottle. You can use a zipper in the back to close the seam. A button or a safety pin also works nicely. Stuff the arms, legs, and head with polyester fiberfill, rags, or old nylons.

As the child is getting ready for bed, fill the bottle with hot water and tuck the bear between the sheets. Your child will look forward to going to bed.

Flannel Sheets in the Winter

For our grandchildren's birthdays, I give them a package of designer flannel sheets and pillowcases. Their mom puts them on the beds when the weather turns cold. They just love these warm, soft sheets that make getting into bed so inviting. It also brings back fond memories of their birthday parties.

Worship Services at Home

There are many times during the year when you might not be able to attend your regular church due to inclement weather, sickness, or being away on a vacation.

Plan your own worship service with the children. Sing familiar hymns and choruses using any instruments that the family can play. One of the children might even like to lead your group in song. Go around the group and share prayer requests. This is a great opportunity to be transparent and reveal where hurts and needs are in the family unit. The children might like to mention friends at school who need prayer. Share blessings from the week. Give an opportunity for prayer. Let the children feel free to pray however they wish. This is a great time to model praying out loud. Our grandchildren love to give devotions on some passage from a previous Sunday school lesson. Dad can always be ready to share from a section of Scripture that he has been studying. In closing, make sure that everyone gets a warm hug with an "I love you."

Family Night

Designate one night a week as family night. Rotate among the family members who will choose the activity for that evening. It might be ice-skating, bowling, roller-skating, frying hamburgers, going to the beach to swim, going out to dinner, etc. These can be very special times when people in a family get to know each other better. Our children always enjoyed family nights because they were so much fun.

Pennies at the Bottom of the Sink

I was able to get our children—and now our grandchildren—to wash the evening dishes by occasionally dropping some pennies into the bottom of the sudsy water. The kids were always thrilled to find these copper treasures.

Grandpa's Treasures

Grandpas have special privileges, and one of them is to make sure that the grandchildren always know that Grandpa has a secret treasure in his shirt pocket. It might be chewing gum, candy, a certificate for something—even some loose change. On occasion, my Bob takes his loose change out of his pocket and divides it among the grandchildren. They like to be around Grandpa because he's so much fun.

Go to the Fun Box

Somewhere near the dining room table have a fun box that contains slips of paper listing activities for the family. The box can be plain, or it can be creatively decorated with bright paper or paint. Make sure that the box has a lid, but make an opening that allows room for a small hand to reach inside.

On slips of paper, the family can write down various activities:

- Renting a video
- Going bowling
- Going to the movies
- Reading a favorite book together
- Going for a walk
- Singing favorite songs
- Making cookies
- Popping popcorn

When things drag around the home and you need to pump a little life into the day, have a family member go over to the box and draw out a slip of paper. Whatever is on that paper becomes the evening's activity. Make sure that only fun ideas are inserted into the box. Once an idea is used, it can be put back into the box if everyone enjoyed the activity. If not, drop in an idea for a new activity for a future draw.

Creating Special Occasions

As a child growing up, I didn't have a lot of fond memories. Our family had more dysfunction than function. However, I do remember my father taking me to a pier and dropping a fishing line over the side. I don't remember us catching any fish, but Dad and I had some precious times together. One of my fondest memories was created when we celebrated the Festival of Lights at Hanukkah time. My Uncle Hy and Uncle Saul would play the violin and piano, respectively. As amateurs, they would make mistakes with a missed string or an out-of-tune key on the piano. But at the conclusion of their playing, we would give them warm applause, thinking they were great.

I have found that these special occasions don't just happen; a successful party is the result of careful planning and organization, and an awareness of just what makes special occasions memorable.

Planning a Successful Party

In all of my organizational books, I stress the importance of having a plan and making the plan work for you. Once I've decided upon a party, I start making lists of both priorities and details for implementing the list. I create a guest list and purchase invitations that reflect the theme or occasion. Then I plan a menu, along with an appropriate shopping list. I jot down what I need to present the food: tablecloths, napkins, flatware, dishes, glassware, and any special serving pieces that the menu might require. If I have to rent any of these items, I contact a rental company (see the Yellow Pages in your phone book) and make those arrangements.

On another list, I jot down details about flowers, candles, and special decorations, along with any appropriate music or individual touches that help make the occasion special.

I know that if I am well-organized when my guests arrive, they will be more relaxed and can rapidly get into the mood for the happening.

Since food is such a vital part of holiday gatherings, I have included some true-and-tried recipes that go along with each chapter. In some cases, they are ones which I have used successfully over the years. Other recipes were given to me by family and friends, and some come from theme magazines or books. Each one has been kept in its original form (with minor changes to reduce fat content while attempting to keep the delicious taste).

We aren't attempting to make you a gourmet cook who must put in hours and hours of preparation time. And most of the ingredients for our recipes are easily found in the typical grocery store.

Good organization, great guests, good food, and an attractive table setting are not the only keys to creating memorable moments. The most important ingredients are thought and caring. The activities should be fun, the food appealing, and the host should be concerned for those who gather—regardless of the event. Memories are what we celebrate.

Let's start with first things first: "But seek first His kingdom and His righteousness; and all these things shall be added to you" (Matthew 6:33). Each day we need to make the commitment to establish God as number one in our lives. If you have not made the decision to give God the number-one spot in your life, do so today; settle that basic question. Establish your priorities in life, and then the activities of each day will fall together in meaningful sequences.

These homemade memories can be made anywhere that people call home: an apartment, a duplex, one bedroom in a house, a condominium, a college dorm, a mobile home, or an estate. These memories are for all types of families—big or small, headed by a single parent or a married couple, with or without children. Wherever home is, you can create memories that will be treasured.

> *Today is the last day of your past and the first day of your future. There's no better time to begin "making memories" with your precious family*—Shirley Dobson.

Birthdays

Thus it came about on the third day, which was Pharaoh's birthday, that he made a feast for all his servants.

—*Genesis 40:20*

When Observed: On the person's date of birth

Earliest Observance: Pharaoh in Genesis 40:20

The practice of marking an individual's exact date of birth came into existence only with the recording of time by a fixed calendar. Originally, birthdays were not celebrated by commoners. It has only been in recent times that general populations have celebrated individual birthdays. In Europe and America an individual's birthday is celebrated with a family dinner or a party with friends and the custom of giving gifts. This is an important occasion, especially for a child.

Different countries share unique traditions. In general, a birthday is a specific time each year to give special praise and recognition to the person whose birth we celebrate. One way to make this a special tradition is to take time out of our busy schedules to do something different. Maybe write a message:

This is your day!

Good news! Psalm 139:13–16 (TEV):

> You created every part of me; you put me together in my mother's womb. I praise you because you are to be feared; all you do is strange and wonderful. I know it with all my heart. When my bones were being formed, carefully put together in my mother's womb, when I was growing there in secret, you knew that I was there—you saw me before I was born. The days allotted to me had all been recorded in your book, before any of them ever began.

Birthdays are always made special in our home—maybe because when I was growing up they never were. I remember when I was 12, I gave myself my first birthday party. My mother was trying to make ends meet after my father's death by opening a small dress shop. We lived in three rooms behind the store, and mother was always busy with customers, doing alterations and book work. Birthday parties were not a priority. I had always wanted a party, so I did it myself. I gave out invitations, cleaned the house, baked a cake, cut flowers, and put up streamers. My friends came and brought presents. I was so embarrassed that I hid in the closet and wouldn't come out. The adult in me could plan the party and organize the attention. I wanted it, but when it came, it was overwhelming. It was then that I decided to make birthdays special for my children someday.

Many times during the year we would talk about our birthdays. I would always (and still do) make the children's favorite meal. Almost every year they would have some kind of birthday celebration.

I'll never forget when our Jenny had her seventh birthday. Of any of us in the family, Jenny loved a party the most and still does, even though she is now a grown woman with three children of her own. We planned for her to invite ten of her closest friends from church and school. She took her invitations and hand-carried them to each person. But unknown to me, she not only invited her ten friends, but also verbally invited anyone who even looked like a friend. After the mothers dropped off their children for the party, we ended up with 24 children. The 12 cupcakes we cut in half, and the children scrambled for the prizes. It was crazy, but that was our Jenny. She couldn't hurt the other children's feelings by not inviting them, so she invited her whole class. It was most definitely a party—and truly a memory for Mom.

Parties with themes can be a lot of fun and will flow well because you have a definite plan. When my Bob turned 50, we had a surprise fiftieth BEARthday party—our theme was teddy bears. The invitations were teddy bears cut out of brown construction paper that said, *"You're invited to Bob's 50th BEARthday.* Bring a teddy dressed in a costume to depict Bob."

The plans took quite a while and, when I got home, Bob was really upset that I had been gone so long. "Where have you been? The phones have rung off the hook; the UPS delivery came. People came by for orders. It's really hard for me to handle this all by myself." Well, I couldn't tell him the truth, or I'd give the whole surprise away. But I sure wanted to say, "I was at Jenny's making *your* birthday invitations." He never caught on, and the party was a surprise.

I filled the room with helium balloons tied to each chair. The centerpiece consisted of a potted plant in a basket with small cloth teddy bears I had stuffed with fiberfill then glue-gunned onto bamboo spears purchased from the Oriental section of the market. I tied three balloons on the handle of the plant basket. A friend made baseball hats with a teddy bear on the bill for each man. I had white T-shirts silk-screened with a big teddy bear and "Bob's 50 BEARthday 1984," which everyone wore to the party.

The high school our children attended had two Poly Bears as their mascots. Jenny, being a cheerleader, called the school asking if we could borrow the two mascots for Bob's BEARthday party. They felt it was an honor to be invited. So we had bears all over the place. When Bob arrived at the party, the two Poly Bears slipped out to escort him in carrying a dozen helium balloons. I wish I had a video of that scene. It was *great!* In they came. We all yelled, "Surprise BEARthday, Bob!" But that was just the beginning.

After dinner and honey buns, each couple stood up with their dressed teddy bear and explained why they dressed it that way. All depicted different qualities of Bob's friendship. We had the Preppie Bear wearing saddle shoes. Bob most generally wears saddle shoes. We had the football referee with a black-and-white shirt and whistle around his neck. Bob spent many years refereeing high school football games to supplement our incomes. We had a teddy studying his Bible wearing glasses. Bob has taught adult and college

Bible studies most of our 39 years of marriage. Our daughter and son-in-law brought a gray-haired Papa bear wearing glasses since they have made Bob a grandpa. On and on the display of teddy bears came.

A longtime friend, Bob Swanson, wrote Bob a song and entertained the guests with his guitar music and song. We all nearly keeled over with laughter. The local newspaper got wind of the affair and came and took pictures and wrote an article, which all of Riverside viewed the next week. So the whole world knew Bob Barnes had turned 50. It was a memory to last a lifetime.

Our daughter gave her husband a surprise birthday party the first year they were married, and everyone came dressed in pink—even the men wore pink shirts. It was a simple thing to do, and yet it made the party a bit different and very creative.

Here's an idea for the working woman. I went to a surprise fortieth birthday party for my friend Yoli Brogger. We all met at 5:00 A.M. at her neighbor's home dressed in our nighties and robes. The working gals put robes over their clothes. We walked down the middle of the street with dawn barely on the horizon, through her front door, down the hall, and into her bedroom yelling, "Surprise!" She was in shock—hair tousled, no makeup. She thought it was a dream as 20 silly mid-life ladies stood at her feet and sang "Happy Birthday." We had such a fun time drinking tea and coffee with birthday cake and fruit at 5:30 A.M. By 7:00 A.M. the presents were opened and the party was over.

Another of our much-loved friends had her surprise birthday party last for 40 days with lunches and brunches provided.

Birthdays don't have to be a surprise. Our son, Brad, isn't big on birthday parties as such. He enjoys quiet family times with favorite foods and warm conversation. We acknowledge that and occasionally have a small party for him.

Other birthday ideas that might enrich your day:

1. *Birthday flag or banner*—Design and create a birthday flag or banner for each family member. Make this flag or banner out of cloth that will last (canvas is great). Place on it the person's favorite colors, sports interests, school activities, hobbies, etc. Fly the flag from sunup to sundown on a pole or hang the banner from a special hook on a fence or on the side of the house. You might even have a special flag raising and lowering ceremony and sing a favorite song, yell a cheer, or dance a dance to start the day off right.

2. *Birthday cup and/or plate*—Designate a special cup and/or plate to be used by the members of your family only on their birthdays. It's a great way to give special honor and recognition to that birthday person.

3. *A song at 9:02 A.M.*—On June 8, a friend of ours was born at 9:02 A.M., and at the exact time each year her family sings "Happy Birthday" to her. In college, she was sure to be in the dorm at that exact time, because she knew she would receive the traditional call. Even today, though married and living in another state, she still looks forward to that traditional call. She now has started the same tradition with her two sons.

4. *Love notes for Daddy*—While baking Dad's favorite German chocolate cake one year, we decided to do something special for him. We wanted to give him a gift that would last all year. We took small strips of paper and made coupons that Dad could redeem anytime during the year. We placed these in a small, colorful tray that he could set on his dresser. We wrote things like:

- Good for one back rub—Jenny
- Good for one fried-chicken dinner—Mom
- Good for one extra hug and kiss—Brad

5. *A special beginning*—Plan special activities for the honored birthday person. Some might be:

- Choose one gift and put it at the birthday person's place at the breakfast table to be opened as soon as his or her day begins.
- Have the birthday person plan the menu for supper (or you might even let the person choose a special restaurant if the budget permits).
- Have clean linens on the birthday person's bed and clean towels in the bathroom.

6. *Weekend celebration*—Try to celebrate your children's birthdays at a hotel that has a pool, game room, and nearby restaurants. Just getting together as a family creates many fond stories for the memory bank.

7. *Creative gifts*—

- Tickets to the zoo
- A beach towel
- New socks
- Art supplies

8. *Un-birthday party*—Pick a date during the warm summer months to have a party with all the birthday trimmings. Who is it

for? No one special—just a reason for family and friends to get together.

9. *Adopted birthday*—If you have an adopted child, you might want to let that child have two birthdays—one for the actual birthday, and another celebrating the day on which he or she came into your home. This second day makes the child feel a special part of a very special family.

10. *A happy "half" birthday*—Make a big deal celebrating your child's half birthday. You can carry out the theme by having a half birthday cake, a half glass of punch, half of a birthday card, etc. Be creative in carrying through the "half" theme.

11. *Birthday letters in a shoe box*—When I was 21, my mother presented me with a very special birthday gift. Wrapped beautifully in a shoe box were 21 letters Mom had written to me. She had started this tradition the first year of my life, and it was her secret until my twenty-first birthday.

The letters contained memories of the funny things I said and did over the years, the struggles during the teenage situations, times we spent together, differences we had, tears shed, and the love we enjoyed. Thanks, Mom, for the best gift in 21 years.

12. *Theme parties*—At our youngest grandchild's (Bradley Joe II) second birthday, we planned a birthday party around animals. We contacted a lady who brought a "petting zoo" to our home—a pony, a calf, two ducks, two pigs, four goats, and a baby lamb. This group of city children had a wonderful day experiencing a little bit of farm life. Maria and Brad carried out the theme beautifully by coordinating the cups, plates, napkins, banners, and streamers to reflect farm animals. My, the flashbulbs went off all afternoon! Upon leaving the event, the parents said that without a doubt this was the most fun that they had ever had at a child's birthday party.

13. *Games that break the ice*—

• Have the guests tell their first name and a word that describes themselves using the first letter of their name. (Example: My name is Christine and I am cute. My name is Chad and I'm charismatic. My name is Bevan and I am believable. My name is Bradley Joe and I'm brave.)

• Have guests tell their first name and when they are going on a vacation and how they are going to get there using the first letter of their name. (Example: My name is Maria and I'm going to Maryland by motorboat.)

• Have guests tell their first name and their favorite beverage using the first letter of their name. (Example: My name is Barbara and I like berry juice.)

• Put 20 wooden clothespins on a clothes hanger. Have the guests remove a clothespin and tell their first names and something special about themselves each time they remove a pin. Guests can only use one hand, and if they drop a pin, they must stop. The person who holds the most pins wins a door prize.

• Have guests introduce themselves by telling one of the following about themselves:

  • Their favorite color
  • Their favorite TV program
  • Their favorite food
  • When they were born, etc.

• Have guests tell their first names and punch their weight into a calculator. They then guess the total weight of all the guests at the party. The person with the closest guess wins a door prize. (If you give prizes to your guests at a birthday party, make sure that every child goes home with at least one prize.)

14. *A rented birthday party*—In many communities there are businesses which provide birthday parties for a fee per guest. They supply everything you need, plus provide food and a birthday cake with punch. Some businesses even throw in a clown or two.

15. *Birthday outings*—Birthdays are a great time to plan a trip to the park, a beach, or the mountains. Or you might go boating or sailing. Use your imagination to create that most unusual birthday theme. Don't get in a rut of doing the same thing each year.

16. *A tenth-birthday box*—On our grandchildren's tenth birthday, they get a big box (like a dishwasher or refrigerator box) full of ten gifts. This is a special benchmark of their lives. We spray-paint the box their favorite color and tie a big ribbon around it with the child's name written in huge letters on the outside of the package. One of the gifts is an envelope with ten new, crisp one-dollar bills (get these at the bank). In addition, we give them nine other gifts that they may have requested for their birthday.

After all the festivities, they get to play in the big box. This is the most fun of all their gifts. They can play in this big box for hours. It soon becomes a plane, a boat, or a train. After it is all over, Bob and I look at each other and say, "Why didn't we just give them a big box to play with?"

17. *A gift for the future*—A tremendous grandparent gift to a grandchild is to go to your local bank and purchase a U.S. Treasury bond made payable to the birthday girl/boy. They will really appreciate that gift when they get older and think of college.

18. *Annual birthday interview*—This acts as a great chronological record for your child's development:

• On each child's birthday, record on an audio- or videocassette an interview with him/her. Ask the birthday person to describe special memories about the past year—happy times, sad moments, fun things that happened, and other meaningful experiences.

• Add to the recording every year at the time of each birthday.

• After each interview, play back the previous years' conversations.

19. *"Do-it-yourself" birthday party*—

• Plan a birthday party for six or eight children, ages ten and younger.

• Look in your cookbook for a yummy gingerbread cookie recipe and assemble the ingredients needed to make it, along with the necessary utensils.

• When the guests arrive, let them help you make gingerbread kids cookies. Each child can then take home the cookie he or she made.

20. *Instant party for a loved one away from home*—

• Bake cookies and arrange them in a box with packets of fruit punch mix, party napkins, and paper cups.

• Wrap the box in birthday paper with a card explaining that you are sending an "instant party."

• Finish with an outer wrapping of brown paper and mail to that special birthday person.

• Instruct the person not to open the package until the day of his or her birthday.

21. *Birthday balloon walk*—Inflate a number of bright balloons. Divide the group of children into two or more equal teams. At the signal, each person must carry the balloon between his knees to the goal line and back. If the balloon breaks, he must come back for a new one and start over. The first team to finish is the winner. A large balloon for each team member would be an appropriate prize.

Variations: 1) Play this as an individual competition, using a stopwatch to time each competitor. The one with the shortest time is the winner. 2) Set up an obstacle course for players to walk through on their way to the goal line.

22. *Questions and answers*—Have guests fill in answers for all the items below. Give them a hint that all answers will contain the words *red, white,* or *blue.*

1. Stop signal . . . . red light
2. President's home . . . . White House
3. Fib . . . . white lie
4. Nursery rhyme . . . . Little Boy Blue
5. Porter at train station . . . . redcap
6. Moby Dick . . . . white whale
7. Architect's plan . . . . blueprint
8. Famous song by Irving Berlin . . . . White Christmas
9. Luncheon special . . . . blue plate
10. Depressing workday . . . . Blue Monday

Birthday Parties on a Budget

- Keep the party small. A good rule to follow is invite the same number of children as the number of years in your child's age.
- Get a family member or a babysitter to help (let grandparents be guests, not helpers).
- Have a backup plan for an outdoor party in case of rain.
- Use color comics for decorations and cartoon bedsheets as tablecloths. Crayons make nice party favors, and kids can use them to decorate white paper tablecloths and paper plates. Children's toys make good decorations: stuffed animals with party hats, a dump truck holding chips or cookies.
- Use creativity with party favors. Wrap peanut-butter play dough or homemade play dough in a plastic bag, tying it shut with a ribbon. Kids can decorate lunch bags and then fill them up as they go on a candy, peanut, or penny hunt.
- Don't plan the party at mealtime; it's more expensive. From 2 to 4 P.M. is a good time.
- Plan activities, but don't expect the children to play all the games. If the kids are having fun, don't interrupt. If they're bored, bring in a new game.
- Have your cake and be able to afford it, too. If a homemade cake has frosting and the child gets to pick the flavors, he's

happy. Licorice, candy, or animal crackers make good sheet cake decorations.

- Don't serve blue icing, red punch, or other things that stain or make children overactive.
- Pick a party theme. Some ideas: beach party, tea party, costume party, dinosaur party, frontier party, scavenger hunt, backyard camp out, detective party.
- An artist party can be fun. Get five or more large boxes for the children to paint or color and make into churches, homes, or cars.
- For children ages five to seven, try a soap bubble party and invite a storyteller.
- Beware of hiring clowns or big characters for toddler parties. Clowns are inappropriate for children younger than three, because small children get frightened. With children ages three and older, it is suggested that the host ask how the clown will dress. Clowns that wear makeup and colorful costumes but no frightening wigs are better. By eliminating the wig, the clown might be able to get the children to stand and talk to him, or at least not run.
- Remember that a party for a child's first couple of birthdays is really for family and friends to celebrate a new life. The child doesn't understand what's going on.
- Don't make your children share their presents.
- Save opening the presents till the end. It's a good way to slow down a party.
- Have a specific ending time for the party. Playing a video is a nice way to keep stragglers who are waiting for rides home occupied. Once everyone is gone, take a few minutes for some hugs and talk about the party. Save the cleanup for later.
- If some members of your family live far away or can't come to the party, make a video recording and send it to them. They will love seeing the party, and it will help your family stay in touch.

Valentine's Day

This is my commandment, that you love one another, just as I have
loved you.
—John 15:12

When Observed: February 14

Earliest Observance: Middle Ages

February 14 has become special in America, as for one day we
return our hearts to love. My earliest recollection of this special day
is from when I was in elementary school. With great anticipation
and thoughtful selection, I chose and signed that special card for
that somewhat secret sweetheart.

Many decades later I still look at February 14 as a special time
for expressing love and affection to those special to me. Everyone
knows that Valentine's Day is that day of the year when friends and
lovers express affection for one another with cards, candy, and
flowers, or through whatever means their imaginations can find.
The symbols for this day are hearts, cupids, and arrows. Red, white,
and pink are this day's colors.

No one is quite sure who St. Valentine was. The early lists of
church martyrs reveal at least three people named Valentine, each
of whom had his feast day on February 14.

Various legends have come down to us, too. Valentine was said to have been imprisoned and, while there, he cured the jailer's daughter of blindness. Another story, in an attempt to associate Valentine more closely with Valentine's Day, has him falling in love with the jailer's daughter and sending her a letter which he signed, "From your Valentine."

In the Middle Ages throughout Europe, there was a belief that birds mated on February 14. This belief that birds chose their mates on Valentine's Day led to the idea that boys and girls would do the same. Even at the turn of the twentieth century in the hills of the Ozarks, folks thought that birds and rabbits started the mating season on February 14—a day which was for people in this region not only Valentine's Day, but Groundhog Day as well.

Some people even give credit for this day to the early Roman feast day of Lupercalia, which was celebrated in February in honor of the pastoral god Lupercus—a Roman version of the Greek god Pan. During this festival the names of young women were put into a box. Youths then drew the names, and the boys and girls so matched would be considered partners for the year which began in March.

The English settlers in the New World brought their Valentine customs with them. Prior to the eighteenth century, original valentine cards of a certain homeliness and simplicity had been exchanged among some colonists. But after 1723, the custom really began to grow with the impact from England valentine writers.

Commercial valentines came out about 1800, and by 1840 were becoming sophisticated. The reduction of postal rates brought about a great increase in the number of valentines sent, and printed valentines became popular. Today, valentine greetings are made for sending to nearly everyone—friend, relative, and sweetheart alike. Valentine's Day is second only to Christmas in the number of greetings sent in the United States.

Christian Activities

As Christians we can certainly celebrate this holiday with our families and friends better if we look at the Bible and see how many times love is used to express the relationship between God and mankind. Our faith is built upon our proper understanding and expression of love. Below are some Scriptures that express God's love to us. May we appreciate our scriptural heritage and through this understanding put into practice a true expression of love to those around us.

> Deuteronomy 6:5—"And you shall love the LORD your GOD with all your heart and with all your soul and with all your might."
> Psalm 18:1—"I love Thee, O LORD, my strength."
> Psalm 116:1—"I love the LORD, because He hears my voice and my supplications."
> Psalm 145:20—"The LORD keeps all who love Him."
> Proverbs 8:17—"I love those who love me; and those who diligently seek me will find me."
> Romans 8:28—"And we know that God causes all things to work together for good to those who love God."

Valentine Ideas

On Valentine's Day we have an opportunity to give of ourselves in love. Homemade valentines with lace, ribbon, craft paper, and glue are almost a lost art. Anyone, even the least artistic person, can create a lovely valentine, but you can also buy prepackaged valentines.

"Good for" coupons make a great valentine for anyone—from children to grandparents. The coupons could include:

- one evening of babysitting
- two hours of yard work or weed-pulling
- one hour of ironing, sewing, or mending
- the preparation of one meal

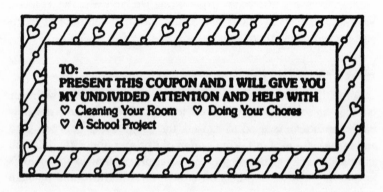

TO: _____
PRESENT THIS COUPON AND I WILL GIVE YOU
MY UNDIVIDED ATTENTION AND HELP WITH
♡ Cleaning Your Room   ♡ Doing Your Chores
♡ A School Project

Give a gift of yourself and your talents as an expression of love. God showed us His love in His Son, Jesus. What an outreach and even a ministry you can create through expressing your love.

Valentine's Day provides children with an opportunity to give from their hearts. One mother in our neighborhood had cookie-baking day with her three girls. They frosted heart-shaped cookies and topped them with jelly beans, coconut, raisins, and nuts and then made up small paper plates filled with loving, homemade cookies and took them to each family on the block. This same idea carried over to other holidays as well: tree-shaped cookies for Christmas, turkey-shaped for Thanksgiving, and cross-shaped for Easter. What this mother taught her girls was more important than how to make cookies. She taught her daughters how to give as Christ gave to us.

Don't think it's "sissy" to give plants or flowers to a man. One wife shared how she sent her husband a bouquet of flowers at work. He wasn't an executive in a high-rise office building, either. It was a sacrifice for her, and she saved for a long time to do it. The other workers all stopped to see who was getting those beautiful flowers. They didn't make fun of him, but admired him and the relationship he and his wife had. If flowers seem a bit too much, try a balloon or box of candy, or pack him a fancy lunch with a heart-shaped sandwich. Write love notes between the lettuce and tomato. He'll find and love them—and hopefully won't eat them.

Valentine's week is a good time to pull out wedding photos and honeymoon pictures. Use this time to reminisce and to recall special memories.

I save my leftover red Christmas candles for Valentine's week, and we have candlelight breakfasts or dinners, children and all. Red napkins and place mats and white lace doilies make nice place settings. A paper or fabric heart wreath can be put on your front door or mailbox the week before Valentine's Day as a sure sign of love and welcome to friends, neighbors, and family.

Valentine's Day gives us an excellent opportunity to reach out to others—to send a note, deliver a handmade valentine, or give a basket of homemade goodies.

Perhaps an apology is due to a friend or family member. Now is the perfect time to settle those differences. A note of apology in love could open the doors for good feelings in the future.

Additional Valentine's Day Ideas

1. *Lend a helping hand*—Make a large red heart with white lace doilies on the edges. In the middle write the words, "I did it because I love you." Take the card and place it next to something you did to show your love for that person:
   - a bed that has been made
   - dishes washed and put away
   - a carpet that has been vacuumed

2. *How Mom and Dad met*—With the family around, have Dad and Mom tell the story of their first date and courtship. They may include:
   - How and where they met
   - Activities and places they enjoyed while dating
   - When they fell in love
   - What qualities attracted them to one another
   - How Dad proposed
   - Humorous stories about their courtship

Have Dad and Mom show pictures of themselves when they were young. As a nice touch, Dad can show the family how he kissed Mom the very first time.

3. *Valentine notes*—Bake a cake and put little notes in it. The children will love this and look forward to it each year. Write some love notes, positive messages, or short Bible verses on strips of paper, fold the papers into small squares, wrap them in foil, and place the notes throughout the cake batter. When the children get a piece of cake, they will love to see if there's a note inside.

4. *Love messages*—
   - Write notes of love to *each* member of your family.
   - Tell them why you love them and appreciate them. Be specific!
   - Tuck notes in their lunchboxes, notebooks, or briefcases, along with special valentine treats.
   - Call your spouse today and say how much you love him or her.
   - Send a fax expressing your love.
   - With red lipstick write "I love you" on your spouse's side of the bathroom mirror.

5. *A dinner by candlelight*—Cook a special meal and eat it on your good dishes with your prettiest glasses and serving ware in the formal dining room (if you have one). Prepare a special dessert with the children's names on the different pieces or a large cake

with a special Valentine's Day message. Select for each of the children a special valentine card—even add a few of your own special words. You might even send out a special invitation to your dinner party a few days ahead of time. It is a good opportunity for the family to dress up. This works best when Dad can help with the preparations.

Keep the children out of the dining room until they are brought in blindfolded. As they take off their blindfolds, their eyes will become large with excitement at seeing this special dinner setting for the first time. During the meal, take turns expressing how important each member is to the family. Let the children know how special they are to Mom and Dad. (By the way, take the phone off the hook.)

6. *Valentine treasure hunt*—

• Buy a package of inexpensive children's valentines.

• Write a different love note on each of 10 to 15 cards, or write one word per card to form a message of love.

• Hide the cards throughout the house, in the car, or in other suitable places.

• Give a written clue on the outside of each envelope directing your "Valentine" to the next card.

• Include a small love gift with the last valentine.

7. *Make a heart-shaped cake*—Just bake a round and a square cake. Face the square one toward you, with the point forward like a playing card diamond. Slice the round cake in half and position the two halves against the diamond's uppermost sides. Frost and serve.

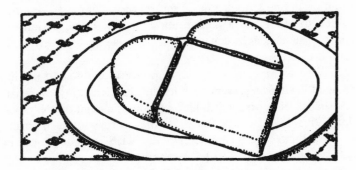

8. *Do-it-yourself candy box*—Instead of giving your sweetie the usual box of chocolates, decorate a box with pretty paper, lace,

buttons, and cut-out hearts. Filled with penny candy, it makes a great low-cost gift, and your Valentine can find other uses for the box after the candy is gone.

9. *A valentine dessert*—Our delicious, no-bake Valentine's Day dessert "box" is made of graham crackers—and the "gift" inside is your family's or friend's favorite ice cream or frozen yogurt! Here are the easy instructions:

• Top a graham cracker square with a scoop of ice cream or frozen yogurt as high and wide as the graham cracker.

• Place four graham crackers on the sides of the ice cream and press lightly, forming a square. Top with another cracker.

• Create a "ribbon" and "bow" with a tube of red cake-decorating gel. Freeze until ready to serve.

10. *A candy-bar "hello"*—On a piece of poster board write your Valentine's Day greetings so the candy bar forms part of the message. Some suggested messages might include:

• "I (mint) to ask you to be my Valentine."
• "Valentine, you stole a (Big Hunk) of my heart."
• "I chews (gum) you to be my Valentine."
• "You're the (Cup 'o Gold) at the end of my rainbow."
• "I'd run a (Marathon Bar) for you, Valentine."

11. *Chinese fortune cookie notes*—

• Buy a bag of Chinese fortune cookies.

• Carefully pull the fortunes out from the cookies with a pair of tweezers.

• Cut up small slips of paper and write your *own* messages of love either in one sentence or on several pieces of paper that must be fitted together like a puzzle. Stick the new messages into the cookies. The messages can also be made clever or funny if the occasion dictates.

12. *Have a heart! (or two)*—Make pretty Valentine earrings in a jiffy by following these very easy instructions: Cut two same-sized heart shapes from cardboard. Using red acrylic paint or nail polish, paint both sides of the hearts. Coat the hearts with clear varnish and allow them to dry completely. Glue each heart to an earring base (available at craft and hobby shops).

13. *Cinnamon cocoa*—For a spicy-good winter and Valentine beverage, add a cinnamon-flavored tea bag to a cup of piping-hot cocoa. Steep for a few minutes, then enjoy!

14. *Hair, hair!*—
• Make a heart-shaped hair ornament by twisting a red pipe cleaner into a heart. Wrap red or white lace ribbon around it and glue on some glitter. When the glue has dried, attach the heart to a barrette or hair clip.

• Save the ribbons from your Valentine's Day gifts. They make perfect hair bows and headbands.

15. *Pink pancakes*—When the family comes to breakfast on Valentine's Day, have pink pancakes already prepared. Just add a little red food coloring to the batter. The children will love it!

16. *Heart sandwiches*—In preparing sandwiches for family members as they go to school and work, take either a large heart-shaped cookie cutter or with a knife shape your bread into a heart. They will love the surprise when they unwrap their sandwiches during the lunch hour. Throw in some chocolate candy kisses for dessert.

17. *Homemade valentines*—Make your own valentines for family members. The handmade ones are still the best.

• Cut an 8½″ × 11″ sheet of construction paper in half.

• Fold each half in half (each full sheet will make two cards).

• Decorate the cover with hearts, pictures, lace, doilies, ribbons, etc.

• Compose a poem or verse for your loved one, or write a short essay on "This Is What You Mean to Me" or "You're Something Special Because . . .".

• Copy the message inside your card.

• Envelopes to fit this size of card can be purchased at stationery stores or can be made by hand.

18. *Fun food tips*—Use a heart-shaped cookie cutter to create fun Valentine's Day treats for your children. Here's how:
Breakfast: Toast bread, then cut it into heart shapes with the cookie cutter. (Don't cut the slices of bread before toasting, or you may have difficulty removing them from the toaster.)
Lunch: Cut bread or toast into slice-size heart shapes for Valentine's Day sandwiches. Note: Use the trimmings to make bread crumbs in a blender or food processor. Freeze the crumbs for use in casseroles and stuffing.

19. *Wrap it up*—Red or pink shopping bags in good condition can be recycled as Valentine gift-wrapping paper. Just cut the handles off the bag and carefully cut the bottom open. On one side, cut the bag from top to bottom, then smooth out the paper.

20. *Valentine cupcakes*—You can make heart-shaped cupcakes easily by using your favorite cupcake recipe. Place paper baking cups in a muffin tin. Put a marble or small ball of foil in each cup between the paper liner and pan. This makes a heart-shaped mold in which to cook cupcakes. Pour batter and bake as usual. Don't fill cups too full or you will lose the heart-shaped effect.

21. *Flowerpot centerpiece*—To make a pretty table decoration, you will need four flowerpots of graduating sizes and an assortment of live plants or silk flowers, whichever you prefer. Stack the flowerpots according to size, placing the largest on the bottom and the smallest on top. Arrange the plants or silk flowers in the top flowerpot and around the edges of the other three pots.

22. *A special grandparents' valentine*—Have your children decorate a red construction-paper heart. Cut out a heart shape from the middle of the valentine. Glue your children's school pictures or other recent photos into the heart shape. If the children make one each Valentine's Day, their grandparents will build a collection of special valentines over the years.

23. *Valentine card construction party*—Start a week ahead of time to gather all the materials and supplies. Unfold one or two card tables and lay out an old sheet or tablecloth to cover the table surface (place in an area of the home where the table can be left up for the week). The family can have a fun time constructing their own very special valentines—a great activity to do before or after school (in lieu of television) or after dinner. Mom and Dad can even get into the swing of things.

24. *A special valentine for Mom*—Husbands and children need to get together and think up something special for Mom. Compose a card that reflects how you love her. Give her a small, inexpensive gift. Hubby might want to call from work to whisper a love message to that special lady in his life. Send or take home a bouquet of flowers or a potted plant.

25. *Valentine tea party*—One mom on Valentine's Day makes a special tea party for her children and their friends. They place at each end of the table Raggedy Ann and Andy. She uses her best dishes and cloth napkins. The other moms are invited, but they sit in the kitchen out of the way. It's first-class for the children and a great idea for teens, too!

26. *Beloved silhouettes—*

• Use a slide projector or Viewmaster to project the head profile silhouette of each person in the family onto a blank wall. A bright lamp with the shade removed also provides a good light source.

• Hold poster board against the wall and trace the silhouette with a broad-tipped pen or marker.

• Cut out each silhouette.

• Cut a heart shape from a sheet of red construction paper or poster board larger than the size of the silhouette.

• Paste each silhouette on a separate heart and display them along a hallway or send them to grandparents for valentines.

Hint: A heart-shaped paper doily may be pasted under the silhouette, using a contrasting color. For instance, use a red heart with a white doily placed on it. Then paste the black silhouette on top of the doily.

Romance Is About the Little Things

Valentine's Day is not automatically the most romantic day of the year. It's there on the calendar, but you have to recognize it and act upon it. It doesn't happen in a void. Here are some additional ideas that will make your day very special:

• Instead of giving roses, this year try something different:

• Buy a different kind of flower.

• Write a love letter.

• Take a love basket to your spouse at work and surprise him or her with a special lunch.

• Do something unique, quirky, or touching.

• Write a poem, or copy one from a book of poetry.

• Fax a poem to your mate at the office (it's okay if someone in the office sees it first—they will know that you are a special person).

• Send a bunch of helium balloons to your mate at his or her job.

• For future reference: Buy an extra bag of Valentine conversation heart candies and save them for use six months later as a surprise.

• Keep your eyes open for pre-Valentine's Day articles in magazines and newspapers. Rip out the articles, circle the best ideas, and plan accordingly. (And don't forget to keep those articles for future reference!) File them in a manila folder with the heading "Valentine's Day."

• Mail him one Valentine's Day card—or mail him 20! Make a huge card. Send a musical greeting card—available in most card shops for just a few dollars.

• Use kids' valentines. Purchase a whole box full of silly puns and clichés, all for a couple of dollars.

  • Mail a box full of them.
  • Fill the empty kitchen sink with them.
  • Fill his briefcase with them.
  • Fill her pillow with them.
  • Tape them all over her car.
  • Mail one-a-day for a month.

• Send her a box filled with Valentine conversation heart candies—a big box.

• Use Valentine conversation heart candies to spell out a romantic message to her. Leave it on the kitchen table or paste it to a piece of construction paper.

• Replace all the Cheerios in the box with Valentine conversation hearts.

• Turn Valentine's Day into a real holiday with your spouse: Take the day off work. Spend the day in bed. Go to the movies. Go out to dinner. Go dancing. Take a drive. Make love. Go for a stroll.

• Send custom valentines of ribbon and lace, tubes filled with heart-shaped confetti or chocolate hearts, heart-shaped baskets filled with hand-painted notes, or anything else you can think of. (These items are available from Ann Fiedler Creations at (310) 838-1857, or write to 333 ½ South Robertson Blvd., Beverly Hills, CA 90211.)

• Create a Valentine's Day concert, just for the two of you. Record an hour's worth of your favorite romantic music. Print a program. List the song titles, along with some personal commentary about the significance of each song to you, or why particular songs remind you of him or her. Send your spouse an invitation to the concert. Dress for the event. Serve sparkling cider and cheese.

• Write "I love you" on the bathroom mirror with a piece of soap.

• Write your mate a note, poem, or letter on one sheet of paper. Cut it into puzzle-shaped pieces. Mail all the pieces to your sweetheart in an envelope—or mail one puzzle piece a day for a week.

• Men, think early and send away for a catalog of beautiful Victorian calling cards, stationery, and note cards for that special lady in your life.

Prescriptions for Romance

• Compliment your mate. Repeat every four to six hours.

• Say "I love you" at least three times today. Repeat dosage every day for the rest of your life.

• The unasked-for gift is most appreciated. The surprise gift is most cherished.

• Pick a wildflower bouquet.

• Run your hands and feet under very warm water before coming to bed.

• Hug at least ten times today. Watch out—it's habit-forming.

• Kidnap your mate! Blindfold her, drive her around town until she is lost; then tell her where you are going: to a movie, to the theater, to a restaurant, skating, or to a ball game.

• Hide 25 little "I love you because . . ." cards all over the house. Write short, romantic notes on index cards, Post-It Notes, or construction paper cut into little hearts. Then hide the notes everywhere: in the *TV Guide,* in pants pockets, in desk drawers, in socks, under magazines, behind pillows, in the tub, in the refrigerator, in the freezer, in the medicine cabinet, in books, in her briefcase, in his car, in the silverware drawer. Some of these notes may remain hidden for months—or even years. So much the better!

Heart-Smart Cocoa Kisses

Light as air, low-fat cookies for you and your Valentine:

Ingredients:

2 egg whites	3 tablespoons cocoa
¼ teaspoon cream of tartar	¾ teaspoon almond extract
⅛ teaspoon salt	⅓ cup finely chopped
⅔ cup sugar	almonds

About two hours before serving:

1. Preheat oven to 200°. Line 2 large cookie sheets with foil. In small bowl with mixer at high speed, beat egg whites, cream of tartar, and salt until soft peaks form. At high speed, gradually beat

in sugar, 2 tablespoons at a time, beating well after each addition. At low speed, beat in cocoa and almond extract until blended. Fold in almonds, reserving 1 tablespoon.

2. Drop mixture by slightly rounded tablespoonfuls onto cookie sheets. Sprinkle tops with reserved almonds.

3. Bake 1 hour and 15 minutes or until set. Cool the cookie sheets on wire racks for 10 minutes. With a metal spatula, carefully loosen and remove kisses from foil; cool completely on wire racks. Store in tightly covered container. Makes about 2 dozen kisses.

Easter

He is not here, but He has risen.
—*Luke 24:6*

When Observed: On the Sunday following the first full moon after the vernal equinox (sometime between March 22 and April 25)

Earliest Observance: Second century

Being brought up in the Jewish faith, I had no early experiences with or recollections of Easter in my childhood. I did have a stuffed Easter bunny, colored eggs, a new dress, and new shoes, but I didn't really observe the religious aspects of Easter until I met and married my husband, Bob. At that time I began to realize that Easter has a much more powerful message than what I had experienced. The symbols for Easter are the resurrection-cross and lilies, and the colors are pastels and purple.

I became aware that no holy day or festival in the Christian year compares in importance with Easter Sunday. That Jesus Christ was resurrected after having suffered and died is the belief most central to the Christian faith. Christians believe that by His dying, Jesus accomplished a reconciliation between God and man. The apostle Paul says:

339

Now if Christ is preached, that He has been raised from the dead, how do some among you say that there is no resurrection of the dead? But if there is no resurrection of the dead, not even Christ has been raised; and if Christ has not been raised, then our preaching is vain, and your faith also is vain (1 Corinthians 15:12–14).

I also learned in Matthew's Gospel that, after the crucifixion, Joseph of Arimathea placed Jesus in his own tomb and rolled a great stone across the entrance. But the Pharisees and Pilate feared that the disciples might come and steal Jesus' body to fulfill His prophecy: "After three days I will rise again." So the tomb was sealed and a guard was placed around the tomb.

On the third day, Mary Magdalene came to the tomb with Mary the mother of James:

And behold, a severe earthquake had occurred, for an angel of the Lord descended from heaven and came and rolled away the stone and sat upon it. And his appearance was like lightning, and his garment as white as snow; and the guards shook for fear of him and became like dead men. And the angel answered and said to the women, "Do not be afraid; for I know that you are looking for Jesus who has been crucified. He is not here, for He has risen, just as He said. Come, see the place where He was lying. And go quickly and tell His disciples that He has risen from the dead; and behold, He is going before you into Galilee, there you will see Him; behold, I have told you" (Matthew 28:2–7).

The feast of Easter was well-established by the second century. There was a great deal of controversy over whether the day should be celebrated on a weekday or whether Easter should always be on a Sunday, regardless of date. In A.D. 325, the Council of Nicaea decided that Easter should fall on the Sunday following the first full moon after the vernal equinox. This calculation was made easier when March 21 was chosen as the date of the vernal equinox.

In the early church, the several days called Pascha commemorated the passion, death, and resurrection of Jesus Christ. By the fourth century, Pascha Sunday had become a separate day which commemorated the glorious resurrection.

In Britain, the feast was named Easter after the Anglo-Saxon goddess of spring, Eastre.

Many of the early settlers of America were Puritans or members of Protestant denominations who didn't want anything to do with pagan religious festivals. The celebration of Easter in this country was therefore severely limited. It is well-known that the Puritans in Massachusetts outlawed the celebration of Christmas, and they also tried to play down the observance of Easter as far as possible.

After the Civil War, the message and meaning of Easter began to be more widely celebrated when the story of the resurrection was used by the Presbyterians as a logical inspiration of renewed hope for all those bereaved by the war.

Since then, Easter has become a major religious and secular celebration. Its joyous customs delight children and adults alike. It is a family day when relatives and friends gather after church services for festive dinners or maybe a park picnic, weather permitting.

Easter heralds the beginning of spring and is generally accompanied by a week's vacation from school.

One of the beautiful religious customs of Easter is the dawn service held by many Christian denominations. These services may well have their origin in the biblical text: "But on the first day of the week, at early dawn, they came to the tomb" (Luke 24:1). The outdoor Easter sunrise service was brought to America by Protestant emigrants from Moravia. The first such service in America was held in Bethlehem, Pennsylvania, in 1741.

Many Christians are torn between the religious significance of the biblical account of Christ's birth, death, and resurrection and the pagan and secular thrust given to these holidays. We struggle with the concept of being in the world but not of the world. Easter and Christmas seem to have been diluted over the past few decades. We want to honor the Scriptures, but we are also bombarded with the Easter bunny, dyeing eggs, egg hunts, Easter clothing, etc. One of the ways a family might want to separate the secular from the religious is to celebrate Easter Saturday and do on that day all those activities which don't fall into the religious function of the season and which are the children's "fun" part of Easter.

Easter Saturday Ideas

1. Decorate and dye your eggs.

2. Hide the eggs in the lawn area of your home or at a friend's home, or go to a park and have an Easter egg hunt. You might even include a "treasure egg" and offer a special prize to the child who discovers it. If your children's ages span several years, you might consider having two separate egg hunts—one for the smaller children and one for the older set.

This hunt can involve your whole family, plus your neighborhood, and friends, or it can be scaled down to include just you and a child. Don't let the lack of numbers discourage you.

3. Inside your "treasure egg" you might want to hide money, a gift, a candy treat, or a small toy.

4. Try decorating the serving table in spring colors and serving light refreshments after the hunt.

5. You and your neighbors or friends might want to join together and hire a clown or magician to come to the party and entertain the children.

6. There are usually some children who don't find any eggs and others who find more than they can carry. This provides a wonderful opportunity to talk about sharing with others.

7. Have an art project in mind that uses the eggshells when they are peeled from the eggs. Since the shells are colored, cracked, and in small pieces, they make excellent material for an Easter mosaic. Assemble a large sheet of poster or construction paper, white glue, and assorted colors of broken eggshells. Trace or draw a simple Easter picture onto your piece of paper. Glue the pieces of colored eggshells onto the paper to fill up your drawing.

8. Use a loaf of unsliced bread and cut the top off, leaving the sides and an attached handle for a basket. Hollow out the bread so Easter goodies can be placed inside. Trim with ribbon. Grind the unused bread for bread crumbs. This becomes an Easter bread basket.

9. Personalize your eggs by enclosing Easter messages in the shells. To blow out the raw eggs, use a sharp needle and poke a small hole in the small end of each egg and a larger hole in the big end. Through the larger hole, puncture the egg yolk with the needle. Hold the egg over a bowl and gently blow through the small

hole to force the raw egg out of the large hole. Rinse shells carefully and thoroughly.

Decorate blown-out eggshells with marking pens, ribbon, lace, or watercolor paints. Write messages on small pieces of paper. Roll them up and carefully place them inside the eggs through the larger hole. Your messages could contain something related to the Easter story.

10. *Egg Tips:*

• If you add two tablespoons of vinegar to the water before cooking your eggs, the egg white from cracked eggs will not leak into the water.

• Puncture the large end of the eggshell with a needle just before cooking to keep eggs from cracking.

• Although fresh eggs can be stored in their cartons in the refrigerator for two to three weeks, hard-boiled eggs should be refrigerated when cooled and used within one week.

• Grate the leftover hard-boiled eggs and place portions in small freezer bags and freeze for later use. Thawed, they provide an excellent garnish for green salads. Grated eggs taste good creamed over toast or added to casseroles—and even make delicious deviled eggs.

• Natural dyes can be put to work at Easter time. You'll have green eggs if you boil them with green grass, red if they're boiled with beets, and yellow if onion skins are in the pot.

11. Double-dipping—Before the Easter bunny became their ambassador, colored eggs were a symbol of springtime. For thousands of years, Ukrainians created elaborately patterned eggs using a wax-resist process. Updated and simplified, the same technique can be used to produce these soft watercolor patterns:

   a. To make a striped egg, dye a raw or hard-boiled egg pale yellow (for rich colors, double or triple the proportion of coloring to water recommended on most food-coloring boxes). Let dry.

   b. Melt beeswax (available at art-supply stores) in a pot. Dip both ends of the egg in wax to prevent them from absorbing the next color.

   c. Place the egg in the green dye for about a minute, then remove and let dry. Dip both ends of the egg deeper in the wax than before, leaving a narrow unwaxed band around the middle of the egg.

d. Place the egg in dark blue to dye the middle stripe. When finished, place the egg in a 250° oven on a cookie sheet lined with waxed paper for about five minutes. Take the egg out and wipe off melted wax with a paper towel. If you used a raw egg, carefully blow out the contents.

To make a half-colored egg, hold an egg partially submerged in a strong dye for about a minute. To create eggs with bands of white, dip-dye both ends, then dip each end deep enough in the wax to cover the dyed areas plus stripes of white beyond them, and proceed as above.

12. You and your family might want to make up a special Easter basket for those friends or neighbors who might be in need of food, clothing, or even a little touch of special loving.

Little Jelly Beans

Little jelly beans
Tell a story true
A tale of our Father's love
Just for me and you.
GREEN is for the waving palms
BLUE for the skies above
BROWN for the soft earth where
People sat hearing of His love.
A SPECKLED bean for fish and sand
RED for precious wine
And BLACK is for the sin He washed
From your soul and mine.
PURPLE'S for the sadness of
His family and friends
And WHITE is for the glory of the
Day He rose again.
Now you've heard the story
You know what each color means
The story of our Father's love
Told by some jelly beans.
So every morning take a bean
They're really very yummy.
Something for the soul, you see.
And something for the tummy.

—Author unknown

Use Easter Saturday to share the secular activities, and reserve Easter Sunday as the day for celebrating and sharing in the death and resurrection of the Lord Jesus Christ.

Christian Activities for Easter Sunday

> And these words, which I am commanding you today, shall be on your heart; and you shall teach them diligently to your sons and shall talk of them when you sit in your house and when you walk by the way and when you lie down and when you rise up (Deuteronomy 6:6,7).

1. Plan with your family to attend an Easter morning sunrise service. Starting the week before, you may want to read as a family a little each day in John 12–20 about the story of the life of Christ leading up to the crucifixion and resurrection. This background will make the sunrise service more meaningful to the children.

2. After a light breakfast, attend a regular church service.

3. Easter is a great time to have the extended family together for lunch or dinner. Rather than one family having full responsibility for food preparation, you might suggest a potluck with various families bringing different parts of the menu. Some families also rotate the location to a different home each year. This way no one family has the continuous responsibility of hosting the meal year after year.

4. When the immediate family is not available for celebration at Thanksgiving and/or Christmas, you might use Easter as the holiday when you come together as a total family. You could even use the symbols of Christmas with an Easter flair. Be creative and see how exciting you can make the theme.

5. Around the dining table you could have the Easter story written out and attached to the name tags or napkin rings. Before blessing the food, have various members of the family read their Scripture and share what that verse means to them.

6. Have your children prepare a drama depicting a segment of the Easter story, and let the other children or adults try to guess what segment they are portraying.

7. Before the day is over, prepare and share a family communion using bread or crackers and grape juice.

Prepare a loaf of bread (unleavened, if possible) and a cup of grape juice so that the family can share in the "one bread" and "one cup." (Read Matthew 26:17–30.) If it is your conviction that only a clergyman can administer communion, you might invite one of your church's staff members to join you in this part of the celebration.

As you take a piece of bread, share with the next person what is so special to you about Easter. Then in a prayer of thanksgiving, express how special Jesus is to you and your family. You might even have several members of the family pray. As in this passage of Scripture, you could close with a song. (If everyone isn't familiar with the song, print copies of the words.)

8. Easter story eggs—To remind your family of the Easter story, prepare an Easter basket with 12 plastic eggs that can be opened. On the outside of the egg write a number (1 to 12) and fill with the corresponding message and Scripture (see chart on page 347). Open one egg each day, starting 12 days before Easter. Read the message aloud to the family and look up the Scripture in the Bible. Pray together, thanking the Lord for that particular aspect of the crucifixion and resurrection. (See next page.)

9. Plan and serve an Easter brunch and invite family, friends, and neighbors.

• Decorations or setting the mood—Place Easter lilies, baskets of tulips, wooden crosses, or spring bouquets around the house. Concentrate on the symbols of the Christian Easter.

• Table setting and centerpiece—Use a pink tablecloth with a white or ecru lace cover, allowing the pink to show through. If a lace cover is unavailable, white or ecru place mats can be used with contrasting pastel-colored napkins. Lay a spring flower across each napkin, or encircle it with a flower ring. At each place setting put a silver or white porcelain eggcup filled with a pastel-colored candle to be lit at the beginning of the meal. For a centerpiece, set an oblong mirror in the center of the table. Place a silver candelabra or silver candlesticks with tall pink or other pastel-colored candles on the mirror. At the base of the candlesticks arrange fresh-cut spring flowers or rings of fresh flowers. Set at each end of the mirror a figurine of Christian orientation (see your local Christian bookstore for ideas and selections).

Message (Front)	Scripture (Back)	Items
1—Jesus rode into Jerusalem on a donkey. The people waved palm branches.	Matthew 21:1–11	Piece of palm branch
2—Mary poured expensive perfume on Jesus' head.	John 12:2–8	Small perfume sample or cloth with perfume
3—Jesus shared the Last Supper with His disciples.	Matthew 26:17–19	Chex cereal
4—Judas betrayed Jesus for 30 pieces of silver.	Matthew 27:3	3 dimes
5—Jesus carried His own cross.	John 19:17	Popsicle stick cut and glued in a cross form
6—Soldiers placed a crown of thorns on Jesus' head.	John 19:2	Small thorny branch
7—Soldiers parted Jesus' garments and cast lots for His coat.	John 19:23	Swatch of burlap and a nail
8—Jesus was nailed to a cross and pierced in His side.	John 19:18,37; John 20:25–29	A nail
9—They gave Jesus vinegar mixed with gall on a sponge to drink.	Matthew 27:34	A small sponge
10—Spices to prepare Jesus for burial.	John 19:40	7 or 8 whole cloves
11—The stone covering Jesus' tomb was rolled away.	John 20:1	A small rock
12—The napkin around Jesus' head was lying separately from His linen clothes. He was not there. He has risen!	John 20:6,7	A scrap of linen-type fabric

Easter Brunch

Ruby Breakfast Juice or *Orange Juice*
Turkey Sausage
Oven-Baked Spinach Mushroom Frittata
Tangerine Flowers or *Mixed Fruit Bowl*
Jam-Filled Scones
Strawberry Coconut Surprise Muffins
Herb Tea

Ruby Red Breakfast Juice

A tasty alternative to orange juice! If the specific brands given in this recipe cannot be located, look for other brands in supermarkets and health-food stores with similar quality of ingredients (as listed in the note below).

Amount: As desired (allow 1 cup or 8 ounces per serving)

Chill and blend together:
2 parts Smuckers Cranberry Juice
1 part Nice 'n Natural Ambrosia Fruit Juice Blend or Hansen's Natural Pineapple-Coconut Juice

Note: These juices are available in many supermarkets. Smuckers Cranberry Juice is made with white grape juice, cranberry juice concentrate, apple juice concentrate, and no sugar. Nice 'n Natural Ambrosia Fruit Juice Blend contains pineapple, orange, and coconut juices with no refined sugars added. No refined sugars are added to Hansen's Pineapple-Coconut Juice.

Orange Juice

If you have access to an economical supply of fresh oranges, make quick work of juicing them with an electric juice squeezer. Plan on the following:

5 pounds oranges per 6 servings (approximately 8 ounces each) (1 4.5-ounce medium orange yields about ⅓ cup juice)

If juice is squeezed in advance, cover tightly and store in a dark container in the refrigerator to minimize vitamin C loss.

To prepare frozen orange juice concentrate, plan on the following amount:

One 12-ounce can orange juice concentrate per 6 servings (1 12-ounce can yields 48 ounces—6 8-ounce glasses)

Turkey Sausage

A tasty alternative to bacon and pork sausage, ground turkey sausage contains ¼ the fat of pork sausage and less than ½ the calories, and ⅕ the fat of bacon with less than ⅓ the calories. Many guests cannot believe they are eating turkey when they are served this recipe!

Amount: 12 patties (serves 6)

   1. Mix together thoroughly with a fork:

1 pound ground turkey
1 teaspoon salt
½ teaspoon nutmeg
½ teaspoon sage
½ teaspoon thyme
⅛ teaspoon cayenne pepper

   2. Shape into 12 small patties. Fry in ungreased skillet or bake at 350° for 10 to 15 minutes in shallow pan until done. Do not overcook or patties will become tough. Oven baking produces juicier patties and is easier when feeding a crowd.

Oven-Baked Spinach Mushroom Frittata

We have turned our Spinach Mushroom Omelette for two into a baked frittata that is easy to make for a crowd. There's no flipping or turning of eggs—just blend all and bake.

Amount: 6 to 8 servings

   1. Steam, drain, and chop spinach; sauté onions and mushrooms in butter until barely tender:

1 head spinach
2 tablespoons melted butter
1 cup sliced fresh mushrooms
2 green onions, chopped

   2. Combine remaining ingredients in order given. Stir in the vegetables and pour into well-buttered 9″ × 13″ pan:

6 large eggs, beaten
6 tablespoons water or milk
¼ teaspoon salt
8 ounces cream cheese, crumbled into small pieces

   3. Bake at 350° for 35 minutes or until a knife comes clean out of center. Serve as desired with avocado wedges, salsa.

Tangerine Flowers

Plan for a colorful fruit garnish on the holiday brunch plate. If the tangerine season has not quite extended into early spring, try this garnish idea as a springboard for your imagination and use another fruit.

1. Score skins of tangerines with sharp knife into six equal wedges around outside of tangerines.

2. Peel the skin petals back ⅔ of the way, leaving intact at the base of tangerines.

3. Carefully loosen center of tangerine and separate sections inside the skin, leaving them intact at the base. Fan them out slightly.

4. Garnish center of tangerine with 1 or 2 slices of kiwi, a parsley sprig, mint leaf, or tangerine leaf.

Mixed Fruit Bowl

Serve a bowl of two, three, or more fresh fruits to go on top of waffles or alongside them. The following are some of our favorite combinations, but only the season need limit your selection. A single fresh fruit, chopped or sliced, is also delicious. You can also top the fruit with whipped cream.

Amount: Allow ½ cup per serving

strawberries, peaches, blueberries
peaches, pineapple
nectarines, pineapple
nectarines, blueberries
peaches, blackberries

If desired sprinkle fruit lightly with crystalline fructose or sugar.

Whipped Cream

Amount: 2 cups (serves 6, ⅓ cup each)

1. In electric mixer on high speed whip for about 30 seconds:

½ pint whipping or heavy cream

2. Add gradually, continuing to whip until thickened:

2 tablespoons mild-flavored honey or crystalline fructose
   (health-food store)

Jam-Filled Scones

Easy-to-make, yummy-to-eat tender morsels! Bake before the frittata.

Amount: 12 to 15 scones (serves 6)

1. Blend together:

2 cups whole-wheat pastry flour (health-food store)
¼ cup crystalline fructose (health-food store)
½ teaspoon cinnamon
½ teaspoon baking powder (low-sodium baking powder from health-food store preferred)
½ teaspoon baking soda
½ teaspoon salt

2. With two table knives or a pastry blender cut butter into dry ingredients until size of small peas:

¼ cup butter

3. Blend in to make a firm dough; knead 8 strokes:

⅔ cup buttermilk

4. Pat dough to ¾" thick. Dip a 2" cookie cutter or rim of glass in flour and cut 2" biscuits out of the dough.
5. Place biscuits on ungreased cookie sheet and let stand 10 minutes; brush with cream or egg yolk for a shiny surface, if desired.
6. Bake at 400° for 12 to 15 minutes.
7. Heat in microwave for about 1 minute:

½ cup jam or preserves

8. Gently slice baked scones in half. Spread bottom halves with about 1½ teaspoons jam; top with other halves and serve.

Strawberry Coconut Surprise Muffins

A delightful breakfast, dessert, or snack muffin. Best served warm.

Amount: 10 medium muffins

1. Spray muffin pan with no-stick cooking spray (Olive Oil Pam Spray preferred).
2. Blend together and let stand for 30 minutes:

1 cup buttermilk
1 cup uncooked rolled oats

3. Blend thoroughly into oat mixture:

1 egg
¼ cup honey or crystalline fructose (health-food store)
¾ cup shredded coconut, unsweetened (health-food store)

4. Blend dry ingredients together in separate bowl:

1 cup whole wheat pastry flour (health-food store)
1½ teaspoons baking powder (low-sodium baking powder from
    health-food store preferred)
½ teaspoon baking soda
½ teaspoon salt

5. Blend dry ingredients into liquid ingredients just until mixed. Do not overmix.
6. Fill muffin cups about half full. Place in center of each:

1 scant teaspoon strawberry preserves

7. Cover preserves on each muffin with dab of remaining dough.
8. Bake at 400° for 20 minutes. Cool 2 minutes or longer (until muffins come out of pan easily).

Herb Tea

With the rich flavors of the menu, serve complementary mild hot drinks of regular and decaffeinated coffee, and spiced herb teas. Purchase 3 or 4 choices of herb teas that are individually packaged in colorful wrappers. Put a pot of piping-hot water on the table with a tray or bowl of herb tea bags, allowing guests to choose and prepare their own. Provide honey, cream, and lemon wedges.

Family Sunrise Service

Ahead of Time

• Choose a special, quiet place from which the sunrise can be seen.

• Prepare a simple carry-along breakfast of boiled eggs, rolls, juice, etc. (If you like, each person's breakfast could be packed in a colorful Easter basket. Surprises could be hidden in the bottom of each basket.)

• Find and mark the Easter story in the Bible.

• Choose one or two songs the whole family can sing about the risen Lord, or take along a cassette player and taped music the family can sing along with.

• The week before Easter, read from a Bible story book or from the Bible the events leading up to the resurrection (Matthew 26 and 27) and discuss them.

• The night before Easter, talk about how the disciples must have felt on the Saturday night before the resurrection; how Jesus' mother must have felt; what Mary Magdalene and those who had known Jesus were feeling.

Our children are like jewels, to be polished by us and given to the Lord.

Easter Morning

• Rise early enough to give the family time to get to your special place just before the sun comes up.

• Wear clothes that can be gotten into quickly (you can get ready for church later). Take warm jackets and blankets.

• Spread a blanket to sit on, then read together about the women going to Jesus' tomb and what they experienced.

• As the sun comes peeping over the horizon, sing or play a victorious song. Then thank God with your eyes wide open for the resurrection and what it means to your family.

• Celebrate by sharing the simple breakfast you have brought with you.

Symbols of Easter

Many times we enjoy the symbols of a special day without really understanding their significance. Easter symbols are especially rich in meaning. Before Easter, discuss as a family the meanings of these symbols we so much enjoy.

• *Spring.* Easter and spring belong together. What a wonderful time to celebrate newness of life and the resurrection when all nature is "rising again."

• *Baby bunnies, chicks, birds.* All newly born creatures remind us of the new birth we have in Christ. Because of Easter, we can become "new creatures" in Him.

• *The green, yellow, pink, and lavender colors of springtime.* These are perfect symbols of Easter. The earth bursts forth into color with the proclamation, "Life wins!" Green also stands for new life, and lavender, the color of royalty, reminds us that Jesus is King of kings and Lord of lords.

• *New clothes.* A new outfit symbolizes the putting away of winter—the time when it seems all nature hides "in the tomb"—and the dressing up of the earth in the lovely new clothes of spring. We, too, because of Christ bursting from the tomb, are "clothed in newness of life."

• *Eggs.* Eggs, of course, are the epitome of promised life—life sealed away for a time before new life literally bursts forth! Eggs also symbolize in Jewish tradition a freewill offering—the giving of more than is demanded. Jesus is God's freewill offering. God gives us far beyond what we deserve or even dare to ask. Jesus is the gift not only of life, but of eternal life.[2]

"Jesus Is Risen"

Try writing messages on the eggs with crayons before dyeing as a reminder of the real meaning of Easter. Examples of messages are:
• Jesus Is Love
• Jesus Loves You
• Praise God
• Love—Forever
• Jesus Died for You
• Born Again
• He Is Risen
• For God So Loved the World

- Love Changes Things
- Hallelujah
- Lord of Lords

Climax the day and evening by renting one of the great classic Easter films on video. Check with your local video rental store on availability.

Easter Sunday Night Dinner

One of my dearest young lady friends, Marita Littauer Noon, describes in her book *Homemade Memories* a wonderful Easter Sunday dinner.[3] She shares recipes that her family has used for many years. Her menu is as follows:

Traditional Easter Sunday Dinner

Easter Ham (or *Turkey* or *Roast Beef*)
Candied Carrots
Rice Pilaf
Lemon Meringue Pie

Marita includes a ham recipe her mother made regularly for Easter and other occasions. It is a basic ham studded with cloves and basted throughout the cooking time with a brown sugar and mustard glaze. With this dinner, a vegetable with a sweet touch is appropriate. The candied carrots come from her grandmother's collection of fine recipes. They are sweet, fresh, and give a nice color to the Easter dinner plate. With the glazed ham and candied carrots, the starch should be light, so a buttery rice pilaf fits the meal perfectly. To top off this colorful menu, Marita suggests lemon meringue pie (one of my Bob's favorites). The yellow color fits in with the Easter scheme, and the fluffy meringue adds to the lightness of the meal.

This is a meal you will want more often than once a year. Since everything involved in making this festive feast is available all year long, why wait for Easter? Celebrate our risen Lord anytime. Christ is risen, indeed!

Timetable

3 hours before serving:
Score the ham.
Prepare the glaze.

2¹/₂ hours before serving:
Place ham in the oven.
Prepare the Lemon Meringue Pie.

2 hours before serving:
Take a rest!

35 minutes before serving:
Prepare the Rice Pilaf.

15 minutes before serving:
Prepare the carrots.

Shopping List

Stock Items

brown sugar
cornstarch
dried minced onion flakes
pepper
eggs
bacon fat

sugar
dried parsley flakes
salt
chicken bouillon cubes
butter
prepared mustard

Special purchases
¹/₂ ham, butt portion
12 medium carrots
3 lemons
vermicelli
white rice (Blue Rose type)
one 9-inch piecrust

Easter Ham(optional)

Preheat oven to 325°.

¹/₂ fully cooked ham, butt portion (usually 6–8 pounds)
whole cloves

½ cup brown sugar
½ cup prepared mustard
3 tablespoons melted bacon fat

Score the fatty portion of the ham to create a diamond-shaped pattern with the diamonds about 1 inch across. Place a clove, pointed side down, into the fat of each diamond shape. Place the ham, fat side facing up, in a roasting pan.

In a small bowl combine the brown sugar, mustard, and bacon fat. Brush the ham with the glaze, coating the fat and the meaty sides lightly with glaze. (There will be quite a bit of glaze left.) Place the ham in the oven and cook 2 to 2½ hours. Brush the ham with more glaze every half hour or until there is no more glaze.

If you are serving a larger crowd and are using a whole ham, score the fatty covering just as for the half ham, double the glaze, and cook 12 to 15 minutes per pound.

Candied Carrots

12 medium carrots
2 tablespoons butter
2 tablespoons brown sugar

Trim and peel or clean the carrots. Slice them into ⅓-inch-thick slices and place the sliced carrots in the top portion of a microwave vegetable steamer. Place a couple of tablespoons of water in the bottom of the steamer, add the top portion, and cover. Cook on high in the microwave for 8 minutes or until carrots reach the desired tenderness. Pour the water out of the bottom portion. Empty the cooked carrots into the bottom portion. Add the butter and brown sugar. Replace the cover and shake the steamer until the carrots are fully covered with the butter and brown sugar. Serve.

Rice Pilaf

An Armenian friend from Fresno, California, first introduced me to rice pilaf. I loved it so much I asked her to show me how to make it. I have since lost her real recipe, but I think she would be happy with my adaptation.

8 tablespoons butter

2 coils of dry, uncooked vermicelli (a fine, spaghetti-like pasta that comes in a coil which slightly resembles a bird's nest. There are several coils per package.)

2 cups white rice (not the quick-cooking kind)

4 cups water

2 chicken bouillon cubes

1 tablespoon dried parsley

1 tablespoon minced onion flakes

1 teaspoon salt

freshly ground pepper

Using a large saucepan, melt the butter over medium heat. Break the coils of vermicelli into little pieces and add them to the melted butter. Cook until the vermicelli has a nice golden color, stirring frequently (about 5 minutes). Add the rice and stir until the rice is nicely coated with butter (about 2 minutes). Add the remaining ingredients and stir to blend. Reduce the heat to low. Cover the pan and cook over low heat until all the liquid is absorbed (about 25 minutes). Stir a couple of times throughout the cooking process. Fluff the rice with a fork before serving.

Lemon Meringue Pie

Amount: one 8-slice pie

Preheat oven to 350°

Filling:

1½ cups sugar

7 tablespoons cornstarch

a dash of salt

1½ cups water

3 beaten egg yolks

grated peel of 1 lemon

2 tablespoons butter

½ cup lemon juice

Using a medium saucepan, combine the sugar, cornstarch, and salt. Stir well, to the point that the cornstarch is completely mixed in with the sugar. Stir in the water. Bring the mixture to a boil over medium heat and cook until the mixture thickens and is translucent, stirring continuously.

Remove the pan from the heat and stir a small amount (about 1 tablespoon) of the sugar mixture into the egg yolks. Pour all of the egg-yolk mixture into the sugar mixture. Return the pan to the heat and bring to a boil, stirring continuously. Once the mixture comes to a boil, remove it from the heat. Stir in the butter. Once the butter has melted and blended, stir in the lemon peel. Set the mixture aside to cool. Stir it occasionally to prevent a film from forming on the top.

Meringue:

4 egg whites
1 teaspoon lemon juice
6 tablespoons sugar

Using an electric mixer, beat the egg whites and the lemon juice together until soft peaks form. Continue beating and add the sugar, 1 tablespoon at a time, until all the sugar has dissolved and the egg whites form stiff peaks.

Pour the lemon filling into the piecrust. Top the filling with the egg-white mixture. Spread the egg whites to the edge of the pastry. Using a spoon, create peaks and valleys in the meringue.

Bake 12 to 15 minutes at 350° or until the meringue is golden brown. (If you are cooking the pie at the same time as the ham, turn up the oven temperature for the 15 minutes needed to brown the meringue, then return it to 325°.) Allow the pie to cool before serving. Cut into 8 pieces and serve.

Marita's Piecrust

Amount: 2 single piecrusts

2 cups regular flour (I use unbleached, although any regular flour will work fine.)
1 teaspoon salt
¾ cup Butter Flavor Crisco (use only Butter Flavor Crisco—very important)
¼ cup water

In a large bowl, combine the flour and salt. Using a pastry blender, mix in the Butter Flavor Crisco until the particles are pea-sized and the mixture looks like coarse oatmeal. Sprinkle the mixture with the water and toss with a fork to combine. Using your hands, reach into the bowl and press the mixture into a ball.

Don't worry if there are little bits that don't mix in. Be careful to handle the dough as little as possible. It is not like bread dough where you must knead it frequently—overhandling makes a piecrust tough.

Use a pastry cloth on the counter and a pastry sleeve on the rolling pin. These are important items for a perfect crust. Sprinkle flour on the pastry cloth and roll the rolling pin in the flour to coat the pastry sleeve.

Once the dough is in a ball, break the ball in half and shape it into another ball. On the pastry cloth, press the ball down until it looks like a thick pancake. Roll the dough with strokes from the center out using the rolling pin. Once the dough is at least 1 inch larger than the edge of the pie plate, stop rolling. Place the pie plate on top of the dough, facedown. Cut the edge of the dough about 2 fingers' width from the edge of the pie plate. Remove the edge pieces. Leave the pie plate on the dough and fold the edges of the pastry cloth over the pie plate. With your hand, reach under the pastry cloth so your hand is in the center of the crust and flip the whole thing over. Peel off the pastry cloth.

Your crust should now be perfectly centered on the pie plate. If it is not, adjust it. Fold under the edges that are hanging over the rim of the pie plate; crimp them to make a pretty edge. To crimp, lightly pinch the edge with both hands. With one thumb and forefinger press the dough inward and with the other thumb and forefinger press out. Continue this technique all around the crust.

Repeat the previous steps for the second crust.

If you are only using one crust, wrap the other tightly in plastic wrap or place in a large zippered storage bag and freeze. The crust will last nicely for several weeks. To bake an empty piecrust, prick it all over with a fork and bake it in a 425° oven 10 to 15 minutes, until golden brown. (Do not bake the crust first if you are using it for an apple pie.)

Kids' Helps

Easter Ham: Older children can stick the cloves into the diamond-
    pattern cuts you have made in the ham. A younger child can mix

the ingredients for the glaze and brush the ham with the glaze before it goes into the oven.

Candied Carrots: Once the carrots are cooked, a child can shake the microwave steamer to coat the carrots with the sugar and butter.

Rice Pilaf: Have a child stir the vermicelli until it is lightly browned. Add the rice and have the child continue stirring while you add the remaining ingredients.

Lemon Meringue Pie: Once all the dry ingredients are in the saucepan, let a child stir them until they are fully blended. Let the child continue stirring while you add the water and the mixture cooks. After you have mixed a small amount of the sugar mixture into the egg yolks, let the child stir while you pour all of the egg yolks into the saucepan and continue to stir while the mixture comes to a boil.

This recipe involves a lot of stirring, so several children may need to take turns. They are apt to need lots of encouragement at this point. Let them drop in the butter pieces while you stir the mixture to blend in the butter.

For the meringue, once you have separated the eggs, let the children take turns beating the egg whites using the electric beater. Once the egg whites have formed soft peaks, add the sugar and continue to beat the egg whites to form stiff peaks.[4]

Mother's Day

Honor your father and your mother, that your days may be prolonged
in the land which the LORD your GOD gives you.

—*Exodus 20:12*

When Observed: Second Sunday in May

Earliest Observance in United States: May 10, 1908; Grafton,
West Virginia

The honoring of mothers can be traced back centuries before
the birth of Christ. But today's second-Sunday-in-May holiday,
commercialized with candy and carnations, was conceived in
America.

The ancient mother goddess Cybele had been the center of an
ancient Greek cult continued by the Romans as the festival of
Hilaria. Later, as Christianity spread, the early church fathers developed ceremonies for the veneration of the Virgin Mary, as well
as reverence for the "Mother Church."

In England on the fourth Sunday of Lent, people might visit the
"Mother Church" of their baptism. Later, young men and women,
working as apprentices and servants, would be given Mid-Lent (or
"Mothering") Sunday to bring to their mothers a kind of rich fruit
cake (similia). More recently, children in the East End of London

would bring nosegays (small bouquets) of violets and primroses to their mothers on Mothering Sunday, after getting the flowers blessed at church.

Amazingly, in Yugoslavia, on one Sunday in December the children will *tie up* Mother till she promises to provide sweets and goodies. (The week before this the parents tie up the children till they promise to be good; the Sunday after the children tie up mother is Dad's turn. A quaint prelude to Christmas . . . .)

The first Mother's Day observance was a church service held in Grafton, West Virginia, on May 10, 1908, to honor motherhood and pay homage to Mrs. Anna Reese Jarvis. Her daughter, Anna M. Jarvis, was instrumental in establishing this day to honor mothers in general, but also to honor her own mother.

The carnation, which has become so traditional and familiar on Mother's Day, was part of this first service. This was one of Mrs. Jarvis's favorite flowers.

By 1911 every state in the Union had adopted its own day for the observance of Mother's Day. On May 9, 1914, a resolution providing that the second Sunday in May be designated Mother's Day was issued by President Woodrow Wilson.

Today, Mother's Day is a popular occasion, warm and joyful in spirit. Flowers and gifts are often the order of the day. Greetings are designed to be sent not only to one's own mother but also to grandmothers, aunts, mothers of wives and sweethearts, and to anyone who merits the accolades of motherhood.

> *You are the mother I received the day I wed your son; and I just want to thank you, Mom, for all the things you've done. You've given me a gracious man with whom I share my life; you are his lovely mother, and I his thankful wife.*—A Thankful Wife

When I think of motherhood, I'm reminded of one great mother of the eighteenth century, Sarah Edwards, whose vital interest in her children's development had a lasting impact. Married to the famous clergyman and theologian Jonathan Edwards, she was the mother of 11 children. At the same time, Sarah maintained a vital and intensely loving marriage.

Writing about the Edwards family, author Elizabeth Dodds says straightforwardly, "The way children turn out is always a reflection on their mother."

Dodds refers to a study done by A.E. Winship in 1900 in which he lists some of the accomplishments of the 1400 Edwards family descendants he located. The Edwards family produced:

   13 college presidents
   65 professors
  100 lawyers and a dean of a law school
   30 judges
   66 physicians and a dean of a medical school
   80 holders of public office
    3 United States senators
    3 state governors
    1 vice president of the United States
    1 controller of the United States Treasury

Winship believed that "much of the capacity and talent, intensity and character of the more than 1,400 of the Edwards family is due to Mrs. Edwards."

How did Sarah Edwards do it? A deeply devout Christian woman, Sarah emerges from the pages of Dodds's book as a firm, patient mother who treated her children with courtesy and love. Samuel Hopkins, a contemporary who spent time in the Edwards' household, said Sarah was able to guide her children without angry words or blows. Unlike many mothers today, Sarah had only to speak once and her children obeyed her.

"In their manners they were uncommonly respectful to their parents. When their parents came into the room, they all rose instinctively from their seats and never resumed them until their parents were seated." These children who were so well-treated by their parents in turn loved and respected them as well as each other.

> *Who ran to help me when I fell,*
> *And would some pretty story tell,*
> *Or kiss the place to make it well?*
> *My mother—Jane Taylor.*

In the management of her busy colonial home, Sarah puts her modern counterparts to shame. We, who have only to press a button to start our many machines, can hardly imagine the sheer physical labor required of the colonial housewife. Sarah had many hard tasks: to see that the candles and clothes were made, the food prepared, the garden planted, the fire stoked, and guests fed and comfortably housed. Contiguously, she taught her children to work and deal with life.

Dodds also portrays Sarah as a keen observer of human nature:

> [She] carefully observed the first appearance of resentment and ill will in her young children, toward any person, whatever, and did not connive at it . . . but was careful to show her displeasure and suppress it to the utmost; yet not by angry, wrathful words, which often provoke children to wrath. . . . Her system of discipline was begun at a very early age and it was her rule to resist the first, as well as every subsequent exhibition of temper or disobedience in the child . . . wisely reflecting that until a child will obey his parents, he will never be brought to obey God.

As a disciplinarian, Sarah clearly defined her boundaries and tolerated no misbehavior from her children. The result was a household that emanated love and harmony.

As Elizabeth Dodds makes abundantly clear in her book, a mother is not merely rearing her one generation of children. She is also affecting future generations for good or ill. All the love, nurture, education, and character-building that spring from Mother's work influence those sons and daughters. The results show up in the children's accomplishments, attitudes toward life, and parenting capacity. For example, one of Sarah Edwards's grandsons, Timothy Dwight, president of Yale (echoing Lincoln), said, "All that I am and all that I shall be, I owe to my mother."

As one ponders this praise, the question arises: Are we women unhappy in our mothering role because we make too little, rather than too much, of that role? Do we see what we have to give our children as minor rather than major, and consequently send them into the world without a healthy core identity and strong spiritual values?

Women like to make sacrifices in one
big piece, to give God something grand.
*   But we can't.*
Our lives are a mosaic of

> *little things, like putting*
> *a rose in a vase on the table.*
> *Sometimes we don't see how much*
> *those things mean.*
>
> —Ingrid Trobisch

It was the great investment of time that mothers like Sarah Edwards and Susanna Wesley made in the lives of their children that garnered each such high praise. One can't teach a child to read in an hour or stretch a child's mind in a few days.

Have we as mothers unwisely left our children's education to school and church, believing that we can fill in around the edges? And would we feel better about ourselves if we were more actively involved in teaching our children? I think so.

A thread runs throughout the whole of life: Only as we invest much will the yield be great. Our children are growing up in a rough, tough world, and they need us to invest a lot of time and energy in their lives. Only then will they—and we—experience significant gain.[1]

Wow! What a mother! I could feel guilty if I compared myself to Sarah Edwards. But I know this: I did the best I knew how to do. Perfect mom? No, not by a long shot. I learned a lot along the way, and I'm still learning. Being open to God's Word and His promises are all the tools I need to be the mother into which God is molding me.

> *God made woman from man's rib—not from his head to top him,*
> *nor from his feet to be walked upon, but from his side to be his*
> *partner in life, from under his arm to be protected by him, and near*
> *his heart to be loved by him.*

The following acrostic is what *Mother* means to me:

M • *Makes Time for Daily Prayer to God*

Matthew 6:33 (KJV) says, "Seek ye first the kingdom of God, and his righteousness; and all these things shall be added unto you." This verse establishes my first priority as a mother: setting aside time each day for prayer.

The prayer basket I made for myself contains my Bible, a pen, a box of tissue, stationery, a few silk flowers in a small jar, and my prayer notebook.

My prayer notebook is a three-ring binder with prayer request sheets, tabs labeled Monday through Sunday, and sheets for sermon notes. (See sample at end of chapter.)

I organized this to give me "more hours in my day" while also spending quality time with my Lord and praying for all the needs of family and friends.

For each day of the week, I've delegated several topics for which to pray. (See sample topic page at end of chapter.) Example: *Monday*—home organization, family. I have a page for each immediate member of the family—Bob, Brad, Craig, Jenny, etc. For each grandchild, I've drawn their handprint on a page and made a heart in the middle. On Monday when I pray for them, I place my hand on theirs, and our hearts beat together as I give the Lord my requests. *Tuesday*—illnesses (my Auntie Phyllis who broke her hip; Brooke, who has M.S.). *Wednesday*—our church pastor and staff people. *Thursday*—self, personal finances. *Friday*—our country, city, state, president. *Saturday*—missionaries at home and abroad. *Sunday*—sermon notes (this is where I record and outline the sermon and any church prayer requests. Later, these requests can be integrated into the proper tab section. Scriptures can be recorded for future reference. See end of chapter for sample page).

My prayer basket goes with me wherever I spend time in prayer: in the backyard under a tree in the summer; by a lake or stream; by the fireplace in the winter with a cup of tea; in an office, bedroom, or perhaps in the bathroom where I know I can be alone. My prayer basket has all the tools I need to "seek first the kingdom of God."

O • *Open to the Lord*

I want to have a heart like Jesus. Psalm 139 (NIV) says it all:

O LORD, you have searched me
    and you know me.
You know when I sit and when I rise;
    you perceive my thoughts from afar.
You discern my going out and my lying down;

you are familiar with all my ways.
Before a word is on my tongue
  you know it completely, O LORD.

You hem me in—behind and before;
  you have laid your hand upon me.
Such knowledge is too wonderful for me,
  too lofty for me to attain. . . .
For you created my inmost being;
  you knit me together in my mother's womb.
I praise you because I am fearfully
    and wonderfully made;
  your works are wonderful,
  I know that full well.
My frame was not hidden from you
  when I was made in the secret place.
When I was woven together in the depths of the earth,
  your eyes saw my unformed body.
All the days ordained for me
  were written in your book
  before one of them came to be. . . .
Search me, O God, and know my heart;
  test me and know my anxious thoughts.
See if there is any offensive way in me,
  and lead me in the way everlasting.

After reading this passage of Scripture, I am amazed that God knows me so intimately. He alone is familiar with all my characteristics, which have become a part of me through my parents and grandparents.

He knows and understands my personality and human behavior more than anyone else. He is fair and just to me. Since He has known me from conception, He knows what's best for me (even when I refuse to listen to God's words).

Through this love He never rejects or despises me. Instead, He begins to create in me a new heart, like His own loving likeness. Through this change of heart, He works on my mind, emotions, and behavior. God understands why I think and feel as I do from day to day as I interface with others around me.

In all these complex activities, He does not condemn me; instead, He comes to change and redirect my values, pride, decisions, thoughts, purpose, and service.

Because of this knowing of me, I want to be open to Him on this very special Mother's Day. I recommit this day to Him and I want to be open to everything He has for me as a wife, mother, and woman.

T • *Trusts in the Lord*

Our hope as mothers is found through spending time with our Bibles to study God's Word. If you aren't already in the habit of having daily devotions with your Lord, why not begin today? Go to your local Christian bookstore and request help in finding just the right devotional for you. It takes 21 days to begin a new habit. Try this for these next 21 days, and you will be amazed at what new zeal you have for life. Set your alarm 10 to 15 minutes earlier each morning. Rise, read, and shine. Trust God to perform a new work in you.

H • *Has Healing in Relationships Through Christ*

A mother seeks forgiveness in relationships so that a healing process can take place. If mother and daughter or mother and son have out-of-order relationships, these must be brought to the surface and bathed in prayer for a complete cleansing.

When my mother went home to be with the Lord at 78 years of age, she left me with two very beautiful gifts: her belief in the Messiah and the knowledge that one day we will be in glory together, and the memory of all the loving times of sweet fellowship we had together.

Guilt feelings can eat you up inside—so clean out the wounds and pour the healing ointment of love and forgiveness inside.

E • *Enriched by the Lord*

Teach us, O Lord, as mothers, so we can teach others. Titus 2:4 says that the older women are to teach the younger women to love their husbands and to be makers of a home. That's what Sarah Edwards did as a mother. As mothers, we can take life experiences and teach them to others and, through it all, we, too, will learn.

Think of someone today whom you can disciple. It might be a son, daughter, a sister, a neighbor, or someone at work. There is always someone you know who knows less about Jesus than you do. Open your eyes and ears and become aware of those all around you who need their lives enriched. Reach out and touch them.

R • *Reaches up to God*

I'm choosing to make God the Lord of my life. This is the best choice I can make; it gives me a purpose and a peace during the tough times.

Let's exchange our earthly desires for heavenly desires. We'll be more alive in death than in life when we do, and our beautiful years of motherhood will never really end if our hearts can daily reach up to God in love and prayer.

I received this letter from our son, Brad, one year on Mother's Day when he was away at college. It is the best gift I ever received from him, and yet it cost only his time.

Thank You, God,

For pretending not to notice that one of Your angels is missing and for guiding her to me. You must have known how much I would need her, so You turned Your head for a minute and allowed her to slip away to me. Sometimes I wonder what special name You had for her. I call her "Mother."

To think of not having her with me is unbearable. I don't know what I would have done without her all these years. She has loved me without reservation—whether I deserved to be loved or not. Willingly and happily, she has fed me, clothed me, taught me, encouraged me, inspired me, and with her own special brand of gentleness reprimanded me. A bit of heaven's own blue, her eyes reflect hope and love for You and her family. She has tried to instill that love in us.

She's not the least bit afraid of work. With her constant scrubbing, polishing, painting, and fixing she has made every house we've lived in, a beautiful home. When I'm confused, she sets me straight. She knows what matters and what doesn't. What to hold on to and what to let go. You have given her an endless supply of love. She gives it away freely yet never seems to run low. Even before I am aware I have a need, she is making plans and working to supply it.

You gave her great patience. She is the best listener I have met. With understanding and determination she always seems to turn a calamity into some kind of success. She urges me to carry my own load in life but is always close by if I stumble under the burden. She hurts when I hurt. She cries when I cry. And she will not be happy until she has seen a smile on my face once more. Although she has taught me to pray, she has never ceased to invoke Your richest blessings upon me.

Thank the other angels for filling in for her while she is away. I know it hasn't been easy. Her shoes would be hard to fill. She has to be one of Your greatest miracles, God, and I want to thank You for lending my mother to me.

You can imagine the tears I shed when I read this. Proverbs 31:28 flashed before me: "Her children arise and call her blessed." Again, God, You are so good when You give me confirmation that all of those endless days and nights of serving my family were recognized by my son, Brad.

These words of encouragement and thanksgiving were all that I needed on this day. Again I say, "It's worth it all, even when it seems like no one notices or cares."

Gifts of Self

None of the following gift suggestions costs anything, yet each is one-of-a-kind and bound to please because it's a gift of yourself. Every day should be a day in which we honor all members of our family, but this day should be extra-special for Mom. These may be the greatest gifts Mom will ever receive.

What the heart gives away is never gone. . . . It is kept in the hearts of others—Robin St. John.

1. *The gift of a compliment*—Perhaps you could make a list of the qualities you admire in your mother: her sense of humor, her survival instinct, her ability to live without impossible expectations. You might praise her cooking, her patience, her intelligence, or her sensitivity.

2. *A gift of thanks*—It's strange how much we take from others and how little we return. A thank you is a simple act—not always

expected and therefore very valuable. Thank Mom for having endured your childhood years that required her constant attention,
for the thousands of meals she cooked, for the tons of laundry she
did—and most important, for just being there.

3. *A gift of affection*—How about a warm embrace, a kiss on
the cheek, a moment of hand-holding? All of us need affection no
matter what our age or how much we protest that it's not our style.

4. *A gift of listening*—Everyone has known the frustration of
wanting to be heard and finding that no one is interested in listening. One of the most valuable things we can do for each other is to
be a good listener.

5. *The gift of a note*—Write your mother a personal note, un-
abashedly sentimental, full of loving thoughts—which may become
her newest family treasure. If you find yourself lacking the right
words, a simple "Mom, I love you" can say so much.

6. *A gift of forgiveness*—People are not perfect. Those closest
to us often seem the least so. We owe them the same forgiveness
we expect for our own imperfections. An act of forgiveness can
start things anew and reunite us as nothing else can.

7. *A gift of laughter*—If so far none of these gifts interest you,
try a gift of laughter. Nothing unites like laughter. Perhaps you can
take Mom out for a day of doing all the crazy things she used to
love—just a day for accumulating new, joyous memories between
mother and daughter or son.

8. *A gift of time*—Make an appointment with Mom so that just
the two of you can spend some time together. You don't need to
plan any activity—just share time. Tell Mom how special she is to
you.

9. *A gift of relaxation*—Tell Mom that she has the evening off.
You're going to prepare supper, set the table, clean off the table,
and wash the dishes. Mom can go read the paper or a good book,
listen to music, watch television, or just take a nap. It's Mom's
night off.

Special Gifts

1. *Special treats*—If you still live at home with Mom, talk with
Dad and plan some special activities for her. Really make a big
deal out of this day.

• Treat Mom with breakfast in bed.

• A delightful gift if you are low on money is to give Mom a cute coupon stating that it is good for clearing off the dinner dishes for a week, doing the ironing for a week, or loading the dishwasher (or washing the dishes by hand) for a week.

• Plan a picnic for Mom.

• Use an oven mitt as the wrapping for a small gift.

• Take Mom to church and share with her how much you appreciate her giving you Christian training. Include a big thank you for the prayers she shares with you each night, etc. After church you can go out for brunch (if you do, be sure to make reservations at least two weeks in advance) or prepare a brunch for her at home. Mom will love the special treatment.

2. *Long-distance appreciation*—If you no longer live at home, you still need to take time to honor Mom.

• Take or send her flowers.

• Take or send her a card.

• If out of town, start early and give her a telephone call. (Since the telephone lines are extremely busy on Mother's Day, you might try to make that call the day before.)

• If you are close enough to see her on this day, set up a time to be with her.

3. *A gift of perfume*—As a family, go to the local mall and purchase some wonderful fragrances, shampoos, and bath oils and put them in a cute basket. Wrap it with cello paper, tie a bow around the top of the wrap, and include a sweet note to Mom. Take the opportunity to make Mom feel very special on this, her day.

4. *Helping hands*—

• Dad or the older children can trace Mother's hands on a folded piece of $8^1/2'' \times 11''$ paper. Draw one hand on the front of the paper and one on the back; the inside of the folded paper will be used for a message.

• Let the smaller children color the hand picture, drawing in Mother's watch, ring, fingernails, etc.

• Help the children compose a note to put inside the paper that expresses appreciation for the loving things that are done by Mother: fixing dinner, ironing, putting on Band-Aids, making repairs on the house, fixing toys, reading stories, etc.

• At the bottom of the page write, "We appreciate you, Mom."

• Give the card to Mom on Mother's Day.

5. *Family card—*

• Fold a large sheet (12″ × 18″) of construction paper in half.

• Decorate the front of the card with a greeting or picture. If Mom has a hobby, perhaps a picture related to that activity would be appropriate.

• Glue a snapshot of each person in the family inside the card and have each person write a message of love under his/her picture. These messages might all begin with "You're special to me because . . ." or "One reason I love you so is . . ." or "I remember when you . . ."

6. *Promise coupons*—Make a coupon book for Mom filled with promises of helpful things you will do. These coupons may be used any time in the next year.

• Cut blank index cards into equal coupon-size pieces.

• On each card write, "This coupon good for . . ." and name one chore or favor:

doing dinner dishes one time

cleaning the garage

raking leaves for one hour

one car wash

one hour of window-washing

one hour of playing Scrabble (or other game of Mom's choice)

one week of feeding the dog

• Save one coupon piece to make an attractive cover for the coupon book.

• Staple all the coupons together and put the coupon book in an envelope.

• Tie a ribbon around the envelope and lay it on Mom's plate before dinner or breakfast.[2]

In many homes, Mother's Day can become most traumatic. Usually the family members want to do something special for Mom, so they try to cook a special breakfast or take Mom out to a restaurant. Many dads are unfamiliar with the kitchen and food preparation, and it can become a disaster where Mom has to intervene and even clean up after her own breakfast.

Keep your ideals high enough to inspire you, and low enough to encourage you.

A trip to a restaurant can be even worse. The wait can be long, the meal hurried, and the service lacking. Many years ago, we as a family said, "No more going out to restaurants on Mother's Day. Let's find a meal that Dad and the children can make—a no-loser menu."

With the help of Sue Gregg and Marita Littauer, I include in this chapter two such menus found in Marita's book *Homemade Memories*.

The first menu features a single surprise breakfast that can be prepared before church, and the second menu includes a lovely dinner for later in the day.

To start out, Dad needs to review the shopping list for both menus to see which items are already in the house and which ones he will need to purchase before Mother's Day.

On the big day, Dad and the children need to get up an hour early. Encourage Mom to stay in bed and get some extra rest, read the Sunday newspaper, and have a cup of fresh-brewed tea or coffee.

Have the children set the table with the prettiest dishes. Cut a few fresh flowers or sprigs of ivy, light some candles, spray a little fragrance in the air, and call Mom to the table when all is ready (serving Mom her breakfast would be fine, too).

Follow the complete timetable for preparing the breakfast, or after church begin preparation of the dinner. If you follow the timetable and directions closely, Mom and the family will have a stress-free Mother's Day.

Mother's Day Breakfast

Freshly Squeezed
Orange Juice
Turkey Sausages
Homemade Apple Pancakes
Serves 4

Timetable

30 minutes before serving:

Set the table.
Put the butter and syrup on the table.

25 minutes before serving:

Start cooking the sausages according to package instructions
or make the sausages yourself with recipe on page 348.

20 minutes before serving:

Turn on the stove to heat the skillet or griddle.
Prepare the pancake batter.

10 minutes before serving:

Cook the pancakes.

5 minutes before serving:

Pour the freshly squeezed orange juice into the glasses.
Place the glasses on the table.

Shopping List

Stock Items

butter	baking powder
sugar	salt
baking soda	Pam (or other nonstick
flour	spray)

Special Purchases

freshly squeezed orange juice (This can be purchased already
squeezed, or you can buy the oranges and squeeze them yourself. Be sure to allow extra time if you are going to squeeze
them yourself.)
sausages—turkey (ones with less fat)
2 apples
1 quart buttermilk

Homemade Apple Pancakes

Serves 4

2 eggs	3 tablespoons butter, melted
1½ cups buttermilk	1½ cups flour

1 tablespoon sugar
1½ teaspoons baking powder
½ teaspoon baking soda

½ teaspoon salt
1 tablespoon lemon juice
2 apples, peeled and grated

Heat skillet or griddle over medium heat.

Use a medium-size bowl and an electric beater (if you have one; if not, use the old-fashioned way of a fork or a wire whisk), and beat the eggs until they are well blended. Add the buttermilk, melted butter, flour, sugar, baking powder, baking soda, salt, and lemon juice and beat until the mixture is smooth. Add the grated apple and stir with a spoon until the batter is well blended.

Test the skillet or griddle to check that it is hot enough. Keep your hand high enough above the hot surface to avoid burning yourself (about five inches) and flick a few drops of water off your fingertips onto the hot surface. If the drops bounce and "dance" on the hot surface, it is hot enough to cook the pancakes. Spray the griddle surface with a light coat of Pam (or any other brand of nonstick spray).

Using a large spoon or a ¼-cup measure, pour the batter onto the hot surface. As each pancake spreads, it should be about 4 inches in diameter. Be careful to keep the pancakes from touching one another. When the pancakes are puffy and full of bubbles, they are ready to be turned over. Once they are turned, cook them for a few more minutes or until they are nicely browned. Serve the pancakes with sausages on individual plates with butter and syrup passed separately.

Kids' Helps

Let the children set the table using the nicest tableware. If they know how to crack eggs, let them crack the eggs and empty them into the bowl. They can beat the eggs and then beat the batter after the remaining ingredients have been added. With your guidance, the other children can turn the sausages to keep them from browning too heavily on one side, and they can pour the pancake batter onto the cooking surface. When the pancakes are ready to be turned over, the children can flip them over.[3]

Whipped Butter

Whipped butter has 20 fewer calories per tablespoon than butter, and is easier to spread. It is simple to make your own with soft butter. The added air whipped into the butter will increase the volume by about one-third. Serve in an attractive bowl or on a small round plate.

Amount: about ⅔ cup

1. Bring to room temperature until very soft, or soften in microwave on simmer for about 35 seconds:

1 cube (½ cup) butter

2. Place butter in small deep mixing bowl and whip vigorously with a wire whisk until light and creamy.

Maple Syrup

Real or pure maple syrup comes from real maple trees! It is admittedly expensive, but a little goes a long way, especially when served with fruit topping alternatives. Allow a serving of 2 tablespoons to ¼ cup per person. A pint will serve 12 to 16 people.[4]

Mother's Day Dinner

Lemon Garlic Roast Chicken
with Potatoes
Table Queen Squash
with Green Peas
Blueberry Buckle
Serves 4

Timetable

2 hours before serving:
Prepare the chicken so it's ready for the oven.
Peel the potatoes.
Prepare the squash so it's ready for the oven.

1½ hours before serving:

Preheat the oven to 350°.

1¼ hours before serving:

Place the chicken in preheated oven.
Prepare the Blueberry Buckle.

1 hour before serving:

Place the squash and the Blueberry Buckle in the oven.
Baste the chicken and potatoes.

30 minutes before serving:

Set the table.
Baste the chicken and potatoes again.

10 minutes before serving:

Cook the peas according to package directions.
Baste the chicken and potatoes a third time.
Remove the Blueberry Buckle from the oven and set aside.

To serve:

Using poultry shears, cut the chicken into fourths. Usually children enjoy the leg portions, while Mom and Dad prefer the larger breast portions. Place the chicken pieces and potatoes on each plate and top with some pan drippings. Turn the squash right-side up so they are like little bowls. Place a squash on each plate and fill the squash bowl with peas. Add a slice of butter to each.

Shopping List

Stock Items

whole garlic
pepper
butter
sugar
flour
milk

salt
olive oil
shortening
egg
baking powder
cinnamon

Special Purchases

3-pound whole chicken
2 table queen or acorn squash

1 10-ounce package frozen peas
1 basket fresh blueberries (1 pint)
1 lemon

Lemon Garlic Roast Chicken with Potatoes

Preheat oven to 350°.

3-pound whole chicken
1 lemon
8 cloves garlic (cloves are the small sections of the whole
   garlic)
salt
pepper
2 tablespoons olive oil
2 tablespoons butter
8 small red potatoes, peeled

Remove the inside pieces from the chicken and rinse it under cold water. Pat the chicken dry with paper towels. Cut the lemon into 8 wedge-shaped pieces. Rub the cut lemons over the outside of the chicken. Combine the lemon pieces with the garlic cloves and place inside the chicken. Generously sprinkle the outside of the chicken with salt and pepper. Place the chicken in a roasting pan and place the potatoes around it. In a small bowl, melt the butter in the microwave (about one minute) and add the olive oil to the butter. Pour the combined butter and olive oil over the chicken and potatoes. Place the chicken in the preheated oven and cook for one hour and 15 minutes, basting frequently with the pan juices. Basting is easiest if you use a bulb baster. Simply insert the tip of the baster into the juices, squeeze the bulb, and release it to draw the juices into the baster. Hold the tip over the chicken and squeeze the bulb again to release the juices over the chicken. The roasting pan may need to be tipped to allow the juices to collect in one corner before using the bulb baster.

Table Queen Squash with Green Peas

2 table queen or acorn squash
1 10-ounce package of frozen peas
butter

Cut the squash in half. Using a spoon, scrape the inside of the squash to remove the seeds. Using a pan large enough to hold the four halves, place the squash open-side down in the pan. Add enough water to cover the bottom of the pan with about ¼ inch of water. Place the squash in the oven and cook for 1 hour. Ten minutes before serving, prepare the peas according to the package instructions. When both the squash and peas are cooked, place each squash, cut-side up, on a plate, fill the bowl of the squash with peas, and top the peas with a slice of butter.

Blueberry Buckle

Preheat oven to 350°.

½ cup shortening, such as Crisco
½ cup sugar
1 egg
2 cups flour
2½ teaspoons baking powder
¼ teaspoon salt
½ cup milk
1 basket fresh blueberries (1 pint)

Topping:

½ cup sugar
½ cup flour
½ teaspoon cinnamon
¼ cup butter

In a large bowl, beat the egg with an electric beater. Add the shortening and sugar and beat well until they are blended and have a creamy texture.

In a small bowl, using a pastry blender, combine the remaining sugar, flour, cinnamon, and butter until they have a crumbly consistency and are well blended. Sprinkle the topping over the blueberries and bake in a preheated 350° oven for 45 to 50 minutes. Let cool slightly before serving. To serve the Blueberry Buckle, cut it into squares and serve on plates. It may be topped with ice cream, if desired.

Kids' Helps

Children can rub the outside of the chicken with the lemons and stuff the inside of the chicken with the combined lemon and garlic. They can sprinkle the chicken with salt and pepper and pour the butter and olive oil over the chicken and potatoes. Older children can peel the potatoes.

Squash are a little bit difficult to work with, but older children can scrape the seeds from the inside of the squash. Once the squash and peas are cooked, children can spoon the peas into the squash bowls.

If they know how, let the children crack the egg for the Blueberry Buckle and empty it into the bowl. They can beat the egg and continue doing all the beating for this recipe. And they can sift the dry ingredients. Let them sprinkle the blueberries over the batter and then sprinkle the topping over the blueberries.[5]

⤚Prayer Requests⤘

Date	Request	Scripture	Update/Answer	Date

∽Sermon Notes ∾

Date: Speaker:

Title:

Text:

✑Notes✑

Subject:

Father's Day

Grandchildren are the crown of old men, and the glory of sons is their
fathers.
—*Proverbs 17:6*

When Observed: Third Sunday in June
Earliest Observance: July 5, 1908; Fairmont, West Virginia

Father's Day is a relatively new holiday in America. It is a day
set aside to honor our living fathers; however, many people do use
this day to remember those fathers who have died. Instilling both
Mother's Day and Father's Day traditions in youngsters is often the
role of the "other" parent. Even though the honoree is not the
parent of the parent, children first need to see an example of lov-
ing-kindness of parents toward each other in order to imitate it.

A number of persons have unconnectedly figured in the growth
of Father's Day. The earliest mention we have of a day for fathers is
July 5, 1908, when a Father's Day service was held in the Central
Church of Fairmont, West Virginia, by Dr. Robert T. Webb at the
request of Charles Clayton.

In 1912 at the suggestion of the Reverend J. H. Berringer, pastor
of the Irvington Methodist Church, the people of Vancouver,

386

Washington, conducted a Father's Day celebration. They believed it to be the first such ceremony.

Another important figure in the "honor fathers" movement was Harry C. Meek, past president of the Uptown Lions Club of Chicago, who said that he first had the idea for Father's Day in 1915. He began to suggest it in speeches before various Lions Clubs, and the notion took hold. Members set the date for Father's Day on the third Sunday in June—the Sunday nearest Meek's birthday. The Lions crowned him "Originator of Father's Day."

Father's Day most influential promoter was Mrs. John Bruce Dodd of Spokane, Washington. Her father, William Jackson Smart, had accomplished the amazing task of raising six children alone after his wife died at an early age. Mrs. Dodd wanted to honor him for this unselfish feat.

President Calvin Coolidge recommended the national observance of this day in 1924, though President Woodrow Wilson had officially approved the idea as early as 1916.

The rose is the official Father's Day flower—a white rose for remembrance, and a red rose as a tribute to a living father.

In 1972 the day finally was established permanently when President Richard Nixon signed a Congressional resolution. His action eliminated the need for an annual designation and put Father's Day on the same continuing basis as Mother's Day. Giving gifts has become a natural part of the occasion, and greetings for fathers, grandfathers, uncles, brothers, sons, other relatives, and friends are widely sent. Father's Day has become another happy occasion for family dinners and gatherings. This day is an occasion to establish more intimate relations between fathers and their children, and to impress upon fathers the full measure of their responsibilities and obligations.

> *I am a family man and I think that family relationships are the purest, cleanest, whitest sand of all*—Bob Benson.

What a Father!

Last year I had some extra time at the Dallas-Fort Worth airport waiting for a connecting flight to California, so I decided to purchase a Sunday morning newspaper. While looking through the classified section, I came upon a tribute to a father from a bereaved daughter. As I read this, I commented to myself, "What a father!"

> This is an open letter to my father which I desire to share with those of you who did not have the privilege of knowing him. J. T. Yates was a war hero of the European Campaign fighting in the Battle of the Bulge. He landed in France on D Day and fought his way across Europe not only as a medic but also as a combat soldier putting his life in jeopardy constantly while trying to save others. He was a man of his own will and lived his life according to his own beliefs and convictions.

> But he was also a hero to me as only a daughter can know and love a father. He was my teacher, whether it be from learning how to survive in the wilderness, to catching a fish, planting a garden, writing a school drama, making science projects, or caring for animals. Unknowingly he strengthened my admiration and appreciation of him. He was my place of safety whenever he held me and cradled me in his big, strong arms. Daddy always tried to give me joy. We made every circus that came to town, walked in every parade, rode in every rodeo, played ball in the park, or took many walks through the zoo. Even at home, he would play games with me, tell me stories, or camp out in the yard. Every year at Christmas, Santa would come to our house and sit me on his knee, yet not one time did I ever suspect that was my dad. They tried to tell me one time that Santa Claus was make-believe but I knew better. I was fortunate to live with him every day for many years. Daddy always let me shine and have all the glory while he stood behind in the shadows. That was his way.

> The world may not have considered him a religious man, but he did believe in God. If he couldn't go to church with me, he always provided me a way. Daddy respected men of the clergy and on Sunday afternoons there was always plenty of food for any of God's people that would visit. His love for children was unsurpassed by no one, and there were lots of wiener roasts and entertainment for all youth. That foundation stayed with me and carried me through the next forty years of my life.

> Daddy was a man of strong convictions. He never turned his head and pretended not to see. He would stand up to any man, stand up for any woman, stand with any child, and stand behind

his beliefs. Daddy was always there when I needed him, and his love was always enough.

If he could, he would have spared me pain, cried my tears to protect all sadness from my eyes. If he could, he would have walked with me everywhere I went to make sure I never chose a wrong turn that might bring me harm or defeat. If he could, he would have shielded my innocence from time, but the time he gave me really wasn't his. He could only watch me grow so he could love me for who I was. But Daddy was a wise man. He knew love couldn't be captured or protected. So he let me take my chances, he gave me my freedom, he let me fight my own battles. I made mistakes but he was always patient.

He was the most generous and giving man of his own self I have ever known, and I hope the legacy he left me will be passed to multitudes of generations.

Thank you, Daddy, for all the times and the nurturing you have given me. The memories will always be in my mind. Now that there will be no more rainbows for us, I will have to let you go, Daddy, but I will always love you. Your daughter, Paula Yates Sugg.[1]

This dad certainly reflected great qualities of character—ones that we all could model for our own lives. Our heavenly Father far exceeds the goodness of our earthly fathers. Unfortunately, many of us may not have had a pleasant experience with our earthly fathers. In some cases, this has prevented us from being able to trust an unseen heavenly Father.

We certainly have the opportunity to experience the abundance of God if we are willing to ask Him. Your Father in heaven is waiting to give you good gifts if you will ask Him.

Today would be a great time to begin trusting your heavenly Father for all your needs. Go to Him in prayer with thanksgiving, adoration, confession, and petition. He is able to meet you where you are.

Spiritual Teachings

Fathers play such a large part in developing the awareness of God's authority. Children learn this by watching their father's everyday words and actions. I have always tried to model in front of (and behind) our children the respect that we give fatherhood. Some of those traits are: love, respect, submission, godliness, speaking at all times with admiration, honoring his position of leadership, and respecting his decision-making responsibilities.

> *If I am an effective father, it is because I have deliberately set as one of my priorities the creation of conditions in my home that will stimulate my children to grow to their full potential*—Gordon MacDonald.

Exodus 20:12 states, "Honor your father and your mother." I've attempted to teach our children at home to give proper honor to their father. We have honored him through obeying him in his position of authority; being careful of language used in the home; and by showing kindness, politeness, discipline, etc. As our children have grown older, they are more in love with their father than ever before. Not because he is always right or sinless, but because children receive blessings by honoring their father. This is not easy at all times, because obedience often isn't easy. We make a deliberate choice to honor our fathers. As mothers, we can be of great assistance to our children and family developing the harmony that is necessary to build a warm and loving family.

I have learned over the years to make every day of the year Father's Day. Fathers play such a large part in making a family successful in the sight of God. Except for God Himself, our next priority is the father of our home. We need to make a deliberate effort each day to find time for the men of our homes. If we don't have a husband or father at home because of some circumstance, we might want to adopt another man to help out in these times. If the children's real father is alive, we need to encourage them to take time on this day to say, "I love you."

A Letter from Our Son

We cherish a letter we received from our son, Brad, while he was in college. It reads:

Dear Mom and Dad,
    As I sit here studying for my finals, I need to take a break and write you a note to express how much I appreciate the time you

have given me over the years. I would not be here studying in college if it wasn't for you giving your time to encourage me along the way. As I think about the money you invested in my college education, I am aware of the many hours that Dad had to work to provide this time in my life.

I remember back to elementary school when you both always attended my school's open house, many times after you had already spent a long day at work. You both took me down to the City Council one evening when I received the award for being the best athlete at East Bluff Park. I also remember you taking me down to the fire station to teach me a lesson after I set fire to my mattress while foolishly playing with matches. I know you weren't happy about that, but you were there.

Remember all the swim meets, and the Little League games that lasted until 10:00 P.M.? It got cold and foggy some evenings, but you were both there cheering me on until the last out.

In junior high you were there with your time and car to take my first girlfriends to school functions. There were more ball games, tournaments, long trips, cold bleachers, sweaty gyms—but you were there.

You really gave a lot of time in high school—attending ball games, transporting me to school and church activities, and sponsoring my youth groups. You were even at the car wash when only a few students showed up, washing and drying cars until you were so tired at day's end. Both of you attended booster club meetings after the football games to catch a glimpse of me on the films making a good catch or tackle.

College wasn't much easier on your schedule. You took time to write me, phone me, and visit me. Parents' weekends at the fraternity house were great with you there. My friends really liked that you were with me. They think you're great! Many of their parents didn't find the time to visit on those weekends. I guess they were too busy, but you weren't. Thanks for all that. You were there.

Yes, Mom and Dad, you always gave me time, but the best thing I remember you giving me was your prayers and godly advice. Many times I could have gone astray, but with each opportunity I looked around and you were there. I will always appreciate the time you gave me. I only hope that one day I will be able to return the favor by giving my wife and children the time you so graciously gave me.

Well, it's time to get back to my marketing notes. I love you both very much.

Love,
Brad

Father's Day Ideas

1. *Designer Dad*—A crayon drawing of Dad translates into an exclusive, designer T-shirt. The artist should use dark colors and a heavy hand with the crayons on a separate piece of paper. DAD must be written in mirror image to appear correctly on the shirt. Place the crayon drawing on a white T-shirt and iron at cotton temperature.

2. *Cards*—Help the children design and make their own Father's Day cards. Dads love homemade cards with handwritten messages. They all say, "I love you."

Never help a child with a task at which he feels he can succeed—M. Montessori.

3. *Just Daddy and Me*—At church you might want to plan a brunch just for the fathers and their daughters. Have each share introductions, good food (physical as well as spiritual), and a fun time with each other. It is their special date on this special day.

4. *Kidnap Dad*—Create a plan for kidnapping your dad from work to have lunch together. (You might need some help from Mom to pull this off.)

5. *Popcorn Pop*—Fix and eat together a bowl of popcorn. (Try it without TV—try conversation instead.)

6. *Gifts of Self*—None of the following gift suggestions costs anything, yet each is one-of-a-kind and bound to please because it's a gift of yourself. Every day should be a day in which we honor all members of our family, but this day should be special just for Father.

• *The gift of a compliment*—Perhaps you could make a list of the qualities you admire in your father: his sense of humor; his survival instinct; his ability to live without impossible expectations; his provision for the family; his godly attributes; his warmth, affection, kindness, and unselfishness.

• *A gift of affection*—How about a warm embrace, a kiss on the cheek, a moment to hold his hand? All of us need affection, no matter what our age or how much we protest that it's not our style.

• *A gift of forgiveness*—People are not perfect. Those closest to us often seem the least so. We owe them the same forgiveness we expect for our own imperfections. An act of forgiveness can start things anew and reunite us as nothing else can.

• *A gift of thanks*—Tell Dad how much you appreciate all that he does for the family. We know that there are days he doesn't feel like going to work but he does. He plays catch and chases our errant throws but never complains. He provides great trips at winter and summer time for our vacations. Gee, Dad, thanks, thanks, thanks!

• *A gift of listening*—Take Dad aside and have him share about his childhood and what were some of his memories, fears, goals, and aspirations. Let Dad just talk about himself, and you be the interested listener. This would be a great time to ask him those questions you always wanted to ask but didn't have the time.

• *A gift of laughter*—Have Dad tell you his best jokes; be prepared to have a few of your own ready. Here are a couple to get started:

Dad: Did you hear about the old lady who told knitting jokes?
Son: No, I haven't.
Dad: She was a real nitwit.

Dad: Did you hear about the thief who stole a calendar?
Daughter: What happened to him?
Dad: He got 12 months.

Dad: Did you hear about the horse who ate an electric wire instead of hay?
Son: That's shocking!
Dad: He went haywire.[2]

7. *Special treats*—If you live at home with Dad, talk with Mom and plan some special activities for him. Really make a big deal out of this day.

• Treat Dad to breakfast in bed.

• A delightful gift if you are low on money is to give Dad a cute coupon stating that it is good for one free washing of the family car, one free back rub, one shoe shine, or free time to read the newspaper with no interruptions.

• Plan a picnic for Dad.

• Take Dad out to brunch after church (be sure to make reservations first).

• Tell Dad he doesn't have to do any work on this special day.

8. *Long-distance appreciation*—If you no longer live at home, you still need to take time to honor Dad.

• Send him a hanging plant for the patio or a plant for his office.

• Give him a telephone call. (Since the telephone lines are extremely busy on Father's Day, you might try to make the call the day before.)

• Send two tickets for a sporting event, musical concert, or some other activity he would enjoy.

9. *Read Proverbs to me*—If you are a teenage boy, ask your father to read the book of Proverbs to you. There are 31 chapters, and you can read one each day. My Bob did this for our son when he was 15, and it provides a great time together for father and son (daughters can also be included).

> *Tis a happy thing to be a father unto many sons*
> —William Shakespeare.

10. *Gifts of special tools*—Many times Dad is in special need of some tools for his garage or automobile. Remember those times when he has said, "I sure wish I had _____, it would make my job so much easier." Those are cue words for a future gift list. Dads are practical in nature and really appreciate practical gifts. Take this opportunity to make Father feel very special on this, his day. The following acrostic is what FATHER means to me:

F • *Faithful Follower of Christ*

An honorable father is a faithful follower of Christ. In Matthew 11:30 (NIV) we read, "For my yoke is easy and my burden is light." If fathers follow Jesus, they will escape from the hard yoke of living by their own laws as they submit to the kindly yoke of Christ Jesus.

Only the man who follows the command of Jesus and lets His yoke rest upon him finds the Lord's burden easy, and under its gentle pressure receives the power to persevere in the right way. The commands of Jesus are hard for the disobedient, but for those who willingly submit, the yoke is easy and the burden is light. Jesus asks nothing of us without first giving us the strength to perform it. His commandments never destroy life; they strengthen and heal it. Our country desperately needs fathers to stand up and be counted. Our sons and daughters need to know who their heavenly and earthly fathers are.

A • *Allows God to Make Him All He Can Be*

One of the hardest lessons about trusting God in our lives is to allow God to be the change agent in dads. Far too often the family wants to be the change agent. Dads need to have space to come to God on His terms and in His timing. It's amazing what happens to Dad when we let God deal with him on His schedule and not ours. In order to do this, we have to concentrate on the positives and let God deal with the negatives.

> *When I was a boy of fourteen my father was so ignorant I could hardly stand to have him around. But when I got to be twenty-one, I was astonished at how much the old man had learned*—Mark Twain.

Become an encourager and cheerleader for Dad. Be excited about his successes. Comfort him when the contract isn't signed, when the deal falls through, and when sickness slows him down. A dad needs permission to fail on occasion. Where else but in the home can he do that? Continue to pray for Dad each day. Encourage the children to be a part of that prayer for Dad's specific needs.

T • *Thanks God for All His Blessings*

In Deuteronomy 8:18 (NIV) we read, "But remember the LORD your God, for it is he who gives you the ability to produce wealth," and Proverbs 28:20 (NIV) states, "A faithful man will be richly blessed."

I never understood the obstacles my father faced until I became one.
I love my father's memory now more than ever—Author unknown.

The beginning of greatness is for a man to realize where everything comes from: God. A godly man will count his blessings, be content where he is, and thank God for all the blessings bestowed upon him. On this special day, we pray that our fathers will have thankful hearts.

H • *Holiness in His Approach to Life*

Peter writes in 1 Peter 1:15, "But just as he who called you is holy, so be holy in all you do." What an awesome command! It isn't a common goal for men of the nineties. If fathers today prayed to be holy, strove to be holy, and were holy, we would have a revival like the world has never seen. We would see marriages healed, differences settled, welfare costs curtailed, and unity displayed in America. The cry is for men to be holy. Their love of God and of man cannot be just symbolic—it has to be completely real. It is not just a mental process, but the giving and commitment of themselves as men to God. As a family, be an encourager to fathers to step out in faith that their God can make them holy. Men can be holy in the nineties. Maybe not easily, but what is easy that has any real value?

E • *Expresses Love to Those Around Him*

When Jesus was asked by a young lawyer in Matthew 22:37,39 (NIV) to name the great commandment, Jesus responded, "Love the Lord your God with all your heart and with all your soul and with all your mind. . . . Love your neighbor as yourself." He stated that we should love God, love others, and love ourselves. If fathers could grasp this triangle of love, we would begin to see men of low self-esteem rise above destructive behavior and move into positions of leadership in their homes. This kind of love is a gift we give to others. We can't buy it. It is a decision we make on a daily basis that someone is valuable and special to us. What better day than this special day to tell Dad that he is special?

In our household we honor special people with a red memory plate that reads, "You Are Special Today." We serve their meal (breakfast, lunch, or dinner) on it, and during the meal each person around the table shares why our honored guest is so special to him or her. After we complete that cycle, we turn to our special guest and say, "Now tell us why you think you are special." At first this request is very threatening, but after a few moments the person usually comes up with a few statements that reveal why he thinks he is special.

Ask yourself why you are special and see how you would answer that question. Our ten-year-old grandson, Chad, gave us a special answer when he was asked to tell us why he is special. Chad replied, "I am special because I am a child of God." He had it absolutely right. We are special because of that eternal relationship with God—we are His children!

R • *Responds to God's Teachings in Scripture*

A father is a man who not only hears God's Word, but who also lets it penetrate into his heart and soul. We want men who will give testimony to what God means in their everyday lives: in marriage, as a father, with a neighbor, at the job, and at church. We desire fathers who are not afraid to be called by Jesus to stand up for His teachings in Scripture—not Sunday Christians, but men who want to live a consistent 24-hours-a-day and seven-days-a-week lifestyle.

A godly father can be trusted because he has endured the tests of the world and has been found true to Christ's calling—a simple man who believes what is revealed in the Holy Scriptures.

The Son of God says this: "I know your deeds, and your love and faith and service and perseverance" (Revelation 2:18,19).

If we had fathers like this, we could say that they reflect all that God intended when He created man in the garden. Our world needs this kind of man. If fathers reflect these attributes, their families, communities, and churches will raise them up as leaders and will call them blessed.

Recently in our local newspaper there appeared a reprint from a previous Ann Landers article dealing with Father's Day; it originally appeared in the *Danbury* (Connecticut) *News-Times*. I thought it had great wisdom for all of us on this day of celebration:

Father

4 Years: My daddy can do anything.

7 Years: My dad knows a lot, a whole lot.

8 Years: My father doesn't know quite everything.

12 Years: Oh, well, naturally Father doesn't know that either.

14 Years: Father? Hopelessly old-fashioned.

21 Years: Oh, that man is out of date. What did you expect?

25 Years: He knows a little bit about it, but not much.

30 Years: Maybe we ought to find out what Dad thinks.

35 Years: A little patience. Let's get Dad's assessment before we do anything.

50 Years: I wonder what Dad would have thought about that. He was pretty smart.

60 Years: My Dad knew absolutely everything.

65 Years: I'd give anything if Dad were here so I could talk this over with him. I really miss that man.

A Special Breakfast for Dad

Father's Day Breakfast

Turkey Sausage
Orange Juice
Crunchy Potato Casserole
Scrambled Eggs with
Easy Salsa (optional)
Toast or Breakfast Biscuits
Serves 6

For Turkey Sausage see recipe on page 348.
For Orange Juice see recipe on page 348.

Crunchy Potato Casserole

2 pounds frozen hash browns
1 stick melted margarine or butter

1 can cream of chicken soup
8 ounces sour cream
10 ounces grated sharp cheese
½ cup chopped onions
dash of salt and pepper
2 cups corn flakes

Mix the above ingredients together and put in a 9″ × 12″ casserole. Top with 2 cups corn flakes (crushed) and one stick melted butter or margarine. Bake uncovered at 375° for 45 minutes. This freezes well.

Scrambled Eggs

Amount: 2 eggs per serving

1. Add to shallow saucepan or frying pan over moderately low heat:

1½ teaspoons olive oil or butter

2. Whisk together thoroughly with a fork in a bowl (per serving):

2 eggs
1 tablespoon water or milk per egg
⅛ teaspoon salt (optional)

> *The liquid whisked into the egg will "stretch" the protein and make it more tender.*

3. Evenly distribute warmed oil or melted butter over surface of the pan and pour in the eggs.
4. When the eggs begin to set, push the cooked eggs to one side with edge of spatula to let uncooked eggs run underneath. You can also gently turn the eggs over, if you like, but don't stir the eggs. Stirring scrambled eggs breaks them up into unpleasantly textured small lumps and pieces.
5. Remove eggs from heat when just barely set on the top—even a bit undercooked. Do not let the eggs brown on the bottom.
6. Cover with a lid until ready to serve.

Quantity cooking tip: For 2 to 3 eggs I use an 8″ pan. If eggs are too shallow in the pan, they cook too fast; if too thick (over 1¼″ deep), they cook too slowly and require too much stirring. To scramble a large quantity, spray a baking pan with a nonstick spray, cover bottom of pan with melted butter or oil, add eggs, and bake in 350° oven. When they begin to cook around the outside edge, gently loosen the eggs and carefully move them. Continue moving the cooked eggs occasionally, until all are scrambled.

Easy Salsa (optional)

This takes the work out of salsa-making, yet provides the home-prepared touch, plus more substance in texture and bulk.

Amount: about 1¼ cups

Blend amounts as desired, to taste:
2 small (Roma size) fresh tomatoes, finely chopped
¼ small onion, finely chopped
2 tablespoons bottled salsa, to taste

Breakfast Biscuits[3]

Amount: 10 biscuits
Preheat oven to 425°.

1. In medium bowl, blend dry ingredients:
2 cups whole-wheat pastry flour or white flour
2½ teaspoons baking powder
½ teaspoon baking soda
½ teaspoon salt

2. Whisk together in a 2-cup measure or small bowl:
1 cup buttermilk
3 tablespoons oil (extra virgin olive oil preferred)

3. Stir liquid ingredients into dry ingredients just until mixed; beat 10 strokes.
4. Drop spoonfuls of dough on ungreased cookie sheet.

5. Bake at 425° for 12 to 15 minutes until lightly golden on the bottom.

A father is the head of a unit of people launched on an exploration of life and all the things God has placed in the world for us to enjoy—Gordon MacDonald.

Independence Day

And you shall know the truth, and the truth shall make you free.
—John 8:32

When Celebrated: Fourth of July
First Celebration: 1776

This is our grand national holiday—the glorious Fourth, when Americans manifest their patriotic enthusiasm in various ways.

The military marks the day by firing a salute of 13 guns and reading the Declaration of Independence. All over the country, church bells are rung in memory of the Liberty Bell that proclaimed independence. This most-famous bell was actually made in England, and around its rim are these prophetic words: "Proclaim liberty throughout the land unto all the inhabitants thereof."

The earliest celebration in 1776 was a very exciting and cheerful occasion. At last the colonies were independent from England. There was yelling and screaming, bonfires were lit, and people paraded and danced in the streets.

Ask not what your country can do you for you; ask what you can do for your country—John F. Kennedy.

The Fourth of July is still celebrated in much the same fashion: there are parades, dancing, and fireworks (some communities are placing certain restrictions due to possible fire dangers).

Since the Fourth of July falls in the summertime and the children are out of school, parents can take their families on outings in the park, in the country, or to the seashore.

This holiday commemorates the formal adoption of the Declaration of Independence by the Continental Congress in Philadelphia on July 4, 1776. Although the resolution for independence was passed by Congress on July 2 and most of the members did not sign the declaration until August 2, the Fourth of July has always been celebrated as the anniversary of national independence. The president of the Congress, John Hancock, did make it official with his signature on that date.

> *A good newspaper and Bible in every house, a good schoolhouse in every district, and a church in every neighborhood, all appreciated as they deserve, are the chief support of virtue, morality, civil liberty, and religion*—Ben Franklin.

As you and your family celebrate this day, you can elect to be an originator of traditions in your family, or you may elect to join in other people's traditions. Either way, it is a wonderful time of the year. Several ideas follow that might help you do something different this year.

Activities

1. *Backyard barbecue*—The theme for decorations is so easy: red, white, and blue. All the way from the invitations to the napkins you can carry through the patriotic colors of our flag. Be sure to send your invitations at least four weeks ahead of the event. People make plans early and need time to decide what they are going to do. Ask your family for suggestions on what the menu will be, what games will be played, and who should be on the guest list. The backyard barbecue can branch out to a park setting if the crowd gets too big. Big is fun for this kind of celebration.

> *Patriotism is your conviction that this country is superior to all other countries because you were born in it*—George Bernard Shaw.

2. *Games*—All kinds of games can be explored for this day. Ask the grandparents what kinds of games they or their parents used to play when they were young. These older and often-forgotten games are a delight. One such old game is called "pick-up sticks" or "Jack straws." Cut any number of sticks of wood $1/2'' \times 1/2'' \times 14''$ and paint them three different colors—red, white, and blue. Throw them in a basket or drop them on the ground in a pile. Ask the children to remove one stick at a time without moving the other sticks. You can make up rules depending on the ages of the children and have colorful prizes for the winners.

A very simple contest that requires only a baseball for equipment is to draw a circle three feet in diameter on the ground and see if anyone can stand at the edge, throw the ball straight up into the air, and have it land back in the circle.

3. *Sack races*—Go to your local grain store and purchase grain sacks (the number you will need depends upon the size of your group). Lay out a course that has a start and a finish line. Have each contestant stand in a sack and hop along the course. The length of the course can vary depending on the ages of participants.

4. *Three-legged race*—This is a similar activity to sack races. However, instead of using a grain bag, have two people stand side by side and tie their inside legs together. The contestants line up behind the starting line and at "Go" they run and hop their way to the finish line.

5. *Pop bottle fill*—You'll need pop bottles of the same size, a large bucket of water, and paper cups. Place the large bucket of water in the center of a circle of adults who are lying on their backs on the grass with their feet pointing away from the bucket of water and their heads about six feet from the water bucket. The adults, while lying down, place pop bottles on their foreheads. The children are given paper cups. The object is to have the children run to the bucket of water, fill their cups with water, hurry to their parent's pop bottle, and try to empty their cups into the bottle. As you can imagine, the adults will get soaked. Of course, the prize goes to the team that fills the pop bottle first.

6. *Egg toss*—This activity carries the anticipation that the next toss will cover someone with egg. You play with a partner. Have the partners line up facing each other (the distance apart depends upon the ages of the players). Young children will stand close to start out, and older children might be six to ten feet apart.

Give each team one raw egg in the shell. At the starter's command, the person holding the egg will toss the egg in an underhand motion to his partner to catch. If the egg breaks, the team is eliminated from the game. If not, the partners stay in the game. (If the egg hits the ground but does not break, the partners stay in the game.)

The starter will give directions for those remaining to step back one giant step. Again, the person makes an underhand toss of the egg. Those who have eggs intact will continue playing the game until one set of partners is left in the game with a good egg. You might want to suggest that the contestants remove their rings. Have some hand towels to clean up any messy egg splashes. You can also substitute water balloons for eggs.

7. *Running events*—These are always great fun for the children. They love to try to win. Be sure to divide the children into age groups so the competition will be fair.

8. *Wheelbarrow races*—Be sure not to have the races too long because the children may not have strong arm muscles. This game is played as a team. One partner holds the other's legs in the air by the ankles and follows behind him as he walks with his hands to the finish line. You might even want to have the partners reverse positions and come back to the start line.

Remember to have plenty of inexpensive prizes available for the winners. Be sure that all children get participant prizes. It's important that everyone leaves feeling that he or she was a winner.

9. *Parade*—Have a family parade. The children love it. Get pots and pans, tambourines, horns, and toy instruments. Small children can carry a flag or tie colored balloons onto strollers, wagons, and tricycles. Everyone could march around the neighborhood and ask others to join in the parade. For country folks, a hayride would be great fun, or decorate horses and have a parade. This is a nice time when small communities can rally together and have fun. A nice ending to the parade would be an ice-cream social or a hot-dog roast.

10. *Plant a tree*—Decide beforehand what kind of tree you want to plant. Where do you want to plant it—at home, at church, in a city park, or at school? If not planted at home, be sure to get permission from the appropriate personnel. Make sure you know how the tree will be taken care of.

This gives you a great opportunity to talk to your children about ecology. This could become a yearly tradition for your family.

After what I owe to God, nothing should be more dear or more sacred than the love and respect I owe to my country—De Thou.

11. *Make a patriotic cake*—Children love to get into the kitchen and bake. Decide the shape and decor for the cake. (Naturally, you will want to use red, white, and blue colors.) Go to your local party store and purchase flags, candles, stars, etc. for decorating the cake. Serve red punch with ice cubes tinted with blue food coloring. As you cut the cake, you might want one of the children to lead the group in saying the Pledge of Allegiance.

12. *Balloon walk*—Inflate a number of red, white, or blue balloons and draw a holiday design on each with a felt-tip pen. Divide the group into two or more equal-size teams. At the signal, each person must carry the balloon between his knees to the goal line and back. If the balloon breaks, he must come back for a new one and start over. The first team to finish is the winner. A large balloon for each team member would be an appropriate prize.

Variations: 1) Play this as an individual competition, using a stopwatch to time each competitor. The one with the shortest time is the winner. 2) Set up an obstacle course for players to walk through on their way to the goal line.

13. *Straw relay*—Cut two or more four-inch-high holiday shapes from construction paper. Divide the group into two or more equal teams. Give each player a drinking straw, and each team one of the paper shapes. One at a time the team members pick up the shape by sucking through the straw, then carry it to the goal line and back. If they drop it, they must start over. The first team to have all players complete the task successfully is the winner.

14. *Beanbag relay*—Make two or more holiday-shaped felt beanbags. Divide the group into two or more equal teams and have each team line up in separate lines with the players one behind the other. Give a beanbag to the first person. Have the team pass the beanbag to the last person in the line and back again. Before each round, the leader calls out the way in which the bag is to be passed: over the head, between the legs, down the right or left. If anyone passes the beanbag incorrectly, it goes back to the front of the line

and that team starts over. The first team to get its beanbag back to the first person in line is the winner.

15. *Paper bag pops*—Give each person a lunch-size paper bag and set out some crayons or felt-tip pens. Have participants decorate their bags appropriately for the holiday. When bags are completed, divide the group into relay teams. The object of the game is for each person at the front of the line to blow up his bag as he runs toward the end of his line. When he reaches the end of the line he is to pop it. If the sack doesn't pop the first time, he must keep trying until he is successful. The next person in each line repeats the action as soon as he hears the previous bag pop. Play continues until player number one is back at the front of the line.

16. *Spear the sweets*—Put holiday-colored jelly beans into two bowls that have been decorated with self-adhesive holiday seals. Divide the group into two equal relay teams and give each team one bowl. The teams line up and each person is given a round wooden toothpick. At the signal, the first person in each line spears a jelly bean with the toothpick and feeds it to the person next to him. He then passes the bowl to the second player who feeds one to the next person, and so on. The team to reach the end of the line first is the winner.

Fourth of July Picnic

Pasta Salad
Coleslaw and *Bean Salad*
Grilled Corn in Husks
Tomato and Red Onion Slices
with *Vinaigrette Dressing*
Hot Dogs and *Hamburgers*
Flag Cake
Three-Layer Chocolate Bars
Banana-Walnut Ice Cream
Fresh Lemonade

Pasta Salad

Amount: 8 servings
Preparation time: 15 minutes

1 pound thin spaghetti
1 8-ounce bottle Italian salad dressing
2¾-ounce jar Salad Supreme salad seasoning
2 chopped celery stalks
1 chopped green pepper
1 thinly sliced onion
1 pint cherry tomatoes
1 6-ounce can pitted ripe olives

1. Cook spaghetti according to package directions. Drain and rinse in cold water.
2. Combine spaghetti, salad dressing, and salad seasoning.
3. Add celery, green pepper, and onion.
4. Chill 3 to 4 hours (may do 3 to 4 days ahead).
5. Just before serving, add tomatoes and olives.

Coleslaw—"Easy to make for a crowd"

Amount: 8 to 10 servings
Preparation time: 20 minutes

1 grated cabbage head
6 grated carrots
1 finely chopped green pepper
1 minced green onion, optional
¼ cup chopped parsley
½ cup Miracle Whip salad dressing
2 tablespoons sugar
1 tablespoon dill weed
1½ teaspoons celery seed
1 tablespoon rice vinegar
salt to taste

Mix all ingredients. Refrigerate.

Bean Salad

Amount: 10 servings (2½ quarts)
Preparation time: 30 minutes
Marinating time: 6 to 8 hours (must do ahead)

Salad

  1 8-ounce can red kidney beans
  1 8-ounce can garbanzos
  1 8-ounce can green beans
  1 8-ounce can yellow wax beans
  1 diced, large green pepper
  2 sliced green onions
  1 4-ounce can sliced, black ripe olives
  2 tablespoons chopped pimiento

Dressing

  ¼ cup vegetable oil
  ¼ cup lemon juice
  ¼ cup honey
  1 tablespoon soy sauce
  1 teaspoon Spice Island salad seasoning

  1. Place dressing ingredients in glass jar and shake to mix.
  2. Drain all beans.
  3. Combine dressing with salad ingredients. Toss well.
  4. Marinate in refrigerator for 6 to 8 hours or overnight. Toss occasionally.

Vinaigrette Dressing

Amount: 12 to 15 servings
Preparation time: 45 minutes

  1 cup olive oil
  2 tablespoons lemon juice
  4 tablespoons vinegar
  2 tablespoons Dijon mustard
  1 minced garlic clove
  1 tablespoon chopped fresh basil
  1 tablespoon chopped fresh tarragon
  1 tablespoon chopped fresh oregano
  Season to taste

Combine above ingredients. Mix well.

Flag Cake—"Serve with pride"

Amount: 12 to 15 servings
Preparation time: 45 minutes

  1 white cake mix
  1 cup heavy cream
  1 tablespoon sugar
  1/2 teaspoon vanilla
  1/2 cup fresh blueberries
  2 cups sliced, fresh strawberries

  1. Mix and bake cake according to package directions in 9″ × 13″ baking dish.
  2. Place cake on attractive serving dish or platter.
  3. Beat cream until soft peaks form. Add sugar and vanilla.
  4. Spread whipped cream in an even layer over top of cake.
  5. Place 2 lines of blueberries at right angles in top left corner to form a 4-inch square. Fill square with additional lines of blueberries. Leave small amount of white cream showing between the berries.
  6. Use overlapping sliced strawberries to form horizontal red stripes from side to side on cake, allowing cream to show for white stripes.
  7. Refrigerate cake until serving time.

Three-Layer Chocolate Bars—"So good they're almost sinful"

Preparation time: 45 minutes
Baking time: 25 to 30 minutes

Crust

  1/2 cup butter
  2 ounces unsweetened chocolate
  1 cup sugar
  1 cup flour
  1 teaspoon baking powder
  1 teaspoon vanilla
  2 eggs
  1 cup chopped nuts

1. Melt the butter and chocolate.
2. Add remaining ingredients. Mix thoroughly.
3. Pour into greased 9″ × 13″ baking dish.

Filling

  1 8-ounce package softened cream cheese
½ cup sugar
2 tablespoons flour
¼ cup softened butter
1 egg
1 teaspoon vanilla
½ cup chopped nuts
1 6-ounce package semisweet chocolate chips

1. Combine and beat filling ingredients, except nuts and chocolate chips, until smooth (about 1 minute).
2. Stir nuts into filling. Pour over crust.
3. Sprinkle chocolate chips on top of filling.
4. Bake at 350° for 25 to 30 minutes.

Frosting

¼ cup butter
2 ounces unsweetened chocolate
2 ounces softened cream cheese
¼ cup milk
3 cups powdered sugar
1 teaspoon vanilla
2 cups miniature marshmallows

1. Melt butter and chocolate.
2. Add cream cheese and milk.
3. Stir in powdered sugar and vanilla.
4. Stir in marshmallows.

To Assemble

1. Frost while hot.
2. Cool and cut into bars.

Banana-Walnut Ice Cream—"Mmm—Good!"

Amount: 1 gallon
Preparation time: 10 minutes
Freezing time: 30 minutes

    4 cups sour cream
    4 cans sweetened condensed milk
    8 cups half-and-half (may use half milk)
    6 mashed or chopped bananas
    1 cup chopped walnuts

    1. Mix all ingredients.
    2. Process in ice-cream freezer.

Fresh Lemonade[1]

Amount: 1 cup
Preparation time: 15 minutes
Cooking time: 2 minutes

For each cup of water, use:
    3–4 tablespoons sugar
    1½ tablespoons lemon juice

    1. Boil water and sugar 2 minutes. Chill.
    2. Add lemon juice.

Invitation

The invitation is written in white ink on a red card outlined with blue-and-gold star stickers. A small American flag may be included.

A firecracker invitation is created by covering an empty tissue roll with red paper. Information is inside and attached to an 8-inch wick of heavy string with a tag that reads "Pull." Hand deliver.

Decorations or Setting the Mood

Line the entrance of your home with several American flags to greet guests with a patriotic spirit.

Clusters of red, white, and blue balloons with crepe paper streamers can decorate the party area.

Table Setting and Centerpiece

The buffet table is covered with a red or white tablecloth. Blue paper napkins are encircled with napkin rings made of white construction paper, affixed with a large gold star. Red and white paper plates and cups complete the table setting.

An "Uncle Sam" hat filled with red and white petunias makes a patriotic centerpiece. A small toy drum with one end removed may be used as a serving dish. Place small flags around the rim. The table can also be enhanced by a watermelon cannon.

Thanksgiving

Always give thanks for everything . . . in the name of our Lord Jesus Christ.

—Ephesians 5:20 TLB

When Observed: Fourth Thursday in November

Earliest Observance: 1621 in Plymouth, Massachusetts

The Pilgrims, who in 1621 observed our first Thanksgiving holiday in Plymouth, Massachusetts, were thankful for their harvest in the New World. They had suffered a perilous journey on the Mayflower, a dreadfully cold winter, and a large number of deaths. By most standards, the first harvest was very mediocre. Many of the first crops were failures. This first Thanksgiving lasted for three days and was celebrated with enthusiasm. The menu was extensive and the food abundant. The Indian braves had added five deer to the store of meat. The pilgrims had venison, duck, goose, seafood, eels, white bread, corn bread, leeks, watercress, and a variety of greens. Wild plums and dried berries were served for dessert. Although turkeys were plentiful, there is no record that they were eaten on this first Thanksgiving holiday.

The first Thanksgiving proclamation was made by Governor Bradford three years after the Pilgrims settled at Plymouth:

To all ye Pilgrims:

Inasmuch as the great Father has given us this year an abundant harvest of Indian corn, wheat, peas, beans, squashes, and garden vegetables, and has made the forests to abound with game and the sea with fish and clams, and inasmuch as he has protected us from the ravages of the savages, has spared us from pestilence and disease, has granted us freedom to worship God according to the dictates of our own conscience; now I, your magistrate, do proclaim that all ye Pilgrims, with your wives and ye little ones, do gather at ye meeting house, on ye hill, between the hours of 9 and 12 in the day time, on Thursday, November ye 29th, of the year of our Lord one thousand six-hundred and twenty-three, and the third year since ye Pilgrims landed on ye Pilgrim Rock, there to listen to ye pastor and render thanksgiving to ye Almighty God for all his blessings.

—William Bradford, Ye Governor of Ye Colony.

Records of subsequent Thanksgiving celebrations are rather sporadic. Many of the later colonies did not adopt this harvest celebration. The first national Thanksgiving proclamation was issued by George Washington in 1789. Mrs. Sarah Josepha Hale of Boston had a great deal of influence on the government toward having this day celebrated across the nation. In 1863 President Abraham Lincoln made a proclamation to establish Thanksgiving Day as a national holiday to be observed on the last Thursday of November. In 1941 Congress changed this to the fourth Thursday in November.

For the last 100 years in America, we have begun to develop some meaningful traditions to make this one of the most memorable of all our holidays. Thanksgiving is warm hearts, good food, family, and lots of conversation. However, some people don't have these kinds of memories.

I was talking with a woman at one of my seminars who had memories of absolutely nothing. Thanksgiving wasn't different from any other day. Today she creates memories, making them on purpose. "We talk about what we can do for others weeks before

Thanksgiving," she said. "The children become a part of special giving times."

Tis the season for kindling the fire of hospitality in the hall, the genial fire of charity in the heart—Washington Irving.

One Thanksgiving a family went to skid row in downtown Los Angeles and helped serve Thanksgiving dinner. They'll never forget that day. It was such a joy that the children suggested they do it again for Christmas.

One year Bob and I were doing a holiday seminar at a very alive church in the heart of a low economic area in El Monte, California. It was November 20, and the church was full. The ladies of the church were in a back room busily pulling food from shopping bags. We were so busy ourselves setting up tables and seminar props that we didn't really take notice of exactly what they were doing.

After the first half of my presentation and the refreshments, the ladies did a wonderful thing. Women came from that back room carrying the most beautiful Thanksgiving "love baskets" filled with the complete ingredients for a Thanksgiving dinner from fruit to turkey and pumpkin pies, 32 baskets in all. They then proceeded to hand them out to each single person there.

As I watched those people come forward to receive their baskets, I saw eyes filled with tears: single working parents, single college students, some people who obviously didn't have finances for such a meal. That church wanted to give and create a memory, and they sure did. Among the group was a young man who played the piano that day for the singing time. His wife had left him with three young children, and he was currently unemployed and living in a small rented apartment. When he went forward to receive his basket, he sobbed with joy. Bob and I were touched by the beauty of that day. We had so much and had taken so much for granted.

If you don't know of a needy family, find one. Call the Salvation Army or a local church and ask them how to get in touch with a needy family. Then decide ways you can help make a special memory for that family this holiday.

Since Thanksgiving preparation can take up such a large part of November, you might want to use one of our calendar pages (see sample at end of chapter) and jot down what needs to be done in little bits and pieces to make this a manageable time rather than a stressful one. Starting with the first week in November, delegate each day to accomplish some of these activities.

First Week in November

As we approach the first week in November, we can begin our holiday organization. Use the "First Week" form at the end of this chapter. Creating memories takes time, and organization for the holidays will give us the time we need.

To polish your silver, add one tablespoon of ammonia to your silver polish. You'll get a super shine, plus it prolongs the shine well into the new year. So do it early and enjoy beautiful silver for the holidays.

Toothpaste on a damp cloth is also good silver polish for the last-minute spoon you forgot that you want to put in the cranberry sauce dish.

Early in the month invite your guests for Thanksgiving dinner. A cheery phone invitation or a written invitation is always welcome.

Second Week in November

Use the "Second Week" form at the end of this chapter to plan this second week. Make up your Thanksgiving dinner menu at the same time you compile your marketing list. You can pick up the dry goods and staples for your meal now (stuffing mix, cranberry sauce, applesauce, water chestnuts, etc.). It's easier on the budget and makes shopping faster later. Check off items on your marketing list as you purchase them. Don't forget the parsley for garnishes. Parsley stays fresh for weeks if rinsed well and wrapped in a paper towel. Put it into a plastic storage bag, pressing the air out and sealing the sack tightly.

Plan your Thanksgiving table setting and centerpiece early. Check your silver pieces, plates, and serving dishes to be sure you have enough for the number of guests you are inviting.

Table decoration can be easy and creative. Take large apples and core out enough to hold a votive candle. Squeeze lemon juice around the cutout area and then insert the candle. The apples can be set in front of each person's place or down the center of the table with autumn leaves, pods, grapes, pears, corn, eggplant, and even squash and nuts. When the candles are lit, you'll have a beautiful harvest display. Plus, after Thanksgiving you can use the parts of the centerpiece for a fruit salad or soup.

If you don't have votive candles, use tall tapers or whatever you have available. (This idea can be used for Christmas with red and green apples.)

Here's an activity with a purpose: Take the children or grandchildren on a harvest walk and collect fall leaves of all sizes. Talk about the different colors and shapes of the leaves. Also collect pods that have fallen from the trees. Carefully put them in a bag or basket and bring them home. The leaves can be dipped in melted paraffin, laid on wax paper, and then used for your harvest table decorations. The pods and small leaves—along with nuts, plastic grapes, small silk flowers, and even an artificial bird—can be used in making a hat for your pumpkin. Find a whole pumpkin that is sort of fat and squatty, but do not cut into it. With a hot-glue gun, glue to the top of the pumpkin a nesting-type material, like gray moss or sphagnum moss. On top of that, glue small leaves, nuts, flowers, a bow, or silk flowers. This can be used as a centerpiece with the apples, figurines of pilgrims, etc.

You and the family will be so proud of this masterpiece, and it will last for several weeks. When Thanksgiving is over, simply pry off the hat and store it until next year to put on top of a new pumpkin.

Speak to one another with psalms, hymns and spiritual songs. Sing and make music in your heart to the Lord, always giving thanks to God the Father for everything, in the name of our Lord Jesus Christ—Ephesians 5:19,20 (NIV).

Name cards can also be completed ahead of time. Every year we, as a family, find verses with a thankfulness theme. Take a 3″ × 5″ card and fold it in half and stand it on the table. On the front write the name of the person who will sit at that place and inside write a Thanksgiving Scripture. When everyone is seated, each person then reads his verse—that can be the table blessing.

Another idea is to place at each person's seat a 3″ × 5″ card and pen and have everyone write something for which they are thankful. These can be read during, before, or after the meal.

On another 3″ × 5″ card have each person write one positive quality about someone else. Examples: "I love you, Uncle Brad, because you make me laugh with your cute jokes," or "I love you, Auntie Christy, because you read to me."

These name cards will give a great opportunity for your family to show God's love, and the Scriptures will put God's Word into the hearts of those who are not in tune with the Lord. The Bible says, "His word will not return void." For 39 years we've been feeding God's Word into my Jewish family through Scripture name cards.

At first they were embarrassed to read them and felt a bit timid, so we would skip those who didn't feel comfortable. But today, 39 years later, the formerly hesitant persons are the ones who ask to read first. I'm excited because I know 39 verses of God's Word have entered their hearts. His Word is sharper than any two-edged sword, and we're trusting God to pierce their hearts with His love. A silent witness can be given in so many ways—especially during the harvest season and on Thanksgiving Day when people are open to talking about being thankful.

Third Week in November

Use the "Third Week" form at the end of this chapter to make any last-minute arrangements for Thanksgiving. If you'll be going out-of-town, ask a neighbor to collect your mail and newspapers. If you are cooking, finalize your menu and entertainment plans.

> *A French proverb tells us: "Gratitude is the heart's memory." And so it is. For when we are thankful, we are thinking not only of blessings of the immediate present, but also of good things received in the past. Especially is this so at Thanksgiving*—Esther Burkholder.

Fourth Week in November

I get so excited by this time—and thankful for all I have done and already accomplished toward being ready for Thanksgiving. Use the form at the end of this chapter for your final planning.

Special holiday events will be happening Thanksgiving weekend. Decide which event you want to attend as a family, then schedule one special event for each child individually.

A few days before any holiday meal, I plan and organize my serving dishes. Then I make out 3" × 5" cards, listing on each card what will go into the empty dish, and I place that card in the bowl.

That way I don't have to try to remember at the last minute what goes into what. It also makes it easy for guests to help with final preparations.

As you gather around the bountiful table, holding hands can make this a special family and friendship time. Colossians 1:3 says, "We give thanks to God, the Father of our Lord Jesus Christ." Have a beautiful turkey day filled with thanksgiving to God, and don't forget to serve the cranberry sauce or to garnish the platter with parsley.

Now put away the fall decorations and start thinking toward Christmas.

Blessings Tied to Serving Food

Thanksgiving Day seems to gather from far and wide groups of people, some friends and some strangers, who pause and give thanks for blessings of health, family, job, business, a free country, and the opportunity to worship freely. Thanksgiving for food extends at this festive time to include giving thanks for other blessings. In Deuteronomy 8:10 (NIV) we read, "When you have eaten and are satisfied, praise the LORD your God for the good land he has given you."

> *Thanksgiving Day comes, by statute, once a year; to the honest man it comes as frequently as the heart of gratitude will allow, which may mean every day, or at least once in seven days*—Edward Sanford Martin.

The act of sharing food is mentioned many times in the Gospels—from the plea to "give us this day our daily bread" in the Lord's Prayer to, "While they were eating, Jesus took bread, gave thanks and broke it, and gave it to his disciples, saying, 'Take and eat; this is my body' " (Matthew 26:26 NIV). Even in other cultures and religions around the world, we find blessings tied to the serving of food.

While there was no specific prayer associated with the first Thanksgiving, there were some American Indian blessings found mentioning the sacred gift of food. One of them stated, "If you see no reason for giving thanks, the fault lies in yourself."

The act of saying grace at mealtime gives individuals a sense of a real connection to God. The sense of being close to God can be more powerful than it is with silent prayer. Our grandson Bevan (age 8) always begins his prayers with, "Father God." When he says that, I know that he is approaching God in a very personal way—far beyond my understanding of the divine when I was eight years old.

When someone orally gives a mealtime blessing, there seems to be an instant presence of God that enters into the group. Food prayers offer a simple way to bring expressions of faith into the family unit. Rotate the offer of such prayers to all the members of the family; praying doesn't have to be left up to the man or adult of the home.

In our family, we hold hands around the table, bow our heads, and join together in prayer. Our youngest grandson, Bradley Joe II (2 years old), loves us to end our prayer with the little chorus, "Amen, Amen." Quite often when we visit the Salvation Army, they will collectively sing a hymn or chorus of thanksgiving for their mealtime grace.

If your family isn't used to saying oral prayers of thanksgiving, you might purchase prepared mealtime prayers. Sharing food and prayers of thanksgiving are great ways to draw a family closer to each other and to the Lord. If this isn't already a habit in your family, Thanksgiving Day is a great time to step out and try something new.

Prayers from Around the World

God most provident, we join all creation in raising to you a hymn of Thanksgiving through Jesus Christ, your Son.

For generation upon generation, peoples of this land have sung of your bounty; we too offer you praise for the rich harvest we have received at your hands. Bless us and this food which we share with grateful hearts. . . .

Praise and glory to you, Lord God, now and forever.

—Traditional Catholic grace

God,
We thank you for all your gifts
This day, this night—

These fruits, these flowers,
These trees, these waters—
With all these treasures
you have endowed us.
       —Grace from Pakistan

Lord, the yam is fat like meat, the cassava melts on the tongue, oranges burst in their peels, dazzling and bright.

Lord, nature gives thanks.

Your creatures give thanks. Your praise rises in us like the great river.
                                        —West African prayer

A circle of friends is a blessed thing.
Sweet is the breaking of bread with friends.
For the honor of their presence at our board
We are deeply grateful, Lord.
       —Nineteenth-century American grace[1]

A Written Prayer for Thanksgiving

Father God, as I sit down to a Thanksgiving table once again, I want to thank You for Your goodness to me.

Thank You for meeting my needs every day—for food and shelter and clothing. And for many extras You provide that I so often take for granted.

Thank You for family and friends who make my life complete. Thank You that even when we are miles apart, we are bound by the cords of Your love.

And I thank You that I live in a country where I am free to worship You and to read Your Word.

Most of all, I thank You for Your Son, Jesus Christ, who is the "light of the world." When I turned to Him, He flooded the darkness of my soul with the light of Your love.

Thank You that He not only died for my sins, but that He is alive today at Your side—hearing my prayers and preparing a home for me in heaven.

Thank You that He came into this world and took up residence in my life as Savior, Lord, and God.

Thank You for all that You have given me as a Christian: the Holy Spirit who is Your presence in my life, the Bible that is the light to my pathway, Christian friends who encourage and help me.

Thank You that I can face tomorrow with hope because Jesus is living for me.

O, Lord, how truly rich I am! Thank You for all You mean to me.[2]

> *Be thankful unto him, and bless his name. For the LORD is good; his mercy is everlasting; and his truth endureth to all generations—* Psalm 100:4,5 (KJV).

Some Extra Thanksgiving Ideas

How Much Turkey to Buy

For turkeys 12 pounds or smaller, allow about one pound per person. Larger birds have a higher proportion of meat to bone weight. For a 12- to 24-pound turkey, allow about ¾ pound per person. If you want leftovers, allow 2 pounds per person when buying a turkey 12 pounds or smaller. Allow 1½ pounds per person for 12- to 24-pound birds.

Turkey Tips

1. To store a fresh turkey, loosely cover it with waxed paper or foil. Keep the turkey in the coldest part of your refrigerator and cook within three days.

2. You can special-order a turkey from your favorite market. Give them the weight you want and request that it be fresh, not frozen. Pick it up the day before Thanksgiving. You now have a fresh turkey that is ready for the oven.

3. After cooking the turkey, it may be stored three or four days in the refrigerator or frozen and stored up to three months.

4. Keep a frozen turkey in the freezer until you want to cook it. Whole turkeys can be kept frozen for one year, turkey parts for six months.

5. The refrigerator is the best place to thaw your frozen turkey. It keeps meat cold while it defrosts. Allow five hours per pound to thaw.

Roasting Time for Turkeys—Oven Temperature 325°F (165°C)

Size	Stuffed	Unstuffed
8–12 pounds	4–5 hours	3–4 hours
12–16 pounds	4½–6 hours	3½–5 hours
16–20 pounds	5½–7 hours	4½–6 hours
20–24 pounds	6½–7½ hours	5½–6½ hours

These times are guidelines only. The meat thermometer should register 185°F (85°C) in the thickest part of the thigh when done. Juices should run clear when the bird is pierced with a fork between the leg and thigh.

Steps to Standard Turkey Cooking (Option #1)

1. Wash the turkey well and wipe dry with paper towels. Season the cavity of the bird.
2. Stuff with a favorite dressing.
3. Rub olive oil or Crisco all over the turkey.
4. Use a meat thermometer, if possible, placing it in the thickest part of the thigh and being careful not to hit a bone.
5. Sprinkle with salt and pepper.
6. Place the turkey on a rack in a roasting pan with breast up (however, roasting with the breast down makes a turkey moister).
7. Place aluminum foil over the turkey and pan, with the thermometer sticking out for ease of reading.
8. Place turkey and pan in oven set at 325°F (165°C).
9. Remove the foil from the turkey during the last 30 minutes for final browning.
10. Pour the juices over the bird to assist in the browning process. Be very careful that you don't burn yourself when basting the bird.
11. Let the turkey cool at least 30 to 60 minutes before carving.

Perfect-Every-Time Turkey (Option #2)

Trust me with this one. I've been making at least four turkeys a year for 40 years, and this recipe from Adelle Davis is the best I have ever found. The white meat will melt in your mouth.

I always used a meat thermometer, so even with this method I still do—just so I know for sure when the turkey's done.

This is a slow-roasting method, but once in the oven, you can forget the turkey until it comes out.

Choose the desired size of turkey, wash it well, and remove the neck and giblets. Dry turkey with paper towels, salt the cavity, and stuff with brown rice dressing or the dressing of your choice. Rub the outside well with pure olive oil.

Put the turkey breast down (this bastes itself, making the white meat very moist) on a poultry rack in a roasting pan uncovered. Put into a 350° preheated oven for one hour to destroy bacteria on the surface. Then adjust the heat to 200° for any size turkey. This is important. The turkey can go in the oven the day before eating it. (Example: I have a 20-pound turkey. At 5:00 P.M. Thanksgiving Eve I put the prepared turkey in the oven at 350° for one hour. I turn the temperature down to 200° and leave the turkey uncovered until it's done the next day about 10:00 or 11:00 A.M.)

Although the cooking times seems startling at first, the meat is amazingly delicious, juicy, and tender. A turkey cooked the regular time at regular temperatures no longer tastes good. And a turkey cooked at this low temperature slices beautifully and shrinks very little. The turkey cannot burn, so it needs no watching, and vitamins and proteins cannot be harmed at such low heat.

A good rule for timing your turkey is to allow about three times longer than moderate-temperature roasting. For example, a 20-pound turkey normally takes 15 minutes per pound to cook and would take five hours. The slow-cook method takes three times five hours so this equals 15 hours of cooking by the slow method. A smaller turkey cooks for 20 minutes per pound, so an 11-pound turkey takes three hours and 40 minutes. Multiplied by three, that equals 11 hours.

Since the lower temperature requires longer cooking, its use must depend on when you wish to serve your turkey. However, once it's done, it will not overcook. You can leave the turkey in an additional three to six hours and it will be perfect. Thus, your roasting can be adjusted entirely to your convenience. Allow yourself plenty of time, and let your meat thermometer be your guide to when the turkey is done. Your only problem could be if you didn't put the turkey in the oven soon enough.

The meat browns perfectly, and you'll get wonderful drippings for gravy.

Try it—everyone will praise you and your turkey.

Turkey Carving Tips

Just out of the oven, with juices dripping, the turkey looks and smells wonderful. To graciously serve it from platter to plate, try these carving techniques.

1. Remove the drumstick and thigh by pressing the leg away from the body. The joint connecting the leg to the backbone may snap free. If it doesn't, use a sharp knife and cut the leg from the backbone. Cut dark meat completely from the bone structure by following body contour with a knife.

2. Cut drumsticks and thighs apart by cutting through the joint. It's easy to do if you tilt the drumstick to a convenient angle and slice toward the plate. Place thighs on a separate plate.

3. To slice thigh meat, hold the piece firmly on the plate with a fork. Cut even slices parallel to the bone.

4. Remove half the breast at a time by cutting along the breast-bone and rib cage with a sharp knife. Lift meat away from the bone.

5. Place half the breast on a cutting surface and slice evenly against the grain of the meat. Repeat with second half of the breast when additional slices are needed. (An optional method is to turn the bird so you can start with the breast of the turkey and make thin slices. When you have sliced all the meat from one side of the bird, you can rotate the bird so you can slice the other side of the turkey.)

Other Time-Tested Recipes

Chocolate Orange Cheesecake

Amount: 6 to 8 servings

1½ cups graham cracker crumbs
2 tablespoons plus ¾ cup sugar
1 tablespoon Pernigotti cocoa, plus additional for dusting top

1 teaspoon ground cinnamon
¼ cup unsalted butter, melted
8 ounces bittersweet chocolate, chopped
½ teaspoon orange oil
1 pound cream cheese at room temperature
½ cup sour cream
5 eggs

Mix graham cracker crumbs with 2 tablespoons sugar, cocoa, and cinnamon. Gradually add melted butter, stirring until crumbs are evenly coated. Press evenly into bottom and two-thirds of the way up the sides of a buttered springform pan that has been covered on the outside with aluminum foil. Refrigerate until ready to fill.

Melt chocolate in double boiler; remove from heat. Place cream cheese in bowl, beat on medium speed until smooth and fluffy (about 10 minutes). Beat in sour cream, ¾ cup sugar, and orange oil. Add eggs, one at a time, beating in between. Beat for 1 to 2 minutes. Using a rubber spatula, gently stir in the chocolate until blended. Stir slowly for 1 to 2 minutes to dispel bubbles.

Pour batter into prepared pan. Bake at 350° until puffed and no longer shiny (35 to 40 minutes). Center will look wet but will firm up when chilled. Transfer to wire rack to cool. When cool, remove foil and sides of pan.

Cover and refrigerate until firm enough to cut easily (4 to 5 hours or overnight). Sift cocoa generously over cake before serving.

Quick and Easy Popovers

Amount: 12 muffins or 6 popovers

2 eggs
¼ teaspoon salt
1 cup milk
2 tablespoons unsalted butter, melted
1 cup all-purpose flour

Butter 12 standard-size muffin cups or a popover pan. In a bowl combine eggs and salt. Using a whisk, beat lightly. Stir in milk and butter and beat in the flour until just blended. Do not overbeat. Fill each cup about half full and place in a cold oven. Set temperature to 425° and bake for 25 minutes. Reduce heat to 375° and bake until the popovers are golden (10 to 15 minutes longer). They should be crisp on the outside. Quickly pierce each popover with a thin metal skewer or the tip of a small knife to release the steam. Leave in the oven a couple of minutes for further crisping. Remove and serve at once.

Orange Muffins

Amount: 12 standard muffins

- ⅓ cup dried cranberries, chopped
- ⅓ cup plus 2 tablespoons sugar
- 3 tablespoons boiling water
- 1¾ cups all-purpose flour
- ½ cup yellow cornmeal
- 2½ teaspoons baking powder
- ½ teaspoon baking soda
- ½ teaspoon salt
- 2 eggs
- 1 cup milk
- ⅓ cup unsalted butter, melted
- 1 tablespoon grated orange peel

In a small bowl, stir together cranberries and 2 tablespoons sugar. Stir in boiling water; set aside for 15 minutes to soften cranberries. In a large bowl, mix flour, cornmeal, ⅓ cup sugar, baking powder, baking soda, and salt. In another bowl, using whisk, beat eggs lightly. Add milk and melted butter; beat until smooth. Stir in cranberries, their liquid, and grated orange peel. Stir liquid mixture into flour mixture. Divide batter evenly among buttered muffin cups, filling each ¾ full. Bake at 400° until risen and the tops are golden (15 to 20 minutes). Remove from the oven and let cool in pan for 2 to 3 minutes. Serve warm.

Pumpkin Muffins

Amount: 10 muffins

- ½ cup unsalted butter
- ¼ cup sugar
- 2 eggs
- 1⅓ cups all-purpose flour

1 teaspoon baking soda
½ teaspoon salt
1¼ cups Muirhead Pecan-Pumpkin Butter
½ teaspoon pure vanilla extract
2 teaspoons fresh lemon juice
¾ cup currants

In a bowl, beat butter and sugar together until smooth and creamy. Add eggs and beat well. Add flour, baking soda, and salt, and mix until combined. Stir in Pecan-Pumpkin Butter, vanilla extract, lemon juice, and currants. Fill buttered muffin cups ¾ full. Bake in preheated 325° oven until toothpick inserted in center comes out clean (about 25 to 30 minutes). Remove muffins from pan and cool on wire rack.

Pumpkin Waffles

Amount: 4 servings

½ cup canned pumpkin
1½ cups milk
3 eggs, well beaten
2 tablespoons melted butter
1 cup all-purpose flour, sifted
2 teaspoons baking powder
½ teaspoon salt
2 tablespoons sugar
⅛ teaspoon nutmeg

Stir together pumpkin, eggs, milk, and butter. In a separate bowl, combine flour, baking powder, salt, sugar, and nutmeg. Add dry ingredients to pumpkin mixture. Stir until thoroughly combined. Cook according to the directions for your waffle maker. Serve immediately with berry or maple syrup, fresh berries, or ginger whipped cream.

Wild Rice Casserole

Amount: 6 servings

1 package (4 ounces) wild and white rice mix
8 ounces bulk pork sausage
1 cup chopped onion

1 cup chopped celery
1 cup shredded fresh spinach
$^1/_2$ cup pitted olives
$^1/_2$ cup reduced-calorie mayonnaise
$^3/_4$ teaspoon ground sage
$^1/_2$ cup chopped pecans

Prepare rice mix according to package directions. Cook sausage and drain thoroughly.

Cook onion and celery until lightly browned. Add remaining ingredients except pecans. Refrigerate until ready to cook. Preheat oven to 350°. Bake for 30 minutes.

Granny's Stuffing

Amount: 8 to 10 servings

12 slices white bread, dried
1 medium onion, finely chopped
3 ribs celery, finely chopped
$^1/_4$ cup chopped parsley
1 teaspoon poultry seasoning
$^1/_2$ teaspoon salt
$^1/_4$ teaspoon pepper
1 egg, lightly beaten
4 tablespoons melted butter
warm water

Preheat oven to 325°. Break bread into postage-stamp-size pieces in a large bowl. Add onion, celery, and parsley, and mix thoroughly. Sprinkle with poultry seasoning, salt, and pepper, and toss again to mix well. Add egg and mix again. Slowly add warm water, a tablespoon or so at a time, tossing until the bread is very moist, but not dripping, or the stuffing will turn out gummy.

Spoon into greased 8″ × 8″ casserole. Bake for 30 to 45 minutes.

Hot Buttered Cranberry Cider

Amount: 10 servings

$^1/_3$ cup butter, softened
$^1/_3$ cup mild honey
$^1/_2$ teaspoon ginger

¹/₂ teaspoon cinnamon
1 48-ounce bottle cranberry juice cocktail
1 quart cider
cinnamon sticks (optional)

Blend softened butter, honey, and spices. This may be done ahead of time.

When ready to serve, combine cranberry cocktail and cider. Bring to a boil or heat in a party percolator. Have butter mixture beside the pot. To serve, put a small spoonful of honey-butter in each mug or heat-proof punch cup. Fill with hot cranberry cider. Stir with a cinnamon stick.

Fudgey Pecan Pie

Amount: one 9″ pie

¹/₃ cup butter
²/₃ cup sugar
¹/₃ cup cocoa
3 eggs
1 cup light corn syrup
¹/₄ teaspoon salt
1 cup chopped pecans
1 unbaked 9″ piecrust
¹/₂ cup cold whipping cream
1 tablespoon powdered sugar
¹/₄ teaspoon vanilla extract
pecan halves (optional)

Heat oven to 375°. In a medium saucepan over low heat, melt butter or margarine; add sugar and cocoa, stirring until well blended. Remove from heat, set aside. In medium bowl, beat eggs slightly. Stir in corn syrup and salt. Add cocoa mixture; blend well. Stir in chopped pecans. Pour into unbaked piecrust. Bake in a 375° oven for 45 to 50 minutes or until set. Cool. Cover and let stand 8 hours before serving.

Yams in Orange Sauce

Amount: 6 to 8 servings

    1. Bake 6 medium yams in oven until almost tender (about 45 minutes) at 375° (or bake in microwave at full power for 6 to 8 minutes per pound).

    2. Peel and slice potatoes into lightly buttered casserole dish.

    3. Blend together and pour over top of potatoes:

1 cup orange juice
¼ cup honey
2 tablespoons unsalted butter, melted
2 tablespoons cornstarch

    4. Cover and bake at 350° for 30 minutes.

Amandine Green Beans

Amount: 4 servings

    1. Cook green beans whole, or cut diagonally, or French cut lengthwise, as desired:

⅔ to 1 pound fresh green beans (or 10-ounce package, frozen)

    2. Sauté almonds in butter until lightly golden brown and fold in hot cooked beans:

1 tablespoon melted butter
¼ cup slivered or sliced almonds

Those Yummy Leftovers

After looking at that turkey carcass all day, your first inclination is to give it away or throw it away—anything to just get rid of it. But don't. This is the best way to be creative and a great money-saver.

Gently place before one of the men or older boys of the group the carcass on a tray and request them to cut away all the turkey still remaining, and to leave just the bones. As the dishes are being washed by someone, you can be placing a picked-clean carcass in a soup pot.

In about two hours, you'll have delicious stock that can be frozen for soup or prepared the next day. Now you can throw out the carcass. (Be sure to keep it away from family pets. The bones splinter and can get lodged in your pet's throat.)

If after dinner you just can't face that carcass one more minute, put it in a plastic bag and store it in the refrigerator until after breakfast the next day.

Turkey Soup Stock

enough water to cover the carcass (8 to 10 cups)
turkey carcass, broken
any leftover pan juices or gravy
1 onion, quartered
2 large cloves of garlic, whole but peeled and slightly smashed
1 carrot, cut into large pieces
4 to 5 stalks celery, with tops and leaves, cut into large pieces
1 teaspoon dried marjoram
1 teaspoon dried thyme (or fresh sprigs)
½ teaspoon dried sage (or fresh sprigs)
a few sprigs fresh parsley
½ teaspoon salt
½ teaspoon cayenne pepper
freshly ground pepper

In a large pot bring the water to a boil. Add all ingredients. Reduce heat to a low simmer. Cover and simmer for two hours. Remove from heat.

When cool enough, pick out any meat that has fallen off the bones to add later to the soup. Strain, pour into a freezer container, and refrigerate. Once it has cooled, freeze stock or keep refrigerated until ready to make soup. (The fat will rise to the top and make a seal. Remove it when ready to make soup.)

If using fresh beans in the soup, place 1 cup dry beans in 3 cups water in a covered saucepan. Simmer one hour or until tender while stock is cooking. This yields about two cups cooked beans.

Turkey Soup

1 large onion, finely chopped
1 teaspoon olive oil
8 cups turkey or chicken stock (fresh or canned)
1½ cups carrots, sliced into thin circles

1½ cups celery, diced

3 turnips or small rutabagas, halved and sliced thin

3 medium red- or white-skinned potatoes, quartered and sliced thin

1 cup navy or northern (white) beans—fresh, soaked, and cooked or canned, rinsed, and drained

2 to 3 cups leftover turkey, cut into bite-sized pieces

1 to 2 cups leftover cooked green beans

cauliflower (optional)

fresh parsley, finely chopped

parmesan cheese, freshly grated

Using a large pot, sauté onion in oil until limp. Pour in stock and add the rest of the ingredients, including fresh cooked beans (but not canned beans). Don't add the leftover vegetables, parsley, and cheese yet. Cover and simmer for about 30 minutes.

Check to see if the vegetables are tender. Simmer longer, if needed.

When soup is done, add canned beans (if used) and leftover cooked vegetables. Top with grated cheese and chopped parsley.

Turkey Hash

6 medium red- or white-skinned potatoes, cut into ½-inch cubes (about 3 cups)

½ cup turkey or chicken broth (fresh or canned)

1 medium onion, chopped

2 stalks celery, finely chopped (about 1 cup)

1 large clove garlic, minced

1 sweet red pepper, chopped

2 cups cooked turkey, chopped into small pieces

⅛ teaspoon nutmeg

½ teaspoon sage

½ teaspoon thyme

½ teaspoon cayenne pepper

salt

freshly ground pepper

fresh paprika

parsley, minced (optional)

Put potatoes and broth in a 12-inch skillet (preferably nonstick). Cover and simmer for 15 minutes until broth has evaporated and potatoes are tender and lightly browned on one side. Add onion, celery, and garlic and sauté for a few minutes over medium heat, stirring occasionally.

Add the rest of the ingredients, with the exception of the paprika and parsley. Let cook for a few minutes on one side, then flip over in sections. Don't overstir. Add a little oil if pan is too dry.

When celery is tender and hash is browned, serve sprinkled with parsley and paprika.

Mashed Potato Pancakes

Amount: 4 servings

1 clove garlic, minced
½ teaspoon jalapeño pepper, minced
canola oil
2 green onions, finely chopped
2 cups leftover mashed potatoes
1 egg, beaten, or 1 egg white

In nonstick skillet (10- to 12-inch), sauté garlic and hot pepper in a few drops of oil for a minute. Stir in green onions for a few seconds; remove from heat. In a mixing bowl, stir together all the ingredients.

Heat a little oil in a skillet. Drop batter into the pan by spoonfuls, making small 2-inch cakes. Flatten with a spatula, and fry on medium-high heat for approximately 2 minutes per side. Flip over when bottom is brown. Serve with low-fat sour cream or yogurt.

Mediterranean Noodle Turkey Casserole

Amount: 8 servings

1 pound medium egg noodles, uncooked
14½-ounce can low-sodium chicken broth
1 cup skim milk
1 teaspoon salt
¼ cup cornstarch
2 cups chopped, cooked turkey
14-ounce can artichoke hearts, drained and quartered

17¹/₂-ounce jar roasted red peppers, drained and sliced
9 Calamata olives, pitted and sliced
¹/₂ cup grated part-skim mozzarella cheese
¹/₂ cup white wine
1 teaspoon lemon juice
¹/₂ teaspoon black pepper
vegetable-oil cooking spray
2 tablespoons grated parmesan cheese

Prepare noodles according to package directions. Drain.

Stir the broth, milk, salt, and cornstarch together in a large pot or Dutch oven until the cornstarch is dissolved. Cook over medium heat, stirring constantly, until thickened and bubbly. Stir in noodles, turkey, artichoke hearts, red peppers, olives, mozzarella cheese, wine, lemon juice, and black pepper.

Spray a 3-quart baking dish with cooking spray. Spoon noodle mixture into dish. Sprinkle with parmesan cheese. Bake in a 350° oven for about 35 minutes. Let stand 5 minutes before serving.

Other Helpful Thanksgiving Ideas

1. *Chopped onion without tears*—Take the tears out of preparing onions by chopping them in a blender. Cut an onion in quarters or eighths. Fill the blender halfway with water. Add onion pieces. Push the chop button on and off until the onion is chopped to the desired size. Drain onions in a colander. Repeat until you have enough onions for your recipe.

2. *Orange shells*—This is a simple, decorative way to serve your sweet potatoes or yams. Cut oranges in half and remove fruit and pulp. Add the fruit to your holiday punch. Prepare cooked yams or sweet potatoes and spoon into the orange shells. Nestle oranges around turkey on platter. For an extra touch, flute top edges of orange shells with a knife and top with a maraschino cherry (or top with a small marshmallow and place them in the oven until the marshmallow melts).

3. *Unconventional day*—Your family may want to plan a day very different from the traditional family gathering. Your plans might include a trip to the beach (climate permitting), the park, the mountains, or the desert. You might even have hamburgers and hot dogs. Be sure to bring along some thoughts of inspiration to share together.

4. *Rent a cabin*—You might consider renting a cabin for the four-day holiday and invite friends and family to share this special period of time with you. Have each family bring their own bedding and supply meals for one day. In the evening you can spend time getting started on some Christmas decorations—a great way to cement family relationships.

Heap high the board with plenteous cheer, and gather to the feast, and toast the sturdy Pilgrim band whose courage never ceased— Alice W. Brotherton, *The First Thanksgiving.*

5. *Hostess gifts*—If you are going to be a guest in someone's home, plan to take an inexpensive hostess gift. A plate of homemade cookies, stationery, tea towels with a bow tied around them, or even a new turkey baster would be appreciated.

6. *Ask children to help*—This is a great time to include the children in the kitchen. They can help scrub vegetables, dry off lettuce, stir whipped cream, set the table, place ice cubes in drinks, etc. This makes them feel a part of the festivities.

7. *Have a potluck*—If you find yourself too busy to do all the cooking, decide to make your harvest dinner a potluck. Call the guests and assign them each a dish to bring.

8. *Pick chores*—As your guests arrive, have them draw out of a hat a slip of paper that will give them a chore for the day. The slips might read:

- Mash the potatoes.
- Make giblet gravy.
- Put ice cubes in the glasses.

9. *Make "thankful cards"*—Have someone make out a card for each person titled, "I'm thankful for . . ." After dinner, each guest will read a thankful card. This is a great way to focus on the positive things God provides to us. Or you could have a person interview each guest asking the question, "What is the best thing that has happened to you this year, month, week, or today?" This exercise has given us many great times of communication and has brought tears to each of us.

Be joyful always; pray continually; give thanks in all circumstances, for this is God's will for you in Christ Jesus—1 Thessalonians 5:16–18 (NIV).

10. *Make Scripture name cards*—Assign to one of the children or to your husband the task of making individual name cards with a Scripture verse on the back. These verses should be in line with Thanksgiving. (Example: Romans 5:20, "Always give thanks for all things in the name of our Lord Jesus Christ.") You can use 3″ × 5″ cards folded in half, placing the name on the front and the Scripture inside. These will be read by each person as the blessing of thanks before your meal.

11. *Design a centerpiece*—A few days before Thanksgiving, set the table. Make it simple. Use a pumpkin and some fresh fruit around it for a centerpiece. Include three candles in an autumn color using different designed holders (or use votive candles and float them in a glass or bowl of water). Try to use items you already have.

> *Let us come before him with thanksgiving and extol him with music and song*—Psalm 95:2 (NIV).

≈Calendar≈

Month				Year
☐	☐	☐	☐	☐
☐	☐	☐	☐	☐
☐	☐	☐	☐	☐
☐	☐	☐	☐	☐
☐	☐	☐	☐	☐
☐	☐	☐	☐	☐
☐	☐	☐	☐	☐

November: Week 1—Things to Do

Activity   Done (x)

1._____ ☐

2._____ ☐

3._____ ☐

4._____ ☐

5._____ ☐

6._____ ☐

7._____ ☐

8._____ ☐

9._____ ☐

10._____ ☐

11._____ ☐

12._____ ☐

13._____ ☐

14._____ ☐

November: Week 2—Things to Do

Activity   Done (x)

1._____ ☐

2._____ ☐

3._____ ☐

4._____ ☐

5._____ ☐

6._____ ☐

7._____ ☐

8._____ ☐

9._____ ☐

10._____ ☐

11._____ ☐

12._____ ☐

13._____ ☐

14._____ ☐

November: Week 3—Things to Do

Activity   Done (x)

1._____ ☐

2._____ ☐

3._____ ☐

4._____ ☐

5._____ ☐

6._____ ☐

7._____ ☐

8._____ ☐

9._____ ☐

10._____ ☐

11._____ ☐

12._____ ☐

13._____ ☐

14._____ ☐

November: Week 4—Things to Do

Activity   Done (x)

1._____ ☐

2._____ ☐

3._____ ☐

4._____ ☐

5._____ ☐

6._____ ☐

7._____ ☐

8._____ ☐

9._____ ☐

10._____ ☐

11._____ ☐

12._____ ☐

13._____ ☐

14._____ ☐

Hanukkah

I am the light of the world; he who follows Me shall not walk in the darkness, but shall have the light of life.
—John 8:12

When Observed: Celebrated for eight days, beginning the twenty-fifth day of the Hebrew month Kislev (November–December)

Earliest Observance: 165 B.C. in Jerusalem

My background being Jewish, I find it only fitting to share what at one time was a very important part of my childhood: Hanukkah or Chanukah—either spelling is correct.

Many Gentiles today do not know what the story of Hanukkah is all about. Perhaps you have Jewish friends or your children have friends at school who practice the Jewish faith. It's a wonderful learning experience to know why and what people are talking about when they say, "I'm Jewish and we celebrate Hanukkah."

An Eternal Feast of Light

Hanukkah is the commemoration of a miracle whose story has fascinated and inspired generation after generation of Jewish people.

444

Over 20 centuries ago, the land of Judea was under the rule of a Syrian king. For a time, the Jews of Judea were free to practice their customs and observe the laws of the Torah—that is, until the reign of King Antiochus.

Antiochus was determined that all those under his rule believe in the multigod religion of the Greeks, as he did. He sent men to Judea to enforce his command and sent soldiers to the temple in Jerusalem. They burned the Torah scrolls. They ripped the curtains and smashed the beautiful menorah. A Greek idol replaced these things on the temple altar. No longer could the Jews worship in their temple, and some gave in to the king's command to worship other gods.

Near Jerusalem in the town of Modi'in, the leader of the town, Mattathias, rebelled against the king and led many of the townspeople away to the mountains where they hid and organized a small army to fight the Syrians. Mattathias, however, was old and in poor health. Before long, he realized that he would not survive to lead his army. Judah, one of his five sons, was appointed as leader and was given the name Maccabee. His army became known as the Maccabees.

They lacked numbers, experience, and weaponry, but they knew the terrain and were able to surprise the king's soldiers several times. More importantly, they were fighting with God for the freedom to practice their faith.

After three years of fighting, they reached Jerusalem and went to the temple. They found it desecrated and in a state of shambles. The fighters became builders and, after much hard labor, the temple was again ready for worship. On the twenty-fifth day of the month of Kislev on the Jewish calendar, the great menorah was ready to be lit. But only specially purified oil could be used, and there was none to be found. A massive search finally yielded only a day's supply. More oil would have to be obtained from the town of Tekoah, but even using the best horse and fastest rider, it would take eight days to obtain. Nevertheless, the menorah was lit with the knowledge that the temple would soon be in darkness again until the rider returned with more oil.

The next day, the high priest entered the temple. To his amazement, the menorah was still burning. This continued for eight days until the rider returned with the necessary oil. Before long, everyone had heard about the great miracle. God had provided the light! Man's best efforts would have left him in darkness, but God provided the light.

Menorahs will burn for eight days in countless Jewish homes to commemorate and celebrate Hanukkah, the "feast of light." The prophet Isaiah, however, foresaw an even greater miracle of light that was to occur. He proclaimed:

> The people who walk in darkness will see a great light; those who live in a dark land, the light will shine on them. . . . For a child will be born to us, a son will be given to us; and the government will rest on His shoulders; and His name will be called Wonderful Counselor, Mighty God, Eternal Father, Prince of Peace. There will be no end to the increase of His government or of peace (Isaiah 9:2,6,7).

Of course, this passage speaks of the coming of the promised Messiah of Israel. Many Jews anticipate this as a future event. Many more speak of "when the Messiah comes" as more of a joke or legend than an anticipation. But Isaiah foresaw this, too, and wrote:

> "Keep on listening, but do not perceive; keep on looking, but do not understand." Render the heart of this people insensitive, their ears dull, and their eyes dim, lest they see with their eyes, hear with their ears, understand with their hearts, and return and be healed (Isaiah 6:9,10).

The prophet also foresaw that the Messiah, the Great Light, would be rejected by His own people because of their blindness:

> Who has believed our message? And to whom has the arm of the LORD been revealed? For He grew up before Him like a tender shoot, and like a root out of parched ground; He has no stately form or majesty that we should look upon Him, nor appearance that we should be attracted to Him. He was despised and forsaken of men, a man of sorrows, and acquainted with

grief; and like one from whom men hide their face, He was despised, and we did not esteem Him (Isaiah 53:1–3).

But Isaiah did say that at least some of the people would see the great light about which he had prophesied. God is able to open the eyes of the blind. So it was that some seven centuries after Isaiah's prophecy, a Jewish man by the name of Jochanan (better known by his Greek name John) was able to proclaim about another Jewish man: "In Him was life, and the life was the light of men" (John 1:4). He was speaking of Yeshua (Jesus) of Nazareth.

It didn't stop with John. For nearly 2000 years now, there has always been a small pocket of Jewish people who have accepted that Jesus—who fulfilled all of Isaiah's messianic prophecies and hundreds of other Old Testament messianic prophecies—is the great light that God promised. True, the majority of the Jewish community rejects this idea, but didn't Isaiah say this would be the case?

Hanukkah is the celebration of God's miraculous provision of light. The best efforts of man would have left him in darkness, but God provided the light. So it is with the Messiah. Our own best efforts in life still leave us uncertain and without peace concerning our origin, purpose, or final destiny. Man has accomplished many things but, to the extent that we are unable to understand the above three issues, we walk in darkness. This very darkness, Isaiah proclaimed, was to be illumined by the Messiah.

Has this happened to you? Is your "feast of light" only eight days long, or do you walk in light all year? Do you understand where you came from, why you are here, and where you are going, or are you still one of "the people who walk in darkness"?

John, the New Testament writer, made this assessment concerning the "light of men" he saw in Jesus: "And the light shines in the darkness, and the darkness did not comprehend it" (John 1:5). His words sounds an awful lot like Isaiah's, don't they?

There will be two celebrations in December that won't be all they should be. One will be the celebration of Christmas as a day of presents and Santa Claus. The other will be the celebration for only eight days of God's provision of light. Hanukkah commemorates a wonderful miracle, and it should be celebrated. But wouldn't it be tragic to celebrate only the eight-day feast of light and remain blind to the fact that God, through His Son, the Messiah, has provided the greatest miracle—an eternal feast of light just for the asking? We need to open our eyes—a great light is shining brightly!

Hanukkah and all its food traditions emphasize oil—including the preparation of *latkes,* or potato pancakes, which are served for this holiday around the world.

Ashkenazic Jews from Germany and Eastern Europe celebrate Hanukkah by frying what have become traditional latkes for most Americans. Sephardic Jews, originally from Spain, emigrated to most countries around the Mediterranean, and they, too, prepare versions of fried potato pancakes to mark the occasion.

The food processor is a must for making East European latkes— no more hand grating the potatoes. The food processor has sped up latke preparation so much that the potatoes don't have time to turn dark.

French *galettes*—crisp, golden pancakes made from shredded potatoes—are another variation on traditional latkes. The key to making the best galettes is baking the potatoes before shredding them. Unfortunately, these potatoes still require hand-grating because they become gluey in the food processor. On the other hand, this is one latke you can brown in advance and recrisp in a hot oven at party time.

Gnocchi, Italian potato dumplings, offer another opportunity for advance preparation. After you shape and boil the gnocchi, you can set them aside until almost serving time, then heat them in the oven and serve with any number of sauces. Marinara, Gorgonzola, and pesto sauces each enhance the flavor of gnocchi. If you don't want to bother with a sauce, sprinkle them with freshly grated parmesan cheese.

Gnocchi preparation has inspired intense debate. Some cooks favor including egg yolks, saying they make the dough easier to handle. Others argue against the yolks, saying the finished dumpling is much lighter without them.

In India, hot mashed potatoes are shaped into patties and fried. Seasoned with onions, ginger, bell peppers, and chopped cashews, these *aloo vadai* are a spicy way to celebrate Hanukkah, and you can make the batter and shape the patties in advance. At party time, all you have to do is fry and serve them.

You can even make potato pancakes from sweet potatoes. This popular North African-style recipe is eaten with a hot pepper sauce, such as Tabasco, and a cooling yogurt-and-cucumber raita. Preparation is easy because the food processor does the grating. To make party preparation easier, refrigerate the batter up to four hours before frying the pancakes.

Raita

2 cups yogurt
1 cucumber
3 teaspoons cumin
$1/2$ teaspoon salt
pinch of black pepper
pinch of cayenne pepper (or dash of Tabasco sauce)
chopped parsley

Mix the yogurt and cucumber together and place in the refrigerator for 30 minutes.

Add the other ingredients before serving and garnish with parsley.

Hanukkah Traditions

One of the best parts of this season is the food, especially the latkes. They are crisp and brown and served with homemade applesauce, sour cream, or yogurt.

Latke is a Russian word, meaning "flat cake." Making latkes was adopted because the Jews wanted to serve a dish cooked in oil to symbolize the miracle of Hanukkah.

The symbolism behind the pancakes is threefold. Made initially of flour and water, they served as a reminder of the food hurriedly prepared for the troops as they went to war. The oil used to prepare the pancakes symbolizes the oil that burned for eight days. The eating of latkes commemorates the liberation from Greek rule.

During the eight days of Hanukkah, latkes are eaten daily. They are a delicacy and quite versatile. They can be served for breakfast, brunch, lunch, dinner, or even as a snack. Plain or fancy, they can be eaten with sugar, yogurt, applesauce, or chicken soup. They can be made with buckwheat or potatoes.

It might be fun to have a Hanukkah party for your family, serve latkes and homemade applesauce, and tell the story of Hanukkah. Perhaps you can have candles available or borrow a menorah and show how one candle is lit for every day of Hanukkah. This could be done in an adult Sunday school class, also.

Traditional Potato Latkes

Amount: 26 pancakes

6 medium potatoes (about 2½ pounds), washed thoroughly and cubed
½ medium onion
3 tablespoons flour
2 eggs
1½ teaspoons salt or to taste
¼ teaspoon freshly ground pepper
oil for frying

Mix all ingredients except oil. Place ¼ of the mixture in a food processor and process until coarsely chopped. Repeat until all the ingredients are combined. Work quickly so mixture does not darken.

Heat a scant tablespoon of oil in a nonstick skillet. Cover the bottom evenly. Use a ¼-cup measure to pour the potato batter into the heated skillet and form patties. Fry until crisp and brown; turn and repeat. Drain on paper towels to remove excess oil. Keep latkes warm until all the batter is fried.

French Potato Galettes

Amount: 22 pancakes

6 medium baking potatoes (about 2½ pounds), washed
salt and pepper to taste
2 eggs, slightly beaten
oil for frying

Preheat oven to 400°. Bake potatoes 1 hour. Allow them to cool thoroughly.

Peel cold potatoes. Grate through a grater with large holes. Season to taste with salt and pepper. Add eggs. Toss lightly.

Heat enough oil to cover the bottom of a nonstick skillet. Using a ¼-cup measure, ladle potato mixture to form patties in skillet. Do not crowd. Cook over medium-high heat until pancakes are brown and crisp; turn and repeat. Keep galettes warm while preparing the rest of the batter. Repeat until all the batter is fried.

To make ahead, brown the potato pancakes and set aside. Keep at room temperature. Recrisp by heating in 425° oven.

Indian Potato Patties (Aloo Vadai)

2 large sweet potatoes (about 1 pound), washed and cut into pieces
1½ teaspoons salt, or to taste
½ teaspoon white pepper
5 eggs, slightly beaten
oil for frying

Grate the potatoes in the food processor, using the blade with large holes. Place in a medium mixing bowl and toss with remaining ingredients except oil. Mix well. Cover and refrigerate (up to 4 hours) until frying time.

Heat enough oil to cover the bottom of a large nonstick skillet. Using a ¼-cup measure, ladle into skillet to form patties, but don't crowd. Cook until crisp and brown on one side; turn and repeat. Keep patties warm while cooking remaining batter.

Emilie's Favorite Applesauce

Amount: 3 cups

1½ pounds of tart baking apples (a mixture of different kinds is ideal)
½ teaspoon cinnamon or to taste
¼ teaspoon nutmeg or to taste
½ cup apple juice, apple cider, pineapple juice, or water
1 slice lemon

Wash apples but do not peel. Cut up washed apples and place in a pot. Add fruit juice or cider and spices. If you like a thinner sauce, add a little more fruit juice. Bring to a boil; then reduce heat and simmer for about 10 minutes. Cool; then mix in blender for the best applesauce you have ever tasted. This recipe can be done in a microwave on high for about 5 minutes. If you don't want to use the blender, cook longer until mushy, and then whip with a fork. If you use a Crockpot, cook on low for 4 to 6 hours or until apples fall apart. Whip with a fork.

Other Hanukkah Foods

Holiday Borscht

Amount: 15 cups (12 first-course servings)

  3 bunches medium-size beets (about 2 pounds beets without leaves)
  3 medium-size onions
  1 tablespoon salad oil
  3 extra-large vegetable bouillon cubes (or 6 envelopes of instant vegetable broth and seasoning)
  4 large carrots (about ¾ pound)
  6 medium-size potatoes (about 2 pounds)
  ¼ cup lemon juice
  3 tablespoons sugar
  1 teaspoon salt

About 2½ hours before serving or one day ahead:

   1. Cut off stems and leaves from beets. Reserve beet greens for use in slaw recipe. Rinse beets with cold running water. Peel and cut beets into ¼-inch pieces.

   2. Slice onions thinly. In 5-quart Dutch oven over medium-high heat, cook onions in hot salad oil until golden, stirring occasionally (about 10 minutes). Stir in beets, bouillon, and 2½ quarts water. Increase heat to high; heat to boiling. Reduce heat to low; cover and simmer 30 minutes.

   3. Meanwhile, peel and shred carrots coarsely. Stir carrots into beet mixture; simmer 15 minutes longer or until beets and carrots are tender. If not serving on the same day, cover and refrigerate soup.

About 1 hour before serving:

   4. In 3-quart saucepan over high heat, heat potatoes and enough water to cover them to boiling. Reduce heat to low. Cover and simmer 25 to 30 minutes until potatoes are fork-tender. Drain potatoes; cool until easy to handle.

5. To serve, peel and dice potatoes. Add lemon juice, sugar, and salt to borscht; heat through. Place diced potatoes in soup bowls and top with borscht.

Sweet and Sour Brisket

Amount: 12 main-dish servings

1 4½-pound beef brisket
1 tablespoon salad oil
2 12-ounce jars apricot jam
½ cup chili sauce
¼ cup cider vinegar
1 tablespoon dry mustard
1 teaspoon salt
2 8-ounce packages dried mixed fruit

About 4 hours before serving:

1. Trim excess fat from beef brisket. In 8-quart Dutch oven over medium-high heat, cook brisket in hot salad oil until well browned on both sides.

2. Add 4 cups water to brisket in Dutch oven; heat to boiling. Reduce heat to low; cover and simmer 2½ hours or until meat is fork-tender.

3. When brisket is done, preheat oven to 375°. In 3-quart saucepan, combine apricot jam, chili sauce, vinegar, mustard, and salt over medium heat. Heat until jam melts.

4. Line medium roasting pan (about 14″ × 10″) with foil. Place brisket in pan; reserve cooking fluid. Spread ¾ cup apricot-jam mixture on top of brisket. Bake brisket about 25 minutes or until glaze is lightly browned.

5. Meanwhile, add dried fruit and 2 cups remaining apricot-jam mixture to saucepan. Over high heat, heat to boiling. Reduce heat to low; cover and simmer 20 minutes or until fruit is tender.

6. Slice brisket across the grain and serve with warm fruit sauce.

Cabbage and Beet-Green Slaw

Amount: 12 servings

  1 medium-size head green cabbage (2 pounds)
  1 medium-size head red cabbage (2 pounds)
  1 medium-size red onion
  3/4 cup mayonnaise
  1/4 cup cider vinegar
  2 tablespoons Dijon mustard
  1 teaspoon salt
  1/2 teaspoon coarsely ground black pepper
  3 cups loosely packed beet leaves or spinach leaves

About 4 hours before serving or early in day:

  1. Thinly slice both kinds of cabbage and discard tough ribs; place in large bowl. Cut onion in half lengthwise, then cut each half crosswise into paper-thin slices. Add onion to cabbage.

  2. In small bowl, with wire whisk or fork, mix mayonnaise, vinegar, sugar, mustard, salt, and pepper. Add to cabbage mixture and toss to coat well. Cover bowl with plastic wrap and refrigerate at least 3 hours before serving to allow flavors to blend.

  3. Meanwhile, rinse beet leaves with cold running water and pat dry with paper towels. Cut beet leaves into julienne strips; cover with plastic wrap and refrigerate until ready to serve salad.

  4. To serve, toss julienne beet leaves with cabbage mixture.

Apple and Pear Baskets

Amount: 12 servings

  12 sheets fresh or frozen (thawed) phyllo (about half of a 16-ounce package)
  margarine
  7 medium-size Golden Delicious apples (about 3 1/2 pounds)
  brown sugar
  lemon juice
  7 medium-size Bartlett pears (about 3 1/2 pounds)
  1/2 cup dried cherries or raisins
  2 pints vanilla frozen nondairy dessert

About 3 hours before serving or day ahead:

1. Preheat oven to 375°. On work surface, stack sheets of phyllo (about 17″ by 12″ each), one on top of the other. With knife, cut stack lengthwise in half, then crosswise in half (you will have 48 8½″ by 6″ sheets of phyllo).

2. In small saucepan over low heat, melt 4 tablespoons margarine (½ stick).

3. Lightly brush 6 10-ounce custard cups with melted margarine. Place 2 sheets of phyllo, one on top of the other; brush top sheet with some melted margarine. Arrange phyllo in a custard cup. Place 2 more sheets of phyllo, one on top of the other, and brush top sheet with some melted margarine and place crosswise over phyllo in cup. Crimp edges of phyllo to make a pretty edge. Repeat with 20 more phyllo sheets to make 5 more cups. Keep remaining phyllo covered with damp towels to prevent it from drying out.

4. Place custard cups in jelly-roll pan for easier handling. Bake phyllo cups 10 to 12 minutes until phyllo is crisp and golden. Cool in cups on wire racks about 15 minutes, then carefully remove phyllo cups from custard cups.

5. Repeat with remaining phyllo and melted margarine to make 6 more phyllo cups. If not serving right away, store phyllo cups in tightly covered container or zippered plastic bags until ready to use.

6. Peel and slice apples. In 12-inch skillet over high heat, heat 3 tablespoons margarine, 3 tablespoons packed brown sugar, and 1 teaspoon lemon juice until melted. Stir in the apples to coat them. Continue cooking over high heat until apples are golden brown and softened (about 15 minutes). Remove apples to a bowl.

7. Peel and slice pears. In same skillet over high heat, cook 3 tablespoons margarine, 3 tablespoons brown sugar, and 1 teaspoon lemon juice until melted. Stir in pears and dried cherries to coat them. Continue cooking over high heat until pears are golden and liquid thickens (about 20 minutes). Add pears to apple mixture in bowl. If not serving right away, cover and refrigerate.

8. To serve, reheat fruit mixture. Arrange phyllo cups on platter. Place scoop of frozen nondairy dessert in each phyllo cup; top with warm fruit. Serve immediately.

Surprise Hanukkah Gelt

Amount: 24 candies

  2 4-ounce packages sweet cooking chocolate
  2 1-ounce squares unsweetened chocolate
  ¼ of 12-ounce bag of pretzels
  24 gold and/or silver foil squares (4″ by 4″) (available wher-
    ever chocolate and candy-making supplies are sold)

About 1½ hours before serving or up to 1 week ahead:

  1. Place a 16-inch-long piece of plastic wrap over top of mini muffin pan (with 12 1¾-inch cups); press plastic wrap into each cup. Repeat with a second pan. Set pans aside.

  2. Chop both kinds of chocolate and place in heavy 2-quart saucepan. Over low heat, cook chocolate, stirring frequently, until melted and smooth. Remove saucepan from heat.

  3. Place pretzels in heavyweight plastic bag. Crush pretzels lightly with rolling pin; stir into melted chocolate.

  4. Spoon chocolate mixture into mini muffin-pan cups to fill almost halfway, or place chocolate mixture in a heavyweight plastic bag. With scissors, snip off one corner of bag and squeeze chocolate mixture into mini muffin-pan cups. Gently tap muffin pans on counter to distribute chocolate mixture evenly. Refrigerate 30 minutes or until chocolate is firm and fully set.

  5. Remove pans from refrigerator. Peel plastic wrap from chocolates and trim any rough edges with knife. Wrap each chocolate in a gold or silver foil square.

> *You are the light of the world. A city on a hill cannot be hidden. Neither do people light a lamp and put it under a bowl. Instead they put it on its stand, and it gives light to everyone in the house. In the same way, let your light shine before men, that they may see your good deeds and praise your Father in heaven*—Matthew 5:14–16 (NIV).

Christmas

For today in the city of David there has been born for you a Savior, who is Christ the Lord.

—*Luke 2:11*

When Observed: December 25

Earliest Observance: Early fourth century

Once a year the Christmas season influences both the sacred and secular segments of life. Christmas is everywhere: on the side of buses, in malls, on banners, in music on the radio and television, and in CD music in our living rooms. For approximately 45 days each year our culture confronts Jesus.

You may accept Him or reject Him, but you can't ignore Him because He's everywhere.

For those of us who claim His name, Christmas ushers in a wonderful time of the year. This season speaks of the Truth. Because of God's gift of His Son born in Bethlehem, nothing can separate us from His love. Light, life, and love are again on our side. The world pauses to listen.

We, as Christians, should be witnesses telling others whereby they, too, can find hope, joy, and strength in their lives.

We must be transformed by His grace—not through our efforts but by what Christ did in His birth, life, and death on the cross.

This grace and future hope can be experienced here on earth in the present time. In John 10:10 (NIV), Jesus said, "I have come that they may have life, and have it to the full."

Christmas is the good news of transforming grace. Through Jesus Christ we are freed to take on a life of new meaning—a life that is trusting, hopeful, and compassionate.

Christmas reminds us of why we are here, and the "why" questions of life are often the most important ones we ask. Without that understanding, we just go through the agonizing motions of the world, not realizing or recognizing the significance of this season.

Christmas celebrates the birth of Jesus Christ with the message of peace on earth, goodwill toward men. Luke 2:1–7 says:

> Now it came about in those days that a decree went out from Caesar Augustus, that a census be taken of all the inhabited earth. This was the first census taken while Quirinius was governor of Syria. And all were proceeding to register for the census, everyone to his own city. And Joseph also went up from Galilee, from the city of Nazareth, to Judea, to the city of David, which is called Bethlehem, because he was of the house and family of David, in order to register, along with Mary, who was engaged to him, and was with child. And it came about that while they were there, the days were completed for her to give birth. And she gave birth to her first-born son; and she wrapped Him in cloths, and laid Him in a manger, because there was no room for them in the inn.

Although the commercialization of Christmas is frustrating to many people, the celebration can give a warm glow at a cold time of the year.

People in a hundred languages sing the joys of Christmas and share their respective countries' traditions. Austria gave us "Silent Night"; England contributed the mistletoe ball and wassail; Germany, the Christmas tree; Scandinavia, the Yule candle and Yule log; Mexico, the poinsettia plant. These traditions continue to be celebrated with fresh and innovative ideas.

The biblical narrative of the birth of Jesus contains no indication of the date that the event occurred. Luke's report, however, that the shepherds were "staying out in the fields, and keeping watch over their flock by night," suggests that Jesus may have been born in summer or early fall.

Jesus

The Word of God became flesh . . .
The Son of God became man . . .
The Lord of all became a servant . . .
The Righteous One was made sin . . .
The Eternal One tasted death . . .
The Risen One now lives in men . . .
The Seated One is coming again!

In the third century, efforts were made to determine the actual date of the nativity, but only in a.d. 336 was definite mention made of December 25.

The early Puritans in America felt that they could not celebrate this day for which there was no biblical sanction. Generally speaking, feelings toward Christmas were divided according to religious denomination.

The diminishing objection to Christmas after 1750 was brought about by the rapid growth of America as a whole. In 1836, Alabama was the first state to grant legal recognition to Christmas. By 1890, all the states and territories had made similar acknowledgment. Christmas is the only annual religious holiday to receive official secular sanction.

November and December
Weekly Activity Schedule

No matter how often we tell ourselves that this year is going to be different, that we're going to stop giving so much, eating so much, and expecting so much—it just doesn't seem to happen that way.

Disappointments and expectations seem greater than at any other time of the year. Families are not really the picture-perfect photos we see portrayed in magazines and on greeting cards.

Hearts are never quite as giving and forgiving as we would like them to be. Feelings get hurt and tensions run high.

There is a lot to do, and it's all being added to a schedule which may have been just barely workable before the holidays. Jobs, car pools, meals, laundry, illness, homework, etc., still exist and need attention. Use the "Week 1" form at the end of this chapter to help you get organized.

Our world doesn't stop because the calendar says it's holiday time, so be kind to yourself and ask for help. Keep those goals and expectations realistic and spend time celebrating the part of Christmas that means the most to you. If you don't have time to bake this year and you've always done it, don't do it. Find a good bakery or pay a teen to bake for you.

> *There is a time for everything, and a season for every activity under heaven*—Ecclesiastes 3:1 (NIV).

Second Week in November

It takes so little time to save time. The selection of your Christmas cards can be made in October or the first part of November. But the best way is to have purchased your cards at the 50-percent-off discounts right after the previous Christmas. Christmas cards are personal selections and should be thought through. Does the card say what you feel as a family? What message do you want to convey? With rising postal costs and increasingly busy schedules, many people have geared down on card-giving, and correspondence in general. Christmas-card-sending may be the only news we send or receive all year.

If you send cards, you will receive them. Nothing takes the stress out of a hectic day in December like sitting down with a letter or note from an old friend. It's a gift in itself. However, with every card you send, take the time to jot a few lines of what's happening. A card with just a signature is cold and impersonal. I feel that if you are going to take the time and expense to send out cards, there should be more than just a card with a signature.

Keep an updated record of the cards you send. We've provided a "Christmas Card Record" chart at the end of this chapter. As you receive cards, check to see if the return addresses are the same as what you have. Make any changes right away so you are sure to have the correct address for next year.

If you don't want to invest in cards, send postcards. The postage is less and there's room enough for a personal message.

If you have a lot of family news, consider photocopying a letter. This may be important to do the year you have moved, added a new baby, or done something truly newsworthy. Otherwise, keep your messages short.

Set up a Christmas-card station if room is available, or set up a card table and have everything collected in one spot: stamps, colored pens, address labels, address book, etc. You can address your envelopes ahead of time and write notes as you have time here or there. Don't forget to recruit help from the family and work together.

If you use printed cards, write a short note to add a personal touch, or have the children sign their names by themselves. Ten minutes of your time to write a note can mean more than a gift. Enclose a photo to friends whom you haven't seen for a year or more. I have an album of Christmas photos from friends, and we have watched children grow through these pictures.

We use and market a beautiful Christmas memory book for keeping 25 years of Christmas memories. For each year there is a spot for a holiday family photo, for the Christmas card sent that year, and for a written account of the year's events.

We think these books are so special that we make them available at all our seminars. It also makes a perfect wedding gift. If we had started one when we first married, we would be well into our second book. I'll never forget the story of a young bride, Cecila, married to Dr. Dick Patchett, an ophthalmologist. She purchased one of our Christmas Memory Books and was so excited as she showed the book to her new husband. He looked it over and then asked, "Where's the second book?" "What do you mean, second book?" bubbled Cecila. "We'll be married more than 25 years, and one won't be enough." She quickly got another book.

We take our family Christmas photo every Thanksgiving. That is one time we all seem to be together. It's fun, too, if you can coordinate your clothing. Be creative and do your own thing. Include the pets, teddy bears, and favorite dolls or toys.

Make up your Christmas gift list early in November. Be sure to list everyone you want to remember—from the newspaper boy to your dentist. Don't forget anyone who has been special to you and extra helpful this past year.

We've given you a chart to help organize the gift-giving dilemma. (See "Gifts Given" chart at end of chapter.) This helps me to remember who gets what. I do a lot of food and food basket giving. I need that list by my side as I put together my holiday love baskets. You can also refer back to your list to make sure you aren't repeating gifts.

We've also given you a chart for recording gifts received. (See "Gifts Received" chart at end of chapter.) With all the excitement on Christmas morning, it's hard to remember who gave you what. Keep a record of each gift as it's opened. Then, once a thank you has been written, check the appropriate blank.

It's still early November, and if you didn't buy your gift wrap after Christmas last year, now is the time to do it. Keep a good supply of scotch tape; gift tags; red, green, and white ribbon; and lots of tissue paper.

Gift tags can be made ahead of time from last year's Christmas cards—a great cut-and-paste project for children. Tags can also be made from matching wrapping paper cut into different shapes: stars, angels, teddy bears, squares, hearts, etc.

Continuing into the first week of November, you should seriously be purchasing Christmas gifts—especially those which need to be mailed out of state or out of the country. We will cover rules for mailing in another section.

Third Week in November

Check your Christmas-card list. Update names and addresses and decide if you will send one to everyone you know or just to those people who live out of town.

People will start hunting for gift ideas for you and other members of the family (see end of chapter). Make a "wish list" for yourself. I really struggle with this, but Bob and the children have no problem making up their lists, and it's wonderful to know what they want and/or need. I am learning not to be bashful with my wishes. Remember to update sizes for the children when telling grandparents so exchanges are kept to a minimum.

Bake early and freeze food, if possible. It will make your last-minute list go a lot easier. Rolls, breads, and even some desserts freeze beautifully.

Fourth Week in November

It's only the fourth week in November, so let's get a good jump on organization.

Find shipping boxes, wrap, and ship all out-of-state Christmas gifts, if possible, before December 1.

If you haven't already done so, send out any holiday invitations for parties, potlucks, Christmas teas, open houses, or any gatherings you are planning. By doing this early, people will make their plans around yours. (See "Hospitality Sheet" chart at end of chapter.)

Advent will begin soon, so if you plan on having an Advent wreath with candles or Advent calendars for the children, get them out now. If you plan to purchase an Advent calendar this year, look for a Christ-centered one—try your Christian bookstore. Find one that has Scriptures and/or tells the Christmas story. As each window is opened, it will give you and the family an opportunity to follow the events leading up to Christ's birth.

Check your church calendar, newspaper, or community bulletin for special Advent events.

Glory to God in the highest, and on earth, peace to men on whom his favor rests—Luke 2:14 (NIV).

First Week of December

Finish up Christmas-gift shopping and don't forget the gift wrap, batteries, film, tree-ornament hooks, or any other items you might need. Did you remember to put on your gift list a small remembrance for your postal person, receptionist, church secretary, trashman, dentist, doctor, pediatrician, or any other person who has served you well this past year?

Once you have made your major purchases, remind yourself you are finished so you won't be tempted to buy more than you intended just because you suddenly get the Christmas spirit! Leave some things such as stocking stuffers until the last minute if it makes you happy to be a part of the hustle and bustle.

Pamper yourself. Think about your holiday wardrobe. Does anything need to be cleaned, hemmed, pressed, or altered? Do you need to add new accessories to freshen up the old basic Christmas dress? Schedule time for a mid-December hair appointment, manicure, or maybe a massage. Do whatever time and finances will allow, but do treat yourself to a rejuvenating experience, if at all possible. And try to get plenty of sleep and exercise.

How to Spend Within Your Holiday Means

By Thanksgiving at the latest, realistically estimate how much you can afford to spend. Then, make out a list of people to whom you want to give gifts, what you would like to buy for each person, along with the approximate price of the item. A quick total may show that you must scale back on the amount spent for each person or trim the number of people on your list. Take the list with you when you shop and stick to it!

Don't forget to budget for the "hidden costs" of Christmas. These include tree decorations, gift wrap, Christmas cards, and postage, and any entertaining you do.

To avoid being haunted by the ghosts of Christmas credit past, use cash or a check whenever possible. Using cash slows down your spending and forces you to weigh your purchases more carefully.

If you must use charge cards, clip half an index card to the back of the credit card. Each time you use it, enter the amount of your purchase on the index card and keep a running total, so that you are continually aware of how much you will have to come up with when the bills start rolling in during January.

Say no to holiday charge accounts that allow you to buy now and delay payment until February (unless you have an assured bonus or other cash reserve coming to cover your bill). The allure of "free money" is a trap you would be wise to avoid.

Ensure that you will be able to do next year's buying in cash by estimating how much your Christmas spending will be, dividing that amount into 12 monthly allotments, and then setting aside that amount each month in either a Christmas club or a money market account.

Plan your holiday entertaining menus for Christmas Eve and/or Christmas Day. If you have room in your freezer, purchase your turkey early. If you are having a fresh turkey, goose, or ham, place your order now.

Decide what table linens you will be using and Scotchguard them; it's a great fabric protector. Spills will be easier to remove.

Keep candles in the freezer until ready for use. That way they don't have a tendency to drip or spark when lit.

Plan several baking days and put these on your calendar. Have at least one day with the children to make those special Christmas cookies and gingerbread men. That way mentally you will be prepared for the mess—dough, powdered sugar, colored frosting, coconut, and sugar all over the children. Let it be fun for them. How proud they will be when they serve a plate of their own creations!

Your days or evenings of cooking can be spent making and freezing hors d'oeuvres, casseroles, fruitcakes, plum puddings, or anything else which should have time to mellow. Not only will the food mellow, but you will also feel mellower because you've gotten a good start on a busy holiday.

Begin addressing Christmas cards if you haven't already.

Having trouble with candles standing up? Twist a rubber band around the base before inserting the candle into the holder. Or keep candles firmly in place by putting a little florist's clay in the holder.

When candles drip on your pretty tablecloths, fear not. Lay paper towels on the ironing board over and under the drips and iron the wax spots with a medium-to-hot iron. Keep moving the paper towels until the wax is absorbed into them. Presto! The wax is gone and the cloth is saved.

Put up Christmas decorations such as wreaths, garlands, candles, nativity scenes, front-door decorations, and bows. String up the outdoor lights. This is a good project for teenagers—they love climbing ladders and getting on roofs. They could make themselves available to do it for the neighborhood and make extra Christmas money or do it as a ministry to people in the church. A cup of hot cider and Christmas cookies is good payment for a hardworking, hungry teen.

The Story of Santa Claus

Many people do not know that there is a special story about who Santa Claus really was. There was a special Christian man who lived a long time ago. His name was Nicholas, and we call him St. Nicholas because saint means "someone who belongs to God." In St. Nicholas's town there were many poor children. They didn't have enough food, clothes, or toys. St. Nicholas used his money to buy food, clothes, and toys for the poor children. He didn't want them to be embarrassed by his gifts, so he gave them secretly.

St. Nicholas also told everyone about Jesus and how much God loved them. Many people became Christians because of what St. Nicholas said. Then some mean people who hated Jesus put St. Nicholas in jail to keep him from telling people about Jesus and helping people. St. Nicholas continued to tell people about Jesus until the mean people finally had him killed.

Because of how much St. Nicholas loved Jesus, and because of the many gifts he gave the poor children in his town, we still remember St. Nicholas at Christmastime. All of the gifts he gave and all of the gifts we give are to remind us of the very best gift anyone ever gave . . . when God the Father gave His only Son, Jesus Christ, to us for our salvation.

—Gretchen Passantino, *Discipleship Journal*

Review your list again for holiday entertaining and menu planning. Keep filling the freezer with yummy baked items. What special love gifts these are for friends and neighbors—especially for the busy working woman whose time is so limited.

A fun idea is to give a favorite recipe and with it include one or two ingredients. One of my favorites is a triple-chocolate-cake recipe. Everyone loves it, and it's so easy—only three steps and five minutes. This is one I couldn't live without for any last-minute special dessert.

I give the recipe and include a package of chocolate chips, a box of chocolate pudding, and the box of chocolate cake mix.

Emilie's Triple Chocolate Fudge Cake

Amount: 10 to 12 servings

Prepare 1 3⅜-ounce package of chocolate pudding mix (cooked type) as directed on package. Blend chocolate cake mix (dry mix) into hot pudding. Pour ingredients into prepared oblong pan, 13″ × 9½″ × 2″.

Sprinkle with ½ cup semisweet chocolate pieces and ½ cup chopped nuts. Bake 30 to 35 minutes at 350°. Serve warm with whipped cream or ice cream—also delicious plain.

Following are great recipes for Christmas Spiced Tea and Holiday Wassail. Make a double batch and divide it into small, attractive jars. Put on a holiday label with instructions and tie a red ribbon around each jar. Your gift recipient will love it and enjoy the special thought for the holiday season.

Christmas Spiced Tea

Amount: makes 1½ quarts

1 cup instant tea (dry) (can use decaffeinated)
2 cups dry lemonade mix (orange flavor)
3 cups sugar (may use 1½ cups sugar substitute and 1½ cups sugar)
½ cup red hots (candy)
1 teaspoon cinnamon
½ teaspoon powdered cloves
½ package dry lemonade mix (8 ounces)

To one cup of hot water, add one heaping tablespoon of mix.

Gifts don't have to be expensive. The effort and love that you put into your homemade gifts will be especially appreciated.

Make a batch of bran muffins. You can give the recipe, a muffin tin, and six muffins in the tin. Wrap the tin with clear cellophane wrap, tie a bell and pretty bow on top, and share your love of muffins with your family and friends.

The word became flesh and made his dwelling among us. We have seen his glory, the glory of the One and Only, who came from the Father, full of grace and truth—John 1:14 (NIV).

When I have a holiday party, open house, or tea, I serve my Holiday Wassail. It has received lots of compliments and makes the house smell festive and wonderful.

Holiday Wassail Recipe

1 gallon apple cider
1 large can pineapple juice (unsweetened)
3/4 cup strong tea (herb tea optional)

In a cheesecloth sack put:

1 tablespoon whole cloves
1 tablespoon whole allspice
2 sticks cinnamon

This is great cooked in a Crockpot. Let it simmer slowly for four to six hours. You can add water if it evaporates too much. Your house will smell wonderful, and friends and family will love it!

Second Week of December

Finish wrapping your Christmas presents and update your gift list. This will lessen last-minute gift-wrapping. Do you have a good hiding place for the children's gifts? If not, consider asking a neighbor to swap hiding places with you.

If you made any catalog purchases, check your orders. Has everything arrived? If not, call the customer service department and inquire. Remember your quiet and gentle spirit! The customer service representatives may be frazzled and not as organized as you are. Shop for necessary gift substitutes or have Plan B ready if the order doesn't arrive in time.

The time frame for decorating is a personal or family decision. We like to have our decorations up for the whole month, so we begin early. Our tree goes up by the second week in December. It may be fun to get a few things out each day for a week or so, culminating your efforts with the trimming of the tree. This makes it easier for the busy woman and fun for the kids, too.

The Candy Cane

I searched through the town, looking at all the "trappings" of the season, the santas and the reindeer, the stockings and the elves, hoping to find the real meaning of Christmas. Then, there it was . . . the candy cane. The legend is that it was invented by a Christian in England in the seventeenth century. At that time, the government would not let people celebrate Christmas. So, a candy maker made candy shaped like a shepherd's crook to be a secret symbol of Jesus. The white stripe represented the purity of Jesus and the red stripe represented His life that He gave for each of us. The candy was a double gift: a sweet treat and a symbol of Christmas.

My friend, Ginny Pasqualucci, keeps her decorations up well into January because she loves Christmas so much. Recently, she went to the Holy Land for Christmas. They had us over for dinner on January 29 for a full Christmas evening, complete with Bing Crosby singing "White Christmas," with all the decorations still up and gifts under their two trees. It was wonderful. So do whatever you prefer—it's kosher.

Remember those replacement bulbs for your light strings? Do you have enough for tree-trimming day, plus ornament hangers for the ornaments?

Make tree-trimming a special time of fun. Play Christmas tapes and light a few candles if it is during the evening. Make an easy meal, or you could have a cookie-and-hot-spiced-tea platter ready for "halftime." This is a good time to pull a casserole from the freezer for dinner.

If you are planning a Christmas Eve potluck or buffet, review your menu. This can become a tradition. One week before, each family member can plan a dish to serve. Prepare the dish a day or two ahead. After Christmas Eve services, spread out the buffet near the tree on snack tables. You can have a sing-along, read the Bible, and serve communion.

The Christmas breakfast brunch menu, if you're serving one, should be checked. Make sure you have all the ingredients you need in your pantry.

Plan your table settings and centerpiece.

Thank you, God, for quiet places far from life's crowded ways, where our hearts find true contentment and our souls fill up with praise— Author unknown.

Third Week of December

The countdown continues. Double-check your shopping lists, supplies, menus, etc. You may have parties to attend yourself. Save the invitations until you have written your thank-you notes. Take a baked goodie, some Christmas Spiced Tea, or a handmade ornament as a hostess gift.

If your tree didn't go up last week, this may be the week to put it up. You may want to invite friends to help make it a festive event. String fresh popcorn or cranberries (this takes patience).

Check your holiday calendar for this week and next, including special church services that you will want to attend. Are you beginning to feel overwhelmed—hustled, hurried, and hassled? If so, prioritize events and extend regrets to those you really don't have to attend. You need time for yourself if you are going to enjoy the next two weeks. It's okay to say no.

Make a list of holiday telephone calls you want to make to family and friends and begin making them now. The circuits will be very busy on Christmas Eve and Christmas Day, and you don't want to spend all your time dialing the phone.

But the angel said to them, "Do not be afraid. I bring you good news of great joy that will be for all the people. Today in the town of David a Savior has been born to you; he is Christ the Lord"—Luke 2:10–11 (NIV).

Many families have a birthday cake for Jesus. This can be made ahead and frozen. One mom shared an idea with her family of having a birthday cake for Jesus complete with candles. They decided to do it after the presents were opened on Christmas morning. Another family has a very simple party at the end of Christmas Day—with packages all opened, paper everywhere, and dirty dishes. They take ten minutes and sing "Happy Birthday, Jesus," blow out the candles on a cake, and have a quiet family communion. The eating of the cake is not what is important. That can be done another day if tummies are too full. The purpose is to focus on the real meaning of Christmas.

Christmas Week

There's not much left to do—we have our plan, and the plan is working.

Go over the menus and supplies one more time. Any last-minute purchases necessary? Shop for groceries.

Try to keep normal routines, if possible, because small children sense the excitement and can be overwhelmed. Schedule reading times with them. Our grandchildren love the Christmas story all year long—they love to hear it over and over. Talk about what the true meaning of Christmas is—how we give gifts just as the wise men brought gifts to the Christ child.

Place the wrapped gifts under the tree, if you haven't already done so. If you open most of the gifts on Christmas Day, consider letting each child open one early. It may be the most appreciated gift.

Keep the list of gifts received up-to-date as each present is opened. This makes writing thank-you notes much easier.

Check your stocking-stuffer items and have them ready to fill on Christmas Eve—late. If Santa comes to your house, leave a snack for him—and don't forget a carrot for Rudolph!

Set your Christmas Eve and/or Christmas Day tables a few days ahead. Put out those serving dishes labeled with the $3'' \times 5''$ cards.

Relax and enjoy yourself and your family. Have a very Merry Christmas. You've worked hard and planned well. You deserve a blessed Christmas.

Parcel Post Shopping Hints

This is the time of year when post office lobbies draw crowds.

The U.S. Postal Service's first rule at this time of year is "the earlier the better." Here are additional tips for ensuring that your mail arrives in time for the holidays.

1. *Containers*—The postal service says fiberboard boxes, such as those available at grocery stores and other retailers, are ideal. Popular-sized boxes and mailing envelopes or bags are available at stationers and post office branches.

2. *Packing*—Cushion box contents with crumpled newspaper. Place the paper around all sides, corners, top, and bottom so the contents won't move, even if you shake the box. Foam shells, "popcorn," and padding are sold for cushioning and may be worth the investment if the items you're planning to send are particularly fragile. Mark the package in three places if the contents are fragile: above the address, below the postage, and on the reverse side.

Padded mailing envelopes or bags are ideal for small items, including books. Avoid using twine, cord, or string. No wrapping paper is allowed on the outside of packages. With boxes, brown paper is not necessary. Put a slip of paper with the name and address of the recipient inside the box, as well as on the outside.

3. *Sealing*—Close the carton with one of the three recommended types of tape: pressure-sensitive, nylon-reinforced paper, or glass-reinforced pressure sensitive. No scotch tape, please!

4. *Addressing*—Use smudge-proof ink. Put the recipient's name and address in the lower right portion of the package. Cover the label with clear tape to waterproof. Put your return address in the upper left corner of only one side of the package. Remove all other labels from the box. Use correct zip codes—a wrong zip code can delay delivery.

5. *Christmas cards*—Holiday cards must be in standard-size envelopes at least 3½″ high and 5″ long. If the card is extra large, you will have to pay extra postage. If in doubt, have the envelope measured by a postal clerk.

Mail not only early in the month, but also early in the day. If you are mailing across the continent, the U.S. Postal Service advises allowing eight to ten days for packages and cards.

When mailing a gift-wrapped present, stuff the package into a dry cleaning plastic bag with crumpled newspapers outside the bag as buffers. That way the newsprint won't rub off on the wrapping paper. Protect the bow from being crushed by covering it with a plastic berry basket—the type strawberries come in.

Surviving the Stress of Shopping

Busy women today don't even want to think about Christmas until after Thanksgiving. We simply haven't had the time to get into stores to shop. We have had meetings to attend and deadlines to meet. The teacher whose energies went into the classroom and who postponed shopping until school was out is now faced with a dilemma. Even many retailers who have been busy selling to others haven't had time themselves to buy gifts. We all share a common expression: "Help!" However, there is hope. Organization is the key to the task. We all have limited time. Every minute we spend in the stores must have a purpose. Before we begin, we must plan our shopping strategy.

She will give birth to a son, and you are to give him the name Jesus, because he will save his people from their sins—Matthew 1:21 (NIV).

1. In your mind review all the stores in a center or mall. Perhaps a better idea is to write them down: bookstore, china shop, hardware store, jewelry store, clothing shop, etc. Hopefully you can accomplish the majority of your shopping in one trip.

2. Make a list based on the shops within a particular mall. Work your way around mentally, jotting down specific people.

3. Take advantage of wrapping services and/or gift boxes, ribbon, and tissue. Have as many gifts as you can ready to place under the tree when you arrive home.

4. Do two things at once. If, for example, you purchase clothing for three people which includes gift-wrapping, allow the clerks to finish the packages while you visit other shops. Circle back at the end of the day and collect your packages.

5. Decide before you go out if this year you are purchasing "one big gift" or lots of little things. Each year I do things a bit differently.

6. Give something an unusual touch. For example, if you are giving a cookbook, wrap it in a tea towel or add an apron or muffin tin. If it's a piece of jewelry, include a nightshirt. Compress your gift into a can or a jar.

Christmas Prayer
May the spirit of giving
Go on through the year,
Bringing love, laughter,
Hope, and good cheer.
Gifts wrapped with charity,
Joy, peace, and grace,

Ribboned with happiness,
A tender embrace.
   —Norma Woodbridge

7. Think in categories: How many golfers, skiers, and tennis players are on your list? If buying for one, buy for three. What about duplicate gifts? Can you give all your neighbors a soup mix or the gourmet cheese or spiced-mustard jar? Absolutely! Many times one stop will take care of five or six gifts.

8. You can also use the phone to your advantage. Call your florist to make up a unique silk arrangement in a basket of soaps and hand cream, etc. The shop will often wrap and deliver the baskets for you. And anyone would love to receive a pretty holiday arrangement with a candle to use as a Christmas table centerpiece.

9. For the hard-to-please and those people who have everything, a gift certificate for a restaurant, ice cream shop, or fast-food restaurant (children love that) are always a hit.

10. Take a few breaks during your shopping to review your list and collect your thoughts. Plan a coffee, tea, or lunch break. You will also need to make periodic trips to lock the packages in your car.

11. Don't leave the shopping area until you are sure you have accomplished all you wanted to do in that spot. Retracing your steps or making second trips isn't practical.

12. Ask a teenager or a friend who loves to shop to pick something up for you.

13. Remember to keep it simple. The love you put into each gift will be what lasts. This season is the time for warmth, fellowship, shared experiences, and hospitality.

14. Hire your teenagers to help out by running errands, wrapping gifts, tying bows, preparing food, sending out party invitations, etc. This is a great teaching time for them.

15. Plan a family conference time when you all can decide what items rate as top priorities. Reconfirm what needs to be done and what's not so meaningful this year. If the front-door wreath or a nativity scene on the mantel are essential, put these on the list of "to dos." If, on the other hand, no one cares about making gingerbread cookies, scratch them off the list.

16. As a group, decide how much is to be spent on presents. There is no point in starting the new year with huge bills and a lot of guilt.

17. Keep your sense of humor and perspective. Make it fun. The whole point is to see the season in terms of memories and lasting values. What is the heart of the celebration? If togetherness and a spirit of giving are concepts you want to teach, preserve, and nurture, build on these for this month of Christmas.

18. Spend time together making cookies, framing photographs to give to grandparents, assembling baskets of goodies for the neighbors, directing and filming your own Christmas video, or just gathering around the fireplace for hot cider and good talk. These are the times you will treasure long after the gift wrap and food scraps have gone into the trash.

> *Suddenly a great company of the heavenly host appeared with the angel, praising God and saying, "Glory to God in the highest, and on earth peace to men on whom his favor rests"*—Luke 2:13–14.

How to Keep Holidays Stressless

Here are a few hints and tips to keep your holidays more stress-free.

1. Ask your family members to share their favorite holiday memory. You may be surprised how few meals and toys they mention. We did this at our church Christmas party one year and, to my surprise, very few people could recall special holiday memories. If this is the case, create some memories. Make your time count. A memory lasts forever, but toys get broken.

2. Settle family matters before holiday time. Families are often separated by divorce or geographic distance, and disputes can arise. Try to make all the arrangements well ahead of time. If you have out-of-town guests, decide where they will stay and let them know before they arrive if they will need a hotel room. Share your time equally and fairly with each set of grandparents, or take turns from year to year. Avoid overcommitment—it can make for situations where people are overtired and overreact.

3. Don't gain weight. Feeling fat in party clothes can really add to your stress and tension. Overeating can make you feel absolutely

awful. Try to schedule the same exercise you normally do. If you are not exercising now, make it a goal for the new year.

There will be a great deal of extra goodies around, so be selective about what you eat. Stick to the things that are worth it—like your favorites that you see only at holiday time.

Only go past the part of the food table where the fruit or veggie platter is. If you decide now not to overdo it, you won't have to make a New Year's resolution later to lose weight.

4. Remember what really matters. As Christians, Christmas is the time for celebrating the birth of Christ, and everything else comes after that special celebration. The hassles will take care of themselves.

5. Watch your finances carefully. Talk about tension and depression! Overspending will do it, especially if you've overcharged and have those bills to look forward to later. Ask the Lord to help you in this area so you won't get caught up in the spirit of things and buy much more than you budgeted for.

Remember that a handmade gift or baked item can be more valuable than an expensive present. Special phone calls or a coupon for an "after-Christmas lunch treat" can mean as much to friends as an expensive gift they may or may not use or like. Set your budget and stick to it. Many people have a special Christmas fund set aside. That makes it easy and, when that's gone, it's gone. Otherwise, spread your purchases over a period of time and charge only the amount you intend to spend. That's why we suggest you begin your gift shopping early in November so it doesn't all come at once.

6. It's okay to say no. You would like to do it all, be everywhere, and see everything. But for today's busy woman, it just can't be. Don't be afraid to say, "No, we need this time together as a family," or "No, I can't bake the extra cookies, but I'd be happy to buy some." Don't feel guilty about those things you simply cannot do.

7. Plan some time for yourself. You can read a book, listen to a music tape, take a bubble bath by candlelight, get a good haircut, have your nails polished, or maybe even buy yourself a new nightgown, blouse, or holiday sweater. By taking care of yourself, that last-minute hassle about your appearance won't happen.

8. Christmas will come regardless if you have done everything on your lists or not. Do those things which really matter and let the others fall where they may.

Family, friends, and above all, the true meaning of Christmas, are what count. Remember: 85 percent of our stress is caused by disorganization.

> *So they [the shepherds] hurried off and found Mary and Joseph, and the baby, who was lying in the manger*—Luke 2:16.

Decorating and Entertaining Ideas

The most important entertaining you will do this year, and especially during the Christmas season, will be for your own family. In our home it's a special time for all of us. I bring out what china, crystal, and silver I have for these family times. The children have learned to handle the dishes gently, and it makes for treasured learning times. Even if you don't have these kinds of items, bring out your best—whatever it is: paper, plastic, metal, china, or crystal. Don't let the lack of things prevent you from decorating and entertaining.

1. *Sheets for tablecloths*—I have fun mixing and matching my table settings. Here are a few ideas I use to make my tables creative and different. Regardless of what the holiday may be, I use sheets for making tablecloths and napkins. I'll take the saucer from my set of eight dishes to the store to look for sheets that might match or coordinate. Many times I'll find a sheet on sale that will work perfectly. I keep my eyes open all year for white sales, and I've found some great bargains.

To make one tablecloth and 12 napkins for a standard-size table, use a king-size flat sheet. If you don't want so many napkins, or if you have a small table, you can use a full- or queen-size sheet. A twin sheet will do if you don't want matching napkins. (You can make six napkins out of one yard of coordinating fabric. Cut each napkin 15″ square.) It is quite alright to leave the sheet's border on the tablecloth, if you wish. People don't usually go around to see if you have a border on the other side.

Measure the length and width of your table and add six inches to hang over each side. Then add one inch for a turn-under hem. Cut your tablecloth out first. Then make your napkins out of the remainder. A nice size for napkins is 18″ square, but you may want a smaller napkin.

If you are making a round tablecloth, fold the sheet in half and cut a string the length of the radius of your table plus the six-inch drop and one-inch hem. Mark your half-circle cutting line with pins or chalk. Cut your napkins out right next to each other. It's always nice to finish the napkins with lace or eyelet embroidery.

I continue to look for Christmas sheets, but so far haven't found any with poinsettias, holly, or red-and-green prints or stripes. Many times I have to settle for holiday fabric such as taffeta, felt, or even lace panel curtains. I bought a lace panel curtain at K-Mart for $5.99 one year and made a tablecloth. I also made six napkins and one lace runner from it.

A green or red felt fabric tablecloth is great for Christmas. You can buy felt by the yard. It doesn't have to be hemmed, and it's nice and wide so no sewing is needed. Also, today's new felt is completely washable. It looks beautiful as is, or you can add a plaid runner, taffeta overcloth, or even holiday place mats. Napkin rings can be made with taffeta ribbon by tying a bow around the napkin.

2. *Napkin rings*—Cover empty toilet paper rolls with lace and cut the rolls 2″ to 3″ in width for simple but nice napkin rings.

Paint wooden clothespins red, green, or white to clip on your napkins. Names can be personalized with a paint pen from the craft store.

Using quilted fabric, cut a boot, star, or angel, leaving an opening at the top for a napkin. The fabric can be sewn or glue-gunned together.

Cookie cutters (plastic or metal) make great napkin rings. You can find them in gourmet stores, kitchen sections of department stores, and catalogs. They come in all shapes.

Napkin rings can be made out of many different materials. One year we were having 26 people for our family Christmas dinner. I was using an old standby poinsettia fabric tablecloth I had used previously, but I wanted to jazz it up a bit. I found some wooden napkin rings—cheap! I bought some red silk poinsettia flowers (small version), cut off the long stem, and glue-gunned the flower to the plain wooden rings. It was sensational with my green napkins, but the best part was I had 26 matching napkin rings for less than 25 cents each. I've used them for the past four years. They store well and keep their shape as long as I put them in my numbered storage boxes.

If you want to go fancy, start collecting china napkin rings. Buy two to four each year until you have enough for your table, or let your family know you're collecting them. It's a great gift idea.

Here's an idea for a Christ-centered napkin ring. Take your paper towel tube and cut it in two-inch widths. Then cut each ring so it opens. Write a Scripture inside and, with your glue gun or regular glue, cover the outside with ribbon, leaving tails long enough on each side of the opening to tie a bow. Slide your napkin through the ring. When your family members or guests untie the bow, there in front of their eyes will be God's Word. If you have each person read his or her verse, it can become the prayer of blessing.

3. *China collection*—Thirty-nine years ago when Bob and I were married, I shared with my family that I would like to collect china cups and saucers. Since that time, I have received over 37 gifts of beautiful cups and saucers, all different. I use them often, letting our guests pick out a favorite they would like to use that evening. I also have several different dinner plates that don't match, and it's so much fun to set a table with all the different plates and cups. They have become conversation pieces. I have also found some great buys on china plates at garage and estate sales. It's a fun hobby, and I use the plates and cups often.

I found a terrific buy at a bargain store. They were selling solid-red ceramic plates at 88 cents each. I use these red plates for Christmas with the green felt tablecloth and the red poinsettia napkin rings. The red plates come out again for Valentine's Day with pink and white napkins, and again on the Fourth of July for our red, white, and blue patio party. It's been a great investment.

4. *Centerpieces*—For a centerpiece, it's attractive to arrange several different-size candles at different heights (maybe six to ten candles). When lit, they make a beautiful arrangement, and yet it is so simple.

Tie a plaid Christmas bow around the base of your candles or around the candle holder itself. You can change the ribbons and bows for all seasons and holidays.

A pretty centerpiece is a wreath set on a glass plate on the table with candles in the center. Use your creativity with pinecones, poinsettias, flowers, ribbon, moss, ivy, and holly.

Make Christmas trees, gingerbread men, or small stuffed teddy bears in Christmas fabrics. Tie a bow around the neck of each bear.

These can be placed against each person's water glass as a gift to remember the evening in your home.

Teddy bears are universal and versatile. They can be used for hugging, loving, and sharing. Write a Scripture verse on a piece of paper and roll it up and insert it through the ribbon around teddy's neck. Not only do your guests take home a teddy bear, but they also take home God's Word.

Two Holiday Menus

Emilie's Orange Chicken
Brown Rice or Almond Brown Rice
Holiday Tomatoes & Steamed Broccoli
Tossed Salad with Emilie's Olive Oil Dressing
Carrot Bran Muffins
No-Bake Honey Cheesecake

Baked Parmesan Chicken
Brown or Wild Rice Pilaf
Christmas Red & Green Beans
Tossed Salad with Emilie's Olive Oil Dressing
Lemon Ginger Muffins
Ambrosia

Emilie's Orange Chicken

Amount: 4 to 6 servings

1. In a saucepan combine and heat while stirring until butter and jelly are melted and sauce is smooth:

1 cup orange juice
½ cup (1 stick) butter
½ cup red currant jelly
¼ cup Worcestershire sauce
2 large cloves garlic, crushed
1 tablespoon Dijon mustard

1 teaspoon powdered ginger
3 dashes Tabasco sauce

2. Cool sauce.
3. Place in baking pan:

1 whole chicken, skinned and quartered, or 8 skinless chicken
   breast pieces

4. Pour sauce over all; marinate in refrigerator for 2 to 3 hours.
5. Preheat oven to 350°.
6. Cover chicken and bake for 1 hour. Uncover, increase temperature to 400° and continue to bake, basting frequently until chicken is an even dark brown.

Baked Parmesan Chicken

Amount: 6 servings

1. Melt in baking pan at about 250°:

½ cup (1 stick) butter

2. Meanwhile, mix in blender until small bread crumbs are formed; pour into shallow bowl:

1 slice whole wheat bread (or as needed to make 1 cup)
2 sprigs parsley (or about ¼ cup minced)
½ cup parmesan cheese
⅛ teaspoon salt
⅛ teaspoon garlic powder

3. Skin and remove visible fat from chicken:

2 pounds boneless chicken breast pieces

4. Coat pieces of chicken in melted butter in pan, then coat with crumb mixture; lay single layer in remaining butter in pan.
5. Garnish with paprika and bake uncovered at 350° until tender (about 1 hour); baste 2 or 3 times during baking. Cover with foil if chicken begins to brown too much before it's done.

Reduced Fat Version (reduces the calories of fat by 29%!):
1. Reduce parmesan cheese to 3 tablespoons.
2. Omit the butter. Dip chicken pieces before coating with crumbs in nonfat milk (amount as needed).

3. Spray baking pan with no-stick cooking spray (Olive Oil Pam Spray preferred).

Brown Rice

Chewy, flavorful, and so easy to prepare! For company, add a dollop of sour cream to dress up each serving of Brown Rice or Almond Brown Rice.

Amount: 3 cups (4 to 6 servings)

1. Place together in a saucepan that has a tight-fitting lid, bring to a boil, and boil uncovered for 5 minutes:

2 to 2½ cups water
1 cup long-grain brown rice (see note below)
up to 1 teaspoon salt (optional)

2. Turn heat very low, cover pan with a tight-fitting lid, and simmer for 50 to 65 minutes. Do not lift lid during cooking. If you do, you will get sticky rice. To test for doneness, insert a spoon straight down through the rice to the bottom of the pot and press a bit of rice to one side. If no unabsorbed water remains, taste the rice to see if it is tender. If not done, cover and cook another 10 minutes or until done.

Note: Long-grain brown rice is less chewy and sticky than medium- or short-grain brown rice, and is closer to the texture of white rice. Most people prefer this texture.

Almond Brown Rice

A simple, yet delightful, variation on plain brown rice. Use the whole wheat kernel or berry, not ground or milled wheat.

Amount: 4 cups (6 to 8 servings)

1. Follow the recipe for Brown Rice with these changes:

use 2½ cups water
add ¼ cup whole wheat kernels (from health-food store) or
  wild rice
add ¼ cup almonds (chopped, slivered, or sliced)

2. For a little gourmet flare of added flavor, sauté almonds in 1 tablespoon butter and add to the cooked rice. For color, sauté a

chopped green onion with the almonds during the last minute, or garnish cooked rice with fresh chopped parsley.

Do not forget to entertain strangers, for by so doing some people have entertained angels without knowing it—Hebrews 13:2 (NIV).

Wild Rice Pilaf

Amount: About 4 cups (6 to 8 servings)

1. Sauté for 20 minutes over moderately low heat in skillet, stirring often:

¼ cup melted butter
1 cup uncooked wild rice
½ cup chopped or slivered almonds
6 to 8 small fresh mushrooms, sliced (or 4-ounce can, drained)—add during last 5 minutes of sautéing

2. While rice is sautéing, bring to a boil in saucepan:

3 cups chicken broth (add ½ teaspoon salt if broth is unsalted)

3. Place rice in casserole dish and pour the hot broth over rice. Add water chestnuts, cover, and bake 1½ hours at 350°.

8-ounce can sliced water chestnuts, drained and rinsed (optional)

4. To serve, top rice with:

¼ cup chopped fresh parsley or 1 to 2 chopped green onions (lightly sautéed in water for 2 minutes).

Brown Rice Pilaf

Amount: 4½ cups (6 servings)

1. Optional: Brown the rice, wheat, almonds (see amounts in step 2), stirring frequently over medium heat:

2 tablespoons butter, melted
2 tablespoons light olive or canola oil (health-food store)

2. Place in saucepan, bring to boil, and boil uncovered for 5 minutes:

1¼ cups long-grain brown rice

¼ cup whole wheat kernels (health-food store) or wild rice, or
¼ cup more brown rice

¼ cup slivered or chopped almonds

3 cups water or chicken broth

4 teaspoons Sue's "Kitchen Magic" seasoning (use chicken
broth, not water, if this seasoning is not available)

2 teaspoons Worcestershire sauce or soy sauce

3. Cover with tight fitting lid, reduce heat to very low, and simmer 50 to 60 minutes or until all the water is absorbed and rice is tender. Do not remove lid or stir during cooking as this tends to produce sticky rice.

4. While rice cooks, lightly sauté 2 chopped green onions for a minute or two in 1 or 2 tablespoons water.

5. Fold green onions into rice just before serving. Fresh chopped parsley or freeze-dried or fresh chives can be used in place of green onions.

Holiday Tomatoes

These are so easy to make that you don't need an exact recipe.

Amount: Prepare 1 to 2 halves per serving (depending on size of tomatoes)

1. Cut tomatoes in half.
2. Place in blender and crumble until fine:

1 soft whole-wheat bread slice, broken (or amount desired)

a sprig of fresh parsley (to make about a tablespoon when
minced)

3. Pour into mixing bowl and blend in:

parmesan cheese (amount desired)

about ½ teaspoon sweet basil leaves

4. Spread about 1 tablespoon of the crumb mixture over top of each tomato half and drizzle each with:

1 teaspoon butter

5. Set in baking pan and bake at 350° for 12 to 15 minutes.

Broccoli

Cook it right and you will have the brightest green vegetable imaginable! The secret is to not cook it as long as most cookbooks recommend.

Amount: 6 servings

1. Clean and trim off tough outer skin of stalk, leaving as much of stalk end as desired:

2 pounds broccoli

2. Place vegetable steamer basket over boiling water, add broccoli, cover, and steam for 10 minutes.
3. Serve with:

juice of ½ lemon

Alternative cooking method:

1. Bring to a boil enough water to cover the broccoli.
2. Add broccoli, return to boil quickly over high heat, cover, and boil 40 to 60 seconds. That's all!
3. Drain immediately.

Christmas Red & Green Beans

Easy! Easy! Easy!

Amount: 8 to 10 servings

1. Sauté onion and pepper in oil until soft:

1 to 2 tablespoons olive oil
1 onion, chopped
1 green pepper, chopped

2. Drain and combine in casserole dish with:

2 1-pound cans green beans, drained or two 10-ounce packages frozen cut green beans
2 1-pound cans baby tomatoes

3. Optional—Brown, drain thoroughly, and add:

6 slices bacon, broken in pieces

4. Cover and bake at 350° for 30 minutes.

Emilie's Olive Oil Dressing

Emilie's best dressing recipe. Always a winner!

Amount: 1³/₄ cups

1. Mash together with tip of knife and put into a pint jar:

3 cloves garlic, pressed
1 teaspoon salt
scant ¹/₂ teaspoon pepper

2. Add and shake well:

1 cup olive oil
¹/₂ cup wine vinegar
juice of 1 lemon (about ¹/₄ cup)

3. Chill thoroughly before serving.

Carrot Bran Muffins

Amount: 12 large muffins

1. Spray muffin pan with no-stick cooking spray (Olive Oil Pam Spray preferred)
2. To soften raisins, cover with warm water and let stand 5 to 10 minutes:

¹/₂ cup raisins

3. Blend together and let stand for 5 minutes to soften bran:

¹/₂ cup boiling-hot water
1¹/₂ cups unprocessed wheat bran (this is not bran cereal, but plain bran without sugar, sodium, or any other ingredient added—available at supermarkets and health-food stores)

4. Blend together thoroughly with wire whisk:

¹/₄ cup oil, optional
¹/₂ cup honey or crystalline fructose (health-food store)
1 or 2 eggs, or 2 or 3 egg whites

5. Mix in:

1 cup grated fresh carrots, or unpeeled grated zucchini
1 cup buttermilk
bran mixture

6. Blend dry ingredients together in a separate bowl:

1½ cups whole-wheat pastry flour (health-food store)
1½ teaspoons baking soda
1 teaspoon salt
1 teaspoon cinnamon

7. Blend dry ingredients into liquid ingredients just until mixed, but do not overmix.
8. Gently fold in:

raisins, drained
½ cup chopped walnuts

9. Fill muffin cups evenly, each almost full, and bake at 350° for 20 to 25 minutes. Allow to cool 2 or more minutes until muffins can easily be removed from pan.

Lemon Ginger Muffins

Amount: 10 large or 12 medium muffins

1. Spray muffin pan with no-stick cooking spray (Olive Oil Pam Spray preferred)
2. Prepare and set aside:

2 tablespoons fresh grated lemon peel
2 tablespoons finely chopped fresh ginger

3. Blend together and let stand (mixture will foam up):

1 cup plain yogurt or buttermilk
1 teaspoon baking soda

4. Blend well in a separate bowl:

¼ cup soft butter or oil, optional
½ cup honey or crystalline fructose (health-food store)

5. Add to honey mixture, blending thoroughly:

2 large eggs, or 4 egg whites
grated lemon and chopped ginger

6. Mix into honey-egg mixture alternately:

yogurt or buttermilk mixture
2 cups whole-wheat pastry flour (health-food store)—mix in ⅔
   cup at a time

7. Fill muffin cups almost full. If making 10 large muffins, fill
the two center muffin cups halfway with water.
   8. Bake at 375° for 18 to 20 minutes.
   9. While muffins bake, blend together:

¼ cup fresh-squeezed lemon juice
1 tablespoon honey or crystalline fructose (health-food store)

10. Cool muffins for 5 minutes. Dip top and bottom of each
muffin in lemon juice mixture.

Ambrosia

So simple to make, yet so sweetly delicious!
Amount: 6 servings

1. Toast about 8 minutes at 325° in shallow pan until lightly-
browned:

½ cup medium shred coconut, unsweetened (health-food
   store)

2. Meanwhile, combine in mixing bowl:

3 medium oranges or 2 mangoes, peeled and cut in chunks
3 cups pineapple chunks, unsweetened (fresh, or canned that
   have been drained)
6 tablespoons raisins
1 tablespoon crystalline fructose (health-food store) or 1 to 2
   tablespoons sugar

3. Fold in toasted coconut and thoroughly chill in refrigerator
to blend flavors before serving.

No-Bake Honey Cheesecake

Amount: 6 to 9 servings

1. Stir gelatin into water and let stand 5 minutes to soften:

¼ cup cold water (room temperature is okay)
1 package (2 teaspoons) unflavored gelatin

2. Meanwhile, mix together in blender:

1 egg
⅓ cup mild-flavored honey (a lighter color usually indicates milder flavor)
1 teaspoon vanilla extract

3. Gradually add, blending until no lumps remain:

8 ounces cream cheese, softened

4. Blend in until smooth:

½ cup lowfat or nonfat plain yogurt
½ cup sour cream or light sour cream

5. Dissolve softened gelatin by bringing just to a boil over medium heat, stirring constantly, or on full power in microwave 40 to 60 seconds.
6. Thoroughly mix dissolved gelatin into remaining ingredients in the blender; pour mixture into an 8″ or 9″ square pan; chill until set.
7. For graham cracker topping, blend together:

¼ cup graham cracker crumbs
1 tablespoon crystalline fructose (health-food store) or 2 tablespoons sugar
1 tablespoon melted butter

8. Sprinkle crumb topping over cheesecake anytime during chilling process or just before serving.[1]

If you want to serve a traditional turkey for your main Christmas entrée, go back to the Thanksgiving chapter to find recipes and tips.

Ideas for Holiday Leftovers

My very favorite part of a big Christmas dinner is the leftovers. I will cook a turkey just for that purpose. There is something about the taste of cold turkey snitched in the kitchen on Christmas night or later in the week that is better than any feast ever served in a four-star restaurant. In fact, some of the best meals I've served have been the result of holiday leftovers. Here are some special tips for using leftovers:

1. Freshen rolls by sprinkling with water and heating in the oven, adding butter and garlic powder, if desired.

2. Make TV dinners by placing leftovers in an aluminum pan, covering with foil, and labeling before sticking in the freezer. Perfect for busy days and late suppers.

3. Leftover food should be stored within two hours, which includes serving time. Keep hot foods hot (above 165°) and cold foods cold (below 40°).

4. Freeze leftover gravy in ice-cube trays; pop out cubes and store in plastic bags. Do the same with fruit juices.

5. Freeze leftover water chestnuts tightly covered in their liquid.

6. Bits of jelly and jam can be melted in a small pan over low heat to make a good sauce for waffles, puddings, or ice cream. They also make a nice glaze.

7. Avoid storing different cakes, cookies, or breads in the same container. The flavors mix, and the baked goods don't keep as well.

8. To refresh cookies that are too soft, heat in a 300° oven just before serving. If cookies are too hard, place them in an airtight container and add a piece of apple or bread. It will take a day or two to soften them.

9. Cooked meats and vegetables should be reheated and added late in the process of assembling a casserole or cooking a soup or stew. This helps retain flavor, texture, and nutritional value.

10. See the Thanksgiving chapter to find additional tips and recipes for leftovers.

Holiday Storage

It's over—now what?

Storage can be a very easy process and will relieve next year's stress when done properly.

Here's what you will need:

• A good supply of white storage boxes 16″ long by 12″ wide by 10″ deep with a lid (check your local stationery store for supplies)
• 1 wide black felt-tip pen
• 3″ × 5″ card file box
• 3″ × 5″ cards

Instead of writing all over the storage box with a description of the contents, simply number your boxes #25A, #25B, #25C, etc. (25 for December 25). Then make out corresponding 3″ × 5″ cards numbered #25A, #25B, #25C, etc. On the left corner of each card write the area where the box is stored. (Examples: garage, attic, cellar, closet in spare room, guest bedroom.) List on the cards exactly what you are storing in each numbered box. These cards can be stored in a 3″ × 5″ file box. When you need an item, just look it up in your file box and go to the storage area where the box is. It's easy, quick, and neat. If you have a computer, this information can be stored in your computer and retrieved very easily. You will actually be excited about storage.

Keep your strings of lights tangle-free by storing them inside empty toilet paper rolls or paper towel rolls. Or wrap them around the outside of empty paper towel rolls after notching the ends of the rolls.

We have 12 filled boxes, four marked trash bags, and four oversized boxes that have 25A, 25B, etc. labels on them. As you can tell, Christmas is big in our home. But when December comes, it's a neat, easy process. I don't have boxes and bags all over the garage floor for the whole month. I take down what I need, when I need it. In August when I begin to prepare for our holiday seminars (which begin in mid-September), I can take those items down from the garage shelves and look through my tablecloths, napkins and props and freshen up those things that need attention. I can add new items and ideas to the old, and it's as easy as pumpkin pie.

Garlands, wreaths, and candles should be stored separately from ornaments. That way, next year you can start your holiday decorating without sorting through boxes of tree decorations. Large items such as wreaths can be stored in plastic trash bags labeled as if they were boxes by stapling a 3″ × 5″ card to the bag.

> *The shepherds returned, glorifying and praising God for all the things they had heard and seen, which were just as they had been told*—Luke 2:20 (NIV).

Traditions

Whether you have had traditions in your past or not, you can begin to implement them in your home, making a rich heritage for you and your children that can be passed on from generation to generation. It's not too late to start now. It makes no difference whether you're a family or an individual—you can still create memories and establish traditions. It's our responsibility to create good family memories and traditions that can be handed down to our children and our children's children. Psalm 71:17–21 says:

> O God, Thou hast taught me from my youth; and I still declare Thy wondrous deeds. And even when I am old and gray, O God, do not forsake me, until I declare Thy strength to this generation, Thy power to all who are to come. For Thy righteousness, O God, reaches to the heavens, Thou who hast done great things; O God, who is like Thee? Thou, who hast shown me many troubles and distresses, wilt revive me again, and wilt bring me up again from the depths of the earth. Mayest Thou increase my greatness, and turn to comfort me.

Dr. James Dobson points out:

> The great value of traditions comes as they give a family a sense of identity, a belongingness. All of us desperately need to feel that we're not just a cluster of people living together in a house, but we're a family that's conscious of its uniqueness, its personality, character and heritage, and that our special relationships of love and companionship make us a unit with identity and personality.

1. *Cookie exchange*—This is a great idea! Who invented it? We're not really sure, but it was definitely a woman with a busy

schedule and truly a stroke of genius! Instead of spending a fortune on ingredients and lots of time making a variety of cookies for the holidays, you can make a large batch of your favorites and swap them for many different kinds.

One of the most fun times I had was at a cookie exchange one morning with our church women. We had hot apple cider and lots of fellowship (this could also be done in the evening or with husbands). I received an invitation that instructed me to bring seven dozen cookies plus my recipe written on a recipe card that would be displayed by my cookie plate.

Our hostess had a lovely table prepared with candles for displaying our cookies. She prepared the hot cider and provided extra recipe cards for those of us who wanted to record other recipes. We were each given a paper tote bag (or you could use a box or tray) for taking cookies home. The tote bags added an extra touch. They aren't expensive, and we felt like kids in a candy store as we filled our bags.

Each one of us then took an equal number of each kind of cookie. We had a great time and went home with enough variety to please our families—not to mention some great recipes.

2. *Christmas cards*—Our Christmas cards begin to arrive early in December. We read and enjoy them at the moment. I then tear off the return address and check it with my address book to keep it current. The card then goes into our Christmas-card basket that I decorate with a holiday bow, holly, or a poinsettia. Our basket begins to fill up, and it stays where it's visible to the family.

After Christmas, this is the one thing we don't store away in boxes—at least not yet. Beginning January 1, we take our card-filled basket to our meal table and, before or after our meal, each member of the family draws out a card. We read the card and who it is from and then offer a prayer for that person or family. This tradition can last well into the new year. Many times I will drop a note to the family saying, "Thank you for your Christmas card. Our family read it today, March 6, and we prayed for you. Blessings from our home to yours!"

3. *Family movies, videos, slides*—It's so much fun to see those old family movies, slides, or photos. Today's family, however, can videotape, so set aside an evening to do just that. It's fun to see how everyone has changed.

4. *Communion*—Christmas Eve or after the Christmas Day festivities are over, gather your family together and take turns sharing the meaning of that Christmas. The Christmas story can be read, and then join in a family communion. A good ending might be to sing "Joy to the World."

5. *Being a witness*—Invite adult friends and/or children's friends to your home to share a December evening with dinner or dessert. Plan songs, games, and some pertinent Scripture, and let them observe your example of Christ's love and the atmosphere of love in your home. Your family can follow up with prayers for the guests during the holiday season and into the new year.

6. *Tree cutting*—In some parts of the United States, you can go to a tree farm and choose and cut your own tree. We do this every year. It's become a fun tradition. In our family we have two perfectionists: our son, Brad, and our son-in-law, Craig. We plan a time when they can go with us so we're sure to bring home the perfect tree! Some tree farms have picnic areas, small zoos, and even offer caroling and hayrides. After we have chosen the tree, we go for a picnic or simple dinner or perhaps come home to cookies and hot cider, or maybe chili or hot soup. This creates a memory and brings the family together. If no tree farms are available in your area, a tree lot will serve the same purpose. It is also fun to take a picture of your tree untrimmed and then one after it's trimmed. You may not trim your tree the day you purchase it. If not, keep it in a bucket of water or wet sand. Hose it down to wash off the dust and dirt. It will keep healthy until the time to bring it into the house for trimming.

7. *Gifts for your neighbors*—Set up a cookie baking day with your children, grandchildren, or Sunday school children so they can experience a day in the kitchen. Bake and decorate the cookies, divide them into equal shares, place the cookies on colorful paper plates, wrap them in clear cello paper, tie with ribbons, and go around the neighborhood distributing the cookies a day or two before Christmas. You can also teach the children about manners as you visit your neighbors. This is a great way to spend a little time with neighbors you don't always visit. Don't be surprised if you get some gifts in return.

8. *Feed the homeless*—Sign up through your church, Salvation Army, or YMCA. In the past, this has been an enjoyable undertak-

ing for our church family. It's a great way to build a better appreciation for the many blessings our family has, and at the same time teaches us to help those who are less fortunate than we are.

9. *Toys for tots*—Many local and civic organizations provide an opportunity for individuals and families to donate toys for distribution to needy families on Christmas Eve. Charles Colson's Prison Ministries has a program called "Angel Tree" where you can choose the name of a prisoner's child who has stated his or her Christmas wish, and you can provide this needy child with a gift. This is a great program available throughout America.

10. *Adopt-a-family*—There are many opportunities where your family can adopt a family in need. Help them with holiday food and gifts—it's a great bridge-builder.

> *On the eighth day, when it was time to circumcise him, he was named Jesus, the name the angel had given him before he had been conceived*—Luke 2:21 (NIV).

Tree-Trimming Party

1. *Special food*—Make it simple: tamales, tacos, hamburgers, pizza, make-your-own Sloppy Joes, spaghetti, Mexican mountains (make-your-own tostadas), etc.

2. *Make tree ornaments*—Use the following: macramé, paper, popcorn, noodles, straw, pipe cleaners, starch, eggshells, paper plates, popsicle sticks, tinsel, aluminum pans, paint, wooden spools, clothespins, string, fabric, cookies, or cranberries. Another idea is to personalize ornaments with a photo or date.

3. *Special music*—As you trim the tree, have your favorite Christmas music playing. Make it soothing enough that you can still have good family conversation. Sing along if you like.

4. *Invite a friend*—Let your children invite friends over so they, too, can experience this fun evening. After many years, many of our children's friends still recall the special time they had trimming our tree with us. Today our invited friends are our grandchildren. They just love coming over to help us with our tree. They are very curious about our ornaments, and want to know where they came from.

5. *Give a dated ornament each year*—All through the year, be looking for that special ornament that reflects the interest or per-

sonality of a family member or close friend. We love to find an ornament that depicts a basketball player, or someone skiing down snowy slopes, Mother cooking in the kitchen, or Dad fishing. Be sure to put the year's date on the ornament. Many of our tree trimmings go back 15 to 20 years in time. When Brad and Jenny got married, we gave each of them their old tree ornaments. They had instant tree trimmings for their first Christmases.

This tree-trimming party has become one of our very favorite Christmas traditions.

The Manger with Baby Jesus

This tradition is probably the sweetest and most meaningful of all. A good friend of ours, Janet Patton from northern California, provided us with a home-built manger, that includes straw and a baby Jesus wrapped in meshed cloth.

As you build a "worship center" on a table in plain view for the whole family, have the following poem written using calligraphy and framed. Place this next to the manger:

With excitement we anticipate the special Christmas morn. Rejoicing daily that our Christ child soon will be born. We'll spread our love throughout our home by preparing a cozy bed. A bed of straw to place his tiny little head.

As each day passes throughout the month we'll add a piece of straw for special love we've spread to one another, special little gifts or deeds and fun surprises to each other.

What fun our family will enjoy as we spread our love around.

On Christmas morn with joy and glee, we'll celebrate the Christmas tree. But most of all rejoice with praise the birthday of our King!

Everything is displayed except Baby Jesus—hide Him away, but be sure to remember where. Next to the empty manger is a pile of straw cut into six-inch pieces. Beginning the first week in December, we gather as a family and talk about the manger and straw. Every day each member of the family does a good deed on his or her own, such as sharing toys happily, helping teacher pass out papers, or taking out trash without being asked. Then everyone puts a piece of straw in the manger. This can be done at the end of each day. Make sure to talk about the happiness you have given to one another.

As the month continues, the straw in the manger grows, and soon a cozy bed of straw fills the manger. Still no Baby Jesus appears. On Christmas Eve, after all the children are nestled in their beds and asleep, Mom and Dad will find Baby Jesus and place Him in His rightful spot. Straw or no straw, Baby Jesus always appears. Some years the manger may not be real cozy, but we have found that December is the best month of all for good behavior. Watch the excitement as the children race on Christmas morning to see if Baby Jesus has arrived. They head straight for the manger even before looking under the tree. Why? Because during the month we have been focusing on the real meaning of Christmas: Jesus' birthday.

Other Christmas Traditions

We had dinner with some friends one evening and, as we walked up to their front door, we saw a banner in the window which said, "Happy Birthday, Jesus." I really loved it! It takes commitment to do something like this. They also had a birthday party for Jesus with cake, candles, and singing. What a beautiful expression of love for the children to experience! Here are a few more ideas to go along with your party:

• Invite neighborhood children and let them be a part of this special birthday party.

• Brings gifts or food which can be given to a needy family.

• Make craft items with a cross or the sign of the fish on them, such as a stuffed fabric heart which can be used as a necklace. Let the children wear these gifts home.

• Make bread-dough hearts and personalize them with a paint pen. Or paint *love, joy, peace,* etc. on them and use them as tree ornaments at home.

• Older children and adults can share testimonies.

• Share memorable Christmases.

• Have communion with friends.

Our friends Bob and Yoli Brogger probably do the best job of making Christmas memories. Their goal is to glorify Jesus during the month of December. Here are a few of their Christ-centered ideas:

• Yoli made a promise candle out of an oatmeal container. She covered the box with red felt then with yellow felt cut a piece in the shape of a flame and glued it onto the top. It looks just like a candle. They fill the box with Scripture promises. Each day of December, every member of the family draws out a promise and reads it around the table or at bedtime.

• They purchased a Christ-centered Advent calendar (one with Scriptures). You can also make these yourself. Each evening after dinner or before bedtime, the family gathers together and opens the appropriate window and reads the Scripture for that day.

• The Brogger family also has an Advent candle. You can use a regular candle and pretend there are numbers written on the side (1 through 25).

Each day of December, light the candle for about five minutes or until it burns down to the next date. They call it their holiday worship time:

1. The candle is lit.
2. The day's Advent calendar door is opened.
3. A Scripture is picked from the promise candle and read.
4. The Baby Jesus manger can be talked about and pieces of straw added.
5. Close with a short prayer.

The candle is then blown out. By Christmas Eve the candle will have burned way down. This is a special event in the Brogger home, and as the children have grown older they have taken the leadership roles.

• From the moment their friends approach their front door, they want them to know that within their home they celebrate something special. Yoli has a grapevine wreath and, in the center of this beautiful wreath, she puts a small nativity scene. Each year Yoli makes a few changes of ribbon, pinecones, or holly, but she always leaves on the nativity scene. As people stand waiting at their door, they can't help but look upon what the real meaning of Christmas is.

• Christmas stockings are always a lot of fun and can be handmade or store-bought. Again, the Brogger family does a very creative thing. They hang up a "joy" stocking. During the month of

December, each family member puts thoughts, prayers, and love notes in the "joy" stocking. Then on Christmas Eve or Christmas Day the notes are pulled out and read. (This would be a great idea to do year-round.)

Singles can start traditions, too. Why not have a party for unmarried and include a spiritual emphasis? Light an Advent candle for five minutes and have a little Advent worship time, or read Scripture on your own each day of the month leading up to the twenty-fifth.

Seven Fun and Free Ways to Celebrate Christmas

Christmas doesn't have to be the season to spend lots of money! Here are ways for you and your kids to celebrate frugally:

1. *Carol at night to spread cheer throughout your neighborhood. Bring a thermos of hot cocoa to keep everyone warm.*
2. *Visit Santa. Instead of heading to the mall, where lines are apt to be long, visit him at a local small store, library, or firehouse.*
3. *Bake Christmas cookies for your child's class at school. If you're pressed for time, make the "slice and bake" variety and decorate them with ready-made frosting.*
4. *Make a wreath from greenery in your own backyard, and let the children decorate it.*
5. *Attend a Christmas pageant at your elementary school—and don't forget to take plenty of pictures.*
6. *Enjoy the holiday lights in your hometown on a nighttime walk. It's fun to see your neighbors' decorations.*
7. *Go to a recital at a local church. Many choirs sing The Messiah and other seasonal music.*

Christmas will be as special or as ordinary as you make it. You can be the architect of memories your children will carry with them for years—memories that will not only strengthen family bonds, but will also deepen their spiritual ties.

One of the most exciting things about traditions is that we can include others in them, even if they're not Christians. People aren't offended if everything is done in love and with a soft and gentle spirit. The Word that is read and vocalized during the month of December is going into the heart. God is honoring all the prayers we have prayed over Christmas meals and Scriptures we have read over the years.

> Love the Lord your God with all your heart and with all your soul and with all your strength. These commandments that I give you today are to be upon your hearts. Impress them on your children. Talk about them when you sit at home and when you walk along the road, when you lie down and when you get up— Deuteronomy 6:5–7 (NIV).

Advent

Rich in Christian tradition and symbolism, the Advent wreath brings beauty, light, and truth to our holiday season. The word *advent* means "coming." In all 39 books of the Old Testament, there is an air of expectancy. Someone is coming! During the Advent season, we anticipate the coming celebration of the birth of our Savior. Using a wreath during Advent season, you can teach and observe much of the symbolism of Christmas.

Advent begins on the fourth Sunday before Christmas and ends on Christmas Eve. A red or purple candle, symbolizing royalty, is lit on each of these four Sundays, and is traditionally accompanied by Scripture reading. A white candle is lit on Christmas Eve, signifying Christ's arrival. The color white speaks of the purity of our Lord. With the lighting of this last candle, the circle is complete, just as we are complete in Christ.

The circle of the wreath reminds us that His kingdom will have no end (Luke 1:33) and that God Himself has no beginning and no end. He has always existed and always will!

The evergreen tell us that Jesus brings eternal life: "For God so loved the world that he gave his one and only Son, that whoever believes in him shall not perish but have eternal life" (John 3:16 NIV).

A white dove on the wreath reminds us that the Holy Spirit descended as a dove.

However plain or elaborate your wreath, remember that God's Word is true. He loves you and sent His only Son into the world that you might have life and have it abundantly (John 10:10)!

Family Advent Worship Time

> The Lord is my light and my salvation—whom shall I fear? (Psalm 27:1 NIV).

Many families have established the Advent wreath as a wonderful tradition during their Christmas season. Here are some guidelines you may want to use:

1. Make a wreath using straw, evergreens, ribbon, etc., and place four red candles and one white candle around it.

2. Fourth Sunday before Christmas—Light the first red candle. Share Isaiah 2:1–5; 11:1–9; 40:3–11 showing the coming of the Messiah.

3. Third Sunday before Christmas—Light the second red candle. Share Luke 1:26–56 and Isaiah 7:13,14 telling of the mother of Jesus.

4. Second Sunday before Christmas—Light the third red candle. Share Luke 2:8–20, telling about the shepherds and angels. Share Matthew 2:1–12, telling about the wise men.

5. Last Sunday before Christmas—Light the fourth red candle. Share Matthew 2:13–23, telling of the flight into Egypt.

6. On Christmas Eve—Light the white and last candle. You may enjoy reading the Christmas story found in Luke 1:26–38 and Luke 2:1–20. Let the candles continue to burn until bedtime.

7. Rejoice! It's the birthday of the King who says, "I am the light of the world" (John 8:12 NIV).

Involve the whole family and take turns lighting and blowing out the candles. We believe this celebration of Christmas is pleasing to the Lord. It has taught our children the meaning of Christmas and helps us all to remember His birth and feel His presence in our homes.

Scripture Readings for the Advent Wreath

The prophecies concerning Christ in the Old Testament which are expressly cited in the New Testament number more than 300!

Here are just a few to choose from to add substance to the lighting of your Advent candles.

Prophecy	Fulfillment
Psalm 72:10	Matthew 2:1–11
Psalm 118:26	Matthew 21:9
Isaiah 7:14	Matthew 1:18; Matthew 1:22,23
Isaiah 9:6,7	John 1:19–34
Isaiah 25:8	1 Corinthians 15:54
Isaiah 28:16	Romans 9:33; 1 Peter 2:6
Isaiah 35:4–6	Matthew 11:4–6
Isaiah 40:3–5	Matthew 3:3; Mark 1:3; Luke 3:4–6
Isaiah 53:3–6,9,12	Luke 22:37; Acts 8:32,33; 1 Peter 2:22
Jeremiah 23:5,6	Romans 3:21,22
Jeremiah 31:31–34	Hebrews 8:8–12; 10:16,17
Micah 5:2–5	Matthew 2:5,6; John 7:42
Zechariah 9:9	Matthew 21:4,5; John 12:14,15
Zechariah 12:10	John 19:37
Malachi 3:1	Matthew 11:10; Mark 1:2; Luke 7:27
Malachi 4:5,6	Matthew 11:13,14; Matthew 17:10–13; Mark 9:11–13; Luke 1:16,17

Christ, the church's one foundation, is the cornerstone of our holidays, the centerpiece of our celebration. May the peace that comes from knowing Christ the Lord be yours as you celebrate a year filled with happy holidays.

November: Week 1—Things to Do

Activity   Done (x)

1._____ □

2._____ □

3._____ □

4._____ □

5._____ □

6._____ □

7._____ □

8._____ □

9._____ □

10._____ □

11._____ □

12._____ □

13._____ □

14._____ □

November: Week 2—Things to Do

Activity   Done (x)

1._____ ☐

2._____ ☐

3._____ ☐

4._____ ☐

5._____ ☐

6._____ ☐

7._____ ☐

8._____ ☐

9._____ ☐

10._____ ☐

11._____ ☐

12._____ ☐

13._____ ☐

14._____ ☐

November: Week 3—Things to Do

Activity   Done (x)

1._____ ☐

2._____ ☐

3._____ ☐

4._____ ☐

5._____ ☐

6._____ ☐

7._____ ☐

8._____ ☐

9._____ ☐

10._____ ☐

11._____ ☐

12._____ ☐

13._____ ☐

14._____ ☐

November: Week 4—Things to Do

Activity	Done (x)
1._____	☐
2._____	☐
3._____	☐
4._____	☐
5._____	☐
6._____	☐
7._____	☐
8._____	☐
9._____	☐
10._____	☐
11._____	☐
12._____	☐
13._____	☐
14._____	☐

December: Week 1—Things to Do

Activity   Done (x)

1._____ ☐

2._____ ☐

3._____ ☐

4._____ ☐

5._____ ☐

6._____ ☐

7._____ ☐

8._____ ☐

9._____ ☐

10._____ ☐

11._____ ☐

12._____ ☐

13._____ ☐

14._____ ☐

December: Week 2—Things to Do

Activity	Done (x)
1.	☐
2.	☐
3.	☐
4.	☐
5.	☐
6.	☐
7.	☐
8.	☐
9.	☐
10.	☐
11.	☐
12.	☐
13.	☐
14.	☐

December: Week 3—Things to Do

Activity   Done (x)

1._____ ☐

2._____ ☐

3._____ ☐

4._____ ☐

5._____ ☐

6._____ ☐

7._____ ☐

8._____ ☐

9._____ ☐

10._____ ☐

11._____ ☐

12._____ ☐

13._____ ☐

14._____ ☐

December: Week 4—Things to Do

Activity   Done (x)

1._____ □

2._____ □

3._____ □

4._____ □

5._____ □

6._____ □

7._____ □

8._____ □

9._____ □

10._____ □

11._____ □

12._____ □

13._____ □

14._____ □

ꙮChristmas Card Recordꙮ

Name	Address	Year	Sent	Rec'd

⮜Gifts Given⮞

Occasion	To	Gift	Year

Gifts Received

Gift	Occasion	To	From	Thank You

∽Shopping List∾

Name	Gift/ Alternate	Size	Store	Cost Budget	Actual

❧Hospitality Sheet❧

Date: _____   Place: _____
Time: _____   Number of Guests: _____
Event: Theme:

Things to Do	✔	Menu	Preparation Time
One Week Before:		Appetizers:	
Three Days Before:		Entree:	
One Day Before:		Side Dishes:	
Day Of:		Salad:	
		Dessert:	
Last Minute:		Drinks:	

Guest List	RSVP Yes No	Notes	Supplies
			Tables/Chairs
			Dishes
			Silver
			Glasses
			Centerpiece

Notes

Chapter 4—Easter

1. Emilie Barnes and Sue Gregg, *Holiday Menus for Busy Women* (Riverside, CA: Eating Better Cookbooks, 1993), pp. 53–60.
2. Gloria Gaither and Shirley Dobson, *Let's Make a Memory* (Waco, TX: Word Books, 1983), pp. 28–34.
3. Marita Littauer, *Homemade Memories; Making Memories that Matter* (Eugene, OR: Harvest House Publishers, 1991), pp. 238–46 (adapted material).
4. Ibid., p. 246.

Chapter 5—Mother's Day

1. Brenda Hunter, "The Value of Motherhood," *Focus on the Family,* 1986, pp. 9–12.
2. Gloria Gaither and Shirley Dobson, *Let's Make a Memory* (Waco, TX: Word Books, 1983), pp. 158–59.
3. Marita Littauer, *Homemade Memories; Making Memories that Matter* (Eugene, OR: Harvest House Publishers, 1991), pp. 248–51.
4. Emilie Barnes and Sue Gregg, *Holiday Menus for Busy Women* (Riverside, CA: Eating Better Cookbooks, 1991), pp. 56–57.
5. M. Littauer, *Homemade Memories,* pp. 252–57.

Chapter 6—Father's Day

1. Paula Yates Sugg, "In Memorial," *The Dallas Morning News* (September 26, 1993).
2. Bob Phillips, *Awesome Good Clean Jokes for Kids* (Eugene, OR: Harvest House Publishers, 1992), pp. 120–21.
3. Emilie Barnes and Sue Gregg, *Eating Better Cookbook* series (Riverside, CA: 1991). Taken from our various self-published cookbooks.

Chapter 7—Independence Day

1. "Very Innovative Parties," Women's Auxiliary to the Alumni Association, School of Dentistry, Loma Linda University, Loma Linda, CA, 1987. You may order it directly from: Very Innovative Parties, Loma Linda University, Dental Auxiliary, P.O. Box 382, Loma Linda, CA 92354.

Chapter 8—Thanksgiving

1. David Briggs, Associated Press, "Mealtime Blessings Give Thought to Food," *The Press-Enterprise,* Nov. 19, 1994, H-3.
2. From a tract published by Good News Publishers, Wheaton, IL.

Chapter 10—Christmas

1. Emilie Barnes and Sue Gregg, *Holiday Menus* (Riverside, CA: Eating Better Cookbooks, 1989), pp. 24–39.